COMMUNICATION RESEARCH MEASURES

Communication
Research Measures
A SOURCEBOOK

Editors
Rebecca B. Rubin
Philip Palmgreen
Howard E. Sypher

Associate Editors

Michael J. Beatty	Howard H. Greenbaum
Sue DeWine	Patricia Kearney
Cal W. Downs	Elizabeth M. Perse
Elizabeth E. Graham	Alan M. Rubin

LEA LAWRENCE ERLBAUM ASSOCIATES, PUBLISHERS
2004 Mahwah, New Jersey   London

This book was originally published in 1991 by The Guilford Press.

Copyright © 2004 by Lawrence Erlbaum Associates, Inc.
All rights reserved. No part of this book may be reproduced in any
form, by photostat, microform, retrieval system, or by any other means,
without the prior written permission of the publisher.

Lawrence Erlbaum Associates, Inc., Publishers
10 Industrial Avenue
Mahwah, New Jersey 07430

Library of Congress Cataloging-in-Publication Data

Communication research measures : a sourcebook / edited by Rebecca B.
Rubin, Philip Palmgreen, Howard E. Sypher.
p. cm. – (The Guilford communication series)
Includes bibliographical references and index.
ISBN 0-8058-5243-3
1. Communication–Research. I. Rubin, Rebecca B. II. Palmgreen,
Philip. III. Sypher, Howard E. IV. Series.
P91.3.C62 1993
302.2'072–dc20 93-23402

Books published by Lawrence Erlbaum Associates are printed on
acid-free paper, and their bindings are chosen for strength and
durability.

Printed in the United States of America

10 9 8 7 6 5 4 3

About the Editors

Michael J. Beatty (Ph.D., Ohio State University, 1976) is Professor of Communication at Cleveland State University, Cleveland, Ohio. His research focuses on communication apprehension, anxiety, persuasion, nonverbal communication, decision making, teacher credibility, and, most recently, relationships between adults and their parents. In addition to books and chapters, he has published numerous articles in journals such as *Communication Monographs, Communication Education, Communication Quarterly, Human Communication Research*, and *Journal of Applied Communication Research*. He serves on several editorial boards and is past editor of *Communication Research Reports*.

Sue DeWine (Ph.D., Indiana University, 1977) is Professor and Director of the School of Interpersonal Communication at Ohio University, Athens. Besides publishing several books and chapters, her research in organizational communication has appeared in *Communication Yearbook, Communication Research Reports, Journal of Applied Communication Research, Communication Education, Journal of Business Communication*, and elsewhere. She has coedited the Instrumentation section of *Management Communication Quarterly*, chaired the Organizational Communication Division of the International Communication Association (ICA), and chaired the Task Force on Instrumentation. In 1990, she was awarded the Outstanding Member Award of the ICA Organizational Communication Division and was named Mentor of the Year by Women in Communications. Her most recent book focuses on her organizational consulting.

Cal W. Downs (Ph.D., Michigan State University, 1963) is Professor of Communication Studies at University of Kansas, Lawrence. Besides publishing several books, his research on communication audits, interviewing, and internal communication has appeared in *Communication Monographs, Management Communication Quarterly, Journal of Business Communication, Personnel, Communication Yearbook*, and *Australian Journal of Communication*. He has served as chair of the Organizational Communication Division of the Academy of Management and ICA. He has been a reviewer for several journals and has headed the ICA Organizational Communication Division Task Force on Instrumentation. He also has consulted with organizations about their internal communication processes and has conducted research internationally.

Elizabeth E. Graham (Ph.D., Kent State University, 1987) is Associate Professor in the School of Interpersonal Communication at Ohio University, Athens. Her research interests include instructional and organizational communication skill development, measurement of communication behavior, and the use of humor in interpersonal conversation. Recent publications have appeared in *Communication Education, Western Journal of Communication,* and *Communication Quarterly.* She serves as the course director for interpersonal communication and teaches interpersonal communication, measurement and statistics, and communication theory. She has served as research committee chair for the Instructional Development Division of the Speech Communication Association (SCA).

Howard H. Greenbaum (Ph.D., Columbia University, 1952) is Distinguished Professor Emeritus of Business at Hofstra University, Hempstead, New York. Earlier, he was senior executive for an industrial organization and served on the financial research staff of the National Bureau of Economic Research. His research on organizational group behavior, measurement and instruction, and communication audits has appeared in the *Academy of Management Journal, Group and Organizational Studies, Journal of Business Communication, Journal of Applied Communication Research,* and *Management Communication Quarterly.* He has served as chair and secretary of the Organizational Communication Divisions of the Academy of Management and ICA, respectively, and serves on several editorial boards. He has received awards by associations for his service to the discipline.

Patricia Kearney (Ed.D., West Virginia University, 1979) is Professor and Deputy Chair of the Speech Communication Department at California State University, Long Beach. Her teaching and research focus on instructional communication, interpersonal communication, and communication theory. Besides publishing books and chapters, her research has appeared in *Communication Education, Human Communication Research, Communication Yearbook, Communication Quarterly,* and elsewhere. Her record of scholarship ranks her as one of the most prolific women researchers in the profession. She has received many awards for her teaching and research. She serves on numerous editorial boards, and recently served as chair of the Instructional Division of ICA.

Elizabeth M. Perse (Ph.D., Kent State University, 1987) is Associate Professor of Communication at the University of Delaware, Newark. Her research focuses on the uses and effects of mass media and newer communication technologies. She has recently investigated the role of gender differences in uses and ownership of communication technologies. Her research has been published in such journals as *Human Communication Research, Journal of Broadcasting and Electronic Media, Communication Research, Journalism Quarterly,* and *Communication Quarterly.* She serves on editorial boards and on the SCA's Mass Communication Division Research Committee. She recently was named among the most productive women scholars in communication.

Philip Palmgreen (Ph.D., University of Michigan, 1975) is Professor in the Department of Communication at the University of Kentucky. He is primarily interested in mass media use and consumption, with particular attention to public communication campaigns. He currently is co-principal investigator on an 8-year project funded by the National Institute on Drug Abuse examining the targeting of televised antidrug public service announcements to at-risk groups, especially high-sensation-seeking young adults. He has published in and served as reviewer for most major communication journals.

Alan M. Rubin (Ph.D., University of Illinois, 1976) is Professor and Director of Graduate Studies in the School of Communication Studies at Kent State University, Kent, Ohio. He has studied the uses and effects of the mass media, including TV and radio news and entertainment, personal and mediated communication, communication and aging, and children and TV. Besides books and chapters, his research has been published in such journals as the *Journal of Broadcasting and Electronic Media* (JOBEM), *Journal of Communication, Communication Research, Critical Studies in Mass Communication, Journalism Quarterly, Communication Monographs,* and *Human Communication Research.* He is past editor of the JOBEM and a former chair and secretary of the Mass Communication Division of SCA and ICA, respectively. He serves on numerous editorial boards and as a consultant to media, education, and industry.

Rebecca B. Rubin (Ph.D., University of Illinois, 1975) is Professor and Director of the Communication Research Center at Kent State University, Kent, Ohio. Her research has focused on interpersonal relationship development, communication competence, and personal and mediated communication. Besides having written or edited several books and chapters, her research has been published in journals such as *Human Communication Research, Communication Monographs, Communication Research, Journal of Broadcasting and Electronic Media, Communication Education,* and *Communication Quarterly.* Her research has placed her as one of the most prolific women researchers in the discipline. She is a past chair of the SCA Instructional Development Division, serves on numerous editorial boards, and is a consultant to government and education in the area of assessment.

Howard E. Sypher (Ph.D., University of Michigan, 1977) is Professor and Chair of the Department of Communication Studies at the University of Kansas. His research, focusing on interpersonal communication and social cognition, has been published in *Communication Monographs, Human Communication Research*, and *Communication Research*. He currently serves as division head of the Interpersonal Communication Division of ICA and serves as coeditor of The Guilford Communication Series.

Preface

Most of us involved in quantitative communication research have at one time or another found that our research required the use of a scale to measure some communication variable we were thinking about including in our theoretical model. But we did not have such a scale, had only dim recollections of "seeing a scale like that somewhere in a journal a few years back," and certainly did not want to go to the trouble of developing and validating such a scale ourselves. Because no sourcebook of communication research measures existed, many of us were forced to do exhausting searches, write other scholars for help, or in some cases reinvent the wheel in order to explore some communication construct. In short, communication scholars have desperately needed a sourcebook of scales on the order of Robinson, Shaver, and Wrightsman's *Measures of Personality and Social Psychological Attitudes*.

This is especially true today, because the development of communication as a discipline has resulted in an explosion of scales tapping various aspects of interpersonal, mass, organizational, and instructional communication. These scales are scattered across a bewildering array of journals, books, dissertations, and research reports, a situation that often hinders awareness of and use of particular measures.

This sourcebook is intended as a partial remedy to the situation, bringing together in one place a variety of scales that measure a number of important communication constructs. In the tradition of the Robinson et al. classic, this volume includes the scales themselves, instructions for administration and scoring, and information on validity and reliability. The scales presented here are drawn from the areas of interpersonal, mass, organizational, and instructional communication—areas in which the use of formal, quantitative scales is particularly well developed. Even with this narrowing of the communication horizon, the profusion of scales available forced us to be selective in deciding which scales to include. This selection was based on stringent criteria of validity, reliability, and use as outlined in the Introduction. However, where space limitations preclude the inclusion of an important or promising scale, we reference it in the appropriate overview chapter discussing the state of formal measurement in a particular area.

Attempts at building a quantitative science in any discipline are, in the final analysis, based on the quality of measurement undergirding the theories and constructs in that area. This book, along with others discussed in the Introduction, reflects the recent important emphasis on developing and improving the measurement base of the communication discipline. None of the editors or associate editors envisioned just how difficult and intimidating the process of producing a sourcebook of this nature would be. But we are satisfied that the hard work over the past four years has been well worth it. We hope that this effort will result in at least an equal amount of labor saved on the part of the scholars, students, and practitioners who find this book useful, and that it will contribute in significant ways to your research efforts.

Philip Palmgreen
Rebecca B. Rubin
Howard E. Sypher

Acknowledgments

We would like to thank the following people who helped research the measures profiled in this volume: Dr. Ira Kaplan at Hofstra University for his contribution to the organizational section; John Gribas at the University of Kansas; Amy Lipka and Lisa E. Travis at the University of Delaware; Matthew Martin, Kevin Einbinder, Gus Schulz, and Lyn Wolfson at Kent State University; Philip Auter at the University of Evansville; and Leda Cooks, Christi Schaller, and Tracy Corrigan at Ohio University.

Contents

Introduction

Part I·of this volume contains summary chapters about four facets of the communication discipline that use quantitative measures. The authors describe the scales and indexes researchers commonly use, identify new or untried measures that may have potential, and comment on measurement issues peculiar to their section. The chapters identify how the editors made their decisions to profile measures. Often these decisions were based on the established validity/reliability track record of the measure. Another criterion was that the measure be developed and used primarily in the communication discipline. New instruments that have great potential for use are also included. (Measures that are profiled in this volume are typed in capital letters when cited in the text and tables.)

Part II includes summaries (what we call profiles) of measures commonly used in communication research. The profiles are organized alphabetically by measure name rather than in categories, not only to facilitate finding specific measures, but because some measures would fall into more than one category. Profile authors (identified on the first page of each profile) have adhered to a standard format for their descriptions. First they describe the background of the measure and what it now looks like. Then they assess the reliability and validity of the measure, providing commentary on the strengths and weaknesses of it. They then give the location of the measure and references used in the profile. And last they provide the actual measure; if the measure was revised since first publication, measure authors provided the most recent version for this volume. In a few cases, the actual measure was not available, so readers are referred to the reference providing the location.

The authors use standard definitions of validity and reliability in their profiles. Kerlinger (1986) and Babbie (1992) provided the definitions and distinctions used here: *Reliability* is the dependability, predictability, stability, or precision of a measure. *Intercoder reliability* is computed for some nominal-data judgments to test the stability of a coding system; two coders assign communication behaviors to categories to see if the two agree. *Inter-rater reliability* does the same for interval- or ratio-data judgments; evaluations are made about the communication on a scale or index. *Test–retest reliability* tests the stability of a measure by correlating scores from two administrations of the measure to the same group of people; if scores change and nothing else has intervened between the two administrations, the measure is unreliable. *Internal consistency* tests a scale's items to see if they are homogenous in nature; this is typically measured via Cronbach's alpha. With *split-half reliability*, half of a measure's items are randomly chosen and correlated with the remaining items; if the reliability coefficient is low, the items are not measuring the same construct consistently.

Validity occurs when a measure is actually measuring what it is supposed to measure. A measure has *face validity* if it appears that the construct to be measured is represented by the items; it relies on common agreement of the mental images people have for the construct. *Content validity* addresses how representative or adequate the content of the measure is: Are all aspects of the construct (substance, matter, topic) represented in the measure? *Criterion-related validity* is guaranteed if the measure is related to an external criterion; if an independent variable measure predicts accurately a dependent measure, this is evidence that the independent variable has criterion-related validity. If two or more related measures are actually related to one another statistically, they have *concurrent validity*. *Construct validity* provides additional information on the meaning of a measure. What exactly is being measured? Often both convergence (correlational evidence from studies using different methods) and discriminability (measures that are unrelated are found uncorrelated with one another) are used as evidence of construct validity. Factor analysis and the multitrait, multimethod approaches are useful for establishing construct validity.

Readers will notice that important measures developed outside the communication field are not included in this volume. For example, organizational communication researchers often use the Job Description Index to measure satisfaction, interpersonal communication researchers use the Role Category Questionnaire to measure construct differentiation, mass communication researchers use the Need for Cognition Scale to measure a person's tendency to engage in and enjoy thinking, and instructional communication researchers use the State–Trait Anxiety Inventory to measure classroom apprehension. Some of these measures are discussed in the section chapters. Others are found in already-published measurement collection volumes or referenced on CD-ROMs. Some measurement sources, besides communication journals (e.g., *Communication Research Reports*), that researchers could use to find additional measures or discussion of measurement issues, include the following:

RESOURCES

Periodicals

Applied Psychological Measurement. (1977–present). Minneapolis: Applied Psychological Measurement.

Educational and Psychological Measurement. (1941–present). Durham, NC: Educational and Psychological Measurement.

Journal of Personality and Social Psychology. (1965–present). Washington, DC: American Psychological Association.

Journal of Personality Assessment. (1971–present). Hillsdale, NJ: Erlbaum.

Journal of Educational Measurement. (1964–present). Washington, DC: National Council on Measurement in Education.

News on Tests. (1979–present). Princeton, NJ: Educational Testing Service.

Psychological Reports. (1955–present). Missoula, MT: Psychological Reports.

Books and Collections

Chun, K-T., Cobb, S., & French, J. R. P., Jr. (1975). *Measures for psychological assessment: A guide to 3,000 original sources and their applications*. Ann Arbor: University of Michigan Survey Research Center, Institute for Social Research.

Emmert, P., & Barker, L. L. (Eds.). (1989). *Measurement of communication behavior*. New York: Longman.

Health and Psychosocial Instruments: HAPI (CD-ROM). (1992). Pittsburgh, PA: Behavioral Measurement Database Services.

Kramer, J. J., & Conoley, J. C. (Eds.). (1992). *Mental measurements yearbook* (11th ed.). Lincoln, NE: University of Nebraska Boros Institute of Mental Measurement.

McReynolds, P. (Ed.). (1968–1975). *Advances in psychological assessment* (6 vols). San Francisco: Jossey-Bass.

McReynolds, P. (Ed.). (1990). *Advances in psychological assessment* (Vol. 7). New York: Plenum Press.

Robinson, J. P., Shaver, P. R., & Wrightsman, L. S. (Eds.). (1991). *Measures of personality and social psychological attitudes*. San Diego, CA: Academic Press.

Spitzberg, B. H., & Cupach, W. R. (1989). *Handbook of interpersonal competence research*. New York: Springer-Verlag.

Tardy, C. H. (Ed.). (1988). *A handbook for the study of human communication: Methods and instruments for observing, measuring, and assessing communication processes*. Norwood, NJ: Ablex.

REFERENCES

Babbie, E. (1992). *The practice of social research* (6th ed.). Belmont, CA: Wadsworth.

Kerlinger, F. N. (1986). *Foundations of behavioral research* (3rd ed.). New York: Holt, Rinehart & Winston.

Part I

MEASUREMENT TRENDS AND ISSUES

Measures of
Instructional Communication

PATRICIA KEARNEY
MICHAEL J. BEATTY

Even though the area of instructional communication is new to our discipline, in the last 10 to 15 years we have seen the development of numerous psychological scales, behavioral (skills) assessments, and qualitative coding schemes. Our tasks of identifying, describing, classifying, and evaluating the multitude of measures available have yielded a fairly exhaustive list of instructional communication measures commonly (and uncommonly) employed in this discipline. There are few measures reported in this chapter that we have not either used ourselves or evaluated based on others' use.

Importantly, we made some criterial decisions up front in an effort to determine which instructional communication measures would receive intensive coverage (i.e., the profiles indexed in the latter part of this volume) and which would receive only cursory attention. Obviously, space limitations prevented us from showcasing them all. Our criteria were similar to those employed by all the authors in this book: sufficient reliability and validity, currency in the field, availability, and high or potentially high use. Moreover, some measures were redundant (in which case, we selected the "best" based on reliability and validity estimates). And, finally, some assessments did not lend themselves easily to our format: coding systems, teacher (or student) profiles, and some classification schemes.

The major criterion for including the remaining measures overviewed in this chapter was simple: They all had to be instructionally relevant. Thus, we began to sort through all the journals and edited texts of the past 15 years that regularly publish instructional communication research, including *Communication Education*, *Communication Yearbook*, and regional communication journals. Some of the measures discussed in this chapter overlap in

Note. Measures that are profiled in this volume (in Part II) are typed in capital letters when cited in the text or tables.

emphasis with other areas of the discipline (e.g., most of the assessments of communication apprehension, nonverbal behavior, and decision rule use orientation). Nevertheless, we included them here as well in an effort to show students, teachers, and researchers both the constructs and the assessments that we normally use in instructional communication research. Moreover, we believe that most of those overlapping measures have instructional communication as their roots. What you will find in this chapter is a fairly extensive list of over 80 instructional communication measures frequently (or only occasionally) used in our discipline. We organized these measures according to the following major instructional themes: learning outcomes, teacher behaviors and characteristics, student behaviors and characteristics, communication skills assessment, and communication apprehension.

LEARNING OUTCOMES

Table 1 provides a variety of measures of students' learning in the classroom. Instructional communication researchers have focused on both affective and cognitive learning outcomes. In the past, we argued that affect (or liking) should be a primary outcome of teacher communication variables, and, as expected, a number of studies substantiated that claim. Most of that research relied on J. F. Andersen's AFFECTIVE LEARNING measure, a scale we profile in this volume. Some practitioners have criticized the scale for problems associated with face validity; other researchers have attempted to strengthen the measure by adding or deleting particular items. Nevertheless, the original Andersen scale remains the most reliable, valid, and parsimonious measure of both lower- and higher-order affective learning. We encourage readers to examine our profile for a more intensive explanation of that conclusion.

At the same time researchers were able to link relevant teacher communication variables with affective learning, they reasoned further that affect should be an important motivator of students' cognitive learning. That is, when students *like* the subject matter (and often the teacher, too), they should also be more willing to learn, use, and generalize the information or skills beyond the traditional classroom. Unfortunately, efforts to test that relationship have been problematic, and no completely satisfactory solution has been obtained to date.

The fact remains that no completely valid means of measuring cognitive learning exists. Students themselves complain that examination scores, course grades, and grade point averages only partially reflect what they have learned. Moreover, we know that grades can be based on what students know *before* they enroll in a course, students' prior history and attitudes toward the course content or teacher, arbitrary or irrelevant grading practices in the course (attendance), invalid and unreliable test items, subjective grading procedures,

TABLE 1. Learning Outcomes Measures

Affective learning
AFFECTIVE LEARNING
Teacher Evaluation (affect toward teacher and class) (Norton & Nussbaum, 1980)
Teacher Evaluation (affect toward teacher, course, and discipline) (McCroskey, Holdridge, & Toomb, 1974)

Cognitive learning
Free Recall (S. Booth-Butterfield, 1988a)
Learning Loss (Richmond, McCroskey, Kearney, & Plax, 1987)
Short-Term Information Acquisition (Andriate, 1982)
Short-Term Recall (Beatty, Behnke, & Froelich, 1980; Beatty, Behnke, & Goodyear, 1979; Beatty & Payne, 1984; Kelley & Gorham, 1988)
Self-Reported Cognitive Learning (Richmond, McCroskey, Kearney, & Plax, 1987)

Grades
Grade point average (Davis & Scott, 1978)
Instructor-determined "judgment" grades and scores on objective exams (Harper & Hughey, 1986)
Standardized course examinations/tests (Andersen, 1979; Elliot, 1979; Nussbaum, 1983; Nussbaum & Scott, 1980)
Student self-reports (Richmond & McCroskey, 1984)

and so on. Even when standardized cognitive learning measures across multiple-section courses have been developed, we know that students are not all taught the same objectives, nor are they all taught the content in the same way. And, of course, by limiting ourselves to standardized courses within a specific area, we are unable to generalize the results across disparate content areas. (For a more in-depth explanation of these issues, see McCroskey & Richmond, 1992, pp. 106–108.)

One of two alternatives remain in our attempts to assess cognitive learning reliably and validly. The first is commonly employed in the educational literature: short-term (and long-term) recall tests. The most recent example of this approach in instructional communication is Kelley and Gorham's (1988) experimental study of teacher immediacy and student recall. Students were given four groups of six items (three unrelated words and three numbers) and then asked to recall each sequence. Whereas this procedure assessed short-term information acquisition and retrieval, we know that it is somewhat removed from what really occurs in the classroom. The second alternative is more subjective and depends on students', as opposed to teachers', assessments of learning. This second procedure relies on students' reports of how much they have learned from a given teacher or course (Richmond, McCroskey, Kearney, & Plax, 1987).

To measure students' reports of their own learning, students are asked two questions: "On a scale of 0–9, how much did you learn in this class, with 0 meaning you learned nothing and 9 meaning you learned more than

in any other class you've had?" and "How much do you think you could
have learned in the class had you had the ideal instructor?" (Richmond et al.,
1987). By subtracting the response to the first question from the second, a
learning loss score is obtained. This latter score is used to eliminate any
possible bias resulting from students who might have been forced to take a
class in a disliked content area. This procedure (a) allows us to look at learning
beyond simple recall of information, (b) involves the students' own perceptions of what they have learned (potentially more valid than teachers' perceptions), and (c) provides a basis for comparing learning across a wide variety
of classes, teachers, and disciplines. On the other hand, this self-report assessment lacks objectivity and standardization and, most important, breaks with
tradition by moving evaluation from the teacher to the student.

TEACHER BEHAVIORS AND CHARACTERISTICS

Whereas learning outcomes may be the primary dependent variable examined in the instructional communication literature, the teacher has been
targeted as the primary independent variable. In fact, Table 2, which lists a
variety of measures of teacher communication behaviors and characteristics,
is the most extensive table in this chapter. Researchers have examined the
ways that teachers gain affinity, establish credibility, communicate concern
or power, engage in nonverbal or verbal behaviors of approach (immediacy),
self-disclose, "misbehave," and rely on individual communicator styles to
teach. Some of these variables are assessed qualitatively and, thus, rely on
difficult content analytic coding schemes (e.g., a number of the teacher communicator style variables, including humor and use of narratives). Others
evolved from qualitative data and were eventually classified as scaled "typologies" (e.g., affinity seeking, behavior alteration techniques and messages,
good and poor teacher profiles, and teacher misbehaviors). Some of these and
still others emerged from affiliated areas, such as interpersonal and organizational communication and persuasion (e.g., affinity seeking, teacher satisfaction, and teacher credibility).

Throughout our history of researching relevant teacher behaviors and
characteristics, we have become increasingly concerned about the use of
perceptual measures versus observational assessments. Advocates of perceptual measures claim that perceptions are valid indicators of what happens
in the classroom. That is, we might argue that teachers themselves are their
own best judge of what they normally do across students, classes, and time.
And even when teachers are unable or unwilling to accurately report what
they do, we can rely on students' perceptions. After all, what students select
as important teacher characteristics may be more relevant than what outside observers might record. Proponents of observational assessments argue

TABLE 2. Teacher Behaviors and Characteristics

Teacher affinity and credibility
Affinity-Seeking Strategies (adapted for classroom teachers) (McCroskey & McCroskey, 1986)
Communication Support Instrument (Hill, Rouner, & Bahniuk, 1987; Hill, Bahniuk, & Dobos, 1989)
Teacher Communication Concerns (Staton-Spicer & Darling, 1986)
TEACHER CREDIBILITY
Teacher Credibility Characteristics (Powers, Nitcavic, & Koerner, 1990)
Teacher Orientations Toward Self, Students, and the Profession (Powers et al., 1990)

Teacher power
BEHAVIOR ALTERATION TECHNIQUES
Behavior Alteration Techniques: Prosocial and Antisocial; Constructed and Selected (Kearney, Plax, Sorensen, & Smith, 1988)
Perceived Power Measure (Richmond, McCroskey, Davis, & Koontz, 1980)
Relative Power Measure (Richmond, McCroskey, Kearney, & Plax, 1987)

Evaluating teachers
Teacher Effectiveness (Norton & Nussbaum, 1980)
Teacher Expectancies (McCroskey & Daly, 1976; revised version, Smythe & Powers, 1978)
Teacher Explicitness (Book, Duffy, Roehler, Meloth, & Vavrus, 1985)
Teacher Feedback (speech performances) (M. Booth-Butterfield, 1989)
Teacher "Misbehaviors" (Kearney, Plax, Hays, & Ivey, 1991)
TEACHER SATISFACTION SCALE (toward teaching and students)
Teacher Self-Disclosure (Nussbaum, Comadena, & Holladay, 1986)
TEACHER SELF-DISCLOSURE INSTRUMENT

Teacher immediacy
Behavioral Indicants of Immediacy (Andersen, 1979)
Coding and Classification System for Teacher Nonverbal Behaviors (Morganstern, 1978)
Coding Scheme for Analyzing Teacher Nonverbal Immediacy Behaviors (Nussbaum, 1983)
GENERALIZED IMMEDIACY SCALE
NONVERBAL IMMEDIACY BEHAVIORS
VERBAL IMMEDIACY BEHAVIORS

Teacher communicator style
COMMUNICATOR STYLE MEASURE (teacher's)
Dramatic Teacher Style (Norton & Nussbaum, 1980; Javidi, Downs, & Nussbaum, 1988)
Teacher Communication Style (Kearney & McCroskey, 1980; Kearney, 1984)
Teacher Humor (Gorham & Christophel, 1990)
Teacher Humor (Nussbaum et al., 1986)
Teacher Narratives (Nussbaum et al., 1986)

that both teachers and students are potentially unreliable in their self- or other-reports. Only by observing what actually goes on in the classroom can we accurately report what teachers say and do. That either/or debate has been virtually resolved with the realization that there is "more than one way to skin a cat." Both approaches are potentially valid and reliable; selecting one over the other depends primarily on (a) the questions asked, (b) accessibility of teachers, students, and classrooms, and (c) administrative constraints (e.g., expense, length of time to execute the study, and other compromises).

STUDENT BEHAVIORS AND CHARACTERISTICS

Compared to our table of measures assessing teacher behaviors and characteristics, Table 3's list of student measures is relatively brief. Moreover, only three from the entire list focus exclusively on students' *communication* behaviors: students' clarifying tactics (signaling noncomprehensions), comforting skills, and communication concerns. The rest focus primarily on psychological constructs (e.g., test anxiety, student motivation, and locus of control), categories of student misbehaviors, and students' projected willingness to comply with teacher demands. Although those student variables can be (and often are) influenced by a number of important teacher communication behaviors, we need to examine students themselves as active, acting communicators in the teacher–student classroom exchange.

Specifically, we recommend not only that researchers begin to examine teacher immediacy, teacher self-disclosure, teacher credibility, and teacher communication style, but that they begin to look at potentially relevant student communication behaviors as well. For instance, it might be interesting to examine the influence of students' immediacy on relevant teacher outcome variables (e.g., reciprocal immediacy, teacher attention, teacher praise, and teacher compliance). What impact do different types and amounts of student self-disclosure have on teachers' willingness to change a grade or course requirement? How much student talk is "too much" in the classroom? To what extent do teachers appreciate student-initiated interactions outside the classroom? In what ways do students approach teachers for help?

Along these lines, Darling (1989) has begun to examine an extremely important student communication behavior, students' clarifying tactics. In her observations of actual classroom interactions, Darling identified a number of ways that students attempt to tell the teacher how and why they are unable to understand a concept or principle currently being taught. Other researchers have begun to examine the ways students attempt to resist teacher compliance-gaining strategies (Burroughs, Kearney, & Plax, 1989; Kearney, Plax, & Burroughs, 1991). While some of those techniques are more be-

TABLE 3. Student Behaviors and Characteristics

Misbehaviors and resistance

Categories of Student Misbehaviors (Kearney, Plax, Sorensen, & Smith, 1988)

Children's Reasons for Compliance–Resistance (Howie-Day, 1977; McQuillen & Higginbotham, 1986)

STUDENT RESISTANCE STRATEGIES

Unwillingness/Willingness to Comply (college student resistance) (Kearney, Plax, Smith, & Sorensen, 1988)

Student learning problems

Categories of "Understanding" Problems (Kendrick & Darling, 1990)

Locus of Control (Levenson, 1974, 1981)

Signaling Non-Comprehensions (student clarifying tactics) (Darling, 1989)

Students' Communication Concerns (Hiemstra & Staton-Spicer, 1983)

Student Learning Style Instrument (Potter & Emanuel, 1990)

STUDENT MOTIVATION SCALE

Test Anxiety Inventory (Emery & Krumboltz, 1967)

Other

Comforting Communication Skills Assessment (Applegate, 1978; revised, Burleson, 1982)

Decision Rule Use Orientation (Beatty, 1987, 1988a)

Picture Sociometric Interview (peer attractiveness ratings) (Moore & Updegraff, 1964; Stohl, 1982)

haviors of avoidance or reluctant compliance, others reveal a variety of ways that students attempt to actively resist their teacher demands.

In any case, the argument justifying attention to student communication variables is compelling. Teachers are not the only communicators in the classroom. In fact, they may not even be the more important ones.

COMMUNICATION SKILLS ASSESSMENT

Table 4 lists a variety of measures that assess particular communication skills (e.g., listening, adapting to others, pronunciation, speech clarity, expressing feelings, and describing another's view). None of the instruments assesses students' knowledge of communication theory and principles; instead, all are designed to measure individuals' actual speaking and/or listening skills. For the most part, these measures were designed for and are used currently as diagnostic tools. That is, because these instruments assess actual observable, behavioral communication skills, they can be used by teachers and trainers to determine appropriate remediation, instruction, and practice. Of course, any of these measures could be used for research purposes as well.

TABLE 4. Communication Skills Assessment

Articulation Test for Intelligibility (Duker, 1974)
Children's Communicative Competence (preschool assessment) (Stohl, 1983)
Communication Competency Assessment Instrument (Rubin, 1982a, 1982b)
Communication Competence Self-Report (Rubin, 1985)
COMMUNICATIVE ADAPTABILITY SCALE
Coping Mechanisms Instrument (Rosenfeld, 1983)
Kentucky Comprehensive Listening Test (Bostrom & Waldhart, 1983)
Student Nonverbal Behaviors (Andersen, Andersen, & Mayton, 1985)
Watson–Barker Listening Test (Watson & Barker, 1984)

Importantly, these instruments can serve as the pedagogical framework for teaching basic communication competency skills. The Communication Competency Assessment Instrument (CCAI) (Rubin, 1982a), for instance, relied on those requisite skill areas adopted and endorsed by the Speech Communication Association. By examining the 19 competency areas included in the CCAI and, concomitantly, the 57 examples representing those areas, teachers and trainers can more efficiently and accurately focus their instruction on relevant communication skills.

MEASURES OF COMMUNICATION APPREHENSION

Communication apprehension (CA) can be conceived as either a trait or a state variable. That is, persons may be apprehensive across all or most communication situations (trait) or their anxieties may be associated with particular contexts (generalized-context CA), individuals (person–group CA), or even more state-like, particular persons at a given point in time (situational CA). Table 5 reveals a rather lengthy list of assessments all apparently measuring one single construct, communication apprehension.

The most popular and most valid measure of trait-like communication apprehension is McCroskey's PERSONAL REPORT OF COMMUNICATION APPREHENSION (PRCA-24). The PRCA-24 is also acceptable for examining apprehension in generalized contexts, such as public speaking, interpersonal interactions, group situations, and meetings. To assess apprehension in specific situations, we recommend a relatively new measure, the "Form–State" component of the COMMUNICATION ANXIETY INVENTORY (CAI), developed by S. Booth-Butterfield and Gould. Previously, the State Anxiety Inventory (SAI) was used by researchers to assess state anxiety, but because of the SAI's inaccessibility of and copyright restrictions, the CAI is a good alternative. Researchers interested in measuring receiver apprehensions should use Wheeless's RECEIVER APPREHENSION TEST (RAT). The reliability estimates are consistently high for all these recommended instruments, and all have substantial construct and predictive validity.

TABLE 5. Measures of Communication Apprehension

Avoidance [or Approach] Behavior Scale (S. Booth-Butterfield, 1988b)
Behavioral Assessment of Speech Anxiety (Mulac & Sherman, 1974)
Behavioral Disruption Index (M. Booth-Butterfield, 1986)
Classroom Apprehension about Participation Scale (Neer, 1987)
COMMUNICATION ANXIETY INVENTORY
Measure of Elementary Communication Apprehension (Garrison & Garrison, 1979)
Measures of Situational "Causes" of Communication Apprehension (Beatty, 1988b)
Performance/Communication Orientation Measure (Motley, 1990)
Personal Report of Communication Apprehension (McCroskey, 1970)
PERSONAL REPORT OF COMMUNICATION APPREHENSION (PRCA-24)
Personal Report of Communication Apprehension (PRCA-25) (McCroskey, 1978)
Personal Report of Communication Fear (McCroskey, Andersen, Richmond, & Wheeless, 1981)
Personal Report of Public Speaking Anxiety (McCroskey, 1970)
RECEIVER APPREHENSION TEST
Self-Appraisal of [Speech] Performance (Pelias & Pelias, 1988)
Shy Scale (McCroskey et al., 1981)
Social Reticence Scale (Jones & Russell, 1982)
SPEAKERS' PERCEPTIONS OF SITUATIONAL CAUSES OF ANXIETY
State Anxiety Scale (5-item version) (O'Neil, Spielberger, & Hansen, 1969)
State–Trait Anxiety Inventory (Spielberger, Gorsuch, & Lushene, 1970)
UNWILLINGNESS-TO-COMMUNICATE SCALE
Willingness to Communicate (McCroskey & Richmond, 1987)

In this chapter we provide a brief overview of some important issues that dominate the thinking of instructional communication research today. At the same time, we present various measures available for research and pedagogical purposes. We close by recommending that researchers and teachers employ a variety of means of assessing particular variables. By using more than one operationalization of a given construct, particularly if that assessment involves both quantitative and qualitative approaches (i.e., data triangulation), we are in a better position to interpret the meaningfulness of our results. Similarly, we might expect teachers to assess students' learning outcomes (including skills attainment) by relying on more than a single objective exam or a solitary speech performance. We recommend that teachers employ several different indicators in their efforts to assess, reliably and accurately, student learning.

REFERENCES

Andersen, J. F. (1979). Teacher immediacy as a predictor of teaching effectiveness. *Communication Yearbook*, 3, 543–559.
Andersen, P. A., Andersen, J. F., & Mayton, S. M. (1985). The development of

nonverbal communication in the classroom: Teachers' perceptions of students in grades K-12. *Western Journal of Speech Communication, 49*, 188–203.

Andriate, G. S. (1982). Teacher communication and student learning: The effects of perceived solidarity with instructor and student anxiety proneness. *Communication Yearbook, 6*, 792–810.

Applegate, J. L. (1978). Four investigations of the relationship between social cognitive development and person-centered regulative and interpersonal communication (Doctoral dissertation, University of Illinois at Urbana-Champaign, 1978). *Dissertation Abstracts International, 40/01-B*, 489.

Beatty, M. J. (1987). Cognitive backlog and decision rule use. *Communication Research Reports, 4*, 79–81.

Beatty, M. J. (1988a). Increasing students' choice-making consistency: The effect of decision rule-use training. *Communication Education, 37*, 95–105.

Beatty, M. J. (1988b). Situational and predispositional correlates of public speaking anxiety. *Communication Education, 37*, 27–39.

Beatty, M. J., Behnke, R. R., & Froelich, D. L. (1980). Effects of achievement incentive and presentation rate on listening comprehension. *Quarterly Journal of Speech, 66*, 193–200.

Beatty, M. J., Behnke, R. R., & Goodyear, F. H. (1979). Effects of speeded speech presentations on confidence-weighted and traditional comprehension scores. *Communication Monographs, 46*, 147–151.

Beatty, M. J., & Payne, S. K. (1984). Listening comprehension as a function of cognitive complexity: A research note. *Communication Monographs, 51*, 85–89.

Bell, R. A., & Daly, J. A. (1984). The affinity-seeking function of communication. *Communication Monographs, 51*, 91–115.

Book, C. L., Duffy, G. G., Roehler, L. R., Meloth, M. S., & Vavrus, L. G. (1985). A study of the relationship between teacher explanation and student metacognitive awareness during reading instruction. *Communication Education, 34*, 29–36.

Booth-Butterfield, M. (1986). Stifle or stimulate? The effects of communication task structure on apprehensive and non-apprehensive students. *Communication Education, 35*, 337–348.

Booth-Butterfield, M. (1989). The interpretation of classroom performance feedback: An attributional approach. *Communication Education, 38*, 119–131.

Booth-Butterfield, S. (1988a). Inhibition and student recall of instructional messages. *Communication Education, 37*, 312–324.

Booth-Butterfield, S. (1988b). Instructional interventions for reducing situational anxiety and avoidance. *Communication Education, 37*, 214–223.

Bostrom, R. N., & Waldhart, E. S. (1983). *The Kentucky Comprehensive Listening Test*. Lexington, KY: The Kentucky Listening Research Center.

Burleson, B. R. (1982). The development of comforting communication skills in childhood and adolescence. *Child Development, 53*, 1578–1588.

Burroughs, N. F., Kearney, P., & Plax, T. G. (1989). Compliance-resistance in the college classroom. *Communication Education, 38*, 214–229.

Darling, A. L. (1989). Signalling non-comprehensions in the classroom: Toward a descriptive typology. *Communication Education, 38*, 34–40.

Davis, G. F., & Scott, M. D. (1978). Communication apprehension, intelligence, and achievement among secondary school students. *Communication Yearbook, 2,* 457–472.

Duker, S. (1974). *Time compressed speech.* Metuchen, NJ: Scarecrow Press.

Elliot, S. (1979). Perceived homophily as a predictor of classroom learning. *Communication Yearbook, 3,* 585–602.

Emery, J. R., & Krumboltz, J. D. (1967). Standard versus individualized hierarchies in desensitization to reduce test anxiety. *Journal of Counseling Psychology, 14,* 204–209.

Garrison, J. P., & Garrison, K. R. (1979). Measurement of communication apprehension among children: A factor in the development of basic speech skills. *Communication Education, 28,* 119–128.

Gorham, J., & Christophel, D. M. (1990). The relationship of teachers' use of humor in the classroom to immediacy and student learning. *Communication Education, 39,* 46–62.

Harper, B. H., & Hughey, J. D. (1986). Effects of communication responsiveness upon instructor judgment grading and student cognitive learning. *Communication Education, 35,* 147–156.

Hiemstra, G. E., & Staton-Spicer, A. Q. (1983). Communication concerns of college undergraduates in basic speech communication courses. *Communication Education, 32,* 29–37.

Hill, S. E. K., Bahniuk, M. H., & Dobos, J. (1989). The impact of mentoring and collegial support on faculty success: An analysis of support behavior, information adequacy, and communication apprehension. *Communication Education, 38,* 15–33.

Hill, S. E. K., Rouner, D., & Bahniuk, M. H. (1987, May). *Mentoring and other communication support systems in the academic setting: Development of an instrument.* Paper presented at the meeting of the International Communication Association, Montreal.

Howie-Day, A. M. (1977). Meta persuasion: The development of reasoning about persuasive strategies (Doctoral dissertation, University of Minnesota, 1977). *Dissertation Abstracts International, 38/06-B,* 2833.

Javidi, M., Downs, V. C., & Nussbaum, J. F. (1988). A comparative analysis of teachers' use of dramatic behaviors at higher and secondary educational levels. *Communication Education, 37,* 278–288.

Jones, W. H., & Russell, D. (1982). The social reticence scale: An objective instrument to measure shyness. *Journal of Personality Assessment, 46,* 629–631.

Kearney, P. (1984). Perceptual discrepancies in teacher communication style. *Communication, 13,* 95–108.

Kearney, P., & McCroskey, J. C. (1980). Relationships among teacher communication style, trait and state communication apprehension and teacher effectiveness. *Communication Yearbook, 4,* 533–551.

Kearney, P., Plax, T. G., & Burroughs, N. F. (1991). An attributional analysis of college students' resistance decisions. *Communication Education, 40,* 325–342.

Kearney, P., Plax, T. G., Hays, E. R., & Ivey, M. J. (1991). College teacher misbehaviors: What students don't like about what their teachers say and do. *Communication Quarterly, 39,* 309–324.

Kearney, P., Plax, T. G., Smith, V. R., & Sorensen, G. (1988). Effects of teacher immediacy and strategy type on college student resistance to on-task demands. *Communication Education, 37*, 54–67.

Kearney, P., Plax, T. G., Sorensen, G., & Smith, V. R. (1988). Experienced and prospective teachers' selections of compliance-gaining messages for "common" student misbehaviors. *Communication Education, 37*, 150–164.

Kelley, D. H., & Gorham, J. (1988). Effects of immediacy on recall of information. *Communication Education, 37*, 198–207.

Kendrick, W. L., & Darling, A. L. (1990). Problems of understanding in classrooms: Students' use of clarifying tactics. *Communication Education, 39*, 15–29.

Levenson, H. (1974). Activism and powerful others: Distinctions within the concept of internal-external control. *Journal of Personality Assessment, 38*, 377–383.

Levenson, H. (1981). Differentiating among internality, powerful others, and chance. In H. M. Lefcourt (Ed.), *Research with the locus of control construct: Vol. 1. Assessment methods* (pp. 15–63). New York: Academic Press.

McCroskey, J. C. (1970). Measures of communication bound anxiety. *Speech Monographs, 37*, 269–277.

McCroskey, J. C. (1978). Validity of the PRCA as an index of oral communication apprehension. *Communication Monographs, 45*, 192–203.

McCroskey, J. C., Andersen, J. F., Richmond, V. P., & Wheeless, L. R. (1981). Communication apprehension of elementary and secondary students and teachers. *Communication Education, 30*, 122–132.

McCroskey, J. C., & Daly, J. A. (1976). Teachers' expectations of the communication apprehensive child in the elementary school. *Human Communication Research, 3*, 67–72.

McCroskey, J. C., Holdridge, W., & Toomb, J. K. (1974). An instrument for measuring the source credibility of basic speech communication instructors. *Speech Teacher, 23*, 26–33.

McCroskey, J. C., & McCroskey, L. L. (1986). The affinity-seeking of classroom teachers. *Communication Research Reports, 3*, 158–167.

McCroskey, J. C., & Richmond, V. P. (1987). Willingness to communicate. In J. C. McCroskey, & J. A. Daly (Eds.), *Personality and interpersonal communication* (pp. 129–156). Newbury Park, CA: Sage.

McCroskey, J. C., & Richmond, V. P. (1992). Increasing teacher influence through immediacy. In V. P. Richmond, & J. C. McCroskey (Eds.), *Power in the classroom: Communication, control, and concern* (pp. 101–119). Hillsdale, NJ: Erlbaum.

McQuillen, J. S., & Higginbotham, D. C. (1986). Children's reasoning about compliance-resisting behaviors. *Communication Yearbook, 9*, 673–690.

Moore, S., & Updegraff, R. (1964). Sociometric status of preschool children related to age, sex, nurturance-giving and dependency. *Child Development, 35*, 519–524.

Morganstern, B. F. (1978). A nonverbal communication classification system for teaching behaviors. *Communication Yearbook, 2*, 473–485.

Motley, M. T. (1990). Public speaking anxiety qua performance anxiety: A revised model and an alternative therapy. *Journal of Social Behavior and Personality, 5*, 83–104.

Mulac, A., & Sherman, R. A. (1974). Behavioral assessment of speech anxiety. *Quarterly Journal of Speech, 60*, 134–143.

Neer, M. R. (1987). The development of an instrument to measure classroom apprehension. *Communication Education, 36*, 154–166.

Norton, R. W. (1977). Teacher effectiveness as a function of communicator style. *Communication Yearbook, 1*, 525–542.

Norton, R. (1983). *Communicator style: Theory, applications, and measures.* Beverly Hills, CA: Sage.

Norton, R., & Nussbaum, J. (1980). Dramatic behaviors of the effective teacher. *Communication Yearbook, 4*, 565–579.

Nussbaum, J. F. (1983). Systematic modification of teacher behavior. *Communication Yearbook, 7*, 672–684.

Nussbaum, J. F., Comadena, M. E., & Holladay, S. J. (1986, May). *Verbal communication within the college classroom.* Paper presented at the meeting of the International Communication Association, Chicago.

Nussbaum, J. F., & Scott, M. D. (1980). Student learning as a relational outcome of teacher-student interaction. *Communication Yearbook, 4*, 553–564.

O'Neil, H. F., Jr., Spielberger, C. D., & Hansen, D. N. (1969). Effects of state anxiety and task difficulty on computer-assisted learning. *Journal of Educational Psychology, 60*, 343–350.

Pelias, M. H., & Pelias, R. J. (1988). Communication apprehension in the basic course in performance of literature. *Communication Education, 37*, 118–126.

Potter, W. J., Emanuel, R. (1990). Students' preferences for communication styles and their relationship to achievement. *Communication Education, 39*, 234–249.

Powers, W. G., Nitcavic, R., & Koerner, D. (1990). Teacher characteristics: A college level perspective. *Communication Education, 39*, 227–233.

Richmond, V. P., & McCroskey, J. C. (1984). Power in the classroom II: Power and learning. *Communication Education, 33*, 125–136.

Richmond, V. P., McCroskey, J. C., Davis, L. M., & Koontz, K. A. (1980). Perceived power as a mediator of management communication style and employee satisfaction: A preliminary investigation. *Communication Quarterly, 28*, 37–46.

Richmond, V. P., McCroskey, J. C., Kearney, P., & Plax, T. G. (1987). Power in the classroom VII: Linking behavior alteration techniques to cognitive learning. *Communication Education, 36*, 1–12.

Rosenfeld, L. B. (1983). Communication climate and coping mechanisms in the college classroom. *Communication Education, 32*, 167–174.

Rubin, R. B. (1982a). Assessing speaking and listening competence at the college level: The Communication Competency Assessment Instrument. *Communication Education, 31*, 19–32.

Rubin, R. B. (1982b). *Communication Competency Assessment Instrument.* Annandale, VA: Speech Communication Association.

Rubin, R. B. (1985). Validity of the Communication Competency Assessment Instrument. *Communication Monographs, 52*, 173–185.

Smythe, M. J., & Powers, W. G. (1978). When Galatea is apprehensive: The effect of communication apprehension on teacher expectations. *Communication Yearbook, 2*, 487–491.

Spielberger, C. D., Gorsuch, R. L., & Lushene, R. E. (1970). *Manual for the State–Trait Anxiety Inventory*. Palo Alto, CA: Consulting Psychologists Press.

Staton-Spicer, A. Q., & Darling, A. L. (1986). Communication in the socialization of preservice teachers. *Communication Education*, 35, 215–230.

Stohl, C. (1982). Sugar or spice: Teachers' perceptions of sex differences in communicative correlates of attraction. *Communication Yearbook*, 6, 811–830.

Stohl, C. (1983). Developing a communicative competence scale. *Communication Yearbook*, 7, 685–716.

Watson, K. W., & Barker, L. L. (1984). *Watson–Barker Listening Test*. New Orleans: Spectra Communication Associates.

Measures of
Interpersonal Communication

REBECCA B. RUBIN
ELIZABETH E. GRAHAM

Interpersonal communication researchers use a multitude of self-report scales, other-report rating scales, and behavioral coding indexes and schema to measure interaction, the predisposition to interact, or personality factors that affect interpersonal relationships. In this chapter, we name some of the measures that focus on personal communication characteristics and then briefly identify some of the more prominent coding/rating systems used to code interaction. We then identify and discuss some measurement issues relevant to interpersonal communication as well as issues that we faced in evaluating and classifying the instruments used in this discipline.

Determining which measures to profile was difficult. First, we identified most of the measures used in interpersonal communication research. By canvassing all journals containing interpersonal research, abstracts, indexes, yearbooks, and handbooks (and references to measures gleaned from these), we developed a list of over 165 measures. This list was sent to 43 prominent interpersonal researchers, identified as such through either their publications in the area or their position as officer in national/international communication associations. Twenty-three responded with their evaluations of the scales; they also provided references to 30 additional measures. These evaluations provided support for judgments about which measures would be profiled.

This short list was still too long, so we devised and used the following criteria for including and profiling measures: (a) sufficient validity and reliability; (b) a track record of use in communication research; and, lacking (a) or (b), (c) promise for future research (new measures). Hart, Carlson, and Eadie's (1980) Rhetorical Sensitivity Scale, for example, has been used in

Note. Measures that are profiled in this volume (in Part II) are typed in capital letters when cited in the text or tables.

21

the field, but Daly, Vangelisti, and Daughton (1987) wisely observed that high rhetorical sensitivity scores seem to indicate uncertainty about one's feelings rather than competence. Thus, this instrument did not meet all of our criteria for profiling it. Our choices were also guided by numerous instrument reviews in interpersonal communication (see Table 6).

For this summary, we divided all the interpersonal measures into two large sections: Personal Qualities (Table 7) and Social Relationships (Table 8). We identified main themes within each section and listed measures that focus on qualities of a person (P), an interaction other (O), the interaction (I) of P and O, or P's relationship or dyad (D). Measures that focus solely on the interaction (e.g., coding systems) do not appear here; they are briefly discussed below. We then classified the measure in terms of response categories used: Likert (e.g., *strongly agree* to *strongly disagree*), semantic differential (e.g., bipolar adjective scales), frequency (e.g., *always* to *never*), or other. We also tried to classify measures as either trait (enduring predisposition, stable over time) or state (variable depending on the target or other circumstances).

TABLE 6. Reviews of Interpersonal Measures

Baxter (1988)	Dyadic personal relationships, relationship progress or intimacy, and relationship quality
Daly & Diesel (1992)	Communication-related personality variables
Donaghy (1989)	Nonverbal communication measures and coding systems
Harvey, Hendrick, & Tucker (1988)	Self-report measures of marital relationships
Hirokawa (1988)	Group communication coding systems
Leary (1988)	Social avoidance, distress, shyness, interaction anxiousness, social anxiety, social reticence, communication apprehension
Marangoni & Ickes (1989)	Loneliness
Scherer & Ekman (1982)	Nonverbal communication
Spitzberg (1988)	Competence
Spitzberg & Cupach (1989)	Interpersonal competence, social skills, anxiety, assertiveness, empathy, role-taking, apprehension
Tardy (1988a)	Interpersonal attraction
Tardy (1988b)	Marital interaction coding systems
Tardy (1988c)	Self-disclosure rating and coding systems
Tardy (1988d)	Social support, social network structure, and support provided by others
Vangelisti (1991)	Family

TABLE 7. Personal Qualities

Scale name (author, year)	Focus (Who is measured?)[a]	Scale response[b]	Construct[c]
Competence			
AFFINITY-SEEKING INSTRUMENT	SI	L	T
COMMUNICATIVE ADAPTABILITY SCALE	S	F	T
COMMUNICATIVE COMPETENCE SCALE	SO	L	ST
CONVERSATIONAL APPROPRIATENESS SCALE	OI	L	S
CONVERSATIONAL EFFECTIVENESS SCALE	SI	L	S
Conversational Sensitivity Scale (Daly, Vangelisti, & Daughton, 1987)	S	L	T
Conversational Skills Rating Scale (Spitzberg & Hurt, 1987)	SO	SdO	TS
INTERACTION INVOLVEMENT SCALE	SO	O	TS
Intercultural Competence (Ruben, 1976; Koester & Olebe, 1987, 1988)	O	O	T
Intercultural Effectiveness (Hammer, Gudykunst, & Wiseman, 1978)	S	O	T
Rating of Alter Competence Scale (Spitzberg, 1988)	O	L	S
Rhetorical Sensitivity Scale (Hart, Carlson, & Eadie, 1980)	S	O	T
Self-Rated Competence Scale (Spitzberg, 1988)	S	L	S
Style			
Bem Sex Role Inventory (Bem, 1981)	S	O	T
COMMUNICATOR STYLE MEASURE	SO	L	T
Role Category Questionnaire (Crockett, 1965)	S	O	T
Self-Monitoring Scale (Snyder, 1974)	S	O	T
SOURCE CREDIBILITY	O	Sd	T
Nonverbal sending and receiving ability			
Affect Expression Rating Scale (Buck, 1975)	O	O	T
Behavior Indicants of Immediacy Scale (J. Andersen, P. A. Andersen, & Jensen, 1979)	O	L	T
Communication of Affect Receiving Ability Test (Buck, 1976)	S	O	T
GENERALIZED IMMEDIACY SCALE	O	Sd	T
Interpersonal Perception Task (Archer & Costanzo, 1988)	S	O	T
Nonverbal Affiliative Expressiveness (Gudykunst, Chua, & Gray, 1987; Gudykunst & Hammer, 1988)	S	L	S
Nonverbal Immediacy Rating Scheme (Coker & Burgoon, 1987)	O	Sd	S
Profile of Nonverbal Sensitivity (Rosenthal, Hall, DiMatteo, Rogers, & Archer, 1979)	S	O	T

(continued)

23

TABLE 7 *(continued)*

Scale name (author, year)	Focus (Who is measured?)[a]	Scale response[b]	Construct[c]
Touch Avoidance Measure (P. Andersen & Leibowitz, 1978)	S	L	T
Approaching communication			
ARGUMENTATIVENESS SCALE	SO	F	T
Assertiveness Inventory (Lorr & More, 1980)	S	O	T
Conversational Involvement (Bell, 1985)	SO	Sd	S
INTERPERSONAL COMMUNICATION MOTIVES SCALE	S	O	T
Rathus Assertiveness Schedule (Rathus, 1973)	S	O	T
VERBAL AGGRESSIVENESS SCALE	SO	F	T
Willingness to Communicate (McCroskey & Richmond, 1987)	S	F	T
Avoiding communication			
COMMUNICATION ANXIETY INVENTORY	S	OF	ST
PERSONAL REPORT OF COMMUNICATION APPREHENSION	S	O	T
Predispositions Toward Verbal Behavior (Mortensen, Arntson, & Lustig, 1977)	S	O	T
RECEIVER APPREHENSION TEST	S	L	T
Self-Consciousness Scale (Fenigstein, Scheier, & Buss, 1975)	S	O	T
Shyness Scale (Cheek & Buss, 1981)	S	O	T
Social Reticence Scale (Jones & Russell, 1982)	S	L	T
State–Trait Anxiety Scale (Spielberger, Gorsuch, & Lushene, 1970)	S	FO	ST
UCLA Loneliness Scale (Russell, Peplau, & Cutrona, 1980)	S	F	T
UNWILLINGNESS-TO-COMMUNICATE SCALE	S	L	T
Self-disclosure			
Openness Scale (Norton & Montgomery, 1982)	SO	O	T
REVISED SELF-DISCLOSURE SCALE	S	L	ST
Self-Disclosure Inventory (Jourard & Lasakow, 1958)	S	O	T
Empathy			
Emotional Empathy Questionnaire (Mehrabian & Epstein, 1972)	S	L	T
Empathic Concern (Davis, 1983)	S	L	T
FEELINGS OF UNDERSTANDING/ MISUNDERSTANDING SCALE	S	O	ST

[a] S = self; O = other; I = interaction; D = dyad.
[b] L = Likert; Sd = semantic differential; F = frequency; O = other.
[c] T = trait; S = state.

TABLE 8. Social Relationships

Scale name (author, year)	Focus (Who is measured?)[a]	Scale response[b]	Construct[c]
Attraction			
INTERPERSONAL ATTRACTION SCALE	S	L	S
Interpersonal Attraction Scale (McCroskey & Richmond, 1979)	S	L	S
Interpersonal Judgment Scale (Byrne, 1971)	S	O	S
Liking/Loving Scales (Rubin, 1974)	S	O	S
PERCEIVED HOMOPHILY MEASURE	S	Sd	S
Trust			
Dyadic Trust Scale (Larzelere & Huston, 1980)	S	L	S
INDIVIDUALIZED TRUST SCALE	S	Sd	S
Interpersonal Trust Scales (Rotter, 1967)	S	L	T
Solidarity			
ATTRIBUTIONAL CONFIDENCE SCALE	S	O	S
Consensus (DeStephen & Hirokawa, 1988)	S	L	S
INTERPERSONAL COMMUNICATION SATISFACTION INVENTORY	SI	L	ST
INTERPERSONAL SOLIDARITY SCALE	S	L	S
RELATIONAL COMMUNICATION SCALE	O	L	S
Interaction strategies			
Affinity-seeking strategies (Bell & Daly, 1984)	SO	O	S
COMPLIANCE-GAINING TECHNIQUES	S	O	T
Disengagement Strategies (Cody, 1982)	S	O	S
Relationship Maintenance Strategies (Ayres, 1983)	S	O	S
Relationship level			
Relationship Communication Behavior Scales (Knapp, Ellis, & Williams, 1980)	S	L	T
Relationship Closeness Inventory (Berscheid, Snyder, & Omoto, 1989)	D	OL	T
Relationship Events Scale (King & Christensen, 1983)	D	O	S
Relationship World Index—2 (Stephen & Markman, 1983)	S	O	S
Marital			
Dyadic Adjustment Scale (Spanier, 1976)	D	O	T
Marital Satisfaction Scale (Roach, Frazier, & Bowden, 1981)	S	L	S
QUALITY MARRIAGE INDEX	D	LO	T
RELATIONAL DIMENSIONS INSTRUMENT	D	LF	T

[a]S = self; O = other; I = interaction; D = dyad.
[b]L = Likert; Sd = semantic differential; F = frequency; O = other.
[c]T = trait; S = state.

PERSONAL QUALITIES

Personal qualities includes measures that assess personality or social predispositions or tendencies, or report behaviors. These qualities have been studied in interpersonal communication research mainly as independent variables (although some training research might assess them as dependent measures). Included are qualities such as competence, style, nonverbal sending/receiving skills, approaching communication, avoiding communication, self-disclosure, and empathy.

SOCIAL RELATIONSHIPS

Social relationships measures attempt to tap qualities of relationships in dyadic, marital, and group settings. Most often these measures are completed by a relationship partner or by a trained coder. Often these measures are used as dependent variables in interpersonal research. The main themes include attraction, trust, solidarity, interaction strategies, relationship level, and marital measures.

CODING SYSTEMS

Numerous coding/rating systems have been developed in interpersonal communication that we could not consider in this volume, in areas such as nonverbal communication, confirmation, interaction strategies, and group interaction. One of the most prominent nonverbal coding systems is the Facial Action Coding System (Ekman & Friesen, 1978); Ekman, Friesen, and Tomkins (1971) also developed a Facial Affect Scoring Technique, which has been used prolifically in psychology studies but not in communication. Other prominent coding systems include the Kinesics Notation System (Birdwhistell, 1970) and the Bernese Time–Series Notation (Hirsbrunner, Frey, & Crawford, 1983).

The confirmation–disconfirmation rating instrument, developed by Sieburg (1969) and adapted by Kennedy and Garvin (1986; see also Garvin & Kennedy, 1986), allows researchers to identify messages that confirm or disconfirm communication in professional (typically nurse–doctor) relationships.

Compliance-gaining strategies have been the main focus of strategy research. Wiseman and Schenck-Hamlin (1981) created a coding system to classify these strategies. Other strategy coding research has centered on accounting behaviors (McLaughlin, Cody, & O'Hair, 1983), affinity maintenance (Bell, Daly, & Gonzalez, 1987), comforting (Samter & Burleson,

1984), embarrassment reduction (Petronio, 1984), interpersonal conflict (Fitzpatrick & Winke, 1979), power (Falbo & Peplau, 1980), relationship initiation (Baxter & Philpott, 1982), and relationship maintenance (Ayres, 1983).

Tardy (1988b) has reviewed numerous marital interaction coding systems, including Marital Interaction Coding System (Weiss & Summers, 1983), Couples Interaction Scoring System (Gottman, 1979), Relational Coding Systems (Ellis, 1979; Rogers & Farace, 1975), and Patterson's (1982) Family Interaction Coding system. These systems have been used successfully to identify patterns of interaction.

Hirokawa (1988) (a) reviewed the typical coding procedures used and (b) identified issues coders must face in their analysis. The most prominent include the Interaction Process Analysis (IPA) system (Bales, 1950); the RELCOM system (Ellis, 1979; Fisher, 1979); the Group Working Relationships Coding System (Poole, 1983); the Decisions Functions Coding System (Poole & Roth, 1989); the Decision Proposal Coding System (Fisher, 1970); the Social Information Processing Analysis (Fisher, Drecksel, & Werbel, 1979); the Feedback Rating Instrument (Leathers, 1971); and the SYMLOG system (Bales & Cohen, 1979).

MEASUREMENT ISSUES

In the 1970s, we witnessed a boom in interpersonal relationship research. One reason for this was the increase in relationship development theories (e.g., uncertainty reduction, attribution theory, and exchange theories), now helpful in guiding research. A logical outgrowth of theory development is an increase in measurement potential; once concepts are conceived, constructs must be operationally defined. Yet, with the increase in measurement instruments came measurement problems, many of which we noted in the measures we reviewed for this volume. In this section, we outline some of the major issues concerning reliability, validity, and other measurement controversies in interpersonal communication.

Reliability

Throughout our review of interpersonal measures, we noted that most researchers have provided information on a scale's internal consistency. Almost all reports include Cronbach alpha information, most alphas exceeding a .80 "floor." Yet, users sometimes need additional reliability information, which is not presented. For example, test–retest reliability information should be available for all trait measures, but it is not. Split-half reliability information is also rarely reported; this would be necessary for tests that have two forms. We have come to rely on the coefficient alpha, and few scale developers venture further.

We also noted that some measures necessarily have lower reliabilities, yet they may be measuring concepts that are difficult to measure in the first place (Emmert & Barker, 1989). For example, it is easier to measure task attraction (INTERPERSONAL ATTRACTION SCALE) than it is to measure constructs such as friendliness (COMMUNICATOR STYLE MEASURE) or conflict avoidance (RELATIONAL DIMENSIONS INSTRUMENT). Concepts that are more abstract may have lower coefficient alphas.

We also noticed that users of interpersonal measures often adapt the measure to an unintended context or different person, use different response options, or use only a part of a measure. Researchers should reassess reliability of the adapted or abridged measure and provide this information in their report. Reliability estimates are not current when measures are adapted in these ways. Reliability, however, does not guarantee validity.

Validity

In interpersonal communication, we found a dearth of content validity research. Although researchers can never be sure that they have assembled a set of items that reflect the content of a theoretical concept, they must do all that is possible to achieve content validity. Granted, not all forms of validity (e.g., multitrait–multimethod) need to be present in the initial introduction of a measure; however, content and construct validity are both essential in initial stages of measurement development.

Interpersonal communication research could benefit from multiple measurement methods and collection periods. Cappella (1987) argued that researchers need to place temporal or conceptual distance between behavioral self-reports and psychological self-report measures. If not, the covariation between perceptual/psychological self-reports and self-report measures of behavior create the problem of artifactual covariation due to the common methods factor. A multitrait–multimethod form of validity testing would minimize the effect of common methods. Earlier, Sypher (1980) warned us that scales utilizing recalled information about behaviors may not actually be measuring behavior but the person's memory of that behavior, which may be distorted.

Researchers also need to reevaluate measures periodically for what Poole and McPhee (1985) refer to as the "slippage between conception and questionnaire execution" (p. 119). A measure designed 20 years ago may need to be reconceptualized to reflect current thinking and/or attitudes. What is satisfying today may not be later. For example, Norton's QUALITY MARRIAGE INDEX conceptualizes satisfaction as "stability" and "being part of a team." This traditional view of satisfaction may not be current today. Also, items in the Touch Avoidance Measure (P. Andersen & Leibowitz, 1978) might lead respondents to think that sexual preference is being measured.

Measurement and Sample

Baxter (1988) identified three measurement problems with personal relationship research methodology. First, Baxter argued that relationship labels such as "close friends" and "acquaintances" are problematic in that using everyday language to operationalize meanings of relationship intimacy levels is inherently ambiguous. Second, Baxter claimed that much of the personal relationship research uses single-item scales instead of multiple-item indexes, which best tap the complex nature of relationships. Third, Baxter discussed the "ecological fallacy" notion: Relationships take place at the dyadic level, yet they are often measured at the individual level; the information provided by one partner is often generalized to the dyad. This is not a problem if one is actually studying individual perceptions, but often information on dyads is provided by only one of the members.

> [However,] new methods have not proliferated at the same rate as the new theoretical perspective . . . researchers have failed to see that they are working at an individual level to explain essentially dyadic action . . . researchers either have been forced to reframe their innovative research questions into more mundane forms that can be addressed with mainstream individually-focused methods or, even worse, they have used the old methods to provide answers to the new questions, thus violating a host of relevant theoretical and methodological, rather than purely statistical, assumptions. (Duck & Montgomery, 1991, p. 10)

One concern we had when we examined interpersonal measures was that of built-in inconsistencies or errors that are not corrected over time: (a) split infinitives, (b) errors in or mixed verb tense within the same item, (c) gender-specific language, (d) misspellings, (e) mixture of different scale responses (e.g., some Likert, some frequency), (f) inconsistency in the number of response options (e.g., some items scaled on 4 points and some on 5 within the same measure), (g) mixture of affective (feeling or attitude) and behavioral (past or current actions) or cognitive (needs or thoughts) items within the same scale, (h) mix of items about one's self, about a partner, and about their relationship in the same scale, (i) mix of items focused on past, present, and future behaviors in the same scale, and (j) lack of instructions for respondent (e.g., mind-set) and researcher (e.g., to reverse coding or order items randomly) in scale development report. Scale developers should correct their scales when such problems are found and be aware of the above problems when they develop scales.

Scale developers also must more closely consider their sample. Convenience sampling (e.g., college students) is the most prevalent sampling procedure, yet one must remember that this group is different in many ways from the general population. With a college student sample, a "longitudinal" study might last for only 10 weeks. Thus, more scale development research with a generalizable sample is called for.

One additional concern in research circles today is the selection procedure some measures use to identify communication strategies. Burleson et al. (1988) examined potential problems with the selection procedure (selecting options from a checklist) and compared it with the construction procedure where respondents write what they would actually say to those they are trying to persuade. Burleson et al. argued that when people are asked to construct strategies, they create strategies unlike (less prosocial) those that they would check on a provided list of strategies. Conversely, (a) Wheeless, Barraclough, and Stewart (1983) and Sorensen, Plax, and Kearney (1989) argued that the selection and construction methods are equivalent, (b) Seibold (1988) warned researchers not to eschew the selection procedure yet because not all studies use "likelihood of use" as a response mode, (c) Hunter (1988) claimed that the social desirability response tendency does not exist as Burleson et al. suggested, and (d) Boster (1988) suggested that Burleson et al. never actually measured compliance-gaining behavior in their studies so their claim that one method is better than another is yet untested.

All these measurement problems might lead the reader to conclude that interpersonal communication scale developers have been lax, but this is not the case. First, they have taken on some difficult tasks. Measuring qualities of interaction (e.g., INTERPERSONAL COMMUNICATION SATISFACTION INVENTORY), behavior (e.g., COMMUNICATIVE COMPETENCE SCALE), psychological constructs (e.g., Role Category Questionnaire [Crockett, 1965]), motives (e.g., INTERPERSONAL COMMUNICATION MOTIVES SCALE), and relationships (e.g., RELATIONAL DIMENSIONS INSTRUMENT) is no simple task. Second, they have adopted some psychological constructs and created measures with communication orientations (e.g., REVISED SELF-DISCLOSURE SCALE and PERCEIVED HOMOPHILY MEASURE). Third, they have realized the role of the situation in measurement and created state and trait versions of measures when appropriate (e.g., PERSONAL REPORT OF COMMUNICATION APPREHENSION and INTERACTION INVOLVEMENT SCALE). Fourth, some have engaged in elaborate (multistudy) scale development procedures establishing content, construct, and criterion-related validity.

As we have seen here, measurement in interpersonal communication, having received contributions from researchers in psychology, anthropology, sociology, nursing, and other disciplines, is alive and well. A large number of scales, indexes, tests, checklists, and observational coding schemes exist to answer today's research questions. Tomorrow's researchers need to find a way to measure more than individual perspectives—or a way to combine views from dyad members—to answer questions about two or more relationship partners. They will need to rethink and update measures to ensure currency, use more generalizable samples during scale development, and pay close attention to the style and form of the measures they create. Finally, they will need to continue reliability and validity testing of measures.

REFERENCES

Andersen, J. F., Andersen, P. A., & Jensen, A. D. (1979). The measurement of nonverbal immediacy. *Journal of Applied Communication Research, 7*, 153–180.

Andersen, P. A., & Leibowitz, K. (1978). The development and nature of the construct touch avoidance. *Environmental Psychology and Nonverbal Behavior, 3*(2), 89–109.

Archer, D., & Costanzo, M. (1988). *The Interpersonal Perception Task*. Berkeley: University of California Media Center.

Ayres, J. (1983). Strategies to maintain relationships: Their identification and perceived usage. *Communication Quarterly 31*, 62–67.

Bales, R. F. (1950). *Interaction process analysis: A method for the study of small groups*. Cambridge, MA: Addison-Wesley.

Bales, R. F., & Cohen, S. P. (1979). *SYMLOG: A system for the multiple-level observation of groups*. New York: Free Press.

Baxter, L. A. (1988). Dyadic personal relationships: Measurement options. In C. H. Tardy (Ed.), *A handbook for the study of human communication: Methods and instruments for observing, measuring, and assessing communication processes* (pp. 193–228). Norwood, NJ: Ablex.

Baxter, L. A., & Philpott, J. (1982). Attribution-based strategies for initiating and terminating friendships. *Communication Quarterly, 30*, 217–224.

Bell, R. A. (1985). Conversational involvement and loneliness. *Communication Monographs, 52*, 218–235.

Bell, R. A., & Daly, J. A. (1984). The affinity-seeking function of communication. *Communication Monographs, 51*, 91–115.

Bell, R. A., Daly, J. A., & Gonzalez, M. C. (1987). Affinity-maintenance in marriage and its relationship to women's marital satisfaction. *Journal of Marriage and the Family, 49*, 445–454.

Bem, S. L. (1981). *Bem Sex Role Inventory: Professional manual*. Palo Alto, CA: Consulting Psychologists Press.

Berscheid, E., Snyder, M., & Omoto, A. M. (1989). The relationship closeness inventory: Assessing the closeness of interpersonal relationships. *Journal of Personality and Social Psychology, 57*, 792–807.

Birdwhistell, R. L. (1970). *Kinesics and context: Essays on body motion communication*. Philadelphia: University of Pennsylvania.

Boster, F. J. (1988). Comments on the utility of compliance-gaining message selection tasks. *Human Communication Research, 15*, 169–177.

Buck, R. (1975). Nonverbal communication of affect in children. *Journal of Personality and Social Psychology, 31*, 644–653.

Buck, R. (1976). A test of nonverbal receiving ability: Preliminary studies. *Human Communication Research*, *2*, 162–171.

Burleson, B. R., Wilson, S. R., Waltman, M. S., Goering, E. M., Ely, T. K., & Whaley, B. B. (1988). Item desirability effects in compliance-gaining research: Seven studies documenting artifacts in the strategy selection procedure. *Human Communication Research*, *14*, 429–486.

Byrne, D. E. (1971). *The attraction paradigm*. New York: Academic Press.

Cappella, J. N. (1987). Interpersonal communication: Definitions and fundamental questions. In C. R. Berger & S. H. Chaffee (Eds.), *Handbook of communication science* (pp. 184–238). Newbury Park, CA: Sage.

Cheek, J. M., & Buss, A. H. (1981). Shyness and sociability. *Journal of Personality and Social Psychology*, *41*, 330–339.

Cody, M. J. (1982). A typology of disengagement strategies and an examination of the role intimacy, reactions to inequity and relational problems play in strategy selection. *Communication Monographs*, *49*, 148–170.

Coker, D. A., & Burgoon, J. K. (1987). The nature of conversational involvement and nonverbal encoding patterns. *Human Communication Research*, *13*, 463–494.

Crockett, W. H. (1965). Cognitive complexity and impression formation. *Progress in Experimental Personality Research*, *2*, 47–90.

Daly, J. A., & Diesel, C. A. (1992). Measures of communication-related personality variables. *Communication Education*, *41*, 405–414.

Daly, J. A., Vangelisti, A. L., & Daughton, S. M. (1987). The nature and correlates of conversational sensitivity. *Human Communication Research*, *14*, 167–202.

Davis, M. H. (1983). Measuring individual differences in empathy: Evidence for a multidimensional approach. *Journal of Personality and Social Psychology*, *44*, 113–126.

DeStephen, R. S., & Hirokawa, R. Y. (1988). Small group consensus: Stability of group support of the decision, task process, and group relationships. *Small Group Behavior*, *19*, 227–239.

Donaghy, W. C. (1989). Nonverbal communication measurement. In P. Emmert & L. L. Barker (Eds.), *Measurement of communication behavior* (pp. 296–332). New York: Longman.

Duck, S., & Montgomery, B. M. (1991). The interdependence among interaction substance, theory, and methods. In B. M. Montgomery & S. Duck (Eds.), *Studying interpersonal interaction* (pp. 3–15). New York: Guilford Press.

Ekman, P., & Friesen, W. V. (1978). *The Facial Action Coding System: A technique for the measurement of facial movement*. Palo Alto, CA: Consulting Psychologists Press.

Ekman, P., Friesen, W. V., & Tomkins, S. S. (1971). Facial affect scoring technique: A first validity study. *Semiotica*, *3*, 37–58.

Ellis, D. G. (1979). Relational control in two group systems. *Communication Monographs*, *46*, 153–166.

Emmert, P., & Barker, L. L. (1989). *Measurement of communication behavior*. New York: Longman.

Falbo, T., & Peplau, L. A. (1980). Power strategies in intimate relationships. *Journal of Personality and Social Psychology*, *38*, 618–628.

Fenigstein, A., Scheier, M. F., & Buss, A. H. (1975). Public and private self-consciousness: Assessment and theory. *Journal of Consulting and Clinical Psychology, 43,* 522–527.

Fisher, B. A. (1970). The process of decision modification in small discussion groups. *Journal of Communication, 20,* 51–64.

Fisher, B. A. (1979). Content and relationship dimensions of communication in decision-making groups. *Communication Quarterly, 27*(4), 3–11.

Fisher, B. A., Drecksel, G. L., & Werbel, W. S. (1979). Social information processing analysis (SIPA): Coding ongoing communication. *Small Group Behavior, 10,* 3–21.

Fitzpatrick, M. A., & Winke, J. (1979). You always hurt the one you love: Strategies and tactics in interpersonal conflict. *Communication Quarterly, 27*(1), 3–11.

Garvin, B. J., & Kennedy, C. W. (1986). Confirmation and disconfirmation in nurse/physician communication. *Journal of Applied Communication Research, 14,* 1–19.

Gottman, J. M. (1979). *Marital interaction: Experimental investigations.* New York: Academic Press.

Gudykunst, W. B., Chua, E., & Gray, A. J. (1987). Cultural dissimilarities and uncertainty reduction processes. *Communication Yearbook, 10,* 456–469.

Gudykunst, W. B., & Hammer, M. R. (1988). The influence of social identity and intimacy of interethnic relationships on uncertainty reduction processes. *Human Communication Research, 14,* 569–601.

Hammer, M. R., Gudykunst, W. B., & Wiseman, R. L. (1978). Dimensions of intercultural effectiveness: An exploratory study. *International Journal of Intercultural Relations, 2,* 382–393.

Hart, R. P., Carlson, R. E., & Eadie, W. F. (1980). Attitudes toward communication and the assessment of rhetorical sensitivity. *Communication Monographs, 47,* 1–22.

Harvey, J. H., Hendrick, S. S., & Tucker, K. (1988). Self-report methods in studying personal relationships. In S. Duck (Ed.), *Handbook of personal relationships: Theory, research and interventions* (pp. 99–113). New York: Wiley.

Hirokawa, R. Y. (1988). Group communication research: Considerations for the use of interaction analysis. In C. H. Tardy (Ed.), *A handbook for the study of human communication: Methods and instruments for observing, measuring, and assessing communication processes* (pp. 229–246). Norwood, NJ: Ablex.

Hirsbrunner, H. P., Frey, S., & Crawford, R. (1983). *Movement in human interaction: Description, parameter formation, and analysis.* Berne, Switzerland: Department of Psychology, University of Berne.

Hunter, J. E. (1988). Failure of the social desirability response set hypothesis. *Human Communication Research, 15,* 162–168.

Jones, W. H., & Russell, D. (1982). The social reticence scale: An objective instrument to measure shyness. *Journal of Personality Assessment, 46,* 629–631.

Jourard, S. M., & Lasakow, P. (1958). Some factors in self-disclosure. *Journal of Abnormal and Social Psychology, 56,* 91–98.

Kennedy, C. W., & Garvin, B. J. (1986). Confirmation-disconfirmation: A framework for the study of interpersonal relationships. In P. L. Chinn (Ed.), *Nursing research methodology: Issues and implementation* (pp. 221–235). Rockville, MD: Aspen.

King, C. E., & Christensen, A. (1983). The Relationship Events Scale: A Guttman scaling of progress in courtship. *Journal of Marriage and the Family, 45*, 671–678.

Knapp, M. L., Ellis, D. G., & Williams, B. A. (1980). Perceptions of communication behavior associated with relationship terms. *Communication Monographs, 47*, 262–278.

Koester, J., & Olebe, M. (1987). *Behavioral Assessment Scale for Intercultural Communication.* Sacramento, CA: Department of Communication Studies, California State University.

Koester, J., & Olebe, M. (1988). The Behavioral Assessment Scale for Intercultural Communication Effectiveness. *International Journal of Intercultural Relations, 12*, 233–246.

Larzelere, R. E., & Huston, T. L. (1980). The Dyadic Trust Scale: Toward understanding interpersonal trust in close relationships. *Journal of Marriage and the Family, 42*, 595–604.

Leary, M. R. (1988). Socially-based anxiety: A review of measures. In C. H. Tardy (Ed.), *A handbook for the study of human communication: Methods and instruments for observing, measuring, and assessing communication processes* (pp. 365–384). Norwood, NJ: Ablex.

Leathers, D. G. (1971). The Feedback Rating Instrument: A new means of evaluating discussion. *Central States Speech Journal, 22*, 32–42.

Lorr, M., & More, W. W. (1980). Four dimensions of assertiveness. *Multivariate Behavioral Research, 15*, 127–138.

Marangoni, C., & Ickes, W. (1989). Loneliness: A theoretical review with implications for measurement. *Journal of Social and Personal Relationships, 6*, 93–128.

McCroskey, J. C., & Richmond. V. P. (1979, May). *The reliability and validity of scales for the measurement of interpersonal attraction and homophily.* Paper presented at the meeting of the Eastern Communication Association, Philadelphia.

McCroskey, J. C., & Richmond, V. P. (1987). Willingness to communicate. In J. C. McCroskey & J. A. Daly (Eds.), *Personality and interpersonal communication* (pp. 129–156). Newbury Park, CA: Sage.

McLaughlin, M. L., Cody, M. J., & O'Hair, H. D. (1983). The management of failure events: Some contextual determinants of accounting behavior. *Human Communication Research, 9*, 208–224.

Mehrabian, A., & Epstein, N. (1972). A measure of emotional empathy. *Journal of Personality, 40*, 525-543.

Mortensen, C. D., Arntson, P. H., & Lustig, M. (1977). The measurement of verbal predispositions: Scale development and application. *Human Communication Research, 3*, 146–158.

Norton, R., & Montgomery, B. M. (1982). Style, content, and target components of openness. *Communication Research, 9*, 399–431.

Patterson, G. R. (1982). *A social learning approach to family intervention: Vol. 3. Coercive family process.* Eugene, OR: Castalia.

Petronio, S. (1984). Communication strategies to reduce embarrassment: Differences between men and women. *Western Journal of Speech Communication, 48*, 28–38.

Poole, M. S. (1983). Decision development in small groups: II. A study of multiple sequences in decision making. *Communication Monographs, 50,* 206–232.

Poole, M. S., & McPhee, R. D. (1985). Methodology in interpersonal communication research. In M. L. Knapp & G. R. Miller (Eds.), *Handbook of interpersonal communication* (pp. 100–170). Beverly Hills, CA: Sage.

Poole, M. S., & Roth, J. (1989). Decision development in small groups: IV. A typology of group decision paths. *Human Communication Research, 15,* 323–356.

Rathus, S. A. (1973). A 30-item schedule for assessing assertive behavior. *Behavior Therapy, 4,* 398-406.

Roach, A. J., Frazier, L. P., & Bowden, S. R. (1981). The Marital Satisfaction Scale: Development of a measure for intervention research. *Journal of Marriage and the Family, 43,* 537–546.

Rogers, L. E., & Farace, R. V. (1975). Analysis of relational communication in dyads: New measurement procedures. *Human Communication Research, 1,* 222–239.

Rosenthal, R., Hall, J. A., DiMatteo, M. R., Rogers, P. L., & Archer D. (1979). *Sensitivity to nonverbal communication: The PONS Test.* Baltimore, MD: Johns Hopkins University Press.

Rotter, J. B. (1967). A new scale for the measurement of interpersonal trust. *Journal of Personality, 35,* 651–665.

Ruben, B. D. (1976). Assessing communication competency for intercultural adaptation. *Group and Organization Studies, 1,* 334–354.

Rubin, Z. (1974). Liking and loving. In Z. Rubin (Ed.), *Doing unto others* (pp. 163–174). Englewood Cliffs, NJ: Prentice-Hall.

Russell, D., Peplau, L. A., & Cutrona, C. E. (1980). The Revised UCLA Loneliness Scale: Concurrent and discriminant validity evidence. *Journal of Personality and Social Psychology, 39,* 472–480.

Samter, W., & Burleson, B. R. (1984). Cognitive and motivational influences on spontaneous comforting behavior. *Human Communication Research, 11,* 231–260.

Scherer, K. R., & Ekman, P. (Eds.) (1982). *Handbook of methods in nonverbal behavior research.* Cambridge, England: Cambridge University Press.

Seibold, D. R. (1988). A response to "Item desirability in compliance-gaining research." *Human Communication Research, 15,* 152–161.

Sieburg, E. (1969). Dysfunctional communication and interpersonal responsiveness in small groups. *Dissertation Abstracts International, 30,* 2622A. (University Microfilms No. 73-28, 534)

Snyder, M. (1974). The self-monitoring of expressive behavior. *Journal of Personality and Social Psychology, 30,* 526–537.

Sorensen, G., Plax, T. G., & Kearney, P. (1989). The strategy selection-construction controversy: A coding scheme for analyzing teacher compliance-gaining message constructions. *Communication Education, 38,* 102–118.

Spanier, G. B. (1976). Measuring dyadic adjustment: New scales for assessing the quality of marriage and similar dyads. *Journal of Marriage and the Family, 38,* 15–28.

Spielberger, C. D., Gorsuch, R. L., & Lushene, R. E. (1970). *Manual for the State–Trait Anxiety Inventory.* Palo Alto, CA: Consulting Psychologists Press.

Spitzberg, B. H. (1988). Communication competence: Measures of perceived effectiveness. In C. H. Tardy (Ed.), *A handbook for the study of human communication: Methods and instruments for observing, measuring, and assessing communication processes* (pp. 67–105). Norwood, NJ: Ablex.

Spitzberg, B. H., & Cupach, W. R. (1989). *Handbook of interpersonal competence research.* New York: Springer-Verlag.

Spitzberg, B. H., & Hurt, H. T. (1987). The measurement of interpersonal skills in instructional contexts. *Communication Education, 36,* 28–45.

Stephen, T. D., & Markman, H. J. (1983). Assessing the development of relationships: A new measure. *Family Process, 22,* 15–25.

Sypher, H. E. (1980). Illusory correlation in communication research. *Human Communication Research, 7,* 83–87.

Tardy, C. H. (1988a). Interpersonal evaluations: Measuring attraction and trust. In C. H. Tardy (Ed.), *A handbook for the study of human communication: Methods and instruments for observing, measuring, and assessing communication processes* (pp. 269–283). Norwood, NJ: Ablex.

Tardy, C. H. (1988b). Interpersonal interaction coding systems. In C. H. Tardy (Ed.), *A handbook for the study of human communication: Methods and instruments for observing, measuring, and assessing communication processes* (pp. 285–300). Norwood, NJ: Ablex.

Tardy, C. H. (1988c). Self-disclosure: Objectives and methods of measurement. In C. H. Tardy (Ed.), *A handbook for the study of human communication: Methods and instruments for observing, measuring, and assessing communication processes* (pp. 323–346). Norwood, NJ: Ablex.

Tardy, C. H. (1988d). Social support: Conceptual clarification and measurement options. In C. H. Tardy (Ed.), *A handbook for the study of human communication: Methods and instruments for observing, measuring, and assessing communication processes* (pp. 347–364). Norwood, NJ: Ablex.

Vangelisti, A. L. (1991). The pedagogical use of family measures: "My how you've grown!" *Communication Education, 40,* 187–201.

Weiss, R. L., & Summers, K. J. (1983). Marital interaction coding systems—III. In E. E. Filsinger (Ed.), *Marriage and family assessment: A sourcebook for family therapy* (pp. 85–115). Beverly Hills, CA: Sage.

Wheeless, L. R., Barraclough, R., & Stewart, R. (1983). Compliance-gaining and power in persuasion. *Communication Yearbook, 7,* 104–145.

Wiseman, R. L., & Schenck-Hamlin, W. (1981). A multi-dimensional scaling validation of an inductively-derived set of compliance gaining strategies. *Communication Monographs, 48,* 251–270.

Measures of
Mass Communication

ALAN M. RUBIN
ELIZABETH M. PERSE

Mass communication research is, perhaps, the most widespread area of communication study throughout the world. This is evident in the usual meaning for the study of communication outside the United States—mass communication. Mass communication research grows out of different concerns and perspectives. It considers such aspects as historical development of the media; communication policy; structure of media industries; links between media, societal institutions, and political power structures; transnational flow of information; development communication; and audience effects. Here, we discuss only research that focuses on communication effects and audience self-report measurement.

To identify our measures in mass communication, we followed procedures similar to those of some authors in this volume (see Table 9). First we requested input from mass communication researchers via announcements in International Communication Association and Speech Communication Association newsletters, Bitnet requests to many colleagues, and requests in ComServe's MassCom and Methods hotlines. This procedure produced only a few useful responses. We then shifted our attention to the actual scholarly literature, examining the last 10 or more years of major journals that publish quantitative, empirical mass communication research, including: *Communication Research, Human Communication Research, Journalism Quarterly, Journal of Broadcasting and Electronic Media, Journal of Communication, Public Opinion Quarterly*, and several in related disciplines. Besides manual searching in journals and indexes such as the *Social Sciences Citation Index*, we also used CD-ROMs such as *PsychLit* to locate mention and application of scales.

Note. Measures that are profiled in this volume (in Part II) are typed in capital letters when cited in the text or tables.

37

TABLE 9. Mass Communication Measures

Media attitudes and perceptions
Amount of Invested Mental Effort (Salomon, 1983)
Crime-Related Anxiety (Weaver & Wakshlag, 1986)
Enjoyment of Frightening Films (Sparks, 1986)
NEWS CREDIBILITY SCALE
PERCEIVED REALISM SCALE
Perceptions of Program Violence (Greenberg & Gordon, 1972)
Social Presence of Communication Media (Short, Williams, & Christie, 1976)
SOURCE CREDIBILITY—BERLO
TELEVISION AFFINITY SCALE

Media use
Estimates of Exposure to Soap Opera Episodes (Carveth & Alexander, 1985)
Estimates of Exposure to Violent Television (Weaver & Wakshlag, 1986)
Exposure to Television Program Genres (A. M. Rubin & R. B. Rubin, 1982)
GRATIFICATIONS SOUGHT AND OBTAINED SCALES
Gratifications Sought from Remote Control Devices (Walker & Bellamy, 1991)
Gratifications Sought from VCRs (A. M. Rubin & Bantz, 1987)
Music Preference (Christenson & Peterson, 1988; Fink, Robinson, & Dowden, 1985)
POLITICAL MEDIA GRATIFICATIONS SCALE
Television Program Preference (Helregel & Weaver, 1989)
TELEVISION VIEWING MOTIVES SCALE

Media and social relations
AUDIENCE ACTIVITY MEASURES
FAMILY COMMUNICATION PATTERNS SCALE
PARASOCIAL INTERACTION SCALE
Parental Comments and Opinions about Television (Dorr, Kovaric, & Doubleday, 1989)
Television Content Rules (Brown, Childers, Bauman, & Koch, 1990)

Media outcomes and effects
Absorbing Content (Christ & Medoff, 1984)
Aggressive Attitudes (McLeod, Atkin, & Chaffee, 1972)
CULTIVATION INDEX
MEAN WORLD INDEX
Recall from News Exposure (Gunter, 1985)
Victim Responsibility and Sympathy (Linz, Donnerstein, & Penrod, 1984)
Visual Sex and Violence (Hansen & Hansen, 1990)

Media practices
Communication Practices of Journalists (Burgoon, Burgoon, Buller, & Atkin, 1987)
Editor Attitudes about Business and Capitalism (Olien, Tichenor, & Donohue, 1988; Peterson, Albaum, Kozmetsky, & Cunningham, 1984)
Editor Attitudes about Press Freedom Regulation (Anderson, Milner, & Galician, 1988)
Job Satisfaction (Rentner & Bissland, 1990)
Journalistic Professionalism (Idsvoog & Hoyt, 1977; McLeod & Hawley, 1964)
Public Relations Roles (Broom & Smith, 1979)

Related-area measures
Anomie (Srole, 1956)
Arousal (J. A. Russell, 1978)
Bem Sex Role Inventory (Bem, 1981)

(continued)

TABLE 9 (continued)

Contextual Age (A. M. Rubin & R. B. Rubin, 1982)
Eysenck Personality Questionnaire (Eysenck & Eysenck, 1975)
I/E Locus of Control (Rotter, 1966)
Imaginal Process Inventory (Singer & Antrobus, 1970)
Innovativeness (Leavitt & Walton, 1975)
INTERPERSONAL ATTRACTION SCALE
Interpersonal Mistrust (Wrightsman, 1964)
Manifest Anxiety (Taylor, 1953)
Multiple Affect Checklist (Zuckerman & Lubin, 1965)
Need for Cognition (Cacioppo & Petty, 1982)
Psychological Sex Roles (Spence & Helmreich, 1978)
Self-Esteem (Rosenberg, 1965)
Sensation Seeking (Zuckerman, 1979)
Sexual Callousness (Mosher, 1971)
UCLA Loneliness Scale (D. Russell, Peplau, & Cutrona, 1980)
UNWILLINGNESS-TO-COMMUNICATE SCALE

Coding schemes
Agenda Setting (McCombs & Shaw, 1972)
Cultivation (Gerbner & Gross, 1976; Gerbner, Gross, Signorielli, Morgan, & Jackson-Beeck, 1979)
Images of Women in Advertising (Dominick & Rauch, 1972)
Occurrence of News Reports after Censorship (Giffard & Cohen, 1989)
Frequency of News Story Types (Dominick, Wurtzel, & Lometti, 1975)
Sex and Violence in Music Videos (Sherman & Dominick, 1986)

We applied specific criteria when selecting the mass communication measures: (a) origin or application in the mass communication literature, (b) self-report measures, (c) utility or usefulness, (d) established track record (although we considered promising scales), (e) validity, and (f) reliability. We profiled only self-report measures used in surveys and experiments in mass communication research. We did not profile content coding schemes. Except for one measure of involvement and one of political media motivation, we did not profile measures from areas such as political communication (e.g., political activity, efficacy, interest, knowledge, and candidate image) or marketing (e.g., product preference, advertising evaluations, attitudes toward advertising, and purchase intent).

CATEGORIES OF MASS COMMUNICATION MEASURES

In this section we summarize some of the measures we located in the search. We group our list of measures in mass communication into six categories: Media Attitudes and Perceptions, Media Use, Media and Social Relations,

Media Outcomes and Effects, Media Practices, and Related-Area Measures. There are numerous mass communication measures, yet few are widely used across research studies or programs.

Media Attitudes and Perceptions

People's attitudes about media and their content influence exposure and outcomes. We profile several measures that assess believability of media (SOURCE CREDIBILITY SCALE and NEWS CREDIBILITY SCALE), perceived importance of media (TELEVISION AFFINITY SCALE), and perceived realism of media content (PERCEIVED REALISM SCALE). There are other useful perceptual and attitudinal measures including Amount of Invested Mental Effort (Salomon, 1983), Perceptions of Program Violence (Greenberg & Gordon, 1972), and Social Presence of Communication Media (Short, Williams, & Christie, 1976). For example, based on the belief that cognitive processes affect a person's fear reactions, Sparks (1986) developed a 10-item Enjoyment of Frightening Films Scale to assess past experiences with frightening films. Based on the expectation that criminal victimization experience mediates any links between TV viewing and one's sense of personal vulnerability to crime, Weaver and Wakshlag (1986) developed a three-dimensional measure, Crime-Related Anxiety.

Media Use

Media use or utility is a core concept in mass communication. Media exposure also fits in this category, although we delay mention of TV exposure until a later discussion of issues in mass communication measurement. Exposure to other media is often measured rather simply: the number of days in the last week a newspaper was read or the number of films attended in the last month. Webster and Lichty (1991) reported different ways that exposure to broadcast media are measured.

We profile several measures of gratifications sought from different media (TELEVISION VIEWING MOTIVES SCALE, GRATIFICATIONS SOUGHT AND OBTAINED SCALES, and POLITICAL MEDIA GRATIFICATIONS SCALE). Some newer measures uncover gratifications sought from media technologies such as videocassette recorders (A. M. Rubin & Bantz, 1987) and remote-control devices (Walker & Bellamy, 1991). Other measures assess music preference (Christenson & Peterson, 1988; Fink, Robinson, & Dowden, 1985), TV program preference (Helregel & Weaver, 1989), and exposure to TV program genres (A. M. Rubin & R. B. Rubin, 1982). Others estimate exposure to violent TV (Weaver & Wakshlag, 1986) and soap opera episodes (Carveth & Alexander, 1985). Media use is sometimes conceptualized as one part of a communication environment whereby scholars assess alternatives to mass communication (Windahl, Hojerback, & Hedinsson, 1986).

Media and Social Relations

Researchers have developed viable measures to examine relations among media consumers such as TV viewers and between consumers and media content. Some measures, such as the FAMILY COMMUNICATION PATTERNS SCALE, seek to assess social relationships as they link to media use. Other such measures include Parental Comments and Opinions about Television (Dorr, Kovaric, & Doubleday, 1989) and Television Content Rules (Brown, Childers, Bauman, & Koch, 1990). Additional measures such as the PARASOCIAL INTERACTION SCALE and AUDIENCE ACTIVITY MEASURES consider one's sense of involvement with media content and personalities.

Media Outcomes and Effects

A significant part of mass communication research focuses on the effects of exposure to media or media content. Several measures are used as dependent variables in surveys and experiments. The CULTIVATION INDEX and MEAN WORLD INDEX reflect such research whereby exposure to media such as TV is expected to influence viewers. Cultivation researchers also have considered whether TV exposure might produce social reality beliefs (e.g., Gerbner et al., 1977). For example, Pingree (1983) used a variant of the Cultivation Index and reported small correlations between amount of TV exposure and social reality perceptions such as the demographics of the family and of women's and men's work. Using a similar measure, Perse (1986) reported a low correlation between amount of soap opera viewing and social reality perceptions. That index asked respondents to estimate, out of 100, how many women and men were doctors, lawyers, divorced, and so on, and how many people have committed a serious crime. Research by Buerkel-Rothfuss and Mayes (1981) and Carveth and Alexander (1985) used these items separately.

Others considered media outcomes such as aggressive attitudes (McLeod, Atkin, & Chaffee, 1972). News awareness studies use knowledge tests to assess what subjects recall from news exposure (Gunter, 1985). Such tests are created for specific periods and experimental stimuli and must be adapted for future application. Experimental researchers often devise specific measures that pertain to their experimental stimuli. Linz, Donnerstein, and Penrod (1984), for example, assessed victim responsibility and sympathy after subjects viewed a rape trial documentary. Other scales assess impressions of content, such as how absorbing the content is (Christ & Medoff, 1984) or visual sex and violence (Hansen & Hansen, 1990).

Media Practices

Characteristics of media professionals were studied because of concerns about their unintentional or conscious influence on news selection and coverage. Researchers developed indexes to measure journalistic professionalism in print and broadcasting (Idsvoog & Hoyt, 1977; McLeod & Hawley, 1964). Assuming such attitudes affect practices, others focused on attitudes held by editors about business and capitalism (Olien, Tichenor, & Donohue, 1988; Peterson, Albaum, Kozmetsky, & Cunningham, 1984) and press freedom regulation (Anderson, Milner, & Galician, 1988). Other measures evaluated such aspects as job satisfaction (Rentner & Bissland, 1990). Some researchers sought to develop measures to tap the tasks and roles of media practitioners such as the communication practices of journalists (e.g., Burgoon, Burgoon, Buller, & Atkin, 1987) and public relations roles (Broom & Smith, 1979). Researchers usually have not extensively addressed the validity and reliability of such measures, nor have such measures received widespread application (cf. Henningham, 1984; Reagan, Anderson, Sumner, & Hill, 1990).

Related-Area Measures

Communication research, including mass communication research, draws heavily from the work in related social science disciplines such as psychology and sociology. Several such measures were developed or adapted from such disciplines and applied in mass communication research. These include Contextual Age (A. M. Rubin & R. B. Rubin, 1982), Imaginal Process Inventory (Singer & Antrobus, 1970), INTERPERSONAL ATTRACTION SCALE, and UNWILLINGNESS-TO-COMMUNICATE SCALE. Researchers have used several of these measures, including contextual age, unwillingness to communicate (Armstrong & A. M. Rubin, 1989), and interpersonal attraction (McCain, Chilberg, & Wakshlag, 1977; R. B. Rubin & McHugh, 1987), in mass communication studies.

Other measures were drawn directly from fields such as psychology and sociology. These include Anomie (Srole, 1956), Arousal (J. Russell, 1978), Eysenck Personality Questionnaire (Eysenck & Eysenck, 1975), Innovativeness (Leavitt & Walton, 1975), Interpersonal Mistrust (e.g., Wrightsman, 1964), Manifest Anxiety (Taylor, 1953), Multiple Affect Checklist (Zuckerman & Lubin, 1965), Need for Cognition (Cacioppo & Petty, 1982), Psychological Sex Roles (Spence & Helmreich, 1978), and Sexual Callousness (Mosher, 1971). There are numerous additional measures that are drawn from other disciplines and applied widely in communication research. These include I/E Locus of Control (Rotter, 1966), Self-Esteem (Rosenberg, 1965), Sensation Seeking (Zuckerman, 1979), Bem Sex-Role Inventory (Bem, 1981), and the UCLA Loneliness Scale (Russell, Peplau, & Cutrona, 1980).

The use of such measures reflects mass communication's roots in related disciplines and shows the central role of communication in the social sciences. Because mass communication scholars often draw from the literature of related fields, mass communication research itself has become fragmented. We discuss the measurement implications of fragmentation later in the chapter.

CODING SCHEMES

Because we limit our discussion to self-report measures used in surveys and experiments, we have not included content analysis schemes. Content analysis is widely used in mass communication research to explore issues of media ownership, content of news, media images or portrayals of societal groups, and levels of media violence. By conducting a content analysis, a researcher usually assumes that content reflects a communicator's goals and believes that the presentation of messages influences audiences. Content coding schemes have focused on several areas, such as sex and violence in music videos (Sherman & Dominick, 1986), images of women in advertising (Dominick & Rauch, 1972), occurrence of news reports after censorship (Giffard & Cohen, 1989), and frequency of news story types (Dominick, Wurtzel, & Lometti, 1975).

Some content analyses adapt definitions and coding schemes used in earlier research. The Cultural Indicators Project's definition of violence is an example of a widely used operational definition (Gerbner & Gross, 1976). Much content analysis, though, employs operational definitions and content categories developed to answer specific research questions of a particular study, and focuses on the frequency of certain message elements. These studies usually are concerned with decisions about the unit of analysis and category construction. Two important research areas that rely on content analysis are cultivation and agenda setting.

Cultivation

The most comprehensive content analysis scheme is that of the Cultural Indicators Project, whose cultivation hypothesis suggests that media, especially TV, cultivate shared cognitive and affective images of roles and behavior in the surrounding world (Gerbner & Gross, 1976; Gerbner, Gross, Signorielli, Morgan, & Jackson-Beeck, 1979). Cultivation investigators expect that enculturation is the primary function of TV. By presenting images of a mean and violent world and a world that celebrates youth, for example, viewers who consume large amounts of TV come to fear their surrounding environment and see older people as feeble and unable to run their own life.

The investigators locate a "television answer" for their Cultivation Index (to compare with a real-world answer) by analyzing TV content (e.g., the number of violent acts). For example, they ask: "During any given week, what are your chances of being involved in some kind of violence? About 1 in 10? About 1 in 100?" They then survey people's beliefs about viewers' fear of violence, sense of mistrust, or images of people presented in the media, expecting that heavy viewers will more often provide the television answer (i.e., 1 in 10). These researchers have chronicled demographics of TV characters and occurrences of violence.

Although the Cultural Indicators Project's examination of TV violence has been at the heart of many content analytic schemes, its definition of violence has been controversial (Signorielli, 1985). Industry representatives argue that the measure overestimates TV violence because the definition includes comic and accidental violence (Blank, 1977) and ignores "the circumstances under which an action occurs, the acceptability of the action by a culture's norms and mores, and the use of an action as self-protection" (Wurtzel & Lometti, 1987, p. 120).

Agenda Setting

Content analysis is also critical to agenda-setting research (McCombs & Shaw, 1972). Agenda-setting researchers expect the media to affect people's perceptions of the importance of societal issues by influencing our awareness of issues and events. Agenda-setting scholars examine news content and determine the relative coverage of different issues over time. For example, the news media may legitimize certain candidates during a campaign by providing more extensive coverage of their campaigns than of their opponents' campaigns. Consistent with Lippmann's (1949) view that the news media shape our images of the surrounding world, McCombs and Shaw (1977) argued that the more the media present a topic, the more people think about that topic.

Agenda-setting researchers determine people's agendas in several ways, for example (a) asking them to name the most important issue, (b) asking them to rank order a predetermined list of issues, or (c) asking them to rate the importance of each issue from a list (Williams, 1985). These results are then correlated with the results of a content analysis of the media agenda. For the media agenda, researchers can assess the amount of time (e.g., in seconds) in TV newscasts, or the space (e.g., in column inches) in newspapers, devoted to different issues. Researchers have found support for agenda setting but have noted that other variables (e.g., voting intention, campaign interest, and media attention) affect agenda-setting relationships (Williams, 1985).

MASS COMMUNICATION MEASUREMENT ISSUES

Many issues surround measurement in mass communication. We chose to discuss four primary ones here: fragmentation, validity, reliability, and the measurement of TV exposure. Later, we illustrate some of these issues in the measurement of two mass communication constructs.

Fragmentation

Mass communication research encompasses myriad interests and perspectives. The mass communication research literature is fragmented (a) within communication associations and journals, (b) across disciplines (not only in communication but also in psychology, sociology, political science, business and economics, marketing, law, etc.), and (c) across national borders (i.e., many literatures of different languages).

The literature is far-reaching, raising concerns of awareness and generalizability. Instead of systematic development in measurement we encountered fragmentation and compartmentalization in many languages and cultures. This problem may be partially remedied by the growth and expansion of computer-generated databases and technology. Fragmentation means that useful measures are not being further applied, tested, and developed, sometimes even beyond one's own research program let alone across disciplinary subdivisions, other disciplines, and other countries.

International Nature

The international nature of mass communication research raises concerns about the abilities of researchers to be aware of, to be able to apply, and to adapt the inquiries of others to their own research programs. For example, agenda setting has been examined in North America, Europe, and Asia, sometimes with similar but also contrasting measures. Measures are sometimes shared but are often quite diverse. Similar comments apply to uses and gratifications and to cultivation research.

Traditions

Another reason for the fragmentation in mass communication research is the applied research tradition, which does not stress external validity of measurement. The emphasis on problem solving led to the development of specific measures to answer specific questions. Hence, there is little measurement development beyond an individual research problem. Issues of reliability and cross-study validity checks are ignored. The need to access and generalize to certain populations led to widespread use of telephone surveys in applied research and development and of simple, few, or single-item survey measures.

Utility

Utility reflects concerns about awareness, application, and adaptability. Often we either do not learn about a measure or do not learn about the utility of a measure to other research questions or cultures. When we do, some useful measures have been applied in other cultures, extending our knowledge and awareness of them. Such extension, often via translation or adaptation to specific research forms (e.g., experiments vs. telephone interviews), helps us achieve deeper knowledge of a measure's external validity. Because of such fragmentation, the utility and generalizability of research studies and findings are concerns.

Validity

External validity and internal validity constitute a second major issue. Given the lack of financial support, in particular, many mass communication studies, especially in the United States, use nonprobability sampling techniques. Such techniques limit generalizability. However, the application and replication of studies across research settings improves the external validity of results. This is beneficial, especially for many U.S. studies, which tend to rely on purposive or convenience samples as compared with, for example, many European mass communication studies. Too often, though, mass communication researchers seem unconcerned with external validity or go well beyond the warranted boundaries of a selective sample.

In mass communication, we have paid even less attention to internal validity. Often, the scope of our statements about measurement validity is limited to face or content validity (i.e., the measures appear to assess the concept adequately, or expert judges have determined that the items represent the dimensions of the concept). Or, we simply reference past research practice in using or applying measures. Occasionally, we progress to the arenas of concurrent validity, as we test our measures against similar measures. Rarely, though, do we establish construct validity. Too often, we fail to consider the conceptual meaning of our concepts. We have come to believe many "truths" about media effects such as violence, aggression, and learning without having paid enough attention to the construct validity of our measures.

Content analysis coding schemes also are not immune to concerns about validity. Disagreements about the definition of "violence" highlight the importance of face validity. Krippendorff (1980) discussed validity issues central to content analysis. For example, sampling affects external validity, and we should use alternate measures of similar constructs to establish convergent and discriminant validity of operational definitions.

Reliability

We have been somewhat better, at least in some respects, about the third issue, reliability of measures. Most researchers report scale homogeneity scores (e.g., Cronbach coefficient alphas), although the practice varies greatly. Sometimes, though, this is done with an occasional abuse, such as arguing that a low alpha is acceptable because an index consists of items intending to measure different aspects of the complex concept (in which case Cronbach's alpha is inappropriate), or reporting an alpha only after a reviewer or editor has requested it.

Although we have rather consistent measures, at least at their point of application, we have been less observant of considering scale item equivalence (e.g., split-half methods) and stability over time (e.g., test–retest reliability). Of course, stability is only meaningful for certain measures. For example, perceived TV realism, as an attitude or disposition, should be fairly stable over time for adults. Exposure to TV, though, should vary greatly from day to day or season to season because of life-style or time demands.

The practical concerns of some mass communication research may dictate the use of single-item measures or only part of a longer scale. In those cases researchers should attempt to demonstrate reliability by equivalence (comparing the items with other reliable measures) or stability (if appropriate). Researchers can use shortened versions of previously developed scales if they use available methods to correct for attenuation due to unreliability.

Intercoder reliability is important to content analysis. Low coder agreement limits internal and external validity of the measures and the utility of the study's results. Two issues are central to intercoder reliability. First, different methods for determining intercoder reliability are appropriate for different types of data. Second, acceptable levels of intercoder agreement depend on the type of data and the level of measurement (Krippendorff, 1980).

Measuring Television Exposure

Because so many questions of media effects center on the impact of media exposure, the most central issue in mass communication research is how to measure exposure. There is no agreed-on way to measure exposure. Webster and Wakshlag (1985) summarized methods used by researchers and measurement organizations. There are weaknesses in almost every approach.

Salomon and Cohen (1978) provided sound advice when deciding how to measure exposure. They suggested that the validity of the measurement depends on the theoretical perspective of the study.

TV exposure is measured in several ways. Many researchers ask respondents to state how many hours a day they watch TV. Salomon and Cohen (1978) argued that this type of measure is useful when treating viewing as time spent with the medium, especially when it displaces other activities. Because distractions accompany much TV viewing (Bechtel, Achelpohl, & Akers, 1972), general measures do not reflect content assimilation. Here, measures of how much attention people pay to TV or its content might be more appropriate. We profile attention measures in this volume under AUDIENCE ACTIVITY MEASURES. Measures of message discrimination, or messages that are remembered (Clarke & Fredin, 1978; Clarke & Kline, 1974), assess transmission of and attention to content.

TV exposure may also be conceptualized as program choice or content preference. Hawkins and Pingree (1981) and A. M. Rubin, Perse, and Taylor (1988) argued that cultivation effects of TV, for example, are better explained by exposure to certain program types rather than general TV exposure. When testing several operational definitions of TV exposure and program choice, Potter and Chang (1990) concluded that a proportional measure, that is, the ratio of program type exposure to total TV exposure, showed more cultivation effects. Proportional measures may also be useful in estimating selective exposure to certain content (A. M. Rubin & Perse, 1987).

TV exposure is a complex concept. Different measures have theoretical implications and yield different results. This issue also has implications for scholars concerned with exposure to other mass media. Spending time with the radio or with newspapers is not the same, for example, as attentive understanding of content. Researchers must use valid and reliable operational definitions that are consistent with their theoretical perspective. We can only answer questions about construct validity in the context of theoretically grounded research questions.

Applications

To illustrate some of these issues in mass communication measurement, we consider two research areas: source credibility and perceived realism. The research in both areas illustrate the inconsistencies and difficulties encountered when developing measures in mass communication.

Source Credibility

Several researchers have constructed measures of believability of different media. The most widely used of these is the SOURCE CREDIBILITY SCALE, which reduced an initial pool of 83 bipolar adjectives to three source credibility factors referring to the criteria by which receivers evaluate sources: safety (e.g., pleasant–unpleasant), qualification or expertise (e.g., experienced–inexperienced), and dynamism (e.g., aggressive–meek). Although Berlo, Lemert, and Mertz (1970) did not assess validity and reliability, many have used, adapted, or cited this multidimensional measure, which was a substantial development over earlier single-item questions such as "If you got conflicting or different reports of the same news story from radio, television, and the newspapers, which of the three versions would you be most inclined to believe, the one on radio, or television, or newspapers?" (Greenberg, 1966, p. 667).

Other researchers also tried to develop multiple-indicator measures of media credibility. Markham (1968), for example, reduced 55 semantic differential items to evaluate the credibility of TV newscasters to three factors: reliable–logical (e.g., unbelievable–believable), showmanship (e.g., uninteresting–interesting), and trustworthiness (e.g., unfriendly–friendly). He did not specifically mention validity or reliability in his study, nor did Dominick (1976), who used Markham's 13-item credibility scale and supported his three credibility dimensions for commercial clutter on radio news.

Many have factor-analyzed a variety of credibility items derived from Berlo et al. (1970), Markham (1968), McCroskey (1966), and others. Whitehead (1968), for example, factor-analyzed 65 bipolar items for high- and low-credibility speakers on the topic, "What constitutes the public interest in broadcasting?" He located four source credibility dimensions: Trustworthiness (e.g., honest–dishonest), Competence (e.g., experienced–inexperienced), Dynamism (e.g., aggressive–meek), and Objectivity (e.g., objective–subjective). Across the many credibility studies there have been occasional but inconsistent mentions of reliabilities for derived factors, or of face and predictive validity (e.g., Avery & McDermott, 1975; Whitehead, 1968 [did not]; McCroskey & Jenson, 1975 [did]).

Others extended the source credibility research in the news arena. The NEWS CREDIBILITY SCALE identified two factors: Credibility (e.g., accurate–inaccurate); and Social Concerns (e.g., moral–immoral). Gaziano and McGrath (1986) did not report reliability but instead supported construct validity by finding their measure to relate to the choice of which medium to believe. Their measure, though, was criticized by Meyer (1988), who reported a reliable seven-item credibility scale, but then pared down his measure to a less "bulky" five face-valid items.

Credibility researchers seem to have followed Avery and McDermott's (1975) advice: "Differences that exist within respondents and differences in the types of concepts to which the subjects react" produce "inherent limitations in the use of generalizable scales." Therefore, "the currently popular advice to researchers is to 'factor analyze every time'" (p. 220). Many mass communication researchers have embraced this advice, not only for credibility research but for other research as well. There are at least two problems caused by this. First, technique, rather than theory, begins to drive mass communication measurement. Second, results are isolated or restricted to specific samples or measurement items. Mass communication researchers need to consider the conceptual meaning of their constructs and to use measures with established validity and reliability.

Scholars need to consider whether concepts such as media credibility are static. That is, is credibility conceptually identical across media, time, samples, and contexts? If not, we should use specific measures for specific situations. Researchers also could use confirmatory factor analysis to clarify dimensions of credibility drawn from theory.

Perceived Realism

Perceived realism is another example of the lack of consistent scale development and application in mass communication. One's perception of realism mediates whether content can affect people. Various scholars have used measures of perceived realism in their studies. Some have asked one-item questions about realism. Others have asked questions about the believability of specific aspects of TV programs. Such methods might illuminate theoretical issues, but they are difficult to translate to other research contexts.

Three scales used to assess TV's perceived realism show the difficulty of measurement development. Greenberg began using measures of perceived realism in the 1960s. However, not all studies report the items used or their reliabilities. Moreover, there is no consistency in the items chosen to measure the concept. The report of his most widely used scale does not list the items (Greenberg, 1974).

Scholars in the uses and gratifications perspective have used A. M. Rubin's (1981) adaptation of the Greenberg (1974) scale. Hawkins (1977) and Potter (1986) also developed their own scales owing to their beliefs that perceived realism is a multidimensional, not unidimensional, concept. Some researchers have used Hawkins's two dimensions of perceived realism (Magic Window and Social Expectations) in some contexts. Reports, though, have given little information about the scale's measurement properties, making it difficult to evaluate the scale.

The PERCEIVED REALISM SCALE is more conceptually discussed. Potter (1986) sought to differentiate his scale from those used in previous research. It is not clear, though, if all dimensions are tapping "perceived realism" or some other construct such as communication motivation. Few articles have reported the scale, which has been primarily restricted to examining cultivation. We need more research to evaluate this scale's worth in other contexts, as well as that of the other two scales.

Measures of perceived realism require conceptual clarity and development. Scholars should explore the value in treating the construct as uni- or multidimensional. Examinations of convergent and discriminant validity will help clarify whether measures "spill over" to other related concepts. Comparative research using the different scales might also help research derive a parsimonious method of measuring perceived realism.

CONCLUSION

Mass communication research needs to overcome its past limitations and also respond to research questions posed by rapidly changing communication environments by developing new, sound instruments. New questions arise because of the impact of technology on media content, audiences, society, and culture. For example, changes in technology drastically altered media coverage between the Vietnam and Persian Gulf wars. Technology altered space and time constraints on the media. It affected the timeliness and manner of message delivery, the availability of information to the public, and government concerns about control of the press. Such changes produce new questions about the nature of news coverage, press and government credibility, and audience effects.

There is a need to review and reassess the state of measurement in mass communication. Mass communication can benefit from consistency, exploration, and explanation. Fragmentation does not absolve scholars from awareness of existing measures or from conceptual and methodological rigor. Our understanding of theoretical relationships will grow with the development of meaningful and consistently applied measures.

REFERENCES

Anderson, D. A., Milner, J. W., & Galician, M. L. (1988). How editors view legal issues and the Rehnquist Court. *Journalism Quarterly, 65*, 294–298.

Armstrong, C. B., & Rubin, A. M. (1989). Talk radio as interpersonal communication. *Journal of Communication, 39*(2), 84–94.

Avery, R. K., & McDermott, P. J. (1975). Speaker affiliation and station image. *Journal of Broadcasting, 19*, 211–220.

Bechtel, R. B., Achelpohl, C., & Akers, R. (1972). Correlates between observed behavior and questionnaire responses on television viewing. In E. A. Rubinstein, G. A. Comstock, & J. P. Murray (Eds.), *Television and social behavior: Vol. 4. Television in day-to-day life, patterns of use* (DHEW Publication No. HSM 72-9059, pp. 274–344). Washington, DC: U.S. Government Printing Office.

Bem, S. L. (1981). *Bem Sex Role Inventory: Professional manual.* Palo Alto, CA: Consulting Psychologists Press.

Berlo, D. K., Lemert, J. B., & Mertz, R. J. (1970). Dimensions for evaluating the acceptability of message sources. *Public Opinion Quarterly, 33,* 563–576.

Blank, D. M. (1977). The Gerbner violence profile. *Journal of Broadcasting, 21,* 273–279.

Broom, G. M., & Smith, G. D. (1979). Testing the practitioner's impact on clients. *Public Relations Review, 5*(3), 47–59.

Brown, J. D., Childers, K. W., Bauman, K. E., & Koch, G. G. (1990). The influence of new media and family structure on young adolescents' television and radio use. *Communication Research, 17,* 65–82.

Buerkel-Rothfuss, N. L., & Mayes, S. (1981). Soap opera viewing: The cultivation effect. *Journal of Communication, 31*(3), 108–115.

Burgoon, J. K., Burgoon, M., Buller, D. B., & Atkin, C. K. (1987). Communication practices of journalists: Interaction with public, other journalists. *Journalism Quarterly, 64,* 125–132.

Cacioppo, J. T., & Petty, R. E. (1982). The need for cognition. *Journal of Personality and Social Psychology, 42,* 116–131.

Carveth, R., & Alexander, A. (1985). Soap opera viewing motivations and the cultivation process. *Journal of Broadcasting and Electronic Media, 29,* 259–273.

Christ, W. G., & Medoff, N. J. (1984). Affective state and the selective exposure to and use of television. *Journal of Broadcasting, 28,* 51–63.

Christenson, P. G., & Peterson, J. B. (1988). Genre and gender in the structure of music preferences. *Communication Research, 15,* 282–301.

Clarke, P., & Fredin, E. (1978). Newspapers, television and political reasoning. *Public Opinion Quarterly, 42,* 143–160.

Clarke, P., & Kline, F. G. (1974). Media effects reconsidered: Some new strategies for communication research. *Communication Research, 1,* 224–240.

Dominick, J. R. (1976). The effects of commercial clutter on radio news. *Journal of Broadcasting, 20,* 169–176.

Dominick, J. R., & Rauch, G. E. (1972). The image of women in network TV commercials. *Journal of Broadcasting, 16,* 259–265.

Dominick, J. R., Wurtzel, A., & Lometti, G. (1975). Television journalism vs. show business: A content analysis of eyewitness news. *Journalism Quarterly, 52,* 213–218.

Dorr, A., Kovaric, P., & Doubleday, C. (1989). Parent–child coviewing of television. *Journal of Broadcasting and Electronic Media, 33,* 35–51.

Eysenck, H. J., & Eysenck, S. (1975). *Eysenck Personality Questionnaire.* San Diego, CA: Educational and Industrial Testing Service.

Fink, E. L., Robinson, J. P., & Dowden, S. (1985). The structure of music preference and attendance. *Communication Research, 12,* 301–318.

Gaziano, C., & McGrath, K. (1986). Measuring the concept of credibility. *Journalism Quarterly, 63,* 451–462.

Gerbner, G., & Gross, L. (1976). Living with television: The violence profile. *Journal of Communication, 26*(2), 173–199.

Gerbner, G., Gross, L., Eleey, M. F., Jackson-Beeck, M., Jeffries-Fox, S., & Signorielli, N. (1977). TV violence profile no. 8: The highlights. *Journal of Communication*, 27(2), 171–180.

Gerbner, G., Gross, L., Signorielli, N., Morgan, M., & Jackson-Beeck, M. (1979). The demonstration of power: Violence profile no. 10. *Journal of Communication*, 29(3), 177–196.

Giffard, C. A., & Cohen, L. (1989). South African TV and censorship: Does it reduce negative coverage? *Journalism Quarterly*, 66, 3–10.

Greenberg, B. S. (1966). Media use and believability: Some multiple correlates. *Journalism Quarterly*, 43, 665–670.

Greenberg, B. S. (1974). Gratifications of television viewing and their correlates for British children. In J. G. Blumler & E. Katz (Eds.), *The uses of mass communications: Current perspectives on gratifications research* (pp. 71–92). Beverly Hills, CA: Sage.

Greenberg, B. S., & Gordon, T. (1972). Perceptions of violence in television programs: Critics and the public. In G. Comstock & E. A. Rubinstein (Eds.), *Television and social behavior: Vol. 1. Media content and control* (DHEW Pub. No. HSM 72-9057, pp. 244–258). Washington, DC: U.S. Government Printing Office.

Gunter, B. (1985). News sources and news awareness: A British survey. *Journal of Broadcasting and Electronic Media*, 29, 397–406.

Hansen, C. H., & Hansen, R. D. (1990). The influence of sex and violence on the appeal of rock videos. *Communication Research*, 17, 212–234.

Hawkins, R. P. (1977). The dimensional structure of children's perceptions of television reality. *Communication Research*, 4, 299–320.

Hawkins, R. P., & Pingree, S. (1981). Uniform messages and habitual viewing: Unnecessary assumptions in social reality effects. *Human Communication Research*, 7, 291–301.

Helregel, B. K., & Weaver, J. B. (1989). Mood-management during pregnancy through selective exposure to television. *Journal of Broadcasting and Electronic Media*, 33, 15–33.

Henningham, J. P. (1984). Comparisons between three versions of the Professional Orientation Index. *Journalism Quarterly*, 61, 302–309.

Idsvoog, K. A., & Hoyt, J. L. (1977). Professionalism and performance of television journalists. *Journal of Broadcasting*, 21, 97–109.

Krippendorff, K. (1980). *Content analysis: An introduction to its methodology*. Beverly Hills, CA: Sage.

Leavitt, C., & Walton, J. (1975). Development of a scale for innovativeness. In M. J. Schlinger (Ed.), *Advances in consumer research* (Vol. 2, pp. 545–554). Chicago: Association for Consumer Research.

Linz, D., Donnerstein, E., & Penrod, S. (1984). The effects of multiple exposures to filmed violence against women. *Journal of Communication*, 34(3), 130–147.

Lippmann, W. (1949). *Public opinion*. New York: Free Press.

Markham, D. (1968). The dimensions of source credibility of television newscasters. *Journal of Communication*, 18(1), 57–64.

McCain, T. A., Chilberg, J., & Wakshlag, J. (1977). The effect of camera angle on source credibility and attraction. *Journal of Broadcasting*, 21, 35–46.

McCombs, M. E., & Shaw, D. L. (1972). The agenda-setting function of mass media. *Public Opinion Quarterly*, *36*, 176–187.

McCombs, M. E., & Shaw, D. L. (1977). "Agenda setting" and the political process. In D. L. Shaw & M. E. McCombs (Eds.), *The emergence of American political issues: The agenda-setting function of the press* (pp. 149–156). St. Paul, MN: West.

McCroskey, J. C. (1966). Scales for the measurement of ethos. *Speech Monographs*, *33*, 65–72.

McCroskey, J. C., & Jenson, T. A. (1975). Image of mass media news sources. *Journal of Broadcasting*, *19*, 169–180.

McLeod, J. M., Atkin, C. K., & Chaffee, S. H. (1972). Adolescents, parents, and television use: Adolescent self-report measures for Maryland and Wisconsin samples. In G. Comstock & E. Rubinstein (Eds.), *Television and social behavior: Vol. 3. Television and aggression* (DHEW Publication No. 72-9058, pp. 173–238). Washington, DC: U.S. Government Printing Office.

McLeod, J. M., & Hawley, S. E. (1964). Professionalization among newsmen. *Journalism Quarterly*, *41*, 529–538.

Meyer, P. (1988). Defining and measuring credibility of newspapers: Developing an index. *Journalism Quarterly*, *65*, 567–574, 588.

Mosher, D. L. (1971). Sex callousness toward women. In *Technical report of the Commission on Obscenity and Pornography: Vol. 8. Erotica and social behavior* (pp. 313–325). Washington, DC: U.S. Government Printing Office.

Olien, C. N., Tichenor, P. J., & Donohue, G. A. (1988). Relation between corporate ownership and editor attitudes about business. *Journalism Quarterly*, *65*, 259–266.

Perse, E. M. (1986). Soap opera viewing patterns of college students and cultivation. *Journal of Broadcasting and Electronic Media*, *30*, 175–193.

Peterson, R. A., Albaum, G., Kozmetsky, G., & Cunningham, I. C. (1984). Attitudes of newspaper business editors and general public toward capitalism. *Journalism Quarterly*, *61*, 56–65.

Pingree, S. (1983). Children's cognitive processes in constructing social reality. *Journalism Quarterly*, *60*, 415–422.

Potter, J. W. (1986). Perceived reality and the cultivation hypothesis. *Journal of Broadcasting & Electronic Media*, *30*, 159–174.

Potter, J. W., & Chang, I. C. (1990). Television exposure measures and the cultivation hypothesis. *Journal of Broadcasting and Electronic Media*, *34*, 313–333.

Reagan, J., Anderson, R., Sumner, J., & Hill, S. (1990). A factor analysis of Broom and Smith's Public Relations Roles Scale. *Journalism Quarterly*, *67*, 177–183.

Rentner, T. L., & Bissland, J. H. (1990). Job satisfaction and its correlates among public relations workers. *Journalism Quarterly*, *67*, 950–955.

Rosenberg, M. (1965). *Society and the adolescent self-image*. Princeton, NJ: Erlbaum.

Rotter, J. B. (1966). Generalized expectancies for internal versus external control of reinforcement. *Psychological Monographs, 80* (1), 1–28.

Rubin, A. M. (1981). An examination of television viewing motivations. *Communication Research*, *8*, 141–165.

Rubin, A. M., & Bantz, C. R. (1987). Utility of videocassette recorders. *American Behavioral Scientist*, *30*, 471-485.

Rubin, A. M., & Perse, E. M. (1987). Audience activity and television news gratifications. *Communication Research, 14*, 58–84.

Rubin, A. M., Perse, E. M., & Taylor, D. S. (1988). A methodological examination of cultivation. *Communication Research, 15*, 107–134.

Rubin, A. M., & Rubin, R. B. (1982). Contextual age and television use. *Human Communication Research, 8*, 228–244.

Rubin, R. B., & McHugh, M. P. (1987). Development of parasocial interaction relationships. *Journal of Broadcasting and Electronic Media, 31*, 279–292.

Russell, D., Peplau, L. A., & Cutrona, C. E. (1980). The Revised UCLA Loneliness Scale: Concurrent and discriminant validity evidence. *Journal of Personality and Social Psychology, 39*, 472–480.

Russell, J. A. (1978). Evidence of convergent validity on the dimensions of affect. *Journal of Personality and Social Psychology, 36*, 1152–1168.

Salomon, G. (1983). The differential investment of mental effort in learning from different sources. *Educational Psychologist, 18*, 42–50.

Salomon, G., & Cohen, A. A. (1978). On the meaning and validity of television viewing. *Human Communication Research, 4*, 265–270.

Sherman, B. L., & Dominick J. R. (1986). Violence and sex in music videos: TV and rock 'n' roll. *Journal of Communication, 36*(1), 79–93.

Short, J., Williams, E., & Christie, B. (1976). *The social psychology of telecommunications.* London: Wiley.

Signorielli, N. (1985). The measurement of violence in television programming: Violence indices. In J. R. Dominick & J. E. Fletcher (Eds.), *Broadcasting research methods* (pp. 235–251). Boston: Allyn & Bacon.

Singer, J., & Antrobus, J. (1970). *The Imaginal Processes Inventory.* Princeton, NJ: Educational Testing Service.

Sparks, G. G. (1986). Developing a scale to assess cognitive responses to frightening films. *Journal of Broadcasting and Electronic Media, 30*, 65–73.

Spence, J. T., & Helmreich, R. L. (1978). *Masculinity and femininity: Their psychological dimensions, correlates and antecedents.* Austin: University of Texas Press.

Srole, L. (1956). Social integration and certain corollaries: An exploratory study. *American Sociological Review, 21*, 709–716.

Taylor, J. A. (1953). A personality scale of manifest anxiety. *Journal of Abnormal and Social Psychology, 48*, 285–290.

Walker, J. R., & Bellamy, R. V., Jr. (1991). Gratifications of grazing: An exploratory study of remote control use. *Journalism Quarterly, 68*, 422–431.

Weaver, J., & Wakshlag, J. (1986). Perceived vulnerability to crime, criminal victimization experience, and television viewing. *Journal of Broadcasting and Electronic Media, 30*, 141–158.

Webster, J. G., & Lichty, L. W. (1991). *Ratings analysis: Theory and practice.* Hillsdale, NJ: Erlbaum.

Webster, J. G., & Wakshlag, J. (1985). Measuring exposure to television. In D. Zillmann & J. Bryant (Eds.), *Selective exposure to communication* (pp. 35–62). Hillsdale, NJ: Erlbaum.

Whitehead, J. L., Jr. (1968). Factors of source credibility. *Quarterly Journal of Speech, 54*, 59–63.

Williams, W., Jr. (1985). Agenda-setting research. In J. R. Dominick & J. E. Fletcher (Eds.), *Broadcasting research methods* (pp. 189–201). Boston: Allyn & Bacon.

Windahl, S., Hojerback, I., & Hedinsson, E. (1986). Adolescents without television: A study in media deprivation. *Journal of Broadcasting and Electronic Media*, *30*, 47–63.

Wrightsman, L. S. (1964). Measurement of philosophies of human nature. *Psychological Reports*, *14*, 743–751.

Wurtzel, A., & Lometti, G. (1987). Researching television violence. In A. A. Berger (Ed.), *Television in society* (pp. 117–132). New Brunswick, NJ: Transaction.

Zuckerman, M. (1979). *Sensation seeking: Beyond the optimal level of arousal*. Hillsdale, NJ: Erlbaum.

Zuckerman, M., & Lubin, B. (1965). *Manual for the Multiple Affect Adjective Checklist*. San Diego, CA: Educational and Industrial Testing Service.

Measures of
Organizational Communication

CAL W. DOWNS
SUE DeWINE
HOWARD H. GREENBAUM

Communication is a relatively recent academic discipline, and organizational communication has been an important subset of that discipline since 1950. Because communication is acknowledged by academics and managers as fundamentally important in the operation of all organizations, there has been a major push since 1970 to develop instruments helpful in analyzing communication so that we can make interventions to achieve organizational effectiveness.

In 1985, the Organizational Communication Division of the International Communication Association (ICA) established a research task force to identify and critique instruments that had been used in organizational communication research. This task force affiliated with *Management Communication Quarterly* (MCQ) and agreed to generate reviews of instruments used in organizational communication and management research. From its inception (in August 1987) until 1991, every issue of MCQ included an article reviewing one or more instruments developed to measure organizational communication constructs. The task force's intent was to "provide information that fills the current gap, evaluate and compare instruments, stimulate refined research, build on the current foundation, and provide networking and research outlets for scholars" (Greenbaum, DeWine, & Downs, 1987, p. 132). The task force continued to provide this ongoing source of instrumentation review, and this chapter is founded on the work of that task force.

The magnitude of the task of identifying major instruments in organizational communication research was demonstrated in two review articles.

Note. Measures that are profiled in this volume (in Part II) are typed in capital letters when cited in the text or tables.

57

First, Greenbaum and Gardner (1985) identified over 500 instruments that had been cited in communication dissertations and journals. Not all of these, of course, were instruments focusing directly on communication. Of the 500, only about 20% had been used as many as three times, and approximately 80% had been designed by the researcher and used only in that person's research. Second, in a survey of 180 journals over a 5-year period, DeWine and Pearson (1985) generated a list of 209 self-report paper-and-pencil tests that had been reported in communication journals. Neither list is complete.

Five organizational communication practices inhibit the possibility of a complete list. First, organizational communication is a boundary-spanning discipline with very imprecise perimeters. Scholars in communication departments focus on communication in organizations, but so do scholars in the disciplines of business, psychology, sociology, education, health science, journalism, and political science. Some cross-fertilization takes place across disciplines, but often it occurs by accident as one person happens to discover what a colleague from a different discipline is doing. A complete list of instruments would require searching numerous databases in numerous disciplines.

Second, the content of what is covered in organizational communication research is exceedingly broad, yet individual scholars tend to develop specialties on narrow facets of organizational communication. On the one hand, a few instruments are designed to give a comprehensive view of communication in organizations. On the other hand, many instruments examine more limited organizational communication constructs such as competence, communication style, organizational commitment, conflict, source valence, work-group effectiveness, stress, and compliance gaining. So there is a mix of micro- and macrolevel measures.

Third, the study of organizations encompasses other aspects of communication, such as interpersonal communication. In their review of instruments used in communication journals, DeWine and Pearson (1985) discovered that many interpersonal communication instruments were used in organizational research. In fact, many of the instruments identified in the interpersonal chapter of this book have been used by organizational scholars to examine interpersonal issues in the work setting, such as interpersonal attraction, sex roles, and communication apprehension. Interpersonal relationships are a key element in how organizations function, so it is quite natural that organizational researchers would turn to interpersonal relationship constructs to better understand how an organization survives. Studies of superior–subordinate relationships necessarily belong in both domains.

Fourth, sometimes when researchers develop a good instrument to measure organizational communication, they incorporate it into a proprietary consulting practice rather than report it in academic research journals. This makes it difficult for others to use and assess.

Fifth, scholars from many countries develop instruments to measure organizational communication. Furthermore, these instruments often appear in noncommunication publications because their academic home may be in a different discipline. Osmo Wiio's work is a notable exception, and it is known in the United States because of his participation in ICA. Despite efforts by ICA and the World Communication Association (WCA) to develop international networks, most researchers' interactions still tend to be within a national framework.

Because of the large number of instruments used in organizational communication research, determining which measures to include in this volume was somewhat difficult, but the task was made somewhat easier because of the prior work of the ICA task force. Some of the considerations are described below:

1. We gave preference to instruments that comprehensively examine communication in organizations.

2. Whenever several instruments measured the same concept, we gave preference to those developed by communication scholars. For example, the ORGANIZATIONAL IDENTIFICATION QUESTIONNAIRE was selected over three other instruments that measure organizational commitment but were developed outside the communication field.

3. We gave preference to measures that demonstrated reliability and validity. However, in some instances, new measures without such data were included because they seemed to hold promise for future research.

4. We gave preference to organizational communication instruments developed in the field with organizational employees rather than with students or student employees. Because most organizational research uses a natural setting, researchers find it difficult to replicate studies and acquire large samples. Also, they cannot always obtain executive approval of data collection from employees or adjust the research program to work schedules, which restricts instrument development. For example, when a researcher needs to identify sub-constructs of scales, several hundred subjects may be needed for a factor analysis. Such a goal is often unrealistic in an organization.

5. Instruments needed to have a communication component. No attempt was made to draw narrow definitions of organizational communication, yet some judgment calls were made about what instruments constitute organizational communication research instruments. For example, the Job Description Index (Smith, Kendall, & Hulin, 1969) is used as an outcome variable in much satisfaction research, but it was not included in this volume because it lacks a communication component.

Given the above limitations and issues, there is a surprisingly large number of well-developed organizational communication instruments. No attempt has been made to list all the instruments available for organizational communication research, but the ones selected for this chapter satisfied one or more of the criteria listed above. We grouped the instruments into three sections: (a) Comprehensive Instruments, (b) Communication Process Instruments, and (c) Organizational Outcomes Instruments. They are listed in Table 10. The following discussion gives an overview of instruments in each category. Then we examine some of the measurement issues in organizational communication.

COMPREHENSIVE INSTRUMENTS

Six primary instruments examine communication throughout the entire organization. The INTERNATIONAL COMMUNICATION ASSOCIATION AUDIT, the ORGANIZATIONAL COMMUNICATION SCALE, and the COMMUNICATION SATISFACTION QUESTIONNAIRE are profiled in this volume. In addition, the ORGANIZATIONAL COMMUNICATION DEVELOPMENT AUDIT QUESTIONNAIRE and the ORGANIZATIONAL CULTURE SURVEY are standardized measures (to allow ease of scoring and ease of making comparisons across organizations) developed by scholars in the communication discipline. One additional measure is the comprehensive Survey of Organizations by Likert (1967). The scope of this instrument goes far beyond communication (e.g., organizational climate, supervisor leadership, group process, satisfaction); yet it also covers many of the topics covered by communication instruments. Furthermore, it has been used quite extensively, and a rich database has been formed. Taylor and Bowers (1972) reported extensive studies to support its construct, content, and predictive validity.

COMMUNICATION PROCESS INSTRUMENTS

Since the 1970s, instrument development has focused on facets of organizational communication rather than on a comprehensive view of organizational communication. Five of the most popular areas are conflict, mentoring, competence, load, and management communication.

Conflict

Conflict is pervasive in organizations as members experience incompatibilities and inevitably compete for resources, directions for change, career development opportunities, interunit advantage, and organizational allegiances. Some estimate that 20–50% of a manager's time is spent handling

TABLE 10. Organizational Communication Instruments

<u>Comprehensive instruments</u>

COMMUNICATION SATISFACTION QUESTIONNAIRE
INTERNATIONAL COMMUNICATION ASSOCIATION AUDIT
ORGANIZATIONAL COMMUNICATION SCALE
ORGANIZATIONAL COMMUNICATION DEVELOPMENT AUDIT QUESTIONNAIRE
ORGANIZATIONAL CULTURE SURVEY
Survey of Organizations (Likert, 1967)

<u>Communication process instruments</u>

Conflict

Conflict Management Message Style (Ross & Dewine, 1988)
Conflict Management Survey (Hall, 1986)
Conflict Management of Difference (MODE) Scale (Thomas & Kilmann, 1974)
Managerial Grid (Blake & Mouton, 1964)
ORGANIZATIONAL COMMUNICATION CONFLICT INSTRUMENT
Organizational Conflict Inventory (Rahim, 1983)

Team building

Team Excellence Questionnaire (Larson & LaFasto, 1989)
Team Interaction Profile (Wilson Learning, 1985)
TEAM-REVIEW QUESTIONNAIRE

Organizational groups

Input

   Group Atmosphere Scale (Fiedler, 1967)
   Index of Work Cohesion (Price & Meuller, 1986)
   Interpersonal Trust Scale (Chun & Campbell, 1974)
   Measures of Morale (Scott, 1967)

Process

   Group Behavior Questionnaire (Blake & Mouton, 1964)
   Group Procedural Order Questionnaire (Putnam & Wilson, 1982)
   Interaction Behavior Measure (McCroskey & Wright, 1971)

Input–Process

   Decision Involvement Analysis (Thierbach, 1980)
   Group Dimension Description Questionnaire (Hemphill, 1957)

Multistage

   Group Atmosphere Scale (Hanson, 1981)
   GROUP BEHAVIOR INVENTORY
   Job Reaction Questionnaire (Honeywell Inc., 1985)

Mentoring

MENTORING AND COMMUNICATION SUPPORT SCALE
Mentoring Questionnaire (Eubank, 1987/1988)

Competence

COMMUNICATIVE COMPETENCE SCALE
COMMUNICATOR COMPETENCE QUESTIONNAIRE
INTERACTION INVOLVEMENT SCALE
Relational Competence Scale (Cupach & Spitzberg, 1983)

(continued)

TABLE 10 (*continued*)

Load
THREE-DIMENSIONAL COMMUNICATION LOAD SCALE

Management communication
Style
    COMMUNICATIVE ADAPTABILITY SCALE
    COMMUNICATOR STYLE MEASURE
    Focal Person's Communication Survey (Klaus & Bass, 1982)
    Management Communication Style (Richmond & McCroskey, 1979)

Leadership
    Coaching Practices Survey (Mahler, 1963, cited in Morrison, McCall, & DeVries, 1978)
    Desirable Motivational Characteristics (McClelland, 1961)
    Grid Feedback from a Subordinate to a Boss (Blake & Mouton, 1964)
    Leader Effectiveness and Adaptability Description Instrument (Hersey & Blanchard, 1973)
    Leadership Opinion Questionnaire (Fleischman, 1969)
    Management Practices Questionnaire (Miller & Zenger, 1976, cited in Morrison et al., 1978)
    Management Profiling, As Others See You (Daniels, Dyer, & Moffitt, 1975)
    Manager Feedback Program (Hinrichs, 1975)
    Organizational Behavior Describer Survey (Harrison & Oshrey, 1976, cited in Pfeiffer & Jones, 1977)

<u>Organizational outcomes instruments</u>
COMMUNICATION SATISFACTION QUESTIONNAIRE
Job Description Index (Smith, Kendall, & Hulin, 1969)
Organizational Commitment Instrument (Cook & Wall, 1980)
Organizational Commitment Questionnaire (Mowday, Porter, & Steers, 1979)
ORGANIZATIONAL IDENTIFICATION QUESTIONNAIRE
Productivity Audit (Mali, 1978)

conflict of some sort. Its very pervasiveness makes handling conflict "one of the most challenging problems that organizational members face" (Putnam, 1988b, p. 293). These concerns led to the development of a number of instruments used in both research and training. A special edition of MCQ (Putnam, 1988a) reviewed some of the principal conflict measures: Managerial Grid (Blake & Mouton, 1964), Conflict Management Survey (Hall, 1986), Conflict MODE (Thomas & Kilmann, 1974), Organizational Conflict Inventory (Rahim, 1983). Also useful is the Conflict Management Message Style (Ross & DeWine, 1988). However, a conflict instrument with a specific focus on communication is profiled in this volume: the ORGANIZATIONAL COMMUNICATION CONFLICT INSTRUMENT by Putnam and Wilson (1982).

The most widely used conflict instrument is the Conflict Management of Difference (MODE) Scale by Thomas and Kilmann (1974), but it does not have a communication focus. It is based on Blake and Mouton's (1964) grid but is simpler to complete and score than a similar scale by Hall (1986). Respondents consider 30 pairs of items on assertive and cooperative axes. The number of times they select a particular mode determines their conflict management style: collaborating, compromising, competing, accommodating, or avoiding. Womack (1988) reported acceptable validity scores, but the test–retest reliability and intercorrelations are problematic.

Also based on Blake and Mouton's (1964) grid, Hall's (1986) Conflict Management Survey classifies conflict styles in the interpersonal, small group, and intergroup contexts. Scores indicate one of five general orientations to conflict: synergistic, compromise, yield–lose, win–lose, and lose–leave. The instrument is lengthy, and scoring is complex; nevertheless, response to it in training sessions has been very favorable. Schockley-Zalabak (1988) reported satisfactory reliability and validity levels. One controversial point is that, like Blake and Mouton, Hall rank-orders the styles in terms of an ideal method of resolving conflict and some disagree with the rank order.

Rahim (1983), using dimensions of Concern for Self and Concern for Others, also based the Organizational Conflict Inventory II on the work of Blake and Mouton (1964). This measure asks respondents to agree or disagree with 28 Likert-type items and classifies responses according to five styles of conflict management: integrating/collaborative, obliging, compromising, dominating/competing, and avoiding/withdrawal. Weider-Hatfield (1988) (a) concluded that much research has been conducted on the scale's validity, (b) reported Cronbach alphas ranging from .61 to .95 across eight studies, and (c) praised the item analysis work done on the scale.

In the Conflict Management Message Style, Ross and DeWine (1988) developed an instrument that was particularly focused on communication. Therefore, they created 18 Likert-type items revolving around particular message types. Factor analysis of over 1,500 subjects uncovered only three styles: self-oriented messages, issue-oriented messages, and other-oriented messages. More work needs to be done on the reliability of the instrument, but construct validity looks favorable. It has been correlated with Schutz's FIRO-B Scale, and the results indicate that it is indeed valid.

Team Building

Team building is the most common intervention for organizational development and, thus, has important ramifications for scholars in organizational communication. A review of the literature reveals that there are no consistent definitions of what an effective team is or what the processes of building teams are (C. W. Downs & Blubaugh, 1989). Generally, the process of team building starts with some sort of diagnosis with an instrument; and the results are then fed back to the team or group for processing. Although numerous instruments are designed to analyze the status of team interaction, most scholars who develop them hold them in a proprietary manner to use them commercially.

The most notable team-building measure is the Team Excellence Questionnaire (Larson & LaFasto, 1989). It is based on in-depth interviews with nationally recognized leaders from a number of different organizations. The authors are eager to have researchers conduct studies to provide reliability and validity data. It has now been translated into Spanish with the expectation that it will be used abroad. Its items measure eight general factors: Clear Elevating Goal, Results-Driven Structure, Unified Commitment, Collaborative Climate, Standards of Excellence, Competent Team Members, External Support, and Recognition and Principled Leadership. Permission to use this instrument may be obtained from Larson. Another useful instrument is the Team Interaction Profile (Wilson Learning, 1985).

This volume profiles an additional team instrument, the TEAM-REVIEW QUESTIONNAIRE. There is not much analytic data about this measure, but it is profiled because (a) it covers comprehensively variables that obstruct effective teamwork and (b) it is seen as having much research potential. Group interactions have always been important in the organizational process, and in a sense, teams are a special type of group. However, not all groups are teams, and that is why they are treated separately in this review.

Organizational Groups

Taylor and Bowers (1972) called organizational groups the basic building blocks of an organization because an organization is a structure of groups linked together by overlapping memberships into a pyramid through which work flows. Jablin and Sussman (1983) defined an organizational group as a collection of three or more organization members who interact more or less regularly over time, are cognizant of one another, perceive themselves as a group, and are embedded within a network of interlocking tasks, roles, and expectations. Many of the innovations designed to make organizations more effective focus on groups called teams, task forces, or quality circles. Because of their importance in organizations, the evaluation of groups has been recognized as essential for understanding organizations.

Research on group processes has always been a major component of the communication discipline. In this review we selected only those instruments that have an organizational application. The group instruments can be classified according to a systems model of group behavior developed by Greenbaum, Kaplan, and Metlay (1988). The model treats the group as an open system composed of four successive stages: input, process, output, feedback. The most popular instruments measure input and process. Few instruments measure output in the group setting.

Input Instruments

Input measures focus on contributions of individuals to a group's effort. The Group Atmosphere Scale (Fiedler, 1967) is a 10-item measure of group climate. The Index of Work Cohesion Scale (Price & Meuller, 1986) contains only five items, but research with it has reported Cronbach alphas of .88 or higher. The Interpersonal Trust Scale (Chun & Campbell, 1974) contains 25 items measuring four different dimensions; Cronbach alphas (.50 to .60) are not particularly strong. However, the most comprehensive input instrument is the Measure of Morale (Scott, 1967), which evaluates seven dimensions of Group Environment, three of Group Interaction, four of Individual Input, and two of the Task; research has identified factor congruence coefficients ranging from .77 to .97.

Process Instruments

Three instruments measure group process behaviors. The Group Behavior Questionnaire (Blake & Mouton, 1964; Hanson, 1981) is one of the earliest and most successful instruments to measure group process. It contains 23 items that measure four dimensions (including one on Communication), and test–retest reliabilities range from .56 to .86. The Group Procedural Order Questionnaire (Putnam & Wilson, 1982) measures two dimensions of group process and is composed of 48 items; test–retest reliabilities range from .69 to .80. And the Interaction Behavior Measure (McCroskey & Wright, 1971) uses 12 items to measure six different dimensions (the most explicit communication dimension is Verbosity) of group process; reliabilities range from .64 to .92.

Input–Process Instruments

Two measures of input–process have been used in organizational communication research. The Decision Involvement Analysis (Thierbach, 1980) is an 80-item questionnaire that focuses primarily on expertise and involvement of people. Alphas ranged from .83 to .91. The Group Dimension Description Questionnaire (Hemphill, 1957) is another pioneer instrument. Much longer than most, it contains 150 items to measure 13 dimensions of group interactions. Split-half reliabilities range from .28 to .92.

Multistage Instruments

Multistage instruments examine more than one or two group process stages. The Group Atmosphere Scale (Hanson, 1981) has only nine items and measures two dimensions: Satisfaction/Productivity and Tensions. Although the Satisfaction/Productivity dimension seems to focus only on group output, it also refers to group process. Interjudge reliabilities are high, ranging from .85 to .97.

Many other multistage instruments exist, but only two are profiled in this volume. The Job Reaction Questionnaire (Honeywell Inc., 1985) was developed to assess the effects of quality circle participation on employees' perceptions of their work life and the GROUP BEHAVIOR INVENTORY was first used to measure interaction processes within work groups and was subsequently used to measure the impact of organizational interventions.

Mentoring

Whereas it is possible to examine the mentor–protege relationship as an interpersonal one, successful mentoring is now seen as an organizational variable, a way in which organizations can increase their success. Mentoring is "the term given for situations in which an older, more experienced person advises, supports, and encourages a younger or less experienced person" (Collin, 1988, p. 23). An estimated one third of the major U.S. companies now have formal mentoring programs, and researchers have investigated problems inherent in mentor relationships, the impact of such programs on women and nonwhite employees, and their influence on career outcomes.

Although many studies of mentoring have been conducted since 1988, only two standardized measures have been used. Eubank (1987/1988) developed a Mentoring Questionnaire for a dissertation to investigate sex differences in the mentoring process, and Kalbfleisch and Davies (1990) used it to determine how communication competence, self-esteem, and risk in intimacy predict mentoring relationships. The second measure, the MENTORING AND COMMUNICATION SUPPORT SCALE, is so new that it does not yet have an extensive research base, but the authors anticipated increased research using the scale in the near future.

Competence

Communication competence has been examined mainly as an interpersonal construct. Perotti and DeWine (1987) reviewed the COMMUNICATIVE COMPETENCE SCALE, the INTERACTION INVOLVEMENT SCALE, and the Relational

Competence Scale (Cupach & Spitzberg, 1983). Monge, Backman, Dillard, and Eisenberg (1982) modified the communication competence construct and made it appropriate for organizational research in their COMMUNICATOR COMPETENCE QUESTIONNAIRE. It is profiled in this volume.

Load

Almost every organizational communication textbook has a section on communication overload or underload, yet optimum load is rarely mentioned because it is so difficult to measure. Load is a concept defined primarily by transgression (i.e., when things are not going right). Nevertheless, as organizational environments became increasingly complex due to advancing technologies, people were expected to process more information than they did in prior years, and communication overload, often referred to as information overload, became a major problem. Chung and Goldhaber (1991) developed a new THREE-DIMENSIONAL COMMUNICATION LOAD SCALE to measure communication load in terms of quantity, complexity, and equivocality.

Management Communication

The superior–subordinate relationship is often described as the most important communication link in organizations. Consequently, many instruments were designed to gather information about the way managers communicate to subordinates. Although few of these instruments are profiled in this volume, they have potential for use in organizational research. This section provides a brief overview of two kinds of management communication instruments: style and leadership. Leadership-style instruments are reviewed here because many contain communication items.

Style

Communication style has been an important research area because of its critical influence in organizational relationships and also because of its training application. C. W. Downs, Archer, McGrath, and Stafford (1988) reviewed five style instruments that measured different aspects of communication style:

1. The COMMUNICATOR STYLE MEASURE is the most popular measure of communication style for scholars in communication. It is profiled in this volume.

2. Richmond and McCroskey (1979) developed the Management Communication Style scale to investigate style's relationship to employee

satisfaction. The styles reflect boss-centered or subordinate-centered leadership orientations. Respondents to the three questions merely select on a 19-point continuum whether or not their communication style is one that tells, sells, consults, or joins. Reliability estimates have been in the .80–.90 range. Critics have praised it for investigating style in the actual organizational setting, but some have also been uncomfortable with its brevity and the social desirability tendency, which might affect respondents.

3. The COMMUNICATIVE ADAPTABILITY SCALE views competence as the ability to adapt to different social constraints. C. W. Downs, McGrath, Stafford, and Rowland (1990) discovered through factor analysis and canonical correlation that the *Communicative Adaptability Scale* had more stable dimensions than any of the other style instruments they reviewed.

4. Klaus and Bass (1982) developed the Focal Person's Communication Survey to measure how people's perceptions of communication style might be congruent or incongruent. They designed an instrument that people fill out themselves and others fill out about them. Twenty-five Likert-type items break into 11 dimensions: Communication Style (careful transmitter, open/two-way, frank, careful listener, informal), Credibility (trustworthy, informative, dynamic), and Organizational Outcomes (role clarity, job satisfaction, satisfaction with each other). Reliability and validity evidence is limited.

Leadership

Leadership encompasses all the processes through which people in organizations structure their actions to accomplish their goals. Consequently, almost any leadership measure can be used to examine elements of communication.

Morrison, McCall, and DeVries (1978) reviewed 24 instruments that allow both managers and subordinates to rate the manager and thus provide important feedback to managers about their leadership. The sophistication of the empirical and theoretical development of these instruments varies considerably. K. Barge and Schleuter (1988) also reviewed leadership instruments. Potentially useful leadership measures include the following:

1. The Coaching Practices Survey (Mahler, 1963, cited in Morrison et al., 1978), has 62 items that measure nine factors. Many of the items have a Communication dimension (e.g., "How often is your supervisor frank in telling you what he/she thinks?" and "Has your superior used meetings with you and your peers to discuss each person's objectives and goals?"). This instrument is now dated.

2. The Desirable Motivational Characteristics instrument contains 48 items based on achievement motivational work (McClelland, 1961). Sev-

eral items focus on relationships (e.g., "Always tries to watch over and control the subordinate," and "Wants to be the one who gives orders in the department").

3. The Leader Effectiveness and Adaptability Description Instrument (Hersey & Blanchard, 1973) contains 20 items, each used to measure (a) leadership style, (b) style range, and (c) style adaptability. This instrument forms the basis for its authors' later work on situational leadership.

4. The Leadership Opinion Questionnaire (Fleischman, 1969) is one of the pioneering instruments developed to measure Structure (task) and Consideration (relationships) dimensions of leadership. Sample communication items include "Speak in a manner not to be questioned" and "Stress importance of being ahead of other units."

5. The Manager Feedback Program (Hinrichs, 1975) contains 40 items that measure 10 dimensions. Some of the labels used to describe the dimensions are communication oriented: "Maintaining Communication," "Clarity of Job Requirements," "Group Atmosphere," and "General Relations with Manager."

6. The Grid Feedback from a Subordinate to a Boss is a short, simple instrument developed to measure information requests (Blake & Mouton, 1964). Each of 10 dimensions is measured by one item each. A sample item is: "Brings me in to discuss and contribute to the quality of plans."

7. The Management Profiling, As Others See You (Daniels, Dyer, & Moffitt 1975) has 34 items that measure seven dimensions, including Communication, Decision Making, Influence Interactions, and Listening.

8. The Management Practices Questionnaire (Miller & Zenger, 1976, cited in Morrison et al., 1978) contains 76 items. Most of its 13 scales have a communication emphasis. It measures Communicating, Decision Making, Giving Support, Team Building, and Delegating.

9. The Organizational Behavior Describer Survey (Harrison & Oshrey, 1976, published in Pfeiffer & Jones, 1977) contains 25 items that measure Rational–Technical Competence, Verbal Dominance, Emotional Expressiveness, and Consideration. According to Morrison et al. (1978), it has been used extensively to determine the effects of T-groups.

ORGANIZATIONAL OUTCOMES INSTRUMENTS

Although one purpose behind the measurement of organizational communication is merely to understand the processes, a basic thrust of much of the research is to relate communication phenomenon to organizational outcomes such as satisfaction, productivity, and commitment. Of these three, most research has aimed at the relationship between dimensions of Communication and Satisfaction (C. W. Downs, Clampitt, & Laird, 1988).

Many questionnaires measure Satisfaction, but one of the most popular is the Job Description Index (Smith et al., 1969). Lists of descriptors are given for each of five dimensions and respondents put a "Y" beside those items that describe impressions, an "N" beside those that do not describe their impression, and a "?" if they cannot make up their mind. Criticisms of the Job Description Index focus on the unequal number of items per dimension and lack of content validity. Nevertheless, the JDI is often used to measure Satisfaction.

Perhaps there have been too many different means of measuring Satisfaction (Wanous & Lawler, 1972). For example, some measures ask respondents to rate Satisfaction with a number of job facets, which are summed to get a final measure of Satisfaction. Others stress that not all facets are equal so they have respondents indicate a measure of importance at the same time that they rate Satisfaction; therefore, the formula becomes Importance × Satisfaction. Others are not comfortable asking respondents to indicate levels of satisfaction so they have two scales per item, such as "How much do you now get?" and "How much do you want?" or "How much should there be?" They then measure level of satisfaction by subtracting how much one now gets from how much one wants. Whatever the definition, there may be problems with it. Summed scales are weak if not all important facets are mentioned. Subtracting one scale score from another scale score is also questionable. Consequently, some researchers have opted for a single global measure of Satisfaction: "How satisfied are you with your job?"

Although there are many measures of Satisfaction, there are relatively few instruments that measure Productivity. Organizations have many different criteria for measuring Productivity. Mali (1978) outlined a broad approach to what he calls a Productivity Audit and proposed measurement for each of 10 dimensions: Productivity Actions, Performance Standards, Productivity Policies, Equipment Usage/Technology, Organizational Support, Resource Accountability, Benefit Allocations, Accountability Reporting, Productivity Leadership, and Personnel Quality.

Communication has been linked to performance review data or to the general productivity of a work unit, but supporting evidence is anecdotal (C. W. Downs et al., 1988).

A recent trend has been to examine the relationship between communication and organizational *commitment*, and herein lies a fertile field for research. The most frequently used instrument is ·the Organizational Commitment Questionnaire (Mowday, Porter, & Steers, 1979), a 15-item Likert scale. A composite score is used even though the authors identified three dimensions: (a) strong belief in and acceptance of the organization's goals and values, (b) willingness to exert considerable effort on behalf of the organization, and (c) strong desire to maintain membership in the organization. Both reliability and validity data are strong (J. Barge & Schleuter, 1988).

Cook and Wall (1980) developed their Organizational Commitment Instrument in the United Kingdom. It contains nine items, three items on each of three dimensions: Identification, Involvement, and Loyalty. Several research studies, however, have indicated that a two-factor solution may be more realistic (A. Downs, 1991; Varona, 1991).

A commitment instrument that has been developed from the communication field is the ORGANIZATIONAL IDENTIFICATION QUESTIONNAIRE. It is profiled in this volume.

MEASUREMENT ISSUES

Organizational communication research can only be as good as the instruments used, so there must be a continued search for improvement in the instruments. Described here are some of the measurement problems with which researchers must contend as they strive to measure organizational communication constructs.

Conceptual Purity

A lack of conceptual purity is one of the greatest problems in organizational communication instruments. Labeling of instruments and of dimensions of instruments is often circular, leading to confusing conceptualizations. For example, there are "team" instruments, of which Communication is a dimension. At the same time there are "communication audit" instruments of which Teamwork is one dimension. Leadership is one factor of team instruments (e.g., Larson & LaFasto, 1989), whereas Teamwork is one factor of leadership style on other instruments. Communication Climate is one factor of Satisfaction (e.g., COMMUNICATION SATISFACTION QUESTIONNAIRE), but there are climate instruments that list several dimensions parallel to the other dimensions of the *Communication Satisfaction Questionnaire*. Also, the ORGANIZATIONAL CULTURE SURVEY seems to measure some of the same things covered on the INTERNATIONAL COMMUNICATION ASSOCIATION (ICA) AUDIT even though the general headings are different. In sum, there may be standard dimensions of organizational communication concepts, but the different instruments group the concepts in different ways and give them different labels.

Instrument Overlap

The lack of conceptual purity for the instruments results in an amazing amount of overlap across instruments. The item "People I work with are concerned about one another" appears in an instrument measuring culture, but similar items appear in measures of climate, teamwork, leadership, communication satisfaction, and commitment. In fact, many of the instruments share a great many questions and dimensions, which may result in multicollinearity when these measures are used together. Researchers must be aware of what is really being measured.

Reliability

Cronbach's alpha, as a measure of internal reliability, is used for most organizational communication instruments; most of those reported are above .70. These internal reliabilities, however, are often quite different when comparisons are made across samples in different organizations. The nature of the organization does appear to matter, but why it does is uncertain.

Other means of testing reliability, however, are not so common. For example, C. W. Downs and Hazen (1977) reported a relatively high test–retest reliability for the COMMUNICATION SATISFACTION QUESTIONNAIRE, but such reliability data is not reported for most instruments. However, it is difficult to get retest data from members of actual working organizations.

Validity

Organizational communication researchers, in general, provide data about three forms of validity. The face validity of general organizational communication instruments reported here is quite high. Most instruments have been used to diagnose communication in actual organizations, and the responses of organizational members to reports based on these instruments attest to the fact that they give valuable information (DeWine & James, 1988).

Two additional forms of validity information are provided. Criterion-related validity has been established more often for instruments that have a limited scope than for general assessment instruments. Wilson and Waltman (1988), for example, were able to compare the ORGANIZATIONAL COMMUNICATION CONFLICT INSTRUMENT with other conflict instruments, and Potvin (1991/1992) correlated Cheney's ORGANIZATIONAL IDENTIFICATION QUESTIONNAIRE with other organizational commitment instruments. Additional criterion-related studies are warranted. More comprehensive instruments such as the ICA AUDIT or the COMMUNICATION SATISFACTION QUESTIONNAIRE are often too long to combine with other measures to be feasible in a one-time administration.

Investigating the stability of an instrument's factor structure is another means for examining construct validity. Most of the instruments reported here have been investigated through some form of factor analysis, but the factors are not stable across many different types of organizations. For example, Hill, Bahniuk, Dobos, and Rouner (1989) found a three-factor solution for their mentoring instrument when it was used for academic respondents and for respondents from the general population; however, when the instrument was used with a group of managers, a four-factor solution appeared. Similarly, Crino and White (1981) tested the factor structure of the COMMUNICATION SATISFACTION QUESTIONNAIRE and found similar results to those of the authors. However, Clampitt and Gerard (1986) proposed a five-factor solution from their analyses. Internal validity, then, is vital research that must accompany measures.

Triangulation of Data

External validity is also important, and triangulation is often used to confirm that measures are externally valid. Within the discipline of organizational communication, there is a debate about the relative merits of quantitative and interpretive data. The utility of using only a single questionnaire to measure communication in organizations is sometimes questioned. In fact, several instruments are designed to be used in conjunction with other forms of data. Interviews, critical incidents, and observation are part of the original design for the ICA AUDIT because the questionnaire itself may not yield the depth of information needed to give an accurate assessment. C. W. Downs (1988) advocated (a) developing questions that are specific to a particular organization and adding them to the audit and (b) using interviews to get a deeper understanding of the quantitative data. Frequently there are apparent contradictions in the data obtained through different methods, and skillful interpretation is needed in such situations. While the scope of this chapter is merely to report on the instruments, other methods for data collection should not be forgotten.

For example, any standardized instrument that proposes to measure "organizational culture" is open to criticism because many interpretive and constructivist scholars would argue that a standard questionnaire cannot uncover the rituals, myths, and values of the organization. The Organizational Culture Scale (Glaser, Zamanou, & Hacker, 1987) is particularly vulnerable to this criticism, but triangulation allows for a more in-depth view of the culture.

Instrument Bias

Sometimes items on the organizational communication instruments are heavily value laden, so researchers need to identify and perhaps to modify the items to eliminate bias. For example, the TEAM-REVIEW QUESTIONNAIRE has a very definite bias in favor of participative management, but Gribas (1990) found that this type of leadership is not necessarily the preferred style in all organizations. In fact, it was counterproductive in voluntary community theater groups. Similarly, "openness" is a bias of the ICA Audit and the Communication Satisfaction Questionnaire, but the degree of openness and the form that it takes are not necessarily addressed.

Other biases occur in the assumptions about the impact of organizational communication processes on outcome variables such as commitment, satisfaction, and productivity. Perhaps this is more of a point about the use of the instrument than about the nature of the instrument itself. But the instruments are often used to predict a change in one of the outcomes, and care should be exercised not to let the inherent item biases color the research.

Scaling

Instrument developers are constantly seeking ways to improve the scales associated with their instruments. Perhaps the most common form of scale is the Likert scale: Respondents indicate on a 5- or 7-point scale how "satisfied" they are with the content of the item, or how strongly they agree with the statement. Metric fractionated scales, where respondents make a mark on lines within numbers, are a variation of this form. For example, Clampitt (1988) had respondents indicate reactions to an item on a 0–100 scale on the Communication Satisfaction Questionnaire. DeWine and James (1988) recommended that such scales be used on the ICA Audit; however "the use of these scales makes interpretation of results more difficult. In addition, White reported lower reliability for most subscales when fractionation scales were used" (p. 157).

Another popular scaling device has been to ask respondents both *how characteristic* an item is of their organization and how much there *should be*. Assessments of the items are then determined by identifying the gap between the "should be" amount and the "how characteristic amount." This not only makes for a longer questionnaire, but it also is more complicated to score. Wanous and Lawler (1972) reviewed the various combinations well, and C. W. Downs (1988) found that adding the equation type of scale gives a different factor analysis than using just one Likert scale to measure one dimension.

CONCLUSION

Organizational communication measurement certainly cuts across many academic disciplines, and the number of instruments to measure communication in organizations is large indeed. Unfortunately, few of the instruments have been used enough to generate the kind of reliability and validity data needed. By identifying these instruments, perhaps future researchers will build on this foundation and refine the measures. Most encouraging is the fact that a number of these instruments have been translated into languages other than English so that researchers can begin to develop globalized information about communication organizations.

REFERENCES

Barge, J., & Schleuter, D. W. (1988). A critical evaluation of organizational commitment and identification. *Management Communication Quarterly*, 2, 116–133.

Barge, K., & Schleuter, D. W. (1988). *Review of instrumentation on leadership*. Unpublished manuscript.

Blake, R., & Mouton, J. (1964). *The Group Behavior Questionnaire*. Austin, TX: Scientific Methods.

Cheney, G. (1983). On the various and changing meanings of organizational membership: A field study of organizational identification. *Communication Monographs, 50*, 342–362.

Chun, K-T., & Campbell, J. B. (1974). Dimensionality of the Rotter Interpersonal Trust Scale. *Psychological Reports, 35*, 1059–1070.

Chung, C-S., & Goldhaber, G. M. (1991, May). *Measuring communication load: A three-dimensional instrument*. Paper presented at the meeting of the International Communication Association, Chicago.

Clampitt, P. (1988). The Communication Satisfaction Questionnaire. In C. W. Downs, *Communication audits* (pp. 112–132). Glenview, IL: Scott-Foresman.

Clampitt, P. G., & Gerard, D. M. (1986, May). *Communication satisfaction: A useful concept?* Paper presented at the meeting of the International Communication Association, Chicago.

Collin, A. (1988). Mentoring. *Industrial and Commercial Training, 20*(2), 23–27.

Cook, J., & Wall, T. (1980). New work attitude measures of trust, organizational commitment and personal need non-fulfillment. *Journal of Occupational Psychology, 53*, 39–52.

Crino, M. D., & White, M. C. (1981). Satisfaction in communication: An examination of the Downs-Hazen measure. *Psychological Reports, 49*, 831–838.

Cupach, W. R., & Spitzberg, B. H. (1983). Trait versus state: A comparison of dispositional and situational measures of interpersonal communication competence. *Western Journal of Speech Communication, 47*, 364–379.

Daniels, Dyer, & Moffitt, N. (1975). *Instruction manual: Management profiling: As others see you*. Provo, UT: Behavioral Science Resources.

DeWine, S., & James, A. (1988). Examining the Communication Audit: Assessment and modification. *Management Communication Quarterly, 2*, 144–169.

DeWine, S., & Pearson, J. C. (1985, May). *State of the art: Self-report paper and pencil instruments reported in communication journals*. Paper presented at the meeting of the International Communication Association, Honolulu.

Downs, A. (1991). *The relation of communication to commitment in two Australian organizations*. Unpublished master's thesis, University of Kansas, Lawrence.

Downs, C. W. (1988). *Communication audits*. Glenview: Scott-Foresman.

Downs, C. W., Archer, J., McGrath, J., & Stafford, J. (1988). An analysis of communication style instrumentation. *Management Communication Quarterly, 1,* 543–571.

Downs, C. W., & Blubaugh, J. (1989, November). *Issues in teambuilding.* Paper presented at the meeting of the Speech Communication Association, San Francisco.

Downs, C. W., Clampitt, P., & Laird, A. (1988). Communication and organizational outcomes. In G. Goldhaber & B. Barnett (Eds.), *Handbook of organizational communication* (pp. 171–212). New York: Ablex.

Downs, C. W., & Hazen, M. D. (1977). A factor analytic study of communication satisfaction. *Journal of Business Communication, 14,* 63–74.

Downs, C. W., McGrath, J., Stafford, J., & Rowland, J. (1990, August). *A comparison of four communication style instruments.* Paper presented at the meeting of the Academy of Management, San Francisco.

Eubank, R. K. (1988). The effects of same gender and cross gender mentoring on personal development, career advancement, and job satisfaction of female administrators in higher education (Doctoral dissertation, University of South Dakota, 1987). *Dissertation Abstracts International, 49,* 670A.

Fiedler, F. (1967). *A theory of leadership effectiveness.* New York: McGraw-Hill.

Fleischman, F. A. (1969). *Manual for the Leadership Opinion Questionnaire.* Chicago: Science Research Associates.

Francis, D., & Young, D. (1979). *Improving work groups: A practical manual for team building.* La Jolla, CA: University Associates.

Glaser, S. R., Zamanou, S., & Hacker, K. (1987). Measuring and interpreting organizational culture. *Management Communication Quarterly, 1,* 173–198.

Greenbaum, H., DeWine, S., & Downs, C. (1987). *Table of instruments.* Unpublished manuscript.

Greenbaum, H., & Gardner, D. (1985, August). *Location, evaluation, and selection of questionnaires for organizational communication research.* Paper presented at the meeting of the Academy of Management, Boston.

Greenbaum, H., Kaplan, I., & Metlay, W. (1988). Evaluation of problem-solving groups: The case of quality circle programs. *Group and Organization Studies, 13,* 133–147.

Gribas, J. (1990). *Characteristics of short-term teams.* Unpublished master's thesis, University of Kansas, Lawrence.

Hall, J. (1986). *Conflict Management Survey.* Woodlands, TX: Teleometrics International.

Hanson, P. G. (1981). *Learning through groups: A trainer's basic guide.* San Diego, CA: University Associates.

Hemphill, J. K. (1957). Development of the Leader Behavior Description Questionnaire. In R. M. Stogdill & A. E. Coons (Eds.), *Leader behavior: Its description and measurement* (Monograph No. 88). Columbus: Ohio State University, Bureau of Business Research.

Hersey, P., & Blanchard, K. (1973). *Leader adaptability and style inventory: Rationale and analysis of LASI instruments.* Athens: Ohio University, Center for Leadership Studies.

Hill, S. E. K., Bahniuk, M. H., Dobos, J., & Rouner, D. (1989). Mentoring and other communication support in the academic setting. *Group and Organiza-tion Studies, 14,* 355–368.

Hinrichs, J. R. (1975). A feedback program to make manager development hap-pen. *Personnel Journal, 9,* 478–481.

Honeywell Inc. (1985). *Job Reaction Questionnaire user's guide.* Minneapolis: Author.

Jablin, F. M., & Sussman, L. (1983). Organizational group communication: A re-view of the literature and model of the process. *Organizational Communication Abstracts, 8,* 11–50.

Kalbfleisch, P., & Davies, A. (1990, June). *Communication competence, self-esteem, and risk in intimacy: Predictors of mentoring relationships.* Paper presented at the meeting of the International Communication Association, Dublin.

Klaus, R., & Bass, R. (1982). *Interpersonal communication in organization.* New York: Academic Press.

Larson, C., & LaFasto, F. (1989). *Teamwork: What must go right, what can go wrong.* Newbury Park, CA: Sage.

Likert, R. (1967). *The human organization.* New York: McGraw-Hill.

Mali, P. (1978). *Improving total productivity.* New York: Wiley.

McClelland, D. C. (1961). *The achieving society.* Princeton, NJ: Van Nostrand Rein-hold.

McCroskey, J. C., & Wright, D. W. (1971). The development of an instrument for measuring interaction behavior in small groups. *Speech Monographs, 38,* 335–340.

Monge, P., Backman, S., Dillard, J., & Eisenberg, E. (1982). Communicator com-petence in the workplace: Model testing and scale development. *Communica-tion Yearbook, 5,* 505–527.

Morrison, A., McCall, M., & DeVries, D. (1978). *Feedback to managers.* Greensboro, NC: Center for Creative Leadership.

Mowday, R. T., Porter, L. W., & Steers, R. M. (1979). The measurement of orga-nizational commitment. *Journal of Vocational Behavior, 14,* 224–247.

Perotti, V. S., & DeWine, S. (1987). Competence in communication. *Management Communication Quarterly, 1,* 272–287.

Pfeiffer, J. W., & Jones, J. E. (1977). *Handbook for group facilitators.* San Diego, CA: University Associates.

Potvin, T. C. (1992). Employee organizational commitment: An examination of its relationship to communication satisfaction and an evaluation of question-naires designed to measure the construct (Doctoral dissertation, University of Kansas, 1991). *Dissertation Abstracts International, 52,* 4147A.

Price, J. L., & Meuller, C. W. (1986). *Handbook of organizational measurement.* Marsh-field, MA: Pitman.

Putnam, L. (1988a). [Special issue]. *Management Communication Quarterly, 1.*

Putnam, L. (1988b). Communication and interpersonal conflict in organizations. *Management Communication Quarterly, 1,* 293–301.

Putnam, L., & Wilson, C. (1982). Communicative strategies in organizational con-flict: Reliability and validity of a measurement scale. *Communication Yearbook, 6,* 629–652.

Rahim, M. A. (1983). A measure of styles of handling interpersonal conflict. *Acad-emy of Management Journal, 26,* 368–376.

Richmond, V. P., & McCroskey, J. C. (1979). Management communication style, tolerance for disagreement and innovativeness as predictors of employee satisfaction: A comparison of single-factor, two-factor, and multiple-factor approaches. *Communication Yearbook, 3*, 359–373.

Ross, R. G., & DeWine, S. (1988). Assessing the Ross-DeWine Conflict Management Message Style. *Management Communication Quarterly, 1*, 389–413.

Schockley-Zalabak, P. (1988). Assessing the Hall Conflict Management Survey. *Management Communication Quarterly, 1*, 302–320.

Scott, W. E., Jr. (1967). The development of semantic differential scales as measures of "morale." *Personnel Psychology, 20*, 179–198.

Smith, P., Kendall, L., & Hulin, C. (1969). *Measurement of satisfaction with work and retirement*. Chicago: Rand McNally.

Taylor, J. C., & Bowers, D. G. (1972). *Survey of organizations: A machine-scored standardized questionnaire instrument*. Ann Arbor: University of Michigan Institute for Social Research, Center for Research on Utilization of Scientific Knowledge.

Thierbach, G. L. (1980). Decision involvement and job satisfaction in middle and junior high schools (Doctoral dissertation, University of Wisconsin, 1980). *Dissertation Abstracts International, 41*, 9A.

Thomas, K. W., & Kilmann, R. H. (1974). *Thomas–Kilmann Conflict MODE Instrument*. Tuxedom, NY: Xicom.

Varona, F. (1991). *Communication satisfaction and organizational commitment*. Unpublished doctoral dissertation, University of Kansas, Lawrence.

Wanous, J. P., & Lawler, E. E. (1972). Measurement and meaning of job satisfaction. *Journal of Applied Psychology, 56*, 95–105.

Weider-Hatfield, D. (1988). Assessing the Rahim Organizational Conflict Inventory—II (ROCI II). *Management Communication Quarterly, 1*, 350–366.

Wilson, S., & Waltman, M. S. (1988). Assessing the Putnam–Wilson Organizational Communication Conflict Instrument. *Management Communication Quarterly, 1*, 367–388.

Wilson Learning. (1985). *Team Interaction Profile*. Eden Prairie, MN: Author.

Womack, D. F. (1988). Assessing the Thomas–Kilmann Conflict MODE Survey. *Management Communication Quarterly, 1*, 321–349.

Part II

MEASURE PROFILES

Affective Learning

The most frequently used measure of students' affect toward learning in the communication literature is the semantic differential scale developed originally by Scott and Wheeless (1975) and later revised and extended by Andersen (1979). Affective learning refers to one of three domains of learning identified by Bloom (1956) in his taxonomy of learning. Affective learning is defined as an increasing internalization of positive attitudes toward the content or subject matter. An overview of those hierarchical objectives specified for that domain indicate that affect ranges from lower-order levels of selective attention and emotional response to higher-order levels of behavioral commitment to adopt an idea and internalize it as a value (Krathwohl, Bloom, & Masia, 1964). Affect is viewed typically as an important motivator of students' willingness to learn, use, and generalize information and skills beyond the traditional classroom.

Consistent with the original conceptualization of affect, affect is operationalized to include lower-order levels of students' attitudes toward (a) course, (b) subject matter, and (c) instructor, as well as higher-order levels of students' behavioral intentions of, (d) engaging in behaviors taught in the class, and (e) taking additional classes in the subject matter. Each specified affect is followed by four 7-step bipolar scales. Across numerous studies, the affective learning measure has been factored consistently as either a five-factor, two-factor, or one-factor solution. For the five-factor solution, items in each scale set had their primary loadings on the intended factor. Similarly, for the two-factor solution, the first three subscales constituted the Affect dimension with the latter two subscales reflecting behavioral commitment.

Because the interfactor correlations are typically high (above .60), the most parsimonious interpretation of the affective learning measure is a single factor with all items having their primary loadings on the first unrotated factor. Thus, most researchers treat the affective measure as unidimensional; however, the decision to treat the data as multi- or unidimensional should reside with the questions asked and the factor solutions obtained with each individual study.

This 20-item self-report scale is administered to students who are told to respond with a particular teacher and course in mind. Sometimes that teacher and course refer to the class in which the students are completing

Profile by Patricia Kearney.

81

the questionnaire. More recently, however, students were asked to respond to the items with "the class that you attended immediately before this class" (Plax, Kearney, McCroskey, & Richmond, 1986, p. 48). This procedure dramatically increases the sample size of target teachers without having to administer the questionnaire beyond a single, large section class. Moreover, it maximizes variability in subject matter fields and strengthens the representativeness of teachers by including those who would not normally agree to participate in research. The scale takes about 10 minutes to complete.

RELIABILITY

The Affective Learning scale has demonstrated consistently high reliability across secondary and college student samples. Whether or not the factors are treated independently or as a single solution, alpha (or split-half) reliability estimates have ranged from a low of .86 to a high of .98 (Gorham, 1988; Kearney & McCroskey, 1980; Kearney, Plax, & Wendt-Wasco, 1985; Plax et al., 1986; Richmond, 1990).

VALIDITY

Unlike other available measures of affective learning, this particular assessment attempts to reflect the full conceptual range of the construct by including items that measure both lower-order affect (attitudes) and higher-order learning (behavioral commitment). It falls short by failing to include items that assess actual or self-reported behaviors indicative of the highest level of affect. The behavioral commitment scales are rather broad and imprecise, making it potentially difficult to judge (e.g., "in real life situations, your likelihood of actually attempting to engage in behaviors recommended in the course").

Construct validity is evidenced by its continued positive association with other affective-based measures. For instance, students' affect has been consistently and positively associated with teachers' nonverbal immediacy. Students report high affect for those teachers who are nonverbally approachable, friendly, warm, and responsive (Kearney et al., 1985; Plax et al., 1986). Similarly, students report high affect for those teachers who are verbally immediate—teachers who call them by name, who refer to the class as "our" class or what "we" are doing, and who initiate conversations with students outside of class (Gorham, 1988). Moreover, high affect is positively correlated with prosocial messages that teachers use to gain student compliance in the classroom and negatively related to teachers' use of antisocial techniques (McCroskey, Richmond, Plax, & Kearney, 1985; Plax et al., 1986).

COMMENTS

More recently, Richmond (1990) and Gorham (1988) added a third subscale (i.e., taking another course from the same teacher) to the Behavioral Commitment dimension of Affect. Factor analyses of all six subscales, however, revealed that responses to the third Behavioral Commitment scale loaded on the Affect dimension, not on the intended Behavioral Commitment factor. Because no information is gained with this additional sixth subscale, researchers should rely on the original Andersen (1979) five-factor Affective Learning measure.

The Andersen scale has been used over and over again to assess students' affective learning. No study has failed to obtain clean factor structures. No study has failed to demonstrate high reliability estimates across or within each dimension of Affect. While other researchers have offered alternatives, none of those assessments represent the range or universe of the construct as well as this one does. Moreover, the consistent use of this particular measure has been useful in researchers' attempts to make comparative claims across studies that examine the same variable.

LOCATION

Andersen, J. F. (1979). Teacher immediacy as a predictor of teaching effectiveness. *Communication Yearbook*, 3, 543–559.
Kearney, P., Plax, T. G., & Wendt-Wasco, N. J. (1985). Teacher immediacy for affective learning in divergent college courses. *Communication Quarterly*, 33, 61–74.

REFERENCES

Bloom, B. S. (1956). *Taxonomy of educational objectives. Handbook I: Cognitive domain*. New York: David McKay.
Gorham, J. (1988). The relationship between verbal teacher immediacy behaviors and student learning. *Communication Education*, 37, 40–53.
Kearney, P., & McCroskey, J. C. (1980). Relationships among teacher communication style, trait and state communication apprehension and teacher effectiveness. *Communication Yearbook*, 4, 533–551.
Krathwohl, D. R., Bloom, B. S., & Masia, B. B. (1964). *Taxonomy of educational objectives: Handbook II. Affective domain*. New York: David McKay.
McCroskey, J. C., Richmond, V. P., Plax, T. G., & Kearney, P. (1985). Power in the classroom: V. Behavior alternation techniques, communication training and learning. *Communication Education*, 34, 214–226.
Plax, T. G., Kearney, P., McCroskey, J. C., & Richmond, V. P. (1986). Power in the classroom: VI. Verbal control strategies, nonverbal immediacy and affective learning. *Communication Education*, 35, 43–55.

Richmond, V. P. (1990). Communication in the classroom: Power and motivation. *Communication Education, 39*, 181–195.

Scott, M. D., & Wheeless, L. R. (1975). Communication apprehension, student attitudes, and levels of satisfaction. *Western Journal of Speech Communication, 41*, 188–198.

Affective Learning*

Instructions: Please respond to the following scales in terms of the class you are taking which meets *immediately before* the class you are now in. Circle one number on each set of bipolar scales to indicate your judgment or evaluation of the concept/idea about that particular class. Note that in some cases the most positive number is a "1" while in other cases it is a "7."

1. Behaviors recommended in the course:

Good	1	2	3	4	5	6	7	Bad
Worthless	1	2	3	4	5	6	7	Valuable
Fair	1	2	3	4	5	6	7	Unfair
Positive	1	2	3	4	5	6	7	Negative

2. Content/subject matter of the course:

Bad	1	2	3	4	5	6	7	Good
Valuable	1	2	3	4	5	6	7	Worthless
Unfair	1	2	3	4	5	6	7	Fair
Negative	1	2	3	4	5	6	7	Positive

3. Course instructor:

Good	1	2	3	4	5	6	7	Bad
Worthless	1	2	3	4	5	6	7	Valuable
Fair	1	2	3	4	5	6	7	Unfair
Positive	1	2	3	4	5	6	7	Negative

4. In "real life" situations, your likelihood of actually attempting to engage in behaviors recommended in the course:

Likely	1	2	3	4	5	6	7	Unlikely
Impossible	1	2	3	4	5	6	7	Possible
Probable	1	2	3	4	5	6	7	Improbable
Would Not	1	2	3	4	5	6	7	Would

5. Your likelihood of actually enrolling in another course of related content
   if your schedule so permits:

Unlikely	1	2	3	4	5	6	7	Likely
Possible	1	2	3	4	5	6	7	Impossible
Improbable	1	2	3	4	5	6	7	Probable
Would	1	2	3	4	5	6	7	Would Not

Affinity-Seeking Instrument

Affinity seeking is "the active social—communicative process by which individuals attempt to get others to like and feel positive toward them" (Bell & Daly, 1984, p. 91). Bell and Daly assumed that people develop strategies to bring about affinity in their interpersonal relationships, and results of their study indicated that the more people used these strategies, the more they were liked by others.

Bell, Tremblay, and Buerkel-Rothfuss (1987) then created the self-report Affinity-Seeking Instrument (ASI) to tap this ability. They began with more than 100 items, narrowing the field to 25, which were completed by 466 people. Factor analysis produced a two-factor solution: Affinity-Seeking Competence (ASC) (ability to say and do what is necessary to be seen as interpersonally attractive) and Strategic Performance (SP) (ability to play roles to be liked by others).

The ASI consists of 13 items and takes less than 5 minutes to complete. Respondents use a 7-point Likert-type scale, ranging from *very strongly agree* (7) to *very strongly disagree* (1). The ASI is available in both the self-report and other-report version; the two versions are modestly correlated (Bell, Tremblay, & Buerkel-Rothfuss, 1987).

A 28-item Affinity-Maintenance Scale has also been created (Bell, Daly, & Gonzalez, 1987). This typology contains six strategies not included in the original 25-item ASI and does not contain four of the original items. It is used to measure the importance and frequency of strategy use in marital dyads.

RELIABILITY

Bell, Tremblay, and Buerkel-Rothfuss (1987) reported alphas ranging from .85 to .89 for the ASC subscale and from .80 to .87 for the SP subscale. Later research reported an ASC alpha of .81 and a SP alpha of .83 (Buerkel-Rothfuss & Bell, 1987). No data on test—retest or split-half reliability are available.

Profile by Rebecca B. Rubin.

VALIDITY

Bell, Tremblay, and Buerkel-Rothfuss (1987) provided evidence of construct and concurrent validity. First, they tested the stability of the factor structure of the ASI and found the same two-factor solution discovered in their first study. Construct validity was also demonstrated in the significant positive relationship between the ASI and affinity-seeking outcomes and the negative relationships between the ASI and nonrelated measures (e.g., social desirability and public communication apprehension). The study also reported concurrent validity: ASC and SP correlated negatively with shyness and ASC correlated positively with communicator image, happiness, feelings of control, and satisfaction with number of friends. ASC was positively related to assertiveness, interaction involvement, self-esteem, and self-monitoring and negatively to communication apprehension, loneliness, and shyness.

Buerkel-Rothfuss and Bell (1987) provided additional criterion-related validity information. They found that self-reports of ASC predicted evaluations made by strangers after interaction; scores on SP were not predictive and may assess behaviors instrumental in getting ahead instead of behaviors instrumental in getting along with others, as measured by the ASC.

COMMENTS

This is a relatively new instrument and could use additional testing. In particular, researchers must discover the conceptual meaning of the subscales and the relationship between them. Also, future research should reinvestigate the reliability of the scale. The instrument, however, appears useful for tapping an important aspect of social–communicative competence and should be related to constructs such as friendship, loneliness, and need for inclusion.

LOCATION

Bell, R. A., Tremblay, S. W., & Buerkel-Rothfuss, N. L. (1987). Interpersonal attraction as a communication accomplishment: Development of a measure of affinity-seeking competence. *Western Journal of Speech Communication, 51,* 1–18.

REFERENCES

Bell, R. A., & Daly, J. A. (1984). The affinity-seeking function of communication. *Communication Monographs, 51,* 91–115.

Bell, R. A., Daly, J. A., & Gonzalez, M. C. (1987). Affinity-maintenance in marriage and its relationship to women's marital satisfaction. *Journal of Marriage and the Family*, 49, 445–454.

Buerkel-Rothfuss, N. L., & Bell, R. A. (1987). Validity of the affinity-seeking instrument. *Communication Research Reports*, 4(2), 24-30.

Affinity-Seeking Instrument*

Instructions: For each of the following statements, please indicate your perceptions of your general abilities. That is, consider how you generally behave, rather than any specific conversation or event. Circle the letters that represent the following categories:

Very strongly agree	Strongly agree	Agree	Undecided	Disagree	Strongly disagree	Very strongly disagree
VSA	SA	A	U	D	SD	VSD

[Editors' note: Respondents use the above scale to respond to all items.]

1. I seldom know what to say or do to get others to like me.
2. If I put my mind to it, I could get anyone to like me.
3. I have trouble building rapport with others.
4. I have difficulty getting others to want to spend time with me.
5. If I want someone to like me, I can usually create positive feelings between us.
6. I just can't seem to get others to like and appreciate me.
7. I am good at getting others to want to hang around with me.
8. I do not seem to know what to say and do to make myself popular with others.
9. When necessary, I can put on an act to get important people to approve of me.
10. I am not very good at putting on a show to impress others.
11. I am very good at playing roles to draw people to me.
12. I can present myself as more likeable than I really am.
13. I can put on excellent social performances to get others to approve of me.

Note. Items 1–8 are Affinity-Seeking Competence and Items 9–13 are Strategic Performance. Items should be rearranged randomly when used.

Items 1, 3, 4, 6, 8, and 10 should be reverse-scored before summing.

Argumentativeness Scale

Infante and Rancer (1982) conceptualized trait Argumentativeness (ARGgt) as "an interaction of the tendency to approach arguments, ARGap, and the tendency to avoid arguments, ARGav. The tendency to avoid arguments is seen as a debilitating factor, weakening the tendency to approach arguments by the anxiety associated with arguing. This may be expressed: ARGgt = ARGap – ARGav" (p. 73). Argumentativeness predisposes people "to advocate positions on controversial issues and to attack verbally the positions which other people take on these issues" (p. 72).

The Argumentativeness (ARG) Scale was developed in a series of factor-analytic studies (Infante & Rancer, 1982). Forty-five items were written to assess the two components of argumentativeness (ARGap and ARGav) as well as the tendency to be verbally aggressive. Items reflecting verbal aggressiveness were included to test the overlap between argumentativeness and verbal aggression. Argumentativeness was found to be independent of verbal aggressiveness.

People self-report their own argumentativeness by responding to 20 items using Likert-type scales that range from *almost never true* (1) to *almost always true* (5). This scale takes about 5 minutes to complete. Some researchers have adapted the scale to reflect an other-report format (Gorden, Infante, & Graham, 1988). People are classified as high or low in argumentativeness if their score is one standard deviation above or below the mean for the sample. Subjects with scores within one standard deviation of the mean are regarded as moderate in argumentativeness.

RELIABILITY

The ARG Scale appears to be reliable. Infante and Rancer (1982) reported a coefficient alpha of .91 for the 10 approach items and a coefficient alpha of .86 for the 10 avoidance items. Test–retest reliability was .87 for ARGap, .86 for ARGav, and .91 for ARGgt. Rancer, Baukus, and Infante (1985) reported alphas of .86 for ARGap and .84 for the ARGav dimension. Hample and Dallinger (1987), interested in how individuals edit their own arguments, reported coefficient alphas of .86 for ARGap and .79 for ARGav. Infante and Gorden (1985) modified the argumentativeness measure to re-

Profile by Elizabeth E. Graham.

flect an other-report format and requested subjects provide their perceptions of their supervisor's level of argumentativeness. Only five items from
the original argumentativeness scale were used and the coefficient alpha was
.69. Canary, Cunningham, and Cody (1988), interested in conflict strategy
behavior, reported alphas of .83 for ARGap and .79 for ARGav. Collectively,
these results suggest that the ARG Scale is internally consistent.

VALIDITY

Infante and Rancer (1982) provided evidence of convergent, concurrent, and
discriminant validity. To assess convergent validity, the authors measured
the correspondence between (a) the subjects' report of their own argumentativeness and (b) good friends' assessment of the subjects' argumentativeness.
The correlation between self and other reports was statistically significant.
The authors also assessed concurrent validity by correlating the ARG Scale
with other communication predisposition measures: Personal Report of
Communication Apprehension (McCroskey, 1982); Predisposition Toward
Verbal Behavior (Mortensen, Arntson, & Lustig, 1977); and Unwillingness-
to-Communicate Scale (Burgoon, 1976). All correlations were significant
and in the expected direction. Infante and Rancer (1982) also conducted a
behavioral choice study to assess discriminant validity and convergent
validity. Subjects were asked to rate their willingness to participate in four
communication studies: debating, watching and rating TV programs, conversing with a fellow student, and delivering a public speech. The authors
reported a positive correlation between ARGap and debating and a negative relationship between desire to debate and ARGav.

The only serious challenge to the conceptualization and measurement
of argumentativeness was offered by Dowling and Flint (1990). These authors were concerned about the face validity of the ARG Scale insofar as the
ambiguous wording of items on the scale may be a confounding variable.
For instance, in the original measure there is mixed use of the terms argue/
arguing, argument, and content/issues. Dowling and Flint suggested that
this lack of consistency in terms allows respondents to incorporate their own
meaning for argumentativeness rather than the meaning Infante and Rancer
originally proposed. Indeed, changing the wording of the ARG Scale items
produced significantly different results (Dowling & Flint, 1990).

COMMENTS

The ARG Scale has enjoyed a good deal of attention in the literature. Argumentativeness has been equated with employee satisfaction (Gorden, Infante,

& Izzo, 1988; Infante & Gorden, 1985, 1989, 1991) and favorable organizational outcomes (Infante & Gorden, 1985). In addition, argumentativeness has been found to be a strong predictor of effective upward communication (Infante & Gorden, 1987). As Infante, Wall, Leap, and Danielson (1984) have indicated, arguing may be good for you. For instance, high argumentatives are perceived as more skillful at arguing, are more dynamic, and experience more success in college (Infante, 1982). Indeed, Bayer and Cegala (1992) suggested that children's experiences in engaging in argumentative discussions with parents might facilitate the development of children's overall communication competence. Furthermore, argumentativeness is a skill that can be learned through communication skills training (Rancer, Kosberg, & Baukus, 1992). This is a particularly important issue because women are not as argumentative as men (Infante, 1982), yet through training, women could become more argumentative.

Dowling and Flint (1990) noted that the term *argument* carries relational overtones, whereas the term *issues* is content bound. However, the term "issues" only appears in the approach items of the ARG Scale. Dowling and Flint concluded that because "women seem more inclined to define and think of relational aspects of arguments, the ambiguous wording of the original scale invites them to score higher on ARGav and lower on ARGap and ARGgt" (p. 194). It seems that uniform wording of terms such as *argument* and *issues* needs to be employed to avoid some of the problems that Dowling and Flint identified. Although Dowling and Flint (1990) and others (DeWine, Nicotera, & Parry, 1991) raised issues concerning the face validity of the ARG Scale, they were quick to note that the construct and the measure of argumentativeness does have merit. Indeed, the pervasive use of this measure is indicative of its usefulness in the investigation of personality constructs in communication research.

LOCATION

Infante, D. A. (1988). *Arguing constructively*. Prospect Heights, IL: Waveland Press.
Infante, D. A., & Rancer, A. S. (1982). A conceptualization and measure of argumentativeness. *Journal of Personality Assessment, 46*, 72–80.

REFERENCES

Bayer, C., & Cegala, D. (1992). Trait verbal aggressiveness and argumentativeness: Relations with parenting style. *Western Journal of Communication, 56*, 301–310.
Burgoon, J. K. (1976). The Unwillingness-to-Communicate Scale: Development and validation. *Communication Monographs, 43*, 60–69.

Canary, D. J., Cunningham, E. M., & Cody, M. J. (1988). Goal types, gender, and locus of control in managing interpersonal conflict. *Communication Research*, *15*, 426–446.

DeWine, S., Nicotera, A. M., & Parry, D. (1991). Argumentativeness and aggressiveness: The flip side of gentle persuasion. *Management Communication Quarterly*, *4*, 386–411.

Dowling, R. E., & Flint, L. J. (1990). The Argumentativeness Scale: Problems and promises. *Communication Studies*, *41*, 183–198.

Gorden, W. I., Infante, D. A., & Graham, E. E. (1988). Corporate conditions conducive to employee voice: A subordinate perspective. *Employee Responsibilities and Rights Journal*, *1*, 101–111.

Gorden, W. I., Infante, D. A., & Izzo, J. (1988). Variations in voice pertaining to dissatisfaction/satisfaction with subordinates. *Management Communication Quarterly*, *2*, 6–22.

Hample, D., & Dallinger, J. M. (1987). Individual differences in cognitive editing standards. *Human Communication Research*, *14*, 123–144.

Infante, D. A. (1982). The argumentative student in the speech communication classroom: An investigation and implications. *Communication Education*, *31*, 141–148.

Infante, D. A., & Gorden, W. I. (1985). Superiors' argumentativeness and verbal aggressiveness as predictors of subordinates' satisfaction. *Human Communication Research*, *12*, 117–125.

Infante, D. A., & Gorden, W. I. (1987). Superior and subordinate communication profiles: Implications for independent-mindedness and upward effectiveness. *Central States Speech Journal*, *38*, 73–80.

Infante, D. A., & Gorden, W. I. (1989). Argumentativeness and affirming communicator style as predictors of satisfaction/dissatisfaction with subordinates. *Communication Quarterly*, *37*, 81–90.

Infante, D. A., & Gorden, W. I. (1991). How employees see the boss: Test of an argumentative and affirming model of supervisors' communicative behavior. *Western Journal of Speech Communication*, *55*, 294–304.

Infante, D. A., Wall, C. H., Leap, C. J., & Danielson, K. (1984). Verbal aggression as a function of the receiver's argumentativeness. *Communication Research Reports*, *1*, 33–37.

McCroskey, J. C. (1982). *An introduction to rhetorical communication* (4th ed.). Englewood Cliffs, NJ: Prentice Hall.

Mortensen, D. C., Arntson, P. H., & Lustig, M. (1977). The measurement of verbal predispositions: Scale development and application. *Human Communication Research*, *3*, 146–158.

Rancer, A. S., Baukus, R. A., & Infante, D. A. (1985). Relations between argumentativeness and belief structures about arguing. *Communication Education*, *34*, 37–47.

Rancer, A. S., Kosberg, R. L., & Baukus, R. A. (1992). Beliefs about arguing as predictors of trait argumentativeness: Implications for training in argument and conflict management. *Communication Education*, *41*, 375–387.

Argumentativeness Scale*

Instructions: This questionnaire contains statements about *arguing controversial issues.* Indicate how often each statement is true for you personally by placing the appropriate number in the blank to the left of the statement. If the statement is *almost never true* for you, place a "1" in the blank. If the statement is *rarely true* for you, place a "2" in the blank. If the statement is *occasionally true* for you, place a "3" in the blank. If the statement is *often true* for you, place a "4" in the blank. If the statement is *almost always true* for you, place a "5" in the blank. Remember, consider each item in terms of *arguing controversial issues.*

1. While in an argument, I worry that the person I am arguing with will form a negative impression of me.
2. Arguing over controversial issues improves my intelligence.
3. I enjoy avoiding arguments.
4. I am energetic and enthusiastic when I argue.
5. Once I finish an argument I promise myself that I will not get into another.
6. Arguing with a person creates more problems for me than it solves.
7. I have a pleasant, good feeling when I win a point in an argument.
8. When I finish arguing with someone I feel nervous and upset.
9. I enjoy a good argument over a controversial issue.
10. I get an unpleasant feeling when I realize I am about to get into an argument.
11. I enjoy defending my point of view on an issue.
12. I am happy when I keep an argument from happening.
13. I do not like to miss the opportunity to argue a controversial issue.
14. I prefer being with people who rarely disagree with me.
15. I consider an argument an exciting intellectual challenge.
16. I find myself unable to think of effective points during an argument.
17. I feel refreshed and satisfied after an argument on a controversial issue.
18. I have the ability to do well in an argument.
19. I try to avoid getting into arguments.
20. I feel excitement when I expect that a conversation I am in is leading to an argument.

Note. To compute tendency to approach argumentative situations (ARGap), add scores on Items 2, 4, 7, 9, 11, 13, 15, 17, 18, and 20. To compute tendency to avoid argumentative situations (ARGav), add scores on Items 1, 3, 5, 6, 8, 10, 12, 14, 16, and 19. To compute the Argumentativeness trait (ARGgt), subtract the total of the 10 ARGav items from the 10 ARGap items.

---

*Copyright 1982 by Lawrence Erlbaum Associates, Inc. Reprinted by permission.

Attributional Confidence Scale

Clatterbuck (1976, 1979) developed the Attributional Confidence Scale as a way of operationalizing the uncertainty construct developed by Berger and Calabrese (1975). The propositions of uncertainty reduction theory direct researchers to regard the communication that occurs in relational development as the result of the need for confident attributions (Berger & Calabrese, 1975). The process of initial interaction is characterized by direct question asking as well as questioning other people about the targeted other and gathering information by observing the other. By communicating, interactants can make proactive and retroactive attributions about one another. Retroactive attributions attempt to explain past behaviors while proactive attributions are concerned with predicting future behaviors (Berger, 1975).

Clatterbuck (1979) adhered to three guidelines in his effort to develop a reliable and valid measure of attributional confidence. First, retroactive attributions must be highly correlated with proactive attributions because past behaviors generally are reflected in future behaviors. Second, because of the holistic quality of attributions and because the perception of confidence in one item affects confidence levels for other items, retroactive and proactive attributions should be viewed as separate, unidimensional constructs. Third, retroactive and proactive items must be cast in an additive/summative scale.

There are two different versions of the Attributional Confidence Scale (CL7). A 65-item instrument (Clatterbuck, 1979) adapted from the Intimacy Scale (Taylor & Altman, 1966) was designed to measure retroactive attribution. However, proactive attributional confidence is measured by the seven-item CL7 instrument. The items in the CL7 were adapted from the uncertainty construct (Berger & Calabrese, 1975). In view of the ease of administration, the CL7 is the "instrument of choice when attributional confidence is to be measured" (Clatterbuck, 1979, p. 149).

For the CL7, respondents are requested to evaluate how confident they are in giving specific facts about one target person. Scoring is based on a scale of 0% confidence (total guess) to 100% confidence (total certainty). However, 4- to 9-point Likert-type scales have been employed with no sig-

Profile by Elizabeth E. Graham.

nificant reduction in reliability. The CL65 takes about 15 minutes to complete, whereas the CL7 requires only about 1 minute.

Clatterbuck (1979) summarized the results of 17 studies ($N = 1,370$) in which the CLUES instrument was used. A principal-components factor analysis of the CL7 measure revealed that all items loaded .60 or greater on the first factor. In addition, a principal-components factor analysis of the 65 items also indicated that all items loaded .50 or greater on the first factor, which accounted for 60% of the variance. These results suggest a unidimensional instrument.

Clatterbuck (1979) recognized that the CL7 was reflective of an American culture and cautioned users that his conceptualization of attributional confidence was "not necessarily the full story" (p. 156). For this reason, Gudykunst and Nishida (1986) modified the CL7 to better reflect meanings that other cultures have of uncertainty. The expanded version of the CL7 is an eight-item, two-factor measure (high- and low-context cultures) of uncertainty reduction. Response scales range from 0 (totally uncertain) to 100 (totally certain). Gudykunst and Hammer (1988) reported alphas of .93 for the low-context factor for Hispanics and .87 for Caucasians, while the high-context factor yielded an alpha of .88 for Hispanics and .93 for Caucasians. Subsequent research (Hammer & Martin, 1992) employing slightly different versions of this scale, produced similar results.

RELIABILITY

Clatterbuck (1979) reported Cronbach alphas for the CL7 ranging from .76 to .97, and from .95 to .99 for the CL65. Other researchers (Gudykunst, 1985; Kellermann & Reynolds, 1990; Wheeless & Williamson, 1992) reported similar results, providing ample evidence of the internal consistency of the CL7 measure. Sunnafrank (1990) employed a 6-point response format for the CL7 and reported a coefficient alpha of .86. In addition, Douglas (1991) proposed a global measure of the CL7 measure that appears to be both reliable and valid.

VALIDITY

Drawing from the results of 17 studies, Clatterbuck (1979) provided information concerning the construct validity of the CL7. For example, empathy, extraversion, dogmatism, intolerance of ambiguity, self-esteem, neuroticism, and social desirability were found to be unrelated to the CL7 scale. In addition, Clatterbuck hypothesized and found that (a) retroactive attributional confidence (CL65) and proactive attributional confidence (CL7) were positively correlated, (b) attributional confidence was related to interpersonal attraction, (c) attributional confidence was positively correlated with time individuals have known one another, and (d) attributional confidence and perceived similarity were positively correlated.

Although they used a modified version of the CL7, Gudykunst and associates have contributed to the validity of this measure. For example, Gudykunst and Nishida (1984) reported that intercultural interactions are more prone to uncertainty than are intracultural interactions. They also reported that self-monitoring influences attributional confidence. Gudykunst, Yang, and Nishida (1985) investigated the effects of similarity on uncertainty reduction strategies for different cultures (Japan, Korea, and the United States) across three relationship types (acquaintances, friend, and dates). One of their primary findings suggested that "in dating relationships similarity leads to interactive strategy use and this leads to other self-disclosure that in turn influences attributional confidence" (p. 444). In a related manner, Gudykunst and Hammer (1988) reported that the axioms and theorems of uncertainty reduction theory are generalizable across ethnic groups, providing further evidence of the validity of the CL7 measure. Furthermore, Perse and Rubin (1989) reported that parasocial TV relationships mirror social relationships such that relationships with soap opera characters were influenced by the reduction of uncertainty.

COMMENTS

The CL7 scale has a strong conceptual base and evidence suggests that it is a stable and valid instrument. The many different ways this measure has been modified without any noticeable effect on its reliability or ability to measure attributional confidence is a testament to the versatility of the CL7. However, there is evidence to suggest that uncertainty reduction theory may be limited in its explanatory power (Planalp & Honeycutt, 1985; Planalp, Rutherford, & Honeycutt, 1988; VanLear & Trujillo, 1986). Most recently, Sunnafrank (1990) argued that predicted outcome values provide a more encompassing framework for explaining initial interactions; his 10-item scale asks respondents to predict relational outcomes (Sunnafrank, 1988). Future research will likely provide additional information to direct subsequent measurement and conceptualization of attributional confidence.

LOCATION

Clatterbuck, G. W. (1976). Attributional confidence, uncertainty reduction, and attraction in initial interaction (Doctoral dissertation, Northwestern University, 1976). *Dissertation Abstracts International, 37,* 3981.

Clatterbuck, G. W. (1979). Attributional confidence and uncertainty in initial interaction. *Human Communication Research, 5,* 147–157.

REFERENCES

Berger, C. R. (1975). Proactive and retroactive attribution processes in interpersonal communications. *Human Communication Research, 2,* 33–50.

Berger, C. R., & Calabrese, R. J. (1975). Some explorations in initial interaction and beyond: Toward a developmental theory of interpersonal communication. *Human Communication Research, 1,* 99–112.

Douglas, W. (1991). Expectations about initial interaction: An examination of the effects of global uncertainty. *Human Communication Research, 17,* 355–384.

Gudykunst, W. B. (1985). The influence of cultural similarity, type of relationship, and self-monitoring on uncertainty reduction processes. *Communication Monographs, 52,* 203–217.

Gudykunst, W. B., & Hammer, M. R. (1988). The influence of ethnicity, gender, and dyadic composition on uncertainty reduction in initial interactions. *Journal of Black Studies, 18,* 191–214.

Gudykunst, W. B., & Nishida, T. (1984). Individual and cultural influences on uncertainty reduction. *Communication Monographs, 51,* 23–36.

Gudykunst, W. B., & Nishida, T. (1986). Attributional confidence in low- and high-context cultures. *Human Communication Research, 12,* 525–549.

Gudykunst, W. B., Yang, S. M., & Nishida, T. (1985). A cross-cultural test of uncertainty reduction theory: Comparisons of acquaintances, friends, and dating relationships in Japan, Korea, and the United States. *Human Communication Research, 11,* 407–454.

Hammer, M. R., & Martin, J. N. (1992). The effects of cross-cultural training on American managers in a Japanese-American joint venture. *Journal of Applied Communication Research, 20,* 161–182.

Kellermann, K., & Reynolds, R. (1990). When ignorance is bliss: The role of motivation to reduce uncertainty in uncertainty reduction theory. *Human Communication Research, 17,* 5–75.

Perse, E. M, & Rubin, R. B. (1989). Attribution in social and parasocial relationships. *Communication Research, 16,* 59–77.

Planalp, S., & Honeycutt, J. M. (1985). Events that increase uncertainty in personal relationships. *Human Communication Research, 11,* 593–604.

Planalp, S., Rutherford, D. K., & Honeycutt, J. M. (1988). Events that increase uncertainty in personal relationships II: Replication and extension. *Human Communication Research, 14,* 516–547.

Sunnafrank, M. (1988). Predicted outcome value in initial conversations. *Communication Research Reports, 5,* 169–172.

Sunnafrank, M. (1990). Predicted outcome value and uncertainty reduction theories: A test of competing perspectives. *Human Communication Research, 17,* 76–103.

Taylor, D., & Altman, I. (1966). *Intimacy-scaled stimuli for use in studies of interper-*

sonal relationships (Report No. 9). Bethesda, MD: Naval Medical Research Institute. (MF 022.01.03-1002)

VanLear, C. A., Jr., & Trujillo, N. (1986). On becoming acquainted: A longitudinal study of social judgement processes. *Journal of Social and Personal Relationships, 3*, 375–392.

Wheeless, L. R., & Williamson, A. M. (1992). State-communication apprehension and uncertainty in continuing initial interactions. *Southern Communication Journal, 57*, 249–259.

Attributional Confidence Scale*

Instructions: The questions which follow will ask you to express how confident you are that you know a particular fact about the person who is your partner. On these questions, the answers should be written as a percentage, anywhere from 0% to 100%. For example, if you are totally confident that you know a particular fact, you might write 100%. If you were slightly less confident, you might put a number like 93%. On the other hand, if you were not at all confident you might place a very low percentage, like 5% in the answer blank. If you absolutely are unable to answer a question, and the answer would be a guess for which you had no basis at all, you might put 0%. Remember, you may use any evidence as a basis for your guess, even if the person has not explicitly told you the answer. We are interested in your confidence in the guess only; do not give the actual answer to the question.

1. How confident are you of your general ability to predict how he/she will behave? _____
2. How certain are you that he/she likes you? _____
3. How accurate are you at predicting the values he/she holds? _____
4. How accurate are you at predicting his/her attitudes? _____
5. How well can you predict his/her feelings and emotions? _____
6. How much can you empathize with (share) the way he/she feels about himself/herself? _____
7. How well do you know him/her? _____

Audience Activity Measures

Audience activity is a central concept in the uses and gratifications mass communication perspective. It reflects the goal-directed and voluntaristic nature of media use. Scholars now tend to approach activity as a variable rather than an absolute condition of the audience using the media (e.g., Blumler, 1979). In a study of TV news, Levy (1983) suggested that audience members "differ in their orientation to television, its messages and viewing situation" (p. 114).

Audience activity is multidimensional, consisting of several qualitative dimensions that include (a) Selectivity, or choice of communication settings or partners; (b) Intentionality, or purposive desire to seek out a communication setting; (c) Attention, or focus on a communication message; and (d) Involvement, or cognitive, affective, or behavioral responses to the communication (see, e.g., Blumler, 1979; Rubin & Perse, 1987a, 1987b). Blumler (1979) also identified a temporal dimension to activity so that researchers could consider the audience before, during, and after media exposure.

Levy (1983) and Levy and Windahl (1984) introduced several measures of audience activity, namely preactivity (or intentionality), activity during exposure (or attentiveness), and postexposure activity (or involvement). Items are randomly presented within questionnaires and each of the three scales takes less than 2 minutes to complete. Responses to the component items of each scale are summed or averaged.

RELIABILITY

Assessments of scale reliability have considered consistency or homogeneity of items rather than stability. Levy and Windahl (1984) reported a mean interitem correlation of .52 for the three-item Intentionality Scale. Rubin and Perse (1987b) observed a .72 Cronbach alpha for the measure for news viewing. Rubin and Perse (1987a), though, expanded the scale to four items (adding "I plan to see the program from start to finish") and reported a .87 Cronbach alpha for soap opera viewing. Following a factor analysis of 20

Profile by Alan M. Rubin.

viewing intention, attention, immersion, and realism items, Rubin, Perse, and Taylor (1988) deleted one item ("It is important to see a program from beginning to end") from the Levy and Windahl measure and added three items ("I often make arrangements so I don't miss a favorite television program," "I cancel other plans to watch television," and I look forward to watching a favorite television program"). This Intentionality factor had a .87 Cronbach alpha. Perse (1990) reported a Cronbach alpha of .86 for the latter five-item Intentionality Scale.

Levy and Windahl (1984) reported a mean interitem correlation of .37 for the seven-item Attentiveness Scale. Levy (1983) previously reported a Cronbach alpha of .61 for a list of five concurrent behaviors when people watch the news. Based on a factor analysis, Rubin and Perse (1987b) shifted one item ("I talk to others about what's on the news") from this scale to accompany the two items in the postexposure activity measure. They argued that this one item actually reflected involvement with rather than distraction from the message. The resulting six-item scale had a .69 Cronbach alpha. Perse (1990) observed a .75 Cronbach alpha for an expanded nine-item coviewing distractions measure.

Levy and Windahl (1984) reported an interitem correlation of .43 for the two-item postexposure activity measure. Rubin and Perse (1987b) found a .68 Cronbach alpha of these two items plus the "talking to others about what's on the news" attentiveness item to form an index of news involvement. Rubin and Perse (1987a) divided Levy and Windahl's scale into two dimensions for soap opera viewing and reported Cronbach alphas of .86 for their four-item Postviewing Cognition Scale (adding "I think about what happened in the story," "I try to predict what will happen in tomorrow's episode," and "I think about the characters") and .89 for their three-item Postviewing Discussion Scale (adding "I talk about the characters with others" and "I talk with others to try to predict what will happen in the story").

VALIDITY

Levy and Windahl (1984) found that preactivity and postactivity measures correlated ($r = .53$), suggesting "the more useful and gratifying exposure is for postactivities, the more likely it is that individuals will seek out news exposure" (p. 70). They also found that the strongest correlations between the pre- and postactivity measures and measures of news-viewing motivation were with surveillance or information-seeking motivation. Rubin and Perse (1987a) supported this pattern for soap opera viewing, reporting a significant canonical correlation; postviewing cognition, postviewing behavior, and parasocial interaction correlated with an instrumental or goal-directed viewing orientation.

Rubin and Perse (1987b) also found three news-viewing patterns that supported both the variable and goal-directed nature of audience activity: (a) news affinity, selectivity, and cognitive involvement predicted intention to watch the news; (b) viewing to fill time and the lack of news affinity predicted more distractions when watching the news; and (c) viewing intention, information motivation, and perceived news realism predicted involvement with the news. Perse (1990) also found that intentionality, attention, and cognitive involvement correlated with instrumental viewing motives, program selection, perceived realism, and affinity.

COMMENTS

The component measures of audience activity have had a brief period of development yet show heuristic promise as they have evolved and been refined. The items used by Levy and Windahl (1984) are reported below. However, it is important for researchers to note their refinements in subsequent studies. Other measures of attention (e.g., Cegala, 1981; Rouner, 1984) also have been adapted to different mass communication settings with some success (e.g., Perse, 1990; Rubin & Perse, 1987a; Rubin et al., 1988).

LOCATION

Levy, M. R., & Windahl, S. (1984). Audience activity and gratifications: A conceptual clarification and exploration. *Communication Research*, *11*, 51–78.

REFERENCES

Blumler, J. G. (1979). The role of theory in uses and gratifications studies. *Communication Research*, *6*, 9–36.

Cegala, D. J. (1981). Interaction involvement: A cognitive dimension of communicative competence. *Communication Education*, *30*, 109–121.

Levy, M. R. (1983). Conceptualizing and measuring some aspects of audience 'activity'. *Journalism Quarterly*, *60*, 109–115.

Perse, E. M. (1990). Audience selectivity and involvement in the newer media environment. *Communication Research*, *17*, 675–697.

Rouner, D. (1984). Active television viewing and the cultivation hypothesis. *Journalism Quarterly*, *61*, 168–174.

Rubin, A. M., & Perse, E. M. (1987a). Audience activity and soap opera involvement: A uses and effects investigation. *Human Communication Research*, *14*, 246–268.

Rubin, A. M., & Perse, E. M. (1987b). Audience activity and television news gratifications. *Communication Research*, *14*, 58–84.

Rubin, A. M., Perse, E. M., & Taylor, D. S. (1988). A methodological examination of cultivation. *Communication Research, 15*, 107– 134.

Intentionality Scale*

Instructions: Read each statement and indicate whether you *strongly agree, agree*, are *neutral, disagree*, or *strongly disagree* with each.

1. It is important to see the news from beginning to end.
2. I usually plan my evenings so I do not miss the TV news.
3. I usually check the time so that I do not miss the news on television.

Attentiveness Scale*

Instructions: Many people do other things at the same time they watch TV. Below you will find a list of things that you might do while watching the news programs. For each item, indicate how often you are engaged in that activity: very often, often, sometimes, rarely, or never.

1. Reading a book or newspaper.
2. Getting something to eat.
3. Eating.
4. Taking care of children.
5. Doing housework.
6. Talking about what is on the news.
7. Talking about things not on the news.

Postviewing Activity Scale*

Instructions: Read each statement and indicate how often you engage in each activity: very often, often, sometimes, rarely, or never.

1. After the news programs I often think about what I have just seen and heard.
2. I often discuss with others what I have recently watched on TV news.

Behavior
Alteration Techniques

The typology of Behavior Alteration Techniques (BATs), developed and revised by Kearney, Plax, Richmond, and McCroskey (1985), refers to those power resources available to teachers in their attempts to influence students. Unlike other compliance-gaining typologies appropriate for interpersonal contexts, the BATs comprise an inductively derived typology specific to classroom influence. Strategies are operationalized with multiple, rather than single, messages with representative messages derived from experienced elementary and secondary teachers.

Factor analysis revealed that, for generalized influence, the strategies were relatively independent and should be treated as 22 separate variables (Kearney, Plax, Richmond, & McCroskey, 1984; Plax, Kearney, McCroskey, & Richmond, 1986). However, for specific situations and/or particular student misbehaviors, other findings supported a two-factor BAT solution: prosocial and antisocial (Kearney, Plax, Sorensen, & Smith, 1988). The prosocial factor includes 11 BATs: Immediate Reward from Behavior (1), Deferred Reward (2), Reward from Others (4), Self-Esteem (5), Responsibility to Class (15), Normative Rules (16), Altruism (18), Peer Modeling (19), Teacher Modeling (20), Expert Teacher (21), and Teacher Feedback (22). The antisocial factor includes 7 BATs: Punishment from Teacher (7), Punishment from Others (8), Guilt (9), Teacher–Student Relationship: Negative (11), Legitimate—Higher Authority (12), Legitimate—Teacher Authority (13), and Debt (17).

The stability of the two-factor solution has been demonstrated across multiple teacher samples, a variety of student scenarios, and with both construction and selection methods. Whether the researcher relies on 2 or 22 separate variables depends, to a large extent, on the questions asked. For example, a researcher might rely on all 22 BATs in order to determine the full range of options available to experienced, as opposed to prospective, teachers. Alternatively, a researcher may opt for the two-factor structure to provide a more parsimonious solution, optimize variance accounted for, and more meaningfully interpret obtained results.

Profile by Patricia Kearney.

When assessing BAT use in the classroom, teachers are often asked to self-report (or students assess their teacher's) likelihood (or frequency) of using each BAT. Response options range from *extremely likely* (7) to *extremely unlikely* (1). BAT category labels are omitted from the questionnaire and only messages representing each category are supplied. The scale takes about 10 minutes to complete.

RELIABILITY

The 22 categories were originally treated as separate, independent techniques. No reliability estimates are available. More recent research, which illustrates a stable two-factor solution, reveals high reliability with estimates ranging from .74 to .84 for the prosocial items and .81 to .88 for the antisocial techniques (Kearney et al., 1988).

VALIDITY

Two studies speak to the typology's content validity. First, without the potential constraints of situational scenarios or other stimulus conditions, Kearney et al. (1985) had students freely recall the full range of compliance-gaining strategies and messages they had/would use to "get someone to change her/his behavior." These messages were coded into 18 categories. Second, in an effort to elicit strategies specific to and appropriate for classroom use, the same authors (Kearney et al., 1984) asked elementary and secondary teachers to report those techniques they commonly use to alter students' behaviors. In small groups, these same teachers were also asked to "code and categorize" their own messages, resulting in an extended typology of 22 techniques. The full range of techniques available to teachers both overlaps and deviates from traditional typologies more suited to interpersonal contexts.

Evidence of concurrent validity can be found in researchers' attempts to determine the relative superiority of one type of measurement technique to another. Specifically, Sorensen, Plax, and Kearney (1989) and Plax, Kearney, and Sorensen (1990) determined that eliciting and coding individual message constructions was "functionally equivalent" to the strategy checklist procedure.

Finally, the BAT instrument reveals construct validity by its ability to correlate highly with theoretically based variables. Students who report their teachers using primarily prosocial BATs should also indicate greater positive affect, and they do; conversely, they should (and they do) report negative affect toward those teachers they perceive to use antisocial techniques (Plax et al., 1986). Similar relationships have been observed with cognitive learning outcomes (McCroskey, Richmond, Plax, & Kearney, 1985; Richmond, McCroskey, Kearney, & Plax, 1987).

COMMENTS

The BAT instrument has been used with college teachers and students and with junior high/high school teachers/students. It has also been used to differentiate prospective from experienced elementary and secondary teachers (Kearney et al., 1988). It has not been used with elementary and middle school students. Depending on the grade level targeted, messages representing each category may need revision. The original 18-item version of this instrument (Kearney et al., 1985) has been used in organizational contexts to assess superior and subordinate communication. Messages were rewritten to reflect managers' use of compliance-gaining strategies with their employees (see Richmond, Davis, Saylor, & McCroskey, 1984).

LOCATION

Kearney, P., Plax, T. G., Richmond, V. P., & McCroskey, J. C. (1984). Power in the classroom: IV. Alternatives to discipline. *Communication Yearbook, 8,* 724–746.

Plax, T. G., Kearney, P., McCroskey, J. C., & Richmond, V. P. (1986). Power in the classroom: VI. Verbal control strategies, nonverbal immediacy and affective learning. *Communication Education, 35,* 43–55.

Richmond, V. P., McCroskey, J. C., Kearney, P., & Plax, T. G. (1987). Power in the classroom: VII. Linking behavior alteration techniques to cognitive learning. *Communication Education, 36,* 1–12.

REFERENCES

Kearney, P., Plax, T. G., Richmond, V. P., & McCroskey, J. C. (1985). Power in the classroom: III. Teacher communication techniques and messages. *Communication Education, 34,* 19–28.

Kearney, P., Plax, T. G., Sorensen, G., & Smith, V. R. (1988). Experienced and prospective teachers' selections of compliance-gaining messages for "common" student misbehaviors. *Communication Education, 37,* 150–164.

McCroskey, J. C., Richmond, V. P., Plax, T. G., & Kearney, P. (1985). Power in the classroom: V. Behavior alteration techniques, communication training and learning. *Communication Education, 34,* 214–226.

Plax, T. G., Kearney, P., & Sorensen, G. (1990). The strategy selection-construction controversy: II. Comparing pre- and experienced teachers' compliance-gaining message constructions. *Communication Education, 39,* 128–141.

Richmond, V. P., Davis, L. M., Saylor, K., & McCroskey, J. C. (1984). Power strategies in organizations: Communication techniques and messages. *Human Communication Research, 11,* 85–108.

Sorensen, G., Plax, T. G., & Kearney, P. (1989). The strategy selection- construction controversy: A coding scheme for analyzing teacher compliance-gaining message constructions. *Communication Education, 38,* 102–118.

Behavior Alteration Techniques*

Instructions: As a teacher, you will often try to get your students to do things that they may not want to do. Below you'll find a series of statements that a teacher might use in her/his efforts to encourage students to change their behaviors. These statements are grouped into 22 separate categories. Please read all the statements in each category. Then, indicate how likely you would be to use statements of that type for each of the 22 categories to influence your own students. Use a 1–7 scale, with 7 = extremely likely and 1 = extremely unlikely. Respond quickly.

[Editors' note: Respondents use the above scale to indicate their likelihood of using each BAT.]

1. You will enjoy it. It will make you happy. Because it is fun. You will find it rewarding/interesting. It is a good experience. (Immediate Reward from Behavior)
2. It will help you later on in life. It will prepare you for getting a job (or going to graduate school). It will prepare you for achievement tests (or the final exam). It will help you with upcoming assignments. (Deferred Reward from Behavior)
3. I will give you a reward if you do. I will make it beneficial to you. I will give you a good grade (or extra credit) if you do. I will make you my special assistant. (Reward from Teacher)
4. Others will respect you if you do. Others will be proud of you. Your friends will like you. Your parents will be pleased. (Reward from Others)
5. You will feel good about yourself if you do. You are the best person to do it. You always do such a good job. (Self-Esteem)
6. You will lose if you don't. You will be unhappy if you don't. You will be hurt if you don't. It's your loss. You'll feel bad if you don't. (Punishment from Behavior)

---

7. I will punish you if you don't. I will make it miserable for you. I'll give you an "F" if you don't. If you don't do it NOW, it will be homework tonight. (Punishment from Teacher)

8. No one will like you. Your friends will make fun of you. Your parents will punish you if you don't. Your classmates will reject you. (Punishment from Others)

9. If you don't, others will be hurt. You'll make others unhappy if you don't. Your parents will feel bad if you don't. Others will be punished if you don't. (Guilt)

10. I will like you better if you do. I will respect you. I will think more highly of you. I will appreciate you more if you do. I will be proud of you. (Teacher–Student Relationship: Positive)

11. I will dislike you if you don't. I will lose respect for you if you don't. I will think less of you if you don't. I won't be proud of you. I'll be disappointed in you. (Teacher–Student Relationship: Negative)

12. Do it, I'm just telling you what I was told. It is a rule, I have to do it and so do you. It's a school policy. (Legitimate—Higher Authority)

13. Because I told you to. You don't have a choice. You're here to work! I'm the teacher, you're the student. I'm in charge, not you. Don't ask, just do it. (Legitimate—Teacher Authority)

14. It is your obligation. It's your turn. Everyone has to do his/her share. It's your job. Everyone has to pull her/his own weight. (Personal [Student] Responsibility)

15. Your group needs it done. The class depends on you. All your friends are counting on you. Don't let your group down. You'll ruin it for the rest of the class. (Responsibility to Class)

16. The majority rules. All of your friends are doing it. Everyone else has to do it. The rest of the class is doing it. It's part of growing up. (Normative Rules)

17. You owe me one. Pay your debt. You promised to do it. I did it the last time. You said you'd try this time. (Debt)

18. If you do this, it will help others. Others will benefit if you do. It will make others happy if you do. I'm not asking you to do it for yourself; do it for the good of the class. (Altruism)

19. Your friends do it. Classmates you respect do it. The friends you admire do it. Other students you like do it. All your friends are doing it. (Peer Modeling)

20. This is the way I always do it. When I was your age, I did it. People who are like me do it. I had to do this when I was in school. Teachers you respect do it. (Teacher Modeling)

21. From my experience, it is a good idea. From what I have learned, it is what you should do. This has always worked for me. Trust me—I know what I'm doing. I had to do this before I became a teacher. (Expert Teacher)

22. Because I need to know how well you understand this. To see how well I've taught you. To see how well you can do it. It will help me know your problem areas. (Teacher Feedback)

Note. For the situational version, teachers are provided with one or more scenarios of particular student misbehavior types and asked to "Imagine that *you* are the teacher who is trying to influence this particular student's behavior in your classroom." Scale items immediately follow the scenario with the instructions, "How likely would you be to use each of the following strategies to get this student to behave [e.g., work on the assignment, stay in his/her seat, etc.]?"

Category labels (in parentheses) should be omitted from the actual questionnaire during administration.

Communication
Anxiety Inventory

An alternative to the well-known and widely used Personal Report of Communication Apprehension (PRCA) scale (McCroskey, 1982) is the Communication Anxiety Inventory (CAI) developed by Booth-Butterfield and Gould (1986). This inventory really comprises two separate but related scales designed to measure Trait and State communication apprehension. Form Trait "is remarkably similar" to the PRCA-24, assessing persons' predispositions to experience anxiety in three generalized contexts: dyadic encounters, small groups, and public speaking performances (Booth-Butterfield & Gould, 1986). In fact, the authors suggest that Form Trait and the PRCA-24 may be parallel forms.

Form State was devised simply because of the inaccessibility of and copyright concerns associated with the State Anxiety Inventory (Spielberger, Gorsuch, & Lushene, 1970). Form State assesses anxieties people have about communicating at a specific point in time: in a given situation with a given person or persons. By referencing a given communication situation in the instructions for the instrument, Form State can be used to measure anxiety responses at any point in time. Fortunately, the data indicate that Form State can be used as a substitute for the Spielberger et al. State Anxiety Inventory (Booth-Butterfield & Gould, 1986).

On the Form Trait, respondents indicate their levels of communication anxiety by responding to 21 statements that feature four frequency-based response options: *almost never, sometimes, often,* and *almost always*. On the Form State, people report their state anxiety by responding to 20 statements that feature four frequency-based response options as well: *not at all, somewhat, moderately so,* and *very much so*. Whereas the instructions on Form Trait ask respondents to indicate how they *generally* feel about communicating in the various contexts specified, Form State asks them to reference how they felt during a specific communication experience they had just completed. Each scale takes about 5 to 10 minutes to complete.

Profile by Michael J. Beatty.

RELIABILITY

The CAI Form Trait appears to be internally consistent. The overall (21 items) alpha coefficient was .90 and the split-half estimate was .92 (Booth-Butterfield & Gould, 1986). Context alpha coefficients were .65 (dyadic), .85 (small group), and .89 (public speaking), and the split-half estimates were .67 (dyadic), .86 (small group), and .89 (public speaking).

The CAI Form State appears to be internally consistent. In the initial development study, Booth-Butterfield and Gould (1986) reported an alpha coefficient of .91 and a split-half reliability estimate of .92. Later, Booth-Butterfield (1987) and Ayres (1988, 1990) reported similar reliability estimates. Available data indicate that the scale is unidimensional (all loadings greater than .35).

VALIDITY

The CAI Form Trait demonstrates considerable construct validity. The initial factor analysis yielded four factors: the three contexts and a physiological factor (Booth-Butterfield & Gould, 1986). All three context subscores correlated significantly with state anxiety scores referring to the associated contexts.

Evidence of the CAI Form State's construct validity has appeared in the communication apprehension literature. Form State scores have been shown to reflect stress induced by public speaking (Booth-Butterfield, 1987). Furthermore, Form State has demonstrated concurrent validity. Form State scores correlate significantly ($r = .69$) with Spielberger, Gorsuch, and Lushene's (1970) state anxiety measure.

COMMENTS

In addition to providing new items, the CAI Form Trait offers a response format different from the many versions of the PRCA. While the PRCA asks subjects to estimate the degree to which they agree with each item, the CAI Form Trait inquires about the frequency of communication-related anxiety experiences. Because anxiety theory posits both Intensity and Frequency dimensions in conceptualizing anxiety, the CAI serves an important measurement function. Overall, the CAI presents interesting new hypotheses about communication anxiety.

LOCATION

Booth-Butterfield, S., & Gould, M. (1986). The Communication Anxiety Inventory: Validation of state- and context-communication apprehension. *Communication Quarterly, 34*, 194–205.

REFERENCES

Ayres, J. (1988). Coping with speech anxiety: The power of positive thinking. *Communication Education, 37*, 289–296.

Ayres, J. (1990). Situational factors and audience anxiety. *Communication Education, 39*, 283–291.

Booth-Butterfield, S. (1987). Action assembly theory and communication apprehension: A psychophysiological study. *Human Communication Research, 13*, 386–398.

McCroskey, J. C. (1982). *An introduction to rhetorical communication* (4th ed.). Englewood Cliffs, NJ: Prentice Hall.

Spielberger, C. D., Gorsuch, R. L., & Lushene, R. E. (1970). *Manual for the State–Trait Anxiety Measure*. Palo Alto, CA: Consulting Psychologists Press.

Communication Anxiety Inventory*: Form Trait

Instructions: This inventory is composed of 21 statements that describe various communication events. You are asked to respond in terms of how you *generally* feel about these events. Please mark your response in the appropriate blank on the answer sheet. Be sure to give the response that best describes how you *generally* feel:

Almost never	Sometimes	Often	Almost always
1	2	3	4

1. I think I communicate effectively in one-to-one situations.
2. My heart beats faster than usual when I speak out in a small group meeting.
3. I enjoy speaking in public.
4. I avoid talking with individuals I don't know very well.
5. I think I make a poor impression when I speak at a small group meeting.
6. I feel disappointed in myself after speaking in public.
7. I enjoy talking with someone I've just met.
8. My body feels relaxed when I speak during a small group meeting.
9. I avoid speaking in public if possible.
10. My body feels tense when I talk with someone I don't know very well.
11. I speak out during small group meetings.
12. I am terrified at the thought of speaking in public.

---

13. My heart beats faster than usual when I talk with someone I've just met.
14. I enjoy talking at a small group meeting.
15. I make a good impression when I speak in public.
16. I would like to have a job that requires me to talk often on a one-to-one basis.
17. I feel disappointed in my efforts to communicate at a small group meeting.
18. My body feels tense and stiff when I speak in public.
19. When conversing with someone on a one-to-one basis, I prefer to listen rather than to talk.
20. I avoid talking during small group meetings.
21. I look forward to speaking in public.

Scoring: Dyadic = sum Items 1, 4, 7, 10, 13, 16, and 19. Small group = sum Items 2, 5, 8, 11, 14, 17, and 20. Public speaking = sum Items 3, 6, 9, 12, 15, 18, and 21.

Note. Reverse coding of Items 1, 3, 7, 8, 11, 14, 15, 16, and 21 before summing.

Communication Anxiety Inventory*:
Form State

Instructions: The following items describes how people communicate in various situations. Choose the number from the following scale that best describes how you felt during the communication experience you *just completed.*

Not at all	Somewhat	Moderately so	Very much so
1	2	3	4

1. I felt tense and nervous.
2. I felt self-confident while talking.
3. While talking, I was afraid of making an embarrassing or silly slip of the tongue.
4. I worried about what others thought of me.
5. I felt calm when I was talking.
6. I felt ill at ease using gestures when I spoke.
7. I could not think clearly when I spoke.

---

*Copyright 1986 by the Eastern Communication Association. Reprinted by permission.

8. My listener(s) seemed interested in what I had to say.
9. I felt poised and in control while I was talking.
10. My body felt tense and stiff while I was talking.
11. My words became confused and jumbled when I was speaking.
12. I felt relaxed when I was talking.
13. My fingers and hands trembled when I was speaking.
14. I felt I had nothing worthwhile to say.
15. I had a "deadpan" expression on my face when I spoke.
16. I found myself talking faster or slower than usual.
17. While speaking, it was easy to find the right words to express myself.
18. I felt awkward when I was talking.
19. My heart seemed to beat faster than usual.
20. I maintained eye contact when I wanted to.

Note. Reverse coding on Items 2, 5, 8, 9, 12, 17, and 20 before summing.

Communication
Satisfaction Questionnaire

The Communication Satisfaction Questionnaire (CSQ) was developed by C. W. Downs and Hazen (1977) in an attempt to discover the relationship between communication and job satisfaction. Redding (1978) defined communication satisfaction as the "overall degree of satisfaction an employee perceived in his total communication environment" (p. 429), but he also wondered if the concept was multidimensional. Wiio (1976) previously identified four dimensions of communication satisfaction: Job Satisfaction, Message Content, Improvements in Communication, and Channel Efficiency.

Initial items, based on literature reviews and interviews with workers, were given to 225 employees in the military, professional organizations, manufacturing organizations, hospitals, government agencies, and universities (C. W. Downs & Hazen, 1977). Principal-components factor analysis revealed eight stable factors, accounting for 61% of the variance. A revised questionnaire containing five items per factor was administered to 510 employees in California, Illinois, Florida, and Minnesota. Factor analysis revealed the items clustered along the same eight factors.

The 40 items are used with a Likert-type scale ranging from *very satisfied* (1) to *very dissatisfied* (7). Each factor has five items, which are averaged for a factor score. The eight factors deal with satisfaction with communication information, relationships, channels, and climate:

1. *Communication Climate* is one of the strongest dimensions, in that people first think of climate when asked about communication satisfaction. The questions in this section measure communication at the organizational and individual levels, probing whether or not the company's communication is stimulating or motivating and whether it encourages employee identification. The questions also assess the perceived communication competence of employees and the extent to which information flow assists the working process.

2. *Relationship to Superiors* includes the components of upward and downward communication. This dimension measures the openness of su-

Profile by Cal W. Downs.

periors to subordinates as well as superiors' ability to listen. Superior's perceived trust of the employee is incorporated in two of the items.

3. *Organizational Integration* revolves around the information employees receive about their job and related items, such as policies and benefits. Also included is information about what is happening currently, what departments are doing, and personnel news. Information about such matters makes employees feel they have been integrated.

4. *Media Quality* looks at communication as it travels through several channels (e.g., publications, memos, and meetings). Employees are asked about the helpfulness and clarity of these information sources and the quantity of information.

5. *Horizontal and Informal Communication* questions the amount of activity of information networks and the accuracy of the information they contain.

6. *Organizational Perspective* refers to the information given out concerning the corporation and its goals and performance. It also encompasses knowledge about external events such as new government policies, which impact the organization.

7. *Relationship with Subordinates* is only completed by those in supervisory or managerial positions. It taps receptivity of employees to downward communication and their willingness and capability to send good information upward. Superiors are also asked whether they experience communication overload.

8. The *Personal Feedback* dimension contains questions about superiors' understanding of problems faced on the job and whether or not employees feel the criteria by which they are judged are clear.

Three additional items are found in the instrument. One global item asks employees to indicate their level of job satisfaction on a 7-point Likert scale. Then they are asked whether their satisfaction has gone up or down, or remained the same, in the last 6 months. An open-ended question asks respondents to indicate what needs to be changed about communication in the organization to improve their satisfaction. Responses are content-analyzed. The CSQ takes between 20 and 30 minutes to complete.

RELIABILITY

Test–retest (2-week interval) reliability of the CSQ was reported at .94 (C. W. Downs & Hazen, 1977). Coefficient alpha reliabilities for the eight dimensions have been consistently high, ranging from .72 to .96 for studies in the United States (Potvin, 1991/1992) and Australia (A. Downs, 1991).

VALIDITY

Construct validity of the CSQ has been determined primarily through factor analysis. Crino and White (1981) administered the CSQ to 137 supervisors from five textile mills and found the eight factors C. W. Downs and Hazen (1977) developed. However, Clampitt and Girard (1988) argued for a five-factor solution.

Evidence of concurrent validity exists. CSQ factors have been found to be highly correlated with job satisfaction (C. W. Downs & Hazen, 1977), strong predictors of organizational commitment (A. Downs, 1991; Potvin, 1991/1992), and related to turnover (Gregson, 1987) and need fulfillment (Kio, 1979/1980). It is unrelated to demographic variables.

COMMENT

The global measure of job satisfaction is somewhat controversial in view of the Job Description Index in which job satisfaction is treated as multidimensional. The eight CSQ factors are not entirely discrete; high intercorrelations exist among the factors.

The CSQ has become a popular instrument for analyzing communication processes in organizations. It has been the primary research tool in more than 30 dissertations and theses, and it has been translated into Chinese, Dutch, German, Japanese, Spanish, and Turkish. The CSQ has been used in Nigeria, Mexico, Taiwan, Guatemala, Australia, as well as in the United States.

In a review of all the instruments used to measure communication satisfaction, Hecht (1978) commented: "The thoroughness of the construction of this satisfaction measure is apparent. The strategies employed in this study are exemplary" (p. 363).

LOCATION

Downs, C. W., & Hazen, M. (1977). A factor analytic study of communication satisfaction. *Journal of Business Communication, 14,* 63–73.

REFERENCES

Clampitt, P., & Girard, D. M. (1988, May). *Time for reflection: A factor analytic study of the communication satisfaction instrument.* Paper presented at the annual meeting of the International Communication Association, San Francisco.

Crino, M. D., & White, M. C. (1981). Satisfaction in communication: An examination of the Downs–Hazen measure. *Psychological Reports, 49,* 831–838.

Downs, A. (1991). *The relationship between communication and organizational commitment in two Australian organizations.* Unpublished master's thesis, University of Kansas, Lawrence.

Gregson, T. (1987). An empirical investigation of the relationship between communication satisfaction, job satisfaction, turnover, and performance for public accountants (Doctoral dissertation, University of Arkansas, 1987). *Dissertation Abstracts International, 48,* 1254A.

Hecht, M. L. (1978). Measures of communication satisfaction. *Human Communication Research, 4,* 350–368.

Kio, J. B. A. (1980). A descriptive study of communication satisfaction, need satisfaction, and need importance index among Nigerian workers (Doctoral dissertation, University of Kansas, 1979). *Dissertation Abstracts International, 41,* 19A.

Potvin, T. C. (1992). Employee organizational commitment: An examination of its relationship to communication satisfaction and an evaluation of questionnaires designed to measure the construct (Doctoral dissertation, University of Kansas, 1991). *Dissertation Abstracts International, 52,* 4147A.

Redding, W. C. (1978). *Communication within the organization.* New York: Industrial Communication Council.

Wiio, O. (1976, May). *Organizational communication: Interfacing systems in different contingencies.* Paper presented at the annual meeting of the International Communication Association, Portland, OR.

Communication Satisfaction Questionnaire–II*

Introduction: Most of us assume that the quality and amount of communication in our jobs contribute to both our job satisfaction and our productivity. Through this study we hope to find out how satisfactory communication practices are and what suggestions you have for improving them. We appreciate your taking time to complete the questionnaire. It should take 20 to 30 minutes.

Your answers are completely confidential *so be as frank as you wish. This is not a test—your opinion is the only right answer. Do not sign your name; we do not wish to know who you are. The answers will be combined into groups for reporting purposes.*

1. How satisfied are you with your job? (check 1)

    ____ 1. Very satisfied   ____ 5. Somewhat dissatisfied

    ____ 2. Satisfied   ____ 6. Dissatisfied

    ____ 3. Somewhat satisfied   ____ 7. Very dissatisfied

    ____ 4. Indifferent

---

*Copyright 1977 by Cal W. Downs and Mike Hazen. Reprinted by permission.

2. In the past 6 months, what has happened to your level of satisfaction? (check 1)

    ___ 1. Gone up   ___ 2. Stayed the same   ___ 3. Gone down

3. If the communication associated with your job could be changed in any way to make you more satisfied, please indicate how:

    _____

    _____

A. Listed below are several kinds of information often associated with a person's job. Please indicate how satisfied you are with the *amount* and/or *quality* of each kind of information by circling the appropriate number at the right.

Very dissatisfied						Very satisfied
1	2	3	4	5	6	7

[Editors' note: Respondents use the above scale to respond to all items.]

4. Information about my progress in my job
5. Personal news
6. Information about organizational policies and goals
7. Information about how my job compares with others
8. Information about how I am being judged
9. Recognition of my efforts
10. Information about departmental policies and goals
11. Information about the requirements of my job
12. Information about government action affecting my organization
13. Information about changes in our organization
14. Reports on how problems in my job are being handled
15. Information about benefits and pay
16. Information about our organization's financial standing
17. Information about accomplishments and/or failures of the organization

B. Please indicate how satisfied you are with the following (circle the appropriate number at right).

18. Extent to which my superiors know and understand the problems faced by subordinates
19. Extent to which the organization's communication motivates and stimulates an enthusiasm for meeting its goals
20. Extent to which my supervisor listens and pays attention to me
21. Extent to which the people in my organization have great ability as communicators

22. Extent to which my supervisor offers guidance for solving job related problems
23. Extent to which the organization's communication makes me identify with it or feel a vital part of it
24. Extent to which the organization's communications are interesting and helpful
25. Extent to which my supervisor trusts me
26. Extent to which I receive in time the information needed to do my job
27. Extent to which conflicts are handled appropriately through proper communication channels
28. Extent to which the grapevine is active in our organization
29. Extent to which my supervisor is open to ideas
30. Extent to which horizontal communication with other organizational members is accurate and free flowing
31. Extent to which communication practices are adaptable to emergencies
32. Extent to which my work group is compatible
33. Extent to which our meetings are well organized
34. Extent to which the amount of supervision given me is about right
35. Extent to which written directives and reports are clear and concise
36. Extent to which the attitudes toward communication in the organization are basically healthy
37. Extent to which informal communication is active and accurate
38. Extent to which the amount of communication in the organization is about right

C. Answer the following *only if you are a manager or supervisor*. Then indicate your satisfaction with the following.

39. Extent to which my subordinates are responsive to downward directive communication
40. Extent to which my subordinates anticipate my needs for information
41. Extent to which I *do not* have a communication overload
42. Extent to which my subordinates are receptive to evaluation, suggestions, and criticisms
43. Extent to which my subordinates feel responsible for initiating accurate upward communication

Note. Downs recommends that researchers factor-analyze the scale to confirm the existence of the eight dimensions: Communication Climate, Relationship to Superiors, Organizational Integration, Media Quality, Horizontal and Informal Communication, Organizational Perspective, Relationship with Subordinates, and Personal Feedback. Item 1 is a global satisfaction item; Item 2 looks at changes within the last 6 months; Item 3 is open-ended. Academic researchers may use the instrument without permission.

Communicative Adaptability Scale

Duran (1983) defined communicative adaptability as a cognitive and behavioral "ability to perceive socio-interpersonal relationships and adapt one's interaction goals and behaviors accordingly" (p. 320). While early versions of the Communicative Adaptability Scale (CAS) had only two (Zakahi & Duran, 1982) or three dimensions (Duran & Wheeless, cited in Spitzberg, 1988, and in Downs, Archer, McGrath, & Stafford, 1988), Duran's (1983) study increased the content validity of the instrument by including four additional components of communicative adaptability and a total of 60 items.

The resulting 30-item instrument (Duran & Kelly, 1988) taps six dimensions (five items for each dimension) of communicative adaptability: Social Composure (feeling relaxed in social situations), Social Experience (enjoying and participating socially), Social Confirmation (maintaining the other's social image), Appropriate Disclosure (adapting one's disclosures appropriately to the intimacy level of the exchange), Articulation (using appropriate syntax and grammar), and Wit (using humor to diffuse social tension).

Respondents use a 5-point Likert-type scale that ranges from *always true of me* (5) to *never true of me* (1) for each of the 30 items. Respondents require less than 5 minutes to complete the CAS. The scale has been used primarily as a self-report instrument.

RELIABILITY

The internal consistency of the CAS has been good. Duran (1992) reported that in 10 samples, with over 4,000 people, the average alpha for the dimensions were as follows: Social Experience, .80; Social Confirmation, .84; Social Composure, .82; Appropriate Disclosure, .76; Articulation, .80; and Wit, .74. Cupach and Spitzberg (1983) reported an overall scale alpha of .81 and Zakahi and Duran (1984) reported an overall alpha of .79. There are no reported data for split-half or test–retest reliability.

Profile by Rebecca B. Rubin.

VALIDITY

The scale appears to have strong concurrent validity. Social Composure and Social Experience are related to communication apprehension (Duran, 1983), Social Experience and Social Confirmation are related to loneliness (Zakahi & Duran, 1982, 1985), and the physically attractive are viewed as more communicatively adaptive (Zakahi & Duran, 1984). Duran and Kelly (1988) looked at CAS in relationship to interaction involvement and found that (a) Responsiveness was related to Social Confirmation and Appropriate Disclosure, (b) perceptiveness was related to Social Composure and Social Experience, and (c) attentiveness was related to Social Experience. The CAS was also strongly correlated with the two measures of communicative competence and self-esteem; it was unrelated to constructs such as dogmatism, interpersonal attraction, and rating of Alter's anxiety (Cupach & Spitzberg, 1983).

Related research has examined communicative adaptability in relation to communicator style. Social Composure and Social Experience were related to a relaxed, dominant style, and Social Confirmation was related to a friendly, animated style (Duran & Zakahi, 1984). A more recent study examined conversational style in relation to the CAS (Duran & Zakahi, 1990). Articulation was positively related to talk time, Social Composure was positively correlated with conversational turns and use of "other pronouns," Social Confirmation was negatively related to talk time, Social Experience was positively—and Appropriate Disclosure was negatively—related to use of other pronouns.

Criterion-related validity also appears good. College students' perceptions of their roommates' Social Composure, Social Experience, and Articulation influenced roommate satisfaction (desires to change or keep their roommates) (Duran & Zakahi, 1988). Appropriate Disclosure, Social Experience, and Social Confirmation were also main contributors in communication satisfaction in interpersonal interaction (Duran & Zakahi, 1987).

Research has also attempted to establish construct validity. Duran and Kelly (1985) found a significant difference between high and low cognitively complex persons on the Social Experience and Wit dimensions. Also, they discovered that women had higher scores on Social Experience and Appropriate Disclosure; however, the women's higher cognitive complexity scores may have confounded these findings. And shy and not shy persons differed on some of the dimensions (Duran & Kelly, 1989; Prisbell, 1991). Validity studies are summarized in Duran (1992).

COMMENTS

Although Duran (1983) extended the content validity of the earlier scale, the six dimensions of the current instrument still may not tap all dimensions of communication competence. Also, the Social Dimensions of the scale appear unrelated to the Wit and Articulation dimensions, which are not often related to other constructs during concurrent validity studies. In the past, the primary subject population has been college students (Spitzberg & Cupach, 1989) except for the initial study's (Duran, 1983) group of teachers, whose data resulted in a five-factor solution rather than six factors. Future research should involve more nonstudent samples and factor analysis to again test the stability of the factor structure.

LOCATION

Duran, R. L. (1983). Communicative adaptability: A measure of social communicative competence. *Communication Quarterly, 31,* 320–326.

Duran, R. L. (1992). Communicative adaptability: A review of conceptualization and measurement. *Communication Quarterly, 40,* 253–268.

Spitzberg, B. H. (1988). Communication competence: Measures of perceived effectiveness. In C. H. Tardy (Ed.), *A handbook for the study of human communication: Methods and instruments for observing, measuring, and assessing communication processes* (pp. 67–105). Norwood, NJ: Ablex.

REFERENCES

Cupach, W. R., & Spitzberg, B. H. (1983). Trait versus state: A comparison of dispositional and situational measures of interpersonal communication competence. *Western Journal of Speech Communication, 47,* 364–379.

Downs, C. W., Archer, J., McGrath, J., & Stafford, J. (1988). An analysis of communication style instrumentation. *Management Communication Quarterly, 1,* 543–571.

Duran, R. L., & Kelly, L. (1985). An investigation into the cognitive domain of communication competence. *Communication Research Reports, 2,* 112–119.

Duran, R. L., & Kelly, L. (1988). An investigation into the cognitive domain of competence II: The relationship between communicative competence and interaction involvement. *Communication Research Reports, 5,* 91–96.

Duran, R. L., & Kelly, L. (1989). The cycle of shyness: A study of self-perceptions of communication performance. *Communication Reports, 2,* 30–38.

Duran, R. L., & Zakahi, W. R. (1984). Competence or style: What's in a name. *Communication Research Reports, 1,* 42–47.

Duran, R. L., & Zakahi, W. R. (1987). Communication performance and communication satisfaction: What do we teach our students? *Communication Education, 36,* 13–22.

Duran, R. L., & Zakahi, W. R. (1988). The influence of communicative competence upon roommate satisfaction. *Western Journal of Speech Communication, 52,* 135–146.

Duran, R. L., & Zakahi, W. R. (1990, April). *State vs. trait competence and locus of judgment: An investigation into issues of communicative competence.* Paper presented at the meeting of the Eastern Communication Association, Philadelphia.

Prisbell, M. (1991). Shyness and self-reported competence. *Communication Research Reports, 8*, 141–148.

Spitzberg, B. H., & Cupach, W. R. (1989). *Handbook of interpersonal competence research.* New York: Springer-Verlag.

Zakahi, W. R., & Duran, R. L. (1982). All the lonely people: The relationship among loneliness, communicative competence, and communication anxiety. *Communication Quarterly, 30*, 203–209.

Zakahi, W. R., & Duran, R. L. (1984). Attraction, communicative competence and communication satisfaction. *Communication Research Reports, 1*, 54–57.

Zakahi, W. R., & Duran, R. L. (1985). Loneliness, communicative competence, and communication apprehension: Extension and replication. *Communication Quarterly, 33*, 50–60.

Communicative Adaptability Scale*

Instructions: The following are statements about communication behaviors. Answer each item as it relates to your general style of communication (the type of communicator you are most often) in social situations.

Please indicate the degree to which each statement applies to you by placing the appropriate number (according to the scale below) in the space provided.

5 = always true of me
4 = often true of me
3 = sometimes true of me
2 = rarely true of me
1 = never true of me

1. I feel nervous in social situations.
2. In most social situations I feel tense and constrained.
3. When talking, my posture seems awkward and tense.
4. My voice sounds nervous when I talk with others.
5. I am relaxed when talking with others.
6. I try to make the other person feel good.
7. I try to make the other person feel important.
8. I try to be warm when communicating with another.
9. While I'm talking I think about how the other person feels.
10. I am verbally and nonverbally supportive of other people.

11. I like to be active in different social groups.
12. I enjoy socializing with various groups of people.
13. I enjoy meeting new people.
14. I find it easy to get along with new people.
15. I do not "mix" well at social functions.
16. I am aware of how intimate my disclosures are.
17. I am aware of how intimate the disclosures of others are.
18. I disclose at the same level that others disclose to me.
19. I know how appropriate my self-disclosures are.
20. When I self-disclose I know what I am revealing.
21. When speaking I have problems with grammar.
22. At times I don't use appropriate verb tense.
23. I sometimes use one word when I mean to use another.
24. I sometimes use words incorrectly.
25. I have difficulty pronouncing some words.
26. When I am anxious, I often make jokes.
27. I often make jokes when in tense situations.
28. When I embarrass myself, I often make a joke about it.
29. When someone makes a negative comment about me, I respond with a witty comeback.
30. People think I am witty.

Note. Items 1, 2, 3, 4, 15, 21, 22, 23, 24, and 25 are reverse-coded.

Social Composure items are 1–5, Social Confirmation items are 6–10, Social Experience items are 11–15, Appropriate Disclosure items are 16–20, Articulation items are 21–25, and Wit items are 26–30. Items should be rearranged randomly before use.

Communicative Competence Scale

Wiemann (1977) created the Communicative Competence Scale (CCS) to measure communicative competence, an ability "to choose among available communicative behaviors" to accomplish one's own "interpersonal goals during an encounter while maintaining the face and line" of "fellow interactants within the constraints of the situation" (p. 198). Originally, 57 Likert-type items were created to assess five dimensions of interpersonal competence (General Competence, Empathy, Affiliation/Support, Behavioral Flexibility, and Social Relaxation) and a dependent measure (Interaction Management). Some 239 college students used the scale to rate videotaped confederates enacting one of four role-play interaction management conditions (high, medium, low, rude). The 36 items that discriminated the best between conditions were used in the final instrument. Factor analysis resulted in two main factors—general and relaxation—indicating that the subjects did not differentiate among the dimensions as the model originally predicted.

Subjects use the CCS to assess another person's communicative competence by responding to 36 items using Likert scales that range from *strongly agree* (5) to *strongly disagree* (1). The scale takes less than 5 minutes to complete. Some researchers have adapted the other-report format to self-report and partner-report. These formats are available from the author.

RELIABILITY

The CCS appears to be internally consistent. Wiemann (1977) reported a .96 coefficient alpha (and .74 magnitude of experimental effect) for the 36-item revised instrument. McLaughlin and Cody (1982) used a 30-item version for college students to rate their partners after 30 minutes of conversation and reported an alpha of .91. Jones and Brunner (1984) had college students rate audiotaped interactions and reported an overall alpha of .94 to .95; subscale scores had alphas ranging from .68 to .82. Street, Mulac,

Profile by Rebecca R. Rubin.

and Wiemann (1988) had college students rate each other on communicative competence and reported an alpha of .84. The 36-item self-report format version is also reliable: Cupach and Spitzberg (1983) reported an alpha of .90, Hazleton and Cupach (1986) reported an alpha of .91, Cegala, Savage, Brunner, and Conrad (1982) reported an alpha of .85, and Query, Parry, and Flint (1992) reported an alpha of .86.

VALIDITY

Two studies found evidence of construct validity. First, McLaughlin and Cody (1982) found that interactants in conversations in which there were multiple lapses of time rated each other lower on communicative competence. Second, Street et al. (1988) found that conversants' speech rate, vocal back channeling, duration of speech, and rate of interruption were related to their communicative competence scores; they also found that conversants rated their partners significantly more favorably than did observers.

Various studies have provided evidence of concurrent validity. Cupach and Spitzberg (1983) used the dispositional self-report format and found that the CCS was strongly correlated with two other dispositions: communication adaptability and trait self-rated competence. The CCS was also modestly related to situational, conversation-specific measures of feeling good and self-rated competence. Hazleton and Cupach (1986) found a moderate relationship between communicative competence and both ontological knowledge about interpersonal communication and interpersonal communication apprehension. Backlund (1978) found communicative competence was related to social insight and open-mindedness. Douglas (1991) reported inverse relationships between communication competence and uncertainty and apprehension during initial meetings. And Query et al. (1992) found that nontraditional students, those high in communication competence, had more social supports and were more satisfied with these supports.

In addition, Cegala et al. (1982) compared 326 college students' CCS and Interaction Involvement Scale scores. All three dimensions of interaction involvement were positively correlated with the CCS, but only perceptiveness correlated significantly with all five dimensions for both men and women. Responsiveness was related to behavioral flexibility, affiliation/support, and social relaxation, and attentiveness was related to impression management.

COMMENTS

Although this scale has existed for a number of years and the original article has been cited numerous times, relatively few research studies have actually used the CCS. As reported by Perotti and DeWine (1987), problems with the factor structure and the Likert-type format may be reasons why. They suggested that the instrument be used as a composite measure of communicative competence rather than breaking the scale into subscales, and this appears to be good advice. Spitzberg (1988, 1989) viewed the instrument as well conceived, suitable for observant or conversant rating situations, and aimed at "normal" adolescent or adult populations, yet Backlund (1978) found little correlation between peer-perceived competence and expert-perceived competence when using the CCS. The scale has been used only with college student populations.

LOCATION

Wiemann, J. M. (1977). Explication and test of a model of communicative competence. *Human Communication Research, 3*, 195–213.

REFERENCES

Backlund, P. M. (1978). Speech communication correlates of perceived communication competence (Doctoral dissertation, University of Denver, 1977). *Dissertation Abstracts International, 38*, 3800A.

Cegala, D. J., Savage, G. T., Brunner, C. C., & Conrad, A. B. (1982). An elaboration of the meaning of interaction involvement: Toward the development of a theoretical concept. *Communication Monographs, 49*, 229–248.

Cupach, W. R., & Spitzberg, B. H. (1983). Trait versus state: A comparison of dispositional and situational measures of interpersonal communication competence. *Western Journal of Speech Communication, 47*, 364–379.

Douglas, W. (1991). Expectations about initial interaction: An examination of the effects of global uncertainty. *Human Communication Research, 17*, 355–384.

Hazleton, V., Jr., & Cupach, W. R. (1986). An exploration of ontological knowledge: Communication competence as a function of the ability to describe, predict, and explain. *Western Journal of Speech Communication, 50*, 119–132.

Jones, T. S., & Brunner, C. C. (1984). The effects of self-disclosure and sex on perceptions of interpersonal communication competence. *Women's Studies in Communication, 7*, 23–37.

McLaughlin, M. L., & Cody, M. J. (1982). Awkward silences: Behavioral antecedents and consequences of the conversational lapse. *Human Communication Research, 8*, 299–316.

Perotti, V. S., & DeWine, S. (1987). Competence in communication: An examination of three instruments. *Management Communication Quarterly, 1*, 272–287.

Query, J. L., Parry, D., & Flint, L. J. (1992). The relationship among social support, communication competence, and cognitive depression for nontraditional students. *Journal of Applied Communication Research, 20*, 78–94.

Spitzberg, B. H. (1988). Communication competence: Measures of perceived effectiveness. In C. H. Tardy (Ed.), *A handbook for the study of human communication: Methods and instruments for observing, measuring, and assessing communication processes* (pp. 67–105). Norwood, NJ: Ablex.

Spitzberg, B. H. (1989). *Handbook of interpersonal competence research.* New York: Springer-Verlag.

Street, R. L., Jr., Mulac, A., & Wiemann, J. M. (1988). Speech evaluation differences as a function of perspective (participant versus observer) and presentational medium. *Human Communication Research, 14,* 333–363.

Communicative Competence Scale*

Instructions: Complete the following questionnaire/scale with the subject (S) in mind. Circle one of the sets of letters before each numbered question based upon whether you strongly agree (SA), agree (A), are undecided or neutral (?), disagree (D), or strongly disagree (SD). Always keep the subject in mind as you answer.

Strongly agree	Agree	Undecided or neutral	Disagree	Strongly disagree
SA	A	?	D	SD

[Editors' note: Respondents use the above scale to respond to all items.]

1. S finds it easy to get along with others.
2. S can adapt to changing situations.
3. S treats people as individuals.
4. S interrupts others too much.
5. S is "rewarding" to talk to.
6. S can deal with others effectively.
7. S is a good listener.
8. S's personal relations are cold and distant.
9. S is easy to talk to.
10. S won't argue with someone just to prove he/she is right.
11. S's conversation behavior is not "smooth."
12. S ignores other people's feelings.
13. S generally knows how others feel.
14. S lets others know he/she understands them.
15. S understands other people.
16. S is relaxed and comfortable when speaking.
17. S listens to what people say to him/her.
18. S likes to be close and personal with people.

19. S generally knows what type of behavior is appropriate in any given situation.
20. S usually does not make unusual demands on his/her friends.
21. S is an effective conversationalist.
22. S is supportive of others.
23. S does not mind meeting strangers.
24. S can easily put himself/herself in another person's shoes.
25. S pays attention to the conversation.
26. S is generally relaxed when conversing with a new acquaintance.
27. S is interested in what others have to say.
28. S doesn't follow the conversation very well.
29. S enjoys social gatherings where he/she can meet new people.
30. S is a likeable person.
31. S is flexible.
32. S is not afraid to speak with people in authority.
33. People can go to S with their problems.
34. S generally says the right thing at the right time.
35. S likes to use his/her voice and body expressively.
36. S is sensitive to others' needs of the moment.

Note. Items 4, 8, 11, 12, and 28 are reverse-coded before summing the 36 items. For "Partner" version, "S" is replaced by "My partner" and by "my long-standing relationship partner" in the instructions. For the "Self-Report" version, "S" is replaced by "I" and statements are adjusted for first-person singular.

Communicator
Competence Questionnaire

Monge, Backman, Dillard, and Eisenberg (1982) suggested modifications in the communicative competence construct to make it appropriate for organizational research. They developed the Communicator Competence Questionnaire (CCQ) to assess the interaction between persons occupying specific roles within organizational settings. The CCQ is composed of 12 items making up two factors: Encoding and Decoding. In addition, the CCQ is other-oriented and designed to assess either superior or subordinate communicative competence. This is the first instrument designed to examine competence from an organizational rather than an interpersonal perspective.

Supervisors and subordinates are asked to evaluate each other using this scale. Seven encoding items focus on behaviors such as being able to express one's ideas clearly, having a good command of the language, and being easy to understand. Five decoding items focus on skills such as listening, responding to messages, and attentiveness. Two items are negatively worded to serve as a check against response set. Five of the items were adapted from the Communicative Competence Scale (Wiemann, 1977). The 7-point response scale (*YES!*, YES, yes, ?, no, NO, *NO!*) was adapted from the Predisposition toward Verbal Behavior (Mortensen, Arantson, & Lustig, 1977) instrument. Respondents normally require less than 5 minutes to complete the CCQ.

Monge et al. (1982) sampled 220 employees from two large firms. This provided 198 supervisor–subordinate dyads. In a second sample, 60 staff people generated 53 supervisor–subordinate dyads. Subordinates completed questionnaires on their superiors and superiors completed questionnaires for each of their subordinates. Because a MANOVA computed on the mean response vectors for the 12 items in the two sets of evaluation (supervisor and subordinate) resulted in a significant F value, two confirmatory factor analyses were performed. The two subscale factors were Encoding and Decoding.

Profile by Sue DeWine.

RELIABILITY

The CCQ appears to have strong internal reliability. In the Monge et al. (1982) study, the internal reliability of the Encoding and Decoding subscales ranged from .81 to .87 with an average of .85 for both supervisors and subordinates. Smith and DeWine (1989) used a repeated-measures design employing the CCQ to determine subjects' perceptions of competence when male and female subordinates were requesting support. Because a repeated-measures design was employed and all subjects completed the questionnaire four times, a coefficient alpha was computed on the CCQ for each occasion: .93, .91, .93, and .89.

Papa and Tracy (1988) used the CCQ to measure the relationship between communicative ability (competence, listening ability, and interaction frequency) and employee performance with new technology. The two factors, Encoding and Decoding, were highly correlated (.95). Because of this high degree of multicollinearity, competence was treated as a single factor. Reliability for the 12-item scale was extremely high with a coefficient alpha of .98. Communicator competence accounted for 24% of the variance in employee productivity with the new computer system.

VALIDITY

Assessment of convergent validity was undertaken by comparing each competence factor for both supervisors and subordinates with two global, single-item measures of competence (Monge et al., 1982). One item read, "In general my supervisor (subordinate) is a very effective communicator"; the other read, "Overall my supervisor (subordinate) is a competent communicator." All correlation coefficients were high; the mean correlation was .74. The authors claimed that collectively, and individually, these results offered evidence of convergent validity.

In Smith and DeWine (1989), convergent validity was assessed for the CCQ by correlating each factor (Encoding and Decoding) with the same global single items used by Monge et al. (1982). Each of the single items was correlated separately with the scores on the Encoding and Decoding factors. For the female communicator, the correlations ranged from .71 to .86. For the male communicator, the correlations ranged from .66 to .81.

COMMENTS

One of the appealing aspects of this instrument is its focus on "other" evaluation of competence. Spitzberg and Cupach (1985) pointed out the need to investigate the relationships among self, partner, and observer perceptions of conversational skill and competence. Additionally, this instrument is uniquely developed for the organizational context. Competence instruments often focus only on encoding skills (i.e., how the individual expresses him/ herself). This is one of the greatest strengths of this research tool: It also identifies decoding skills (i.e., how well the individual is listening).

LOCATION

Monge, P. R., Backman, S. G., Dillard, J. P., & Eisenberg, E. M. (1982). Communicator competence in the workplace: Model testing and scale development. *Communication Yearbook*, 5, 505–528.

REFERENCES

Mortensen, C. D., Arantson, P. H., & Lustig, M. (1977). The measurement of verbal predispositions: Scale development and application. *Human Communication Research*, 3, 146–158.
Papa, M. J., & Tracy, K. (1988). Communicative indices of employee performance with new technology. *Communication Research*, 15, 524–544.
Smith, G., & DeWine, S. (1989, May). *Requesting help at work and perceived communicative competence of subordinates.* Paper presented at the annual meeting of the International Communication Association, San Francisco.
Spitzberg, B. H., & Cupach, W. R. (1985). Conversational skill and locus of perception. *Journal of Psychopathology and Behavioral Assessment*, 7(3), 207-220.
Wiemann, J. M. (1977). Explication and test of a model of communicative competence. *Human Communication Research*, 3, 195–213.

Communicator Competence Questionnaire*

Instructions: In this series of questions we would like you to describe how your subordinate communicates. Think about his/her behavior in general, rather than about specific situations.
    In responding to the statements below, please use the following scale:

YES!	= very strong agreement	*NO!*	= very strong disagreement
YES	= strong agreement	NO	= strong disagreement
yes	= mild agreement	no	= mild disagreement

                    ? = neutral feelings or don't know

[Editors' note: Respondents use this scale, as demonstrated in Item 1, to respond to all items.]

1. My subordinate has a good command of the language.

    YES!   YES   yes   ?   no   NO   *NO!*

2. My subordinate is sensitive to others' needs of the moment.
3. My subordinate typically gets right to the point.
4. My subordinate pays attention to what other people say to him or her.
5. My subordinate can deal with others effectively.
6. My subordinate is a good listener.
7. My subordinate's writing is difficult to understand.
8. My subordinate expresses his or her ideas clearly.
9. My subordinate is difficult to understand when he or she speaks.
10. My subordinate generally says the right thing at the right time.
11. My subordinate is easy to talk to.
12. My subordinate usually responds to messages (memos, phone calls, reports, etc.) quickly.

Note. This is the Subordinate version. Substitution of the word "Supervisor" throughout will provide the Supervisor version.

Encoding items are Items 1, 3, 5, 7, 8, 9, and 10, and Decoding Items are 2, 4, 6, 11, and 12. Items 7 and 9 are reverse-coded before summing.

Communicator Style Measure

Norton (1978) conceptualized communicator style as "the way one verbally and paraverbally interacts to signal how literal meaning should be taken, interpreted, filtered, or understood" (p. 99). The Communicator Style Measure (CSM) consists of nine independent variables (Dominant, Dramatic, Contentious, Animated, Impression Leaving, Relaxed, Attentive, Open, and Friendly) and one dependent variable (Communicator Image). The independent variables are descriptive of one's style; the dependent variable is the evaluative consequence of the independent variables.

Dominant reflects a tendency to take charge in social situations. Dramatic refers to communicating in a way that highlights or understates content. Contentious represents communicating in a negative combative fashion. Animated refers to "physical, nonverbal cues" (Norton, 1978, p. 100). Impression Leaving defines a person who manifests a visible or memorable style of communicating. Relaxed refers to an absence of tension or anxiety. Attentive involves making sure others know that they are being listened to. Open is "being conversational, expansive, affable, convivial, gregarious, unreserved, unsecretive, somewhat frank, possibly outspoken, definitely extroverted, and obviously approachable" (Norton, 1978, p. 101). Friendly "ranges in meaning from being unhostile to deep intimacy" (Norton, 1978, p. 101). Precise refers to accuracy and correctness. Communicator Image, the dependent variable, refers to whether someone is a "good communicator."

The underlying clusters, dimensions, and predictors of the communicator style construct were investigated in a series of studies. Rather than employ traditional data reduction techniques such as factor analysis, Norton (1978) chose to employ smallest space analysis, which produced two continua. The first continuum was anchored by attentive and friendly (nondirective communication) at one end and by dominant and contentious (directive communicative) at the other end. The second was "anchored by communicative activity, dramatic and animated . . . at one end, and by communicative activity, relaxed" at the other (p. 109). Results of multiple regression analysis revealed that three variables (Animated, Contentious, and Dramatic) failed to predict communicator image. The remaining six vari-

Profile by Elizabeth E. Graham.

ables accounted for 53% of the total variance in communicator image. However, Dominant was the best predictor, accounting for over 30% of the variance by itself.

Participants are requested to assess their own communicator style by responding to 51 items using Likert scales that range from *strongly agree* (1) to *strongly disagree* (4). The CSM-51 requires less than 10 minutes to complete. Initially, 102 Likert items comprise the CSM; however, through refinement Norton reduced the number of items in the measure to 51. An even shorter version of the CSM was proposed by Montgomery and Norton (1981). This version uses a four-sentence description of each variable and a 6-point scale for rating each style variable. Although Norton intended the CSM to be a self-report measure, other formats have also been successfully employed (Duran & Zakahi, 1987; Rubin & Feezel, 1986).

RELIABILITY

Norton (1978) reported the following internal reliabilities for the CSM variables: Friendly, .37; Animated, .56; Attentive, .57; Contentious, .65; Dramatic, .68; Impression Leaving, .69; Open, .69; Relaxed, .71; Communicator Image, .72; and Dominant, .82. Various researchers have reported similar results (Duran & Zakahi, 1984, 1987; Hailey, Daly, & Hailey, 1984; Lamude & Daniels, 1984). In order to boost the reliability to .70, Norton suggested adding 15 parallel items to the friendly construct. The reliabilities of the animated and attentive subscales may also be improved by adding like items to the subscale. These items are available from Norton.

VALIDITY

Norton (1978) provided evidence of content validity by specifying the domain of the communicator-style construct. As much as this is a difficult task with any construct, "the problem is aggravated since there is no established domain of communicator style similar to such heavily validated constructs as attraction, credibility, or empathy" (Norton, 1983, p. 57).

Various studies support the construct validity of the CSM. Communicator style has been positively associated with a host of communication behaviors and perceptions such as attractiveness (Brandt, 1979; Norton & Pettegrew, 1979), communication apprehension (Porter, 1982), communication competence (Eadie & Paulson, 1984), and relationship disengagement strategies (Hailey et al., 1984).

Criterion-related validity was provided by Duran and Zakahi (1987), who report that the CSM significantly discriminates between satisfied and dissatisfied groups. Also, Tardy, Childs, and Hampton (1985) reported that Type A persons are more dominant, contentious, precise, animated, and dramatic communicators than are Type B personalities. And O'Hair, Cody, Goss, and Krayer (1988) concluded that a person's honesty could be predicted from communicator-style components of friendliness, attentiveness, and preciseness.

The CSM has been employed in a variety of contexts. For example, Buller and Buller (1987) and Buller and Street (1991) found that physicians' communicator style has an effect on patient satisfaction. Infante and Gorden (1989) reported that superiors were most satisfied with subordinates who expressed an affirming (friendly, relaxed, and attentive) communicator style. In the instructional environment, teachers' communicator style was positively associated with student learning (Nussbaum & Scott, 1979) as well as ratings of teaching effectiveness (Norton, 1983; Scott & Nussbaum, 1981).

There appears to be an interaction between style and gender. Montgomery and Norton (1981) indicated that men see themselves as more precise than women, whereas women see themselves as more animated than men. Various other researchers reported few differences in the self-reports of men and women (Gudykunst & Lim, 1985; Lamude & Daniels, 1984; Staley & Cohen, 1988).

COMMENTS

The CSM has generated considerable research in the communication discipline as well as in related fields. However, there are some conceptual and methodological issues that have arisen since the introduction of the CSM. For example, Ganster, Petelle, Baker, Dallinger, and Backus (1981) reported a number of problems with the CSM including low nonuniform reliabilities for some of the subscales and multicollinearity among subscales. Most problematic is the failure to specify a nomological network for the style construct. In addition, Sypher (1980) questioned the validity of the CSM, as representative of self-report measures of behavior, noting that the CSM is memory based and therefore not a true indicator of actual behavior. Sypher called this problem "illusory correlation" because "our measures may be tapping semantic similarity rather than actual communication behavior" (p. 84). Furthermore, Sallinen-Kuparinen (1992) noted that the CSM needs to be more sensitive to how different cultures enact communicator style. Although the CSM has great heuristic value (as evidenced by its frequent use), the arguments waged against this measure have some substance. Future research should continue to investigate the reliability and the validity of the measure.

LOCATION

Norton, R. W. (1978). Foundation of a communicator style construct. *Human Communication Research, 4*, 99–112.

Norton, R. W. (1983). *Communicator style.* Beverly Hills, CA: Sage.

REFERENCES

Brandt, D. R. (1979). On linking social performance with social competence: Some relations between communicative style and attributions of interpersonal attractiveness and effectiveness. *Human Communication Research, 5*, 223–237.

Buller, M. K., & Buller, D. B. (1987). Physicians' communication style and patient satisfaction. *Journal of Health and Social Behavior, 28*, 375–388.

Buller, D. B., & Street, R. L. Jr. (1991). The role of perceived affect and information in patients' evaluations of health care and compliance decisions. *Southern Communication Journal, 56*, 230–237.

Duran, R. L., & Zakahi, W. R. (1984). Competence or style: What's in a name? *Communication Research Reports, 1*, 42–47.

Duran, R. L., & Zakahi, W. R. (1987). Communication performance and communication satisfaction: What do we teach our students? *Communication Education, 36*, 13–22.

Eadie, W. F., & Paulson, J. W. (1984). Communicator attitudes, communicator style, and communicative competence. *Western Journal of Speech Communication, 48*, 390–407.

Ganster, D. C., Petelle, J., Baker, D., Dallinger, J., & Backus, D. (1981, May). *Leader communication style: Toward the development of a multidimensional model.* Paper presented at the meeting of the International Communication Association, Minneapolis, MN.

Gudykunst, W. B., & Lim, T. S. (1985). Ethnicity, sex, and self perceptions of communicator style. *Communication Research Reports, 2*, 68–75.

Hailey, J. L., Daly, J. A., & Hailey, J. (1984). Communicator characteristics associated with relationship disengagement strategies. *Communication Research Reports, 1*, 1–6.

Infante, D. A., & Gorden, W. I. (1989). Argumentativeness and affirming communicator style as predictors of satisfaction/dissatisfaction with subordinates. *Communication Quarterly, 37*, 81–90.

Lamude, K. G., & Daniels, T. D. (1984). Perceived managerial communicator style as a function of subordinate and manager gender. *Communication Research Reports, 1*, 91–96.

Montgomery, B. M., & Norton, R. W. (1981). Sex differences and similarities in communicator style. *Communication Monographs, 48*, 121–132.

Norton, R. W., & Pettegrew, L. S. (1979). Attentiveness as a style of communication: A structural analysis. *Communication Monographs, 46*, 13–26.

Nussbaum, J. F., & Scott, M. D. (1979). Instructor communication behaviors and their relationship to classroom learning. *Communication Yearbook, 3*, 561–583.

O'Hair, D., Cody, M. J., Goss, B., & Krayer, K. J. (1988). The effect of gender, deceit orientation and communicator style on macro-assessments of honesty. *Communication Quarterly, 36,* 77–93.

Porter, D. T. (1982). Communicator style perceptions as a function of communication apprehension. *Communication Quarterly, 30,* 237–244.

Rubin, R. B., & Feezel, J. D. (1986). Elements of teacher communication competence. *Communication Education, 35,* 254–268.

Sallinen-Kuparinen, A. (1992). Teacher communicator style. *Communication Education, 41,* 153–166.

Scott, M. D., & Nussbaum, J. F. (1981). Student perceptions of instructor communication behaviors and their relationship to student evaluation. *Communication Education, 30,* 44–53.

Staley, C. C., & Cohen, J. L. (1988). Communicator style and social style: Similarities and differences between the sexes. *Communication Quarterly, 36,* 192–202.

Sypher, H. E. (1980). Illusory correlation in communication research. *Human Communication Research, 7,* 83–87.

Tardy, C. H., Childs, R. J., & Hampton, M. M. (1985). Communication and Type A coronary-prone behavior: Preliminary studies of expressive and instrumental communication. *Perceptual and Motor Skills, 61,* 603–614.

Communicator Style Measure*

Instructions: You have impressions of yourself as a communicator. The impressions include your sense of the way you communicate. This measure focuses upon your sensitivity to the way you communicate, or what is called your communicator style. The questions are not designed to look at *what* is communicated; rather, they explore the way you communicate.

Because there is no such thing as a "correct" style of communication, none of the following items has a right or wrong answer. Please do not spend too much time on the items. Let your first inclination be your guide. Try to answer as honestly as possible. All responses will be strictly confidential.

Some questions will be difficult to answer because you honestly do not know. For these questions, however, please try to determine *which way you are leaning* and answer in the appropriate direction.

The following scale is used for each item:

YES! = strong agreement with the statement
yes = agreement with the statement
?   = neither agreement nor disagreement with the statement
no   = disagreement with the statement
NO! = strong disagreement with the statement

For example, if you agree with the following statement, "I dislike the coldness of winter," then you would circle the "yes" as indicated:

NO!   no   ?   yes   YES!

[Editors' note: The above scale appears to the right of each item, as shown in Item 1.]

Some of the items will be similarly stated. But each item has a slightly different orientation. Try to answer each question as though it were the *only* question being asked. Finally, answer each item as it relates to a *general face-to-face* communication situation—namely, the type of communicator you are most often.

Thank you for helping out.

1. I am comfortable with all varieties of people.   NO! no ? yes YES!
2. I laugh easily.
3. I readily express admiration for others.
4. *What* I say *usually* leaves an impression on people.
5. I leave people with an impression of me which they definitely tend to remember.
6. To be friendly, I habitually acknowledge verbally other's contributions.
7. I am a *very* good communicator.
8. I have some nervous mannerisms in my speech.
9. I am a very relaxed communicator.
10. When I disagree with somebody I am very quick to challenge them.
11. I can always repeat back to a person *exactly* what was meant.
12. The sound of my voice is *very easy* to recognize.
13. I am a very precise communicator.
14. I leave a *definite* impression on people.
15. The rhythm or flow of my speech is sometimes affected by my nervousness.
16. Under pressure I come across as a relaxed speaker.
17. My eyes reflect *exactly* what I am feeling when I communicate.
18. I dramatize a lot.
19. I always find it *very easy* to communicate on a one-to-one basis with strangers.
20. Usually, I *deliberately react* in such a way that people *know* that I am listening to them.
21. Usually I do not tell people much about myself until I get to know them well.
22. *Regularly* I tell jokes, anecdotes and stories when I communicate.
23. I tend to *constantly* gesture when I communicate.
24. I am an *extremely* open communicator.
25. I am vocally a loud communicator.

26. In a small group of strangers I am a *very good* communicator.
27. In arguments I insist upon very precise definitions.
28. In most social situations I generally speak very frequently.
29. I find it extremely easy to maintain a conversation with a member of the opposite sex *whom I have just met.*
30. I like to be strictly accurate when I communicate.
31. Because I have a loud voice I can easily break into a conversation.
32. *Often* I physically and vocally act out what I want to communicate.
33. I have an assertive voice.
34. I readily reveal personal things about myself.
35. I am dominant in social situations.
36. I am very argumentative.
37. Once I get wound up in a heated discussion I have a hard time stopping myself.
38. I am always an *extremely* friendly communicator.
39. I really *like* to listen *very carefully* to people.
40. Very often I insist that other people document or present some kind of proof for what they are arguing.
41. I try to take charge of things when I am with people.
42. It bothers me to drop an argument that is not resolved.
43. In most social situations I tend to come on strong.
44. I am very expressive nonverbally in social situations.
45. The *way* I say something *usually* leaves an impression on people.
46. Whenever I communicate, I tend to be very encouraging to people.
47. I actively use *a lot* of facial expressions when I communicate.
48. I *very frequently* verbally exaggerate to emphasize a point.
49. I am an *extremely attentive* communicator.
50. As a rule, I openly express my feelings and emotions.

51. Out of a random group of six people, including myself, I would probably have a better communicator style than (circle one choice):

5 of them	4 of them	3 of them	2 of them	1 of them	None of them

Note. Only 45 items are scored. Ten subconstructs with four items per subconstruct can be treated as independent variables. One subconstruct, communicator image, can be treated as a dependent variable. Items 1, 2, 12, 25, 31, and 33 are filler items and should be ignored.

It is advisable, although not necessary, to convert all scores for the respective items to z scores and then average them for the subconstruct.

Use the following weights for the responses: YES! = 5; yes = 4; ? = 3; no = 2; NO! = 1. Reverse-coding for items indicated by *R*.

Friendly	3	6	38	46	
Impression Leaving	4	5	14	45	
Relaxed	8R	9	15R	16	
Contentious/Argumentative	10	36	37	42	
Attentive	11	20	39	49	
Precise	13	27	30	40	
Animated/Expressive	17	23	44	47	
Dramatic	18	22	32	48	
Open	21R	24	34	50	
Dominant	28	35	41	43	
Communicator Image	7	19	26	29	51

Compliance-Gaining Techniques

Compliance-gaining research focuses on choices people make about what to say when trying to persuade others to behave in predetermined ways. Marwell and Schmitt (1967) brought together techniques suggested by persuasion researchers and created a questionnaire to elicit people's tendencies to use particular power bases to gain compliance in interpersonal relationships.

Compliance-gaining techniques (CGTs) (Marwell & Schmitt, 1967) do not formally constitute a scale or an index but exist as a format for creating one. Marwell and Schmitt identified 16 power-based compliance-gaining techniques—promise, threat, positive expertise, negative expertise, liking, pregiving, aversive stimulation, debt, moral appeal, positive self-feeling, negative self-feeling, positive altercasting, negative altercasting, altruism, positive esteem, and negative esteem—and asked people how likely they would be to use each in four different situations (job, family, sales, and roommate). Factor analysis resulted in five dimensions: Rewarding Activity, Punishing Activity, Expertise, Activation of Impersonal Commitments, and Activation of Personal Commitments. Most researchers view these factors as descriptive and continue to use all 16 techniques (or multiples of 16) rather than just those that constituted the five Marwell/Schmitt dimensions.

In using CGTs, a scenario is presented to respondents, who are asked to indicate their degree of likelihood of using each of 16 compliance-gaining strategies (created to reflect the techniques) on a 6-point scale, ranging from *definitely would use* to *definitely would not use*. Respondents spend less than 4 minutes on each scenario. Dillard (1988) explained that responses to the 16 messages can be summed to create a unidimensional variable (see Hunter & Boster, 1987), factor-analyzed (Baglan, LaLumia, & Bayless, 1986), or multidimensionally scaled (e.g., Cody & McLaughlin, 1980; Hertzog & Bradac, 1984) to reduce the 16 CGT to fewer dimensions (items are summed or averaged for the dimensions), or used separately as 16 different variables (deTurck, 1985; Sillars, 1980). Cluster analysis (Miller, Boster, Roloff, & Seibold, 1977) and confirmatory factor analysis (Cody,

Profile by Rebecca B. Rubin.

Woelfel, & Jordan, 1983) have also been used to identify strategy dimensions.

Numerous variations on these procedures exist. Miller et al. (1977) used eight-interval Likert-type scales, ranging from *extremely likely* (1) to *extremely unlikely* (8) and most research has adopted this procedure. Hample and Dallinger (1987) created another variation. They wanted to find out why people choose not to use a particular technique, so they gave subjects three messages for each of the 16 CGTs and asked subjects to indicate which ones they would use; for those not used, subjects indicated why they would not use them by choosing one of eight reasons (e.g., not effective and treats other as too negative).

CGTs have generated numerous research investigations in many areas of communication: organizational (Lamude & Lichtenstein, 1985), media (Ragland, 1987), cross-cultural (Neuliep & Hazleton, 1985), educational (Kearney, Plax, Richmond, & McCroskey, 1985), and health (Burgoon et al., 1987). But most research has used interpersonal scenarios (e.g., Dillard, 1988; Hample & Dallinger, 1987; Miller et al., 1977; Sillars, 1980; Tracy, Craig, Smith, & Spisak, 1984; Wiseman & Schenck-Hamlin, 1981).

RELIABILITY

Few researchers have examined the internal consistency of CGTs (mainly because they use the 16 items as single-item indicators). However, Lamude and Lichtenstein (1985) found a Kendall's Coefficient of Concordance of .89 across the four scenarios used. Boster and Levine (1988) found a .81 coefficient alpha for the Miller et al. (1977) "move to the Southwest" scenario and .92 for their "used car" scenario. And Baglan et al. (1986) found two main dimensions of strategies: Antisocial (with an alpha of .76) and Prosocial (with a .51 alpha).

Evidence of test–retest reliability also exists. Burleson et al. (1988) reported test–retest (24 days) reliabilities ranging from .31 to .66 (average of .53) for "likelihood of use" ratings for four situations; the test–retest correlation for grouped data (across the four situations) was .99. Hample and Dallinger (1987) found a test–retest (6 weeks) correlation of .66 for the nine option totals they used.

VALIDITY

Compliance-gaining research has focused on discovering antecedent variables that might help predict strategy selection. Williams and Untermeyer (1988) varied the size of the request in an interpersonal setting. Miller et al.

(1977) varied the interpersonalness and long- versus short-term consequences of the situation. deTurck (1985) used episodes varying in context interpersonalness, relational consequences, and target gender to see sequences of strategies once subjects are told that their first (and second) choices failed. And Boster and Levine (1988) looked for personality variables that might influence strategy choice. One study produced evidence of construct validity: Neuliep (1987) found that Theory X managers preferred antisocial CGTs such as deceit and threat, while Theory Y managers preferred esteem and ingratiation strategies.

COMMENTS

Compliance-gaining techniques make up a highly controversial system (see Wheeless, Barraclough, & Stewart, 1983). Criticism has revolved around the "selection," "checklist," or "frequency of use" procedures (see "Measures of Instructional Communication" for a discussion of these issues). In particular, some claim that the Marwell–Schmitt scheme lacks content validity, lacks external validity, contains a social desirability bias, and is too reactive to the scenarios used.

Wiseman and Schenck-Hamlin (1981) first suggested that the Marwell–Schmitt list was not exhaustive or representative of the strategies persuaders would actually encode if left to themselves. They added five strategies—ingratiation, guilt, direct request, explanation, and deceit—and argued that their inductive technique produced a superior list of strategies. Boster, Stiff, and Reynolds (1985) created strategies from the Wiseman–Schenck-Hamlin data and found the list complemented the Marwell–Schmitt list; they suggested using a combined 24-item strategy list in future research. Cody, McLaughlin, and Jordan (1980) found that a large number of CGTs were not used by respondents in their study. They also claimed an inherent social desirability bias and argued that persuaders would not actually use the prosocial ones that they selected.

Prosocial strategies are chosen more often than antisocial strategies (e.g., Baglan et al., 1986; Ragland, 1987). Burleson et al. (1988) (like Boster et al., 1985, and deTurck, 1985) found that need for social approval is not significantly related to strategy "likelihood of use," but ratings of social appropriateness of the strategies were related to use.

Some have argued that the scenario produces differences in responses (Boster & Levine, 1988; Dillard & Burgoon, 1985) and that number of strategies might be reduced, depending on which scenario is used (Miller et al., 1977). Hertzog and Bradac (1984) analyzed compliance-gaining situations and found five main types; this could very well explain why results are different for different scenarios.

All in all, the Marwell–Schmitt (1967) CGTs have been used in numerous research studies. Researchers should familiarize themselves with the issues involved in scale use and with the procedural options available in the literature.

LOCATION

Marwell, G., & Schmitt, D. R. (1967). Dimensions of compliance-gaining behavior: An empirical analysis. *Sociometry, 30*, 350–364.
Miller, G., Boster, F., Roloff, M., & Seibold, D. (1977). Compliance-gaining message strategies: A typology and some findings concerning effects of situational differences. *Communication Monographs, 44*, 37–51.

REFERENCES

Baglan, T., LaLumia, J., & Bayless, O. L. (1986). Utilization of compliance-gaining strategies: A research note. *Communication Monographs, 53*, 289–293.
Boster, F. J., & Levine, T. (1988). Individual differences and compliance gaining message selection: The effects of verbal aggressiveness, argumentativeness, dogmatism, and negativism. *Communication Research Reports, 5*, 114–119.
Boster, F. J., Stiff, J. B., & Reynolds, R. A. (1985). Do persons respond differently to inductively-derived and deductively-derived lists of compliance gaining message strategies? A reply to Wiseman and Schenck-Hamlin. *Western Journal of Speech Communication, 49*, 177–187.
Burgoon, J. K., Pfau, M., Parrott, R., Birk, T., Coker, R., & Burgoon, M. (1987). Relational communication, satisfaction, compliance-gaining strategies, and compliance in communication between physicians and patients. *Communication Monographs, 54*, 307–324.
Burleson, B. R., Wilson, S. R., Waltman, M. S., Goering, E. M., Ely, T. K., & Whaley, B. B. (1988). Item desirability effects in compliance-gaining research: Seven studies documenting artifacts in the strategy selection procedure. *Human Communication Research, 14*, 429–486.
Cody, M. J., & McLaughlin, M. L. (1980). Perceptions of compliance-gaining situations: A dimensional analysis. *Communication Monographs, 47*, 132–148.
Cody, M. J., McLaughlin, M. L., & Jordan, W. J. (1980). A multidimensional scaling of three sets of compliance-gaining strategies. *Communication Quarterly, 28*(3), 34–46.
Cody, M. J., Woelfel, M. L., & Jordan, W. J. (1983). Dimensions of compliance-gaining situations. *Human Communication Research, 9*, 99–113.
deTurck, M. A. (1985). A transactional analysis of compliance-gaining behavior: Effects of noncompliance, relational contexts, and actors' gender. *Human Communication Research, 12*, 54–78.
Dillard, J. P. (1988). Compliance-gaining message-selection: What is our dependent variable? *Communication Monographs, 55*, 162–183.

Dillard, J. P., & Burgoon, M. (1985). Situational influences on the selection of compliance-gaining messages: Two tests of the predictive utility of the Cody–McLaughlin typology. *Communication Monographs, 52*, 289–304.

Hample, D., & Dallinger, J. M. (1987). Individual differences in cognitive editing standards. *Human Communication Research, 14*, 123–144.

Hertzog, R. L., & Bradac, J. J. (1984). Perceptions of compliance-gaining situations: An extended analysis. *Communication Research, 11*, 363–391.

Hunter, J. E., & Boster, F. J. (1987). A model of compliance-gaining message selection. *Communication Monographs, 54*, 63–84.

Kearney, P., Plax, T. G., Richmond, V. P., & McCroskey, J. C. (1985). Power in the classroom III: Teacher communication techniques and messages. *Communication Education, 34*, 19–28.

Lamude, K. G., & Lichtenstein, A. (1985). The effects of motivational needs and rights situational dimension on compliance gaining strategies. *Communication Research Reports, 2*, 164–171.

Neuliep, J. W. (1987). The influence of Theory X and Theory Y management styles on the selection of compliance-gaining strategies. *Communication Research Reports, 4*, 14–19.

Neuliep, J. W., & Hazleton, V., Jr. (1985). A cross-cultural comparison of Japanese and American persuasive strategy selection. *International Journal of Intercultural Relations, 9*, 389–404.

Ragland, R. A. (1987). How mayor candidates seek endorsements in New Mexico. *Journalism Quarterly, 64*, 199–202.

Sillars, A. L. (1980). The stranger and the spouse as target persons for compliance-gaining strategies: A subjective expected utility model. *Human Communication Research, 6*, 265–279.

Tracy, K., Craig, R. T., Smith, M., & Spisak, F. (1984). The discourse of requests: Assessment of a compliance-gaining approach. *Human Communication Research, 10*, 513–538.

Wheeless, L. R., Barraclough, R., & Stewart, R. (1983). Compliance-gaining and power in persuasion. *Communication Yearbook, 7*, 105–145.

Williams, M. L., & Untermeyer, N. K. (1988). Compliance-gaining strategies and communicator role: An analysis of strategy choices and persuasive efficacy. *Communication Research Reports, 5*, 10–18.

Wiseman, R. L., & Schenck-Hamlin, W. (1981). A multi-dimensional scaling validation of an inductively-derived set of compliance gaining strategies. *Communication Monographs, 48*, 251–270.

Compliance-Gaining Techniques*

[Editors' note: Presented here is only one of Marwell and Schmitt's (1967) four situations; some researchers have used fewer than four scenarios and others have used more than four. Instructions were recreated following

---

*Copyright 1977 by the Speech Communication Association. Reprinted by permission.

Marwell and Schmitt's guidelines and those provided by Miller, Boster, Roloff, and Seibold (1977). The techniques and their meanings are presented here prior to the actual message (in quotation marks). Normally, only the messages are given; however, Miller et al. indicated they included descriptions of the techniques as well. The 8-point response options are presented after each message.]

Instructions: This booklet contains four situations in which persons might find themselves. Every situation has something in common. They are all situations in which one person is trying to induce another to do something. That is, they are situations in which one person is trying to influence, or gain the compliance of, another. Imagine that, in each situation, you are the individual who is trying to persuade the other.

A list of the methods which persons commonly use to get another to do something will follow each situation. For each situation, rate how likely you would be to use each of the 16 message-oriented behaviors to gain compliance from the other hypothetical person described in that situation. Use the following scale and circle the number that best represents your position.

Extremely likely   1   2   3   4   5   6   7   8   Extremely unlikely

Situation B (Family): Your teen-age son, Dick, who is a high school student, has been getting poor grades. You want him to increase the amount of time he spends studying from 6 to 12 hours a week.

How likely are each of the following messages for you?

1. Promise—If you comply, I will reward you.
    "You offer to increase Dick's allowance if he increases his studying."
2. Threat—If you do not comply I will punish you.
    "You threaten to forbid Dick the use of the car if he does not increase his studying."
3. Positive Expertise—If you comply you will be rewarded because of "the nature of things."
    "You point out to Dick that if he gets good grades he will be able to get into a good college and get a good job."
4. Negative Expertise—If you do not comply you will be punished because of "the nature of things."
    "You point out to Dick that if he does not get good grades he will not be able to get into a good college or get a good job."
5. Liking—Actor is friendly and helpful to get target in "good frame of mind" so that he will comply with request.
    "You try to be as friendly and pleasant as possible to get Dick in the 'right frame of mind' before asking him to study."

6. Pregiving—Actor rewards target before requesting compliance.
    "You raise Dick's allowance and tell him you now expect him to study."
7. Aversive Stimulation—Actor continuously punishes target making cessation contingent on compliance.
    "You forbid Dick the use of the car and tell him he will not be allowed to drive until he studies more."
8. Debt—You owe me compliance because of past favors.
    "You point out that you have sacrificed and saved to pay for Dick's education and that he owes it to you to get good enough grades to get into a good college."
9. Moral Appeal—You are immoral if you do not comply.
    "You tell Dick that it is morally wrong for anyone not to get as good grades as he can and that he should study more."
10. Positive Self-Feeling—You will feel better about yourself if you comply.
    "You tell Dick he will feel proud if he gets himself to study more."
11. Negative Self-Feeling—You will feel worse about yourself if you do not comply.
    "You tell Dick he will feel ashamed of himself if he gets bad grades."
12. Positive Altercasting—A person with "good" qualities would comply.
    "You tell Dick that since he is a mature and intelligent boy he naturally will want to study more and get good grades."
13. Negative Altercasting—Only a person with "bad" qualities would not comply.
    "You tell Dick that only someone very childish does not study as he should."
14. Altruism—I need your compliance very badly, so do it for me.
    "You tell Dick that you really want very badly for him to get into a good college and that you wish he would study more as a personal favor to you."
15. Positive Esteem—People you value will think better of you if you comply.
    "You tell Dick that the whole family will be very proud of him if he gets good grades."
16. Negative Esteem—People you value will think worse of you if you do not comply.
    "You tell Dick that the whole family will be very disappointed (in him) if he gets poor grades."

Conversational Appropriateness and Effectiveness Scales

Appropriateness and effectiveness are two components of interpersonal communication competence (Spitzberg & Cupach, 1984). Appropriate behavior is that which receives social rewards and fulfills others' expectations. Effective behavior is that which accomplishes its goal. Spitzberg and his colleagues view both components as necessary for perceptions of communication competence to occur.

Spitzberg and Phelps (1982) began scale development with a 26-item semantic differential instrument that had an unstable factor structure. Spitzberg and Canary (1985) converted the measure to a Likert-type format and added 14 items so that 20 tapped Appropriateness (.91 alpha) and 20 tapped Effectiveness (.85 alpha). These scales were further developed (items reworded for conflict behaviors) by Canary and Spitzberg (1987) and used by third-party observers to rate conflict strategies of interactants. Factor analysis revealed three factors: Effectiveness (goal accomplishment), Specific Appropriateness (specific aspects of the conversation were appropriate), and General Appropriateness (global suitability).

Twenty items comprise each of the two scales. Seven-point Likert-type responses, ranging from *strongly agree* to *strongly disagree*, are used by communicators to indicate level of appropriateness and effectiveness for their partner or for a person they observe during conversation. The scales have been adapted for recalled, immediately preceding, and hypothetical conversations, and each takes less than 3 minutes to complete.

RELIABILITY

Research indicates that the scales are internally consistent. Coefficient alphas for the effectiveness scale have ranged from .87 (Canary & Spitzberg, 1989) to .93 (Canary & Spitzberg, 1987). Alphas for the specific appropriateness

Profile by Rebecca B. Rubin.

subscale have ranged from .74 (Canary & Spitzberg, 1990) to .85 (Canary & Spitzberg, 1987) and for the general appropriateness from .80 (Canary & Spitzberg, 1989) to .92 (Canary & Spitzberg, 1990).

VALIDITY

These scales have been used mainly in studies of conflict, and the results indicate the expected relationship with conflict strategy use. Canary and Spitzberg (1989) found that (a) specific appropriateness was correlated with avoidant and distributive messages, (b) general appropriateness was correlated with integrative tactics and with trust, mutuality, and intimacy, and (c) effectiveness was related to trust, intimacy, and satisfaction. They found earlier that people judge themselves as competent based on perceptions of their own effectiveness, but they judge others as competent on the basis of how appropriate their behavior is (Canary & Spitzberg, 1987). In addition, an actor's and his/her partner's perceptions of competence are significantly related (Canary & Spitzberg, 1990).

COMMENTS

These instruments are relatively new in the field and could benefit from additional research. Factor analysis indicates that some items of the scales load on more than one factor and some items have low factor loadings (e.g., Canary and Spitzberg, 1987, had to eliminate seven such items). The scale developers have not yet provided full information on the construct validity of the scales. Users should factor-analyze the scales and create subscales using only those items loading cleanly on the factors. Also, information on split-half and test–retest reliability would be useful. However, the scales appear to measure communication appropriateness and effectiveness, two important components of interpersonal communication competence.

LOCATION

Canary, D. J., & Spitzberg, B. H. (1987). Appropriateness and effectiveness perceptions of conflict strategies. *Human Communication Research, 14,* 93–118.
Spitzberg, B. H., & Phelps, L. A. (1982, November). *Conversational appropriateness and effectiveness: Validation of a criterion measure of relational competence.* Paper presented at the meeting of the Speech Communication Association, Denver.

REFERENCES

Canary, D. J., & Spitzberg, B. H. (1989). A model of perceived competence of conflict strategies. *Human Communication Research, 15*, 630–649.

Canary, D. J., & Spitzberg, B. H. (1990). Attribution biases and associations between conflict strategies and competence outcomes. *Communication Monographs, 57*, 139–151.

Spitzberg, B. H., & Canary, D. J. (1985). Loneliness and relationally competent communication. *Journal of Social and Personal Relationships, 2*, 387–402.

Spitzberg, B. H., & Cupach, W. R. (1984). *Interpersonal communication competence.* Beverly Hills, CA: Sage.

Conversational Appropriateness Scale*

Instructions: Complete the following items about a person with whom you have just had a conversation. Use the following scale and write one number before each statement to indicate your feelings.

[Editors' note: A blank should appear before each statement number.]

> 7 = Strongly agree
> 6 = Moderately agree
> 5 = Slightly agree
> 4 = Undecided
> 3 = Slightly disagree
> 2 = Moderately disagree
> 1 = Strongly disagree

1. S/he said several things that seemed out of place in the conversation.
2. S/he was a smooth conversationalist.
3. Everything s/he said was appropriate.
4. Occasionally, her/his statements made me feel uncomfortable.
5. Her/his conversation was very suitable to the situation.
6. Some of the things s/he said were awkward.
7. Her/his communication was very proper.
8. S/he said some things that should not have been said.
9. I was embarrassed at times by her/his remarks.
10. Some of her/his remarks were inappropriate.
11. I was comfortable throughout the conversation with her/his remarks.
12. Some of the things s/he said were in bad taste.

---

13. None of her/his remarks were embarrassing to me.
14. S/he said some things that were simply the incorrect things to say.
15. S/he did not violate any of my expectations in the conversation.
16. The WAY s/he said some of her/his remarks was unsuitable.
17. The things s/he spoke about were all in good taste as far as I'm concerned.
18. Some of her/his remarks were simply improper.
19. S/he interrupted me in the conversation.
20. At least one of her/his remarks was rude.

Note. Items 1, 4, 6, 8, 9, 10, 12, 14, 16, 18, 19, and 20 are reverse-coded.

Conversational Effectiveness Scale*

Instructions: Complete the following items about a person with whom you have just had a conversation. Use the following scale and write one number before each statement to indicate your feelings.

[Editors' note: A blank should appear before each statement number.]

7 = Strongly agree
6 = Moderately agree
5 = Slightly agree
4 = Undecided
3 = Slightly disagree
2 = Moderately disagree
1 = Strongly disagree

1. Our conversation was very beneficial.
2. The other person was more active in the conversation than I was.
3. I achieved everything I hoped to achieve in our conversation.
4. It was a useless conversation.
5. I was in control of the conversation.
6. I was effective in the conversation.
7. Our conversation was unsuccessful.
8. I just let the other person talk most of the time.
9. I got what I wanted out of the conversation.
10. The conversation was unprofitable.
11. It was an advantageous conversation.
12. I was an ineffective conversationalist.
13. I didn't know what was going on in the conversation.

14. It was a rewarding conversation.
15. The other person dominated the conversation.
16. I talked most of the time.
17. I found the conversation to be very useful and helpful.
18. The other person controlled the conversation.
19. The conversation went pretty much the way I wanted.
20. The conversation was very unrewarding.

Note. Items 2, 4, 7, 8, 10, 12, 13, 15, 18, and 20 are reverse-coded.

Cultivation Index

Media cultivation research assumes that TV is the main cultural arm of society and that enculturation is TV's primary function. Gerbner and Gross (1976) argued that, as an agency of those in control of society, TV's "chief cultural function is to spread and stabilize social patterns, to cultivate not change but resistance to change" (p. 175). Cultivation adherents approach TV viewing as nonselective, habitual behavior that does not differentiate information and entertainment content. In short, people live in the symbolic world of TV, and "'living' in the world of TV cultivates conceptions of its own conventionalized 'reality'" (Gerbner & Gross, 1976, p. 175). Through TV, a society arrives at a shared cultural community.

Cultivation researchers have argued that experimental and quasi-experimental research techniques are inappropriate to assess the effects of TV exposure (Gerbner & Gross, 1976). Gerbner, Gross, Jackson-Beeck, Jeffries-Fox, and Signorielli (1978) stated they preferred to speak of TV's contributions to cultivating common beliefs rather than the occurrence of effects or impact. They maintained that TV contributes to shifts in personal outlook that may be barely perceptible, and proposed two methods in their analysis to ascertain such shifts.

First, message-system analysis content-analyzes the composition and structure of TV messages. According to Gerbner et al. (1978), "The message system comprising that world (of television drama) presents coherent images of life and society . . . (that are) reflected in the assumptions and values held by the audience" (p. 193). The message-system analysis provides a "television answer" about how TV presents content (e.g., the number of violent or stereotypical portrayals). Gerbner and Gross (1976) stated that "representation in the fictional world signifies social existence; absence means symbolic annihilation" (p. 182).

Second, cultivation analysis examines people's social-reality beliefs, presumably formed from TV viewing. The Cultivation Index (CI), or Victimization Index, gives respondents two choices in questions, one being the "television answer" (based on televised portrayals), and the other representing how things are in the "real world." Heavy TV viewers are expected to choose the television answer more than are light TV viewers. The four ques-

Profile by Alan M. Rubin.

tions are asked by interviewers or can be self-administered; they take less than 2 minutes to complete. Researchers then compute a "cultivation differential," which is the "margin of heavy viewers over light viewers giving the 'television answers' within and across groups . . . indicating conceptions about social reality that viewing tends to cultivate" (Gerbner & Gross, 1976, p. 182).

RELIABILITY

Gerbner and his associates (e.g., Gerbner & Gross, 1976; Gerbner et al., 1977; Gerbner et al., 1978) did not address the reliability of the CI. Hawkins and Pingree (1981) and Pingree (1983) also did not report reliability.

VALIDITY

Gerbner and his associates (e.g., Gerbner & Gross, 1976; Gerbner et al., 1977; Gerbner et al., 1978) did not discuss the validity of the Cultivation Index. As compared with light viewers, Gerbner and associates reported mixed evidence about whether heavy viewers are more afraid to walk alone at night (gammas ranged from .03 to .18) or take more precautions against crime (gammas ranged from .03 to .18); several gammas were near .00 after statistical controls for age, gender, or education. Questioning a primary cultivation assumption about uniform messages, Hawkins and Pingree (1981) noted that content type matters in cultivation relationships. They reported a significant .16 partial correlation (controlling for overall TV viewing and social class) between the CI and crime-adventure viewing. Similarly, Rubin, Perse, and Taylor (1988) noted program-type relationships with their measures of social attitudes. For example, whereas total TV viewing positively predicted perceptions of safety, action-adventure program viewing was a negative predictor.

Gerbner and his colleagues compared the portrayals of men versus women, different occupations such as law enforcers, and, primarily, the depiction of televised violence in their message analyses (e.g., Gerbner & Gross, 1976; Gerbner et al., 1977; Gerbner et al., 1978). After controlling for some demographic and individual characteristics, they noted relationships for their CI about the incidence of violence and law enforcers. Because heavy TV viewers are more likely than light viewers to give the television answer than the real-world answer, heavy viewers overestimated the proportion of people employed as law enforcers and their chances of being a victim of crime (e.g., Gerbner & Gross, 1976; Gerbner et al., 1977).

Others have found similar, statistically significant relationships. Hawkins and Pingree (1981) reported a .25 partial correlation (controlling for social class) between the CI (which they labeled "violence in society") and total TV viewing. Pingree (1983) noted a .18 correlation between the CI (which she labeled "demographics of violence") and total TV viewing.

COMMENTS

Cultivation studies have differed in their definition of heavy and light viewing. For example Gerbner et al. (1978) stipulated that light viewing was 2 hours or less, medium viewing was 2 to 6 hours, and heavy viewing was 6 hours or more each day. Gerbner, Gross, Morgan, and Signorielli (1980) defined light viewing as under 2 hours, medium viewing as 2 to 4 hours, and heavy viewing as more than 4 hours. In addition, typical significant relationships are small with significant gammas between the cultivation differentials being .20 and less, although often consistent (e.g., Gerbner et al., 1978). Reliability and validity require attention. Also, due to changes in crime rates since 1977, options in the questions should be updated.

Researchers have criticized the assumptions and method of cultivation research, including the reduction or elimination of cultivation effects by using demographic controls (e.g., Hirsch, 1980; Hughes, 1980) or controls for residence (Doob & Macdonald, 1979), personality traits (Wober & Gunter, 1982), experience with crime (Weaver & Wakshlag, 1986), or viewers' acceptance of TV reality (e.g., Slater & Elliott, 1982). Cultivation researchers responded to the criticisms and formulated concepts such as mainstreaming, which refers to a "commonality of outlooks that television tends to cultivate" (Gerbner et al., 1980, p. 15). Heavy viewers across demographic groups would share common outlooks, whereas heavy and light viewers within the same demographic groups would have divergent beliefs. Another concept, resonance, refers to the congruence of TV messages with everyday reality, which amplifies cultivation patterns by providing "a coherent and powerful 'double dose' of the television message" (Gerbner et al., 1980, p. 15).

LOCATION

Gerbner, G., Gross, L., Eleey, M. F., Jackson-Beeck, M., Jeffries-Fox, S., & Signorielli, N. (1977). TV violence profile no. 8: The highlights. *Journal of Communication*, 27(2), 171–180.

REFERENCES

Doob, A. N., & Macdonald, G. E. (1979). Television viewing and fear of victimization: Is the relationship causal? *Journal of Personality and Social Psychology, 37*, 170–179.

Gerbner, G., & Gross, L. (1976). Living with television: The violence profile. *Journal of Communication, 26*(2), 173–199.

Gerbner, G., Gross, L., Jackson-Beeck, M., Jeffries-Fox, S., & Signorielli, N. (1978). Cultural indicators: Violence profile no. 9. *Journal of Communication, 28*(3), 176–207.

Gerbner, G., Gross, L., Morgan, M., & Signorielli, N. (1980). The "mainstreaming" of America: Violence profile no. 11. *Journal of Communication, 30*(3), 10–29.

Hawkins, R. P., & Pingree, S. (1981). Uniform messages and habitual viewing: Unnecessary assumptions in social reality effects. *Human Communication Research, 7*, 291–301.

Hirsch, P. M. (1980). The "scary world" of the nonviewer and other anomalies: A reanalysis of Gerbner et al.'s findings on cultivation analysis, part I. *Communication Research, 7*, 403–456.

Hughes, M. (1980). The fruits of cultivation analysis: A reexamination of some effects of television watching. *Public Opinion Quarterly, 44*, 287–302.

Pingree, S. (1983). Children's cognitive processes in constructing social reality. *Journalism Quarterly, 60*, 415–422.

Rubin, A. M., Perse, E. M., & Taylor, D. S. (1988). A methodological examination of cultivation. *Communication Research, 15*, 107–134.

Slater, D., & Elliott, W. R. (1982). Television's influence on social reality. *Quarterly Journal of Speech, 68*, 69–79.

Weaver, J., & Wakshlag, J. (1986). Perceived vulnerability to crime, criminal victimization experience, and television viewing. *Journal of Broadcasting and Electronic Media, 30*, 141–158.

Wober, J. M., & Gunter, B. (1982). Television and personal threat: Fact or artifact? A British survey. *British Journal of Social Psychology, 21*, 239–247.

Cultivation Index*

Instructions: Instructions were not provided but, when self-administered, respondents are asked to read each item and to circle the one response for each that best reflects their own feelings.

1. During any given week, what are your chances of being involved in some kind of violence? About one in ten? About 1 in 100?
2. What percent of all males who have jobs work in law enforcement and crime detection? One percent? Five percent?

---

3. What percent of all crimes are violent crimes like murders, rape, robbery and aggravated assault? Fifteen percent? Twenty-five percent?
4. Does most fatal violence occur between strangers or between relatives or acquaintances?

Note. One in 10, 5%, 25%, and "between strangers" are the television answers for the respective questions.

Family Communication Patterns Scale

Chaffee, McLeod, and Atkin (1971) suggested that how children become socialized to the world partly depends on the ways in which parents and children communicate. They conceptualized family communication patterns (FCP) as two general dimensions that describe family communication structure. Socio-Oriented Family Communication stresses maintenance of harmonious interpersonal relations. Children are encouraged to avoid controversy and repress anger. Concept-Oriented Family Communication values open, controversial discussion. Children are stimulated to express ideas, even if they disagree with others.

The coorientation model (Newcomb, 1953) also explains FCP (Chaffee & Tims 1976). Socio-oriented families are more oriented to interfamily relations than to external topics. Concept-oriented families are more oriented to relations with the outside world than to interpersonal relations in the family. Therefore, FCP affect both communication within the family and how a child views situations outside the home.

Chaffee et al.'s (1971) 11-item scale measures socio- and concept-oriented dimensions. Items ask parents and children about communication in family interactions. Responses are summed to create socio- and concept-FCP scores. When scores exist for both parents and children, responses are usually averaged to create family-level socio- and concept-FCP scores (Ritchie & Fitzpatrick, 1990).

Because early research noted that socio and concept orientations were only slightly correlated, these studies used the FCP Scale to categorize respondents according to a four-cell typology: (a) laissez-faire families emphasize neither type of communication, (b) protective families score high on socio communication only, (c) pluralistic families stress only concept communication, and (d) consensual families score high on both socio and concept communication. Later studies considered mainly socio- and concept-orientation scores.

Investigators have used several related versions of the scale (e.g., Chaffee & McLeod, 1972; Chaffee et al., 1971; Chaffee, McLeod, & Wackman, 1973;

Profile by Elizabeth M. Perse.

Chaffee & Tims, 1976). The version reported by McLeod, Atkin, and Chaffee (1972) is presented here. The scale is adaptable for parents and children. It takes about 5 minutes for parents to complete, and about twice as long for children. Although Chaffee and colleagues did not report response categories, most studies have used 4-point responses that assess frequency (e.g., ranging from *often* to *never*). Some studies have phrased the items as Likert statements and used 5-point response categories ranging from *strongly agree* to *strongly disagree*.

RELIABILITY

Reliabilities for the two dimensions vary depending on the number of items used and the nature of the sample. For the socio-oriented dimension, Cronbach alphas range from .67 (three-item version [Messaris & Kerr, 1983]) to .71 (six-item version [Moore & Moschis, 1981]). Alphas for the concept dimension range from .54 (six-item version [Moore & Moschis, 1981]) to .72 (six-item version [Moschis & Mitchell, 1986]). Morgan, Alexander, Shanahan, and Harris (1990) found reliabilities of .60 (four-item socio-oriented) and .70 (three-item concept-oriented) when using shortened versions of the scale. Ritchie (1991) reported a .61 alpha and a .71 test–retest correlation for seven socio-oriented items, and a .66 alpha and a .66 test–retest correlation for seven concept-oriented items. The items were based on the earlier work by both Chaffee and McLeod. Also using items from that earlier work, Thompson, Pingree, Hawkins, and Draves (1991) observed alphas of .84 and .82 for eight-item measures of socio-orientation and concept orientation.

VALIDITY

The two dimensions of the FCP Scale appear to have face validity. Chaffee et al. (1973) summarized research validating the two-dimensional structure of the FCP Scale. Studies found that average correlations between items within each dimension are substantially larger ($r = .30$) than across-dimension item correlations ($r = .04$). And, an independent Q-sort supported the four-category FCP typology (Chaffee et al., 1973).

Factor analyses have largely supported the two-dimensional FCP structure (e.g., Moore & Moschis, 1981). Allen and Chaffee (1977) observed that a two-factor solution accounting for 46% of the variance replicated the socio- and concept dimensions for a sample of white respondents. A two-factor solution, though, only accounted for 27% of the variance for a black sample; a six-factor solution accounted for more variance (57%). The authors suggested that FCP differed in white and black families.

Concurrent validity for the FCP Scale has been shown in the subscales' relationship to some demographic and media use variables. Reflecting the changing parent–child relationship as children grow, socio-orientation, which focuses on interfamily communication, decreases during adolescence (Chaffee et al., 1971). Concept orientation, which focuses on extrafamily relationships, is more stable. Earlier research also found that socio-orientation scores were higher in families with female children and correlated with other measures of parental control (McLeod, Atkin, & Chaffee, 1972). Wade (1973) found that adolescents from concept-oriented families were more likely to report that they could talk freely with their parents on any subject.

Some studies have provided evidence of construct validity. Socio-oriented families had greater similarity between parent and child TV use (Chaffee et al., 1971), maternal comments during TV viewing that disapproved of imitating TV role models but affirmed the reality of TV programming (Messaris & Kerr, 1983), and evaluations of product consumption based on perceived effects on others leading to higher materialistic attitudes (Moore & Moschis, 1981). As compared with socio-oriented families, concept-oriented families had greater interest and participation in political affairs, greater public affairs TV and newspaper exposure use (Chaffee et al., 1973), more maternal information giving about science, history, and geography during TV viewing (Messaris & Kerr, 1983), greater consumer knowledge (Moore & Moschis, 1981), and more political conversations (Liebes & Ribak, 1992). Concept orientation has been linked to norms that favor coorientational accuracy among family members, and socio-orientation has been linked to norms that favor coorientational congruence of parents (Ritchie, 1991). Thompson et al. (1991) found concept-oriented FCP to be an important predictor of cognitive activities, especially content-centered cognitive efforts.

Tims and Masland (1985) explored the assumption that the FCP Scale represents a stable family communication context that consistently influences children's socialization. Using Lisrel, they tested the stability of socio- and concept subscales in a three-wave, year-long panel study. They found that across-time stability estimates for both scales ranged from .34 to .70, suggesting that FCP subscales are only partially stable over time. Instability may be due to changes in FCP or to measurement error. Tims and Masland also noted that scores were more stable for parents and older adolescents, reflecting changes in how parents talk to children or that younger respondents may have difficulty with the items.

Tims and Masland (1985) also addressed the correspondence between parent and child scores on FCP dimensions. They noted that earlier studies found low correlations between parent and child FCP scores (r = .07 or .12). They found that parent–child across-time FCP correlations were in the .10

to .20 range, suggesting that researchers be cautious if they choose to create family-level FCP measures by summing child and parent scores.

COMMENTS

The FCP Scale has been widely used in several contexts such as mass communication (e.g., Chaffee et al., 1971), family relations (e.g., Abel, 1976), consumer research (Moore & Moschis, 1981), and instructional communication (Van Den Berg, 1975). It is adaptable for use with parents and children. Abel (1976) used FCP statements to code TV families as idea- (concept) or socio-oriented. Researchers should consider age and race of respondents when using the scale, however. And, it may not be valid to generalize from children's responses to family-level FCP.

Ritchie and Fitzpatrick (1990) developed a related measure, the Revised Family Communication Patterns Instrument, which initial analyses have found to correct some of the problems with the earlier scale. Ritchie and Fitzpatrick reported strong evidence of reliability: (a) 3-week test–retest reliabilities for subscales ranged from .64 to .82, (b) subscale Cronbach alphas ranged from .79 to .88, and (c) correlations between parent and child scores were higher than those reported for the original scale.

LOCATION

McLeod, J. M., Atkin, C. K., & Chaffee, S. H. (1972). Adolescents, parents, and television use: Self-report and other-report measures from the Wisconsin sample. In G. A. Comstock & E. A. Rubinstein (Eds.), *Television and social behavior: Vol. 3. Television and adolescent aggression* (DHEW Publication No. HSM 72-9058, pp. 239–313). Washington, DC: U.S. Government Printing Office.

REFERENCES

Abel, J. D. (1976). The family and child television viewing. *Journal of Marriage and the Family, 38*, 331–335.

Allen, R. L., & Chaffee, S. H. (1977). Racial differences in family communication patterns. *Journalism Quarterly, 54*, 8–13, 57.

Chaffee, S. H., & McLeod, J. M. (1972). Adolescent television used in the family context. In G. A. Comstock & E. A. Rubinstein (Eds.), *Television and social behavior: Vol. 3. Television and adolescent aggression* (DHEW Publication No. HSM 72-9058, pp. 149–172). Washington, DC: U. S. Government Printing Office.

Chaffee, S. H., McLeod, J. M., & Atkin, C. K. (1971). Parental influences on adolescent media use. *American Behavioral Scientist, 14,* 323–340.

Chaffee, S. H., McLeod, J. M., & Wackman, D. B. (1973). Family communication patterns and adolescent political participation. In J. Dennis (Ed.), *Socialization to politics: A reader* (pp. 349–364). New York: Wiley.

Chaffee, S. H., & Tims, A. R. (1976). Interpersonal factors in adolescent television use. *Journal of Social Issues, 32*(4), 98–115.

Liebes, T., & Ribak, R. (1992). The contribution of family culture to political participation, political outlook, and its reproduction. *Communication Research, 19,* 618–641.

Messaris, P., & Kerr, D. (1983). Mothers' comments about TV: Relation to family communication patterns. *Communication Research, 10,* 175–194.

Moore, R. L., & Moschis, G. P. (1981). The role of family communication in consumer learning. *Journal of Communication, 31*(4), 42–51.

Morgan, M., Alexander, A., Shanahan, J., & Harris, C. (1990). Adolescents, VCRs, and the family environment. *Communication Research, 17,* 83–106.

Moschis, G. P., & Mitchell, L. G. (1986). Television advertising and interpersonal influences on teenagers' participation in family consumer decisions. In R. J. Lutz (Ed.), *Advances in consumer research* (Vol. 13, pp. 181–185). Provo, UT: Association for Consumer Research.

Newcomb, T. M. (1953). An approach to the study of communicative acts. *Psychological Review, 60,* 393–404.

Ritchie, L. D. (1991). Family communication patterns: An epistemic analysis and conceptual reinterpretation. *Communication Research, 18,* 548–565.

Ritchie, L. D., & Fitzpatrick, M. A. (1990). Family communication patterns: Measuring intrapersonal perceptions of interpersonal relationships. *Communication Research, 17,* 523–544.

Thompson, M., Pingree, S., Hawkins, R. P., & Draves, C. (1991). Long-term norms and cognitive structures as shapers of television viewer activity. *Journal of Broadcasting and Electronic Media, 35,* 319–334.

Tims, A. R., & Masland, J. L. (1985). Measurement of family communication patterns. *Communication Research, 12,* 35–57.

Van Den Berg, S. (1975). Student alienation: Orientations toward and perceptions of aspects of educational social structure. *Urban Education, 10,* 262–278.

Wade, S. E. (1973). Interpersonal discussion: A critical predictor of leisure activity. *Journal of Communication, 23,* 426–445.

Family Communication Patterns Scale:
Parent Version*

[Editors' note: Scale alterations for the Child Version are in parentheses.]

Instructions: Now I would like to read a list of things parents sometimes say to their children. How often do you (your parents) say these things to him/her (you)? For each item, do you (they) say it often, sometimes, rarely, or never?

[Editors' note: The scoring of items is *often* (3), *sometimes* (2), *rarely* (1), *never* (0).]

Socio-oriented

1. Say that your (their) ideas are correct, and he/she (you) shouldn't argue with them.
2. Answer their (your) arguments by saying, "You'll know better when you grow up."
3. Say that he/she (you) should give in on arguments, rather than risk making people angry.
4. Say there are some things that just shouldn't be talked about.
5. Say that he/she (you) shouldn't argue with adults.

Concept-oriented

1. Say that he/she (you) should always look at both sides on an issue.
2. Say that getting his/her (your) ideas across is important, even if others don't like it.
3. Ask for his/her (your) opinion when family is discussing something.
4. Say that every member of your family should have some say in family decisions.
5. Admit that kids know more about some things than adults do.

---

*Reprinted from a U.S. Government document. In the public domain.

Feelings of Understanding/ Misunderstanding Scale

Cahn and Shulman (1984) defined perceived understanding or misunderstanding as a "communicator's assessment of his/her success of [sic] failure when attempting to communicate with another person" (p. 122). The scale was created to help ascertain level of development in new relationships.

Cahn and Shulman (1984) first developed the Feelings of Understanding/Misunderstanding (FUM) Scale by asking 224 respondents to identify adjectives descriptive of perceived understanding, which were then Q-sorted by 182 persons. When ambiguous items were eliminated, 16 remained, 8 descriptive of the perception of being understood, and 8 describing being misunderstood. Factor analysis confirmed the two dimensions.

The FUM Scale consists of eight items to measure perceptions of feeling understood (FU) and eight items to measure perceptions of feeling misunderstood (FM); eight "distractor" items are also included. Respondents use a 5-point scale, ranging from *very little* (1) to *very great* (5), to describe how they feel immediately after trying to make themselves understood by others. FM scores are subtracted from summed FU scores, making the possible range of scores −40 (most misunderstood) to +40 (most understood). Respondents require about 3 minutes to complete the scale. Three different versions exist: Trait—General (target is other people in general), Trait—Relationship (target is a specific person, but one recalls general feelings about communicating with this person), and State (target is a person one has just conversed with).

RELIABILITY

Cahn and Shulman (1984) reported a test–retest reliability of .90 and a Cronbach alpha of .89 for the State version. No additional reliability information is available.

Profile by Rebecca B. Rubin.

VALIDITY

Research indicates some evidence of concurrent validity. In the first study, perceived understanding was significantly related to perceived empathy, while perceived misunderstanding was not (Cahn & Shulman, 1984). In a later work, perceived understanding was strongly related to behavioral impressions created by listeners about members of the opposite sex (Cahn & Frey, 1989).

There is also evidence of criterion-related validity. One study found that perceived understanding was an important predictor of student evaluations of teachers (Cahn, 1984a, 1984b). Cahn (1983) also found that perceived understanding contributed less to interpersonal trust and interpersonal attraction in initial interactions than did other variables. Later research indicated that perceived understanding was more important in relationships that had already developed (Cahn, 1989).

COMMENTS

This is a relatively underused instrument, but one with potential. The instrument may be useful in both researching and counseling marital and other close dyads (Cahn, 1990). The construct appears to be closely related to empathy but on a higher plane. As Laing, Phillipson, and Lee (1966) originally conceptualized the construct, feelings of being understood or misunderstood arise when there is a discrepancy between one's meta-metaperspective and one's own direct perspective of a situation or relationship. These feelings can only be tapped through a self-report measure such as this one.

LOCATION

Cahn, D. D. (1983). Relative importance of perceived understanding in initial interaction and development of interpersonal relationships. *Psychological Reports*, 52, 923–929.

Cahn, D. D., & Shulman, G. M. (1984). The perceived understanding instrument. *Communication Research Reports*, 1, 122–125.

REFERENCES

Cahn, D. D. (1984a). Relative importance of perceived understanding in students' evaluations of teachers. *Perceptual and Motor Skills*, 59, 610.

Cahn, D. D. (1984b). Teacher–student relationships: Perceived understanding. *Communication Research Reports*, 1, 65–67.

Cahn, D. D. (1989). Relative importance of perceived understanding in developing male-female mate relationships. *Psychological Reports, 64,* 1339–1342.

Cahn, D. D. (1990). Perceived understanding and interpersonal relationships. *Journal of Social and Personal Relationships, 7,* 231–244.

Cahn, D. D., & Frey, L. R. (1989). Behavioral impressions associated with perceived understanding. *Perceptual and Motor Skills, 69,* 1299–1302.

Laing, R. D., Phillipson, H., & Lee, A. R. (1966). *Interpersonal perception.* New York: Springer.

Feelings of Understanding/Misunderstanding Scale*: Trait—General Version

Instructions: Recall how you generally feel when talking with (or listening to) other people. The following terms refer to feelings that may be relevant when people attempt to make themselves understood by others. Please indicate the extent to which each term describes how you generally feel when and immediately after trying to make yourself understood by others. Respond to each term according to the following scale:

(1) Very little
(2) Little
(3) Some
(4) Great
(5) Very great

1. Annoyance	13. Sadness
2. Satisfaction	14. Acceptance
3. Self-reliance	15. Humbleness
4. Discomfort	16. Failure
5. Relaxation	17. Comfortableness
6. Shyness	18. Hostility
7. Dissatisfaction	19. Incompleteness
8. Pleasure	20. Happiness
9. Enviousness	21. Compassion
10. Insecurity	22. Uninterestingness
11. Good	23. Importance
12. Attentiveness	24. Assertiveness

Note. Beginning with Item 1, sum every third item (1, 4, 7, 10, 13, 16, 19, and 22) for the FM score; these feelings may be quantified as a single rating ranging from 8 to 40. Beginning with Item 2, sum every third item (2, 5, 8, 11, 14, 17, 20, and 23) for the FU score. Other items are distractors. To determine the FUM score, subtract the FM score from the FU score. FUM may range from −32 to +32. The more positive the score, the more one generally feels understood by others.

Trait–Relationship Version

Instructions: Recall how you generally feel when talking with (or listening to) _____. The following terms refer to feelings that may be relevant when people attempt to make themselves understood by others. Please indicate the extent to which each term describes how you generally feel when and immediately after trying to make yourself understood by the person you specified above. Respond to each term according to the following scale:

[Editors' note: Use same scale, terms, and scoring as in the Trait—General version.]

State Version

Instructions: You have just finished talking with (or listening to) _____. The following terms refer to feelings that may be relevant when people attempt to make themselves understood by others. Please indicate the extent to which each term describes how you generally felt when and immediately after trying to make yourself understood by the person specified above. Respond to each term according to the following scale:

[Editors' note: Use same scale, terms, and scoring as in the Trait—General version.]

Generalized Immediacy Scale

Immediacy refers to those behaviors that reduce physical or psychological distance between people (Mehrabian, 1969). Although the immediacy construct originated in social psychology, immediacy was introduced into the instructional communication area by Andersen (1979). Andersen developed the first self-report instrument as well as a behavioral/ observational index for classroom use. Relying on Mehrabian's conceptual definition of immediacy, Andersen reasoned that immediate teachers are those who communicate closeness, warmth, and overall positive affect toward their students. Behavioral, nonverbal indicants of immediacy include positive head nods; smiles; eye contact; vocal expressiveness; overall body movements and purposeful gestures; direct, relaxed, and open-body positions; and close physical distances. In behavioral terms, immediacy is based on approach–avoidance principles. That is, "people are drawn toward persons and things they like, evaluate highly, and prefer, and they avoid or move away from things they dislike, evaluate negatively, or do not prefer" (Mehrabian, 1971, p. 1). Immediacy, then, is an affectively based construct. Immediate behaviors of approach indicate liking, whereas nonimmediate behaviors of avoidance communicate disliking.

The Generalized Immediacy (GI) Scale measures a general or gestalt impression of an individual's overall level of immediacy (Andersen, 1979). Typically, the GI Scale is used to measure students' perceptions of their teacher's level of immediacy. To assess this gestalt, the immediacy construct is defined conceptually and behaviorally for students in a short paragraph. After reading the explanation, students are then asked to rate their teacher's overall level of immediacy by responding to two sets of semantic differential types of scales (nine items in all) using a 7-point continuum. Across a number of research studies, factor analysis consistently confirms a single-factor solution with all items loading on the first unrotated factor (Andersen, 1979; Andersen, Andersen, & Jensen, 1979; Kearney, Plax, & Wendt-Wasco, 1985; Plax, Kearney, McCroskey, & Richmond, 1986). Therefore, responses to the nine items are summed. The scale only takes a few minutes to complete.

Profile by Patricia Kearney.

RELIABILITY

Reliability estimates for the GI Scale are always high, ranging from .84 to .97 (Andersen, 1979; Kearney et al., 1985; Plax et al., 1986). Test–retest correlation (Day 1 and Day 2) was .81, and when corrected for attenuation, .85 (Andersen et al., 1979).

VALIDITY

Andersen (1979) attempted to validate students' gestalt impressions of their teachers' overall immediacy by having the same students also report their teachers' specific immediacy behaviors. In this second instrument, the Behavioral Indicants of Immediacy (BII) Scale, students indicated the degree to which they perceived their teachers engaging in 15 separate nonverbal behaviors in the classroom. The correlation between the BII and GI scales was .67. The BII correlated at .80 (.92 when corrected for attenuation) with actual observers' ratings of the same teachers' nonverbal immediacy behaviors (Andersen, 1979).

The GI Scale also correlates highly with other affectively based variables. More so than the BII, the GI Scale has been significantly and positively associated with students' affective learning (Andersen, 1979; Andersen, Norton, & Nussbaum, 1981; Kearney et al., 1985; Plax et al., 1986), teacher/student solidarity (Andersen, 1979), and students' willingness to comply with teacher requests or demands (Kearney, Plax, Smith, & Sorensen, 1988).

COMMENTS

Other scales are also available to assess immediacy. For an index of verbal immediacy behaviors, see Gorham (1988). For an index of nonverbal immediacy behaviors, see Richmond, Gorham, and McCroskey (1987). Both instruments are reliable, valid indicators of specific, as opposed to gestalt, perceptions of another's level of immediacy.

LOCATION

Andersen, J. F. (1979). Teacher immediacy as a predictor of teaching effectiveness. *Communication Yearbook, 3*, 543–559.

Andersen, J. F., Andersen, P. A., & Jensen, A. D. (1979). The measurement of nonverbal immediacy. *Journal of Applied Communication Research*, 7, 153–180.

REFERENCES

Andersen, J. F., Norton, R. W., & Nussbaum, J. F. (1981). Three investigations exploring the relationship between perceived teacher communication behaviors and student learning. *Communication Education*, 30, 377–392.

Gorham, J. (1988). The relationship between verbal teacher immediacy behaviors and student learning. *Communication Education*, 37, 40–53.

Kearney, P., Plax, T. G., Smith, V. R., & Sorensen, G. (1988). Effects of teacher immediacy and strategy type on college student resistance to on-task demands. *Communication Education*, 37, 54–67.

Kearney, P., Plax, T. G., & Wendt-Wasco, N. J. (1985). Teacher immediacy for affective learning in divergent college classes. *Communication Quarterly*, 33, 61–74.

Mehrabian, A. (1969). Significance of posture and position in the communication of attitude and status relationships. *Psychological Bulletin*, 71, 359–372.

Mehrabian, A. (1971). *Silent messages*. Belmont, CA: Wadsworth.

Plax, T. G., Kearney, P., McCroskey, J. C., & Richmond, V. P. (1986). Power in the classroom VI: Verbal control strategies, nonverbal immediacy and affective learning. *Communication Education*, 35, 43–55.

Richmond, V. P., Gorham, J. S., & McCroskey, J. C. (1987). The relationship between selected immediacy behaviors and cognitive learning. *Communication Yearbook*, 10, 574–590.

Generalized Immediacy Scale*

Instructions: Immediate behaviors are those communication behaviors that reduce distance between people. Immediate behaviors may actually decrease the physical distance, or they may decrease the psychological distance. The more immediate a person is, the more likely he/she is to communicate at close distances, smile, engage in eye contact, use direct body orientations, use overall body movement and gestures, touch others, relax, and be vocally expressive. In other words, we might say that an immediate person is perceived as overtly friendly and warm.

Please circle the number that corresponds to the word that best describes your agreement with the following statement:

In your opinion, the teaching style of your instructor is very immediate.

Agree	1	2	3	4	5	6	7	Disagree*
False	1	2	3	4	5	6	7	True
Incorrect	1	2	3	4	5	6	7	Correct
Wrong	1	2	3	4	5	6	7	Right
Yes	1	2	3	4	5	6	7	No*

Please circle the number that corresponds to the word that best describes the teaching style of your instructor:

Immediate	1	2	3	4	5	6	7	Not immediate*
Cold	1	2	3	4	5	6	7	Warm
Unfriendly	1	2	3	4	5	6	7	Friendly
Close	1	2	3	4	5	6	7	Distant*

Note. Items with asterisks are reverse-coded before summing.

Gratifications Sought and Obtained Scales

Uses and gratifications (U&G) is an audience-centered approach to mass communication, which holds that understanding why people use media helps explain media choices and consequences. Critics argued that U&G confused its central concepts and was without a theoretical base (e.g., Swanson, 1977). Palmgreen and his associates reacted to those criticisms and began applying the expectancy-value approach to media gratifications (see Palmgreen & Rayburn, 1985b, for a summary). According to this approach, gratifications sought (GS) represent motives for media exposure and are based on expectations about media content. Gratifications obtained (GO), on the other hand, are perceived personal *outcomes*; they are, therefore, sensitive to media content and feedback to influence content expectations.

To apply their expectancy-value approach, Palmgreen, Wenner, and Rayburn (1980) developed two 15-item scales to measure the GS and GO from TV news. The items measured five GS and GO dimensions: General Information Seeking, Decisional Utility, Entertainment, Interpersonal Utility, and Parasocial Interaction. Palmgreen et al. focused on news for three reasons. First, earlier U&G research addressed political information seeking. Second, TV news has a large viewing audience. Third, different network news programs allow for choice based on program distinctions.

These GS–GO scales have been used (a) to test the relationship between GS from TV news and the corresponding GO item for most-watched and least-watched news programs (Palmgreen et al., 1980), (b) to create GS and GO discrepancy scores that distinguish viewers of different news programs (Palmgreen, Wenner, & Rayburn, 1981), and (c) to test specific components of the expectancy-value model (Palmgreen & Rayburn, 1982).

Researchers have used the scale items to measure GO from most-watched TV news programs (Palmgreen et al., 1980) and have adapted them to measure beliefs, evaluations, and importance of TV news features (Babrow & Swanson, 1988; Palmgreen & Rayburn, 1982). Some have used several items to assess GO from videotex (Atwater, Heeter, & Brown, 1985) and from morning news programs (Rayburn, Palmgreen, & Acker, 1984). Some

Profile by Elizabeth M. Perse.

studies have not used Item 2 because it does not load cleanly on a single factor.

Some studies factor-analyzed the items to reduce them to their underlying dimensions (Levy & Windahl, 1984: Palmgreen et al., 1980). Palmgreen et al. (1980) reported a three-factor, varimax-rotated GS that accounted for 48.6% of the total variance: Interpersonal Utility–Surveillance, Entertainment Seeking, and Parasocial Interaction. The three-factor GO from the most-watched news program solution accounted for 55.9% to 60.9% of the total variance. It differed somewhat from the GS factor solution: Interpersonal Utility, Entertainment–Parasocial Interaction, and Surveillance. Levy and Windahl (1984) replicated these factor structures with a Swedish sample, and Babrow and Swanson (1988) did the same with a U.S. college student sample.

Palmgreen et al. (1980) administered the GS–GO scales during telephone interviews. Others have self-administered the scales in questionnaires (e.g., Babrow & Swanson, 1988). Response options for self-administered versions are usually on 7-point scale, ranging from *never applies to me* to *always applies to me*. GS and GO versions are worded similarly (Palmgreen et al., 1980, p. 171), but the differences in wording are important in distinguishing between the two concepts. The Palmgreen et al. (1980) GS scale is reported here. Researchers should order the items randomly when collecting data. Each of the scales takes less than 5 minutes to complete.

RELIABILITY

Studies that use summed GS and GO scores report that the scales and their dimensions are internally consistent. Palmgreen and Rayburn (1985a) observed a .83 alpha for the sum of GS from TV news items and a .85 alpha for the sum of GO from the most-watched news program. Babrow and Swanson (1988) reported the internal consistency of three-item indicators of three GS dimensions: Information (alpha = .85), Entertainment (.57), and Parasocial–Interaction (.69).

Rayburn et al. (1984) reported that the 14-item version of the GS–GO scales is somewhat stable over time. Test–retest correlations were .65 for GS and .71 for GO. The scales have been used reliably with U.S. adults (Palmgreen et al., 1980), college students (Babrow & Swanson, 1988), older adults (Goodman, 1990), and Swedish adults (Levy & Windahl, 1984).

VALIDITY

In testing expectancy-value models, studies provide construct validity for the GS–GO scales. First, the correlation between corresponding GS and GO items is stronger than that between noncorresponding items (Palmgreen et al., 1980). Second, the GS and GO factor structures differ, suggesting that GS are not the same as GO (Palmgreen et al., 1980). Third, people report higher GO from their most-watched news program than from competing programs (Palmgreen et al., 1981). Fourth, a GO discrepancy model can predict most-watched evening (Palmgreen et al., 1981) and morning (Rayburn et al., 1984) news programs. GS are also related positively to news exposure (Palmgreen & Rayburn, 1982) and planning to watch the news (Levy & Windahl, 1984), whereas GO from the news relate to news program satisfaction (Palmgreen & Rayburn, 1985a).

COMMENTS

The scale items were derived from news theory and research. It might be useful to assess content validity now that TV news options have increased via cable. Because of similar wording of GS and GO items, researchers should take precautions to prevent response bias and be careful that instructions are clear so respondents can distinguish between measures. Such wording has been adapted to measure GS and GO in different levels of abstraction (e.g., GS from TV news and GO from specific news programs) and at the same level (e.g., GS and GO from TV news). Although similar factor-analysis methods have yielded similar solutions, Dobos and Dimmick (1988) noted that different statistical packages and rotation methods may yield different factor structures.

LOCATION

Palmgreen, P., Wenner, L. A., & Rayburn, J. D., II. (1980). Relations between gratifications sought and obtained: A study of television news. *Communication Research*, 7, 161–192.

REFERENCES

Atwater, T., Heeter, C., & Brown, N. (1985). Foreshadowing the electronic publishing age: First exposures to Viewtron. *Journalism Quarterly*, 62, 807–815.

Babrow, A. S., & Swanson, D. L. (1988). Disentangling antecedents of audience exposure levels: Extending expectancy-value analyses of gratifications sought from television news. *Communication Monographs*, 55, 1–21.

Dobos, J., & Dimmick, J. (1988). Factor analysis and gratification constructs. *Journal of Broadcasting and Electronic Media*, 32, 335–350.

Goodman, R. I. (1990). Television news viewing by older adults. *Journalism Quarterly, 67*, 137–141.

Levy, M. R., & Windahl, S. (1984). Audience activity and gratifications: A conceptual clarification and exploration. *Communication Research, 11*, 51–78.

Palmgreen, P., & Rayburn, J. D., II. (1982). Gratifications sought and media exposure: An expectancy value model. *Communication Research, 9*, 561–580.

Palmgreen, P., & Rayburn, J. D., II. (1985a). A comparison of gratification models of media satisfaction. *Communication Monographs, 52*, 334–346.

Palmgreen, P., & Rayburn, J. D., II. (1985b). An expectancy-value approach to media gratifications. In K. E. Rosengren, L. A. Wenner, & P. Palmgreen (Eds.), *Media gratifications research: Current perspectives* (pp. 61–72). Beverly Hills, CA: Sage.

Palmgreen, P., Wenner, L. A., & Rayburn, J. D., II. (1981). Gratification discrepancies and news program choice. *Communication Research, 8*, 451–478.

Rayburn, J. D., II, Palmgreen, P., & Acker, T. (1984). Media gratifications and choosing a morning news program. *Journalism Quarterly, 61*, 149–156.

Swanson, D. L. (1977). The uses and misuses of uses and gratifications. *Human Communication Research, 3*, 214–221.

Gratifications Sought Scale*

Instructions: We are interested in why people watch TV news. Here are 15 reasons other people have given. As I read each reason, please tell me how much that reason applies to you. If the reason very definitely applies, give it a 5; if it does not apply at all, give it a 1; if it applies somewhere in between, give it a 2, 3, or 4, depending on how much it applies.

General Information Seeking
1. I watch TV news to keep up with current issues and events.
2. I watch TV news so I won't be surprised by higher prices and things like that.
3. I watch TV news because you can trust the information they give you.

Decisional Utility
4. I watch TV news to find out what kind of job our government officials are doing.
5. I watch TV news to help me make up my mind about the important issues of the day.
6. I watch TV news to find out about issues affecting people like myself.

Entertainment
7. I watch TV news because it's often entertaining.

---

8. I watch TV news because it's often dramatic.
9. I watch TV news because it's often exciting.

<u>Interpersonal Utility</u>
10. I watch TV news to support my own viewpoints to other people.
11. I watch TV news so I can pass the information on to other people.
12. I watch TV news to give me interesting things to talk about.

<u>Parasocial Interaction</u>
13. I watch TV news because the newscasters give a human quality to the news.
14. I watch TV news to compare my own ideas to what the commentators say.
15. I watch TV news because the reporters are like people I know.

Note. Instructions for GO items read: "Now we'd like to know to what extent the network evening news programs provide you with some of the things we've just been talking about, when you get a chance to watch them. I want you to tell me how much each statement applies to the news program you ordinarily watch the most, using the same 5-point scale that we used before." Respondents then reply to the same, but slightly reworded, items used to measure GS. For example, Item 6 is: "TV news helps me find out about issues affecting people like myself."

The scale items should be ordered randomly and category headings removed before administering.

Group Behavior Inventory

Originally developed to evaluate interaction processes within work groups, the Group Behavior Inventory (GBI) was subsequently used to measure the impact of organizational interventions (Friedlander, 1966). Most of the items were generated from interviews with group members in organizations with verbatim comments being rephrased into questions. Additional items were developed from observations of staff meetings and from the literature on group behavior.

The GBI is made up of 81 questions, and has been refined to 71 questions. The first 57 items are answered on a Likert scale, with response options ranging from *strongly agree* (1) to *strongly disagree* (5). Items 58 to 81 focus on meetings and are answered with a semantic differential scale or are filled in. The original questionnaire was administered to 91 people across 12 work groups. Factor analysis of the responses identified nine factors that account for 70% of the total variance. Although many would now claim that a sample of 91 is not large enough to permit factor analysis of 81 items, the factor structure is reported as follows:

1. Group Effectiveness is described by perceptions of effective problem solving through a creative, realistic team effort.
2. Approach to versus Withdrawal from Leader indicates the degree to which group members can establish an unconstrained and comfortable relationship with the leader.
3. Mutual Influence describes groups in which members see themselves as having influence with one another.
4. Personal Involvement and Participation describes the degree to which members want, expect, and achieve active participation.
5. Trust vs. Competitiveness indicates the degree to which members collaborate to put the group above individuals and have confidence in the group.
6. General Evaluation of Meetings measures a general perception that the meetings are good or bad, weak or strong, worthwhile or worthless.

Profile by Howard H. Greenbaum, with assistance from Ira Kaplan.

178

7. Submission to Leader versus Rebellion describes how groups react when disagreements arise.
8. Leader Control measures the degree to which leaders control through one way communication.
9. Role and Idea Conformity investigates whether conformity takes precedence over creativity.

RELIABILITY

Friedlander (1966) measured the internal consistency of the factors using the Kuder–Richardson Formula 20 and also obtained test–retest reliabilities with an intervention of 6 months. For Factors 1 through 6, the internal consistencies varied from .71 to .91 and the test–retest reliabilities ranged from .64 to .81. These are respectable. However, both the internal consistencies and test–retest reliabilities for Factors 7 through 9 fell in the .50 range and were judged too low for utilization.

VALIDITY

Both Friedlander (1966, 1967, 1968) and Boss (1983) claimed that the GBI is a valid measure of group interactions. They pointed to the original factor analysis, to its ability to measure changes in group performance after interventions, and to its agreement with Likert Profile of Organizational and Performance Characteristics and another measure designed to determine honesty in communication and mutual trust. These three tests were administered prior to an intervention and at repeated intervals thereafter. Scores on the two other instruments were identical to those on the GBI in both the pattern of responses and the statistically significant changes. However, claims for validity are ameliorated by research indicating low reliabilities for some dimensions.

COMMENTS

Friedlander and Boss have used the GBI extensively to measure changes in work groups after interventions. More recently, Smith (1984) used a modified version of the GBI, retaining about half the items. His objectives were to determine which aspects of the manager's behavior and the team processes were associated with perceived group effectiveness. Although the size of the sample is not known, Smith's analysis of the modified instrument identified seven factors similar to the ones found by Friedlander. Many studies using the GBI are now somewhat dated, but perhaps the greatest testimony to the utility of the GBI is Kaplan and Greenbaum's (1989) report that other investigators have referred to the GBI in developing instruments of their own (e.g., Kilmann, 1974; White & Mitchell, 1976; Woodman & Sherwood, 1980).

LOCATION

The GBI may be obtained for a nominal fee from the Library of Congress, Photo-duplication Service, Washington, DC, by requesting Document ADI-8787.

REFERENCES

Boss, R. W. (1983). Team building and the problem of regression: The personal management interview as an intervention. *Journal of Applied Behavioral Science, 19*, 67–83.

Friedlander, F. (1966). Performance and interactional dimensions of organizational work groups. *Journal of Applied Psychology, 50*, 257–265.

Friedlander, F. (1967). The impact of organizational training laboratories upon the effectiveness and interaction of ongoing work groups. *Personnel Psychology, 20*, 289–307.

Friedlander, F. (1968). A comparative study of consulting processes and group development. *Journal of Applied Behavioral Science, 4*, 377–379.

Kaplan, I. T., & Greenbaum, H. H. (1989). Measuring work group effectiveness: A comparison of three instruments. *Management Communication Quarterly, 2*, 424–448.

Kilmann, R. H. (1974). The effects of interpersonal values on laboratory training: An empirical investigation. *Human Relations, 27*, 247–265.

Smith, P. B. (1984). Social service teams and their managers. *British Journal of Social Work, 14*, 601–613.

White, S. E., & Mitchell, T. R. (1976). Organization development: A review of research content and research design. *Academy of Management Review, 1*, 57–73.

Woodman, R. W., & Sherwood, J. J. (1980). Effects of team development intervention: A field experiment. *Journal of Applied Behavioral Science, 16*, 211–227.

Group Behavior Inventory*

Instructions: Think of the past two or three department meetings that you have attended. The following questions apply to the meetings or the group which attended these meetings.

---

*Reprinted from a U.S. Government document. In the public domain.

[Editors' note: Items 1–57 are scored on a 5-point scale with 1 as *strongly agree* and 5 as *strongly disagree*. Items 58–71 are fill-in or semantic-differential-type questions.]

1. Most material covered in meetings is introduced by the chairman.
2. There is a destructive competitiveness among members of the group.
3. Meetings do not come to grips with the real problems.
4. The chairman is oriented toward a "human relations" approach.
5. Meetings are primarily a means of information dissemination.
6. There is trust and confidence in each other among members of the group.
7. Group meetings should be discontinued.
8. Policies from higher levels hinder the effectiveness of the group.
9. Group meetings result in creative solutions to problems.
10. There is open examination of issues and problems at group meetings.
11. The group is an effective problem-solving team.
12. Divergent ideas are discouraged at group meetings.
13. There is no point in raising critical problems at group meetings.
14. I expect decisions on important matters to be made at group meetings.
15. The chairman is oriented toward production and efficiency.
16. Meetings do not formulate future policy.
17. Members are more intent on satisfying the chairman than in optimizing the potential output of the group.
18. The goals of the group are clear cut.
19. Group members are willing to listen to and to understand me.
20. The group should have an "expert" on hand to settle certain questions.
21. Meetings are not effective in discussing mutual problems.
22. It is important to be on friendly terms with other members.
23. There are too many personal opinions raised at meetings, as opposed to the department point of view.
24. Meetings are trivial.
25. Conflict within the group is submerged, rather than used constructively.
26. I expect little from group meetings.
27. The chairman offers new approaches to problems at meetings.
28. There is open examination of relationships among group members.
29. Group meetings should be continued.
30. The policies under which the group works are clear cut.
31. The criterion for evaluating ideas in the group is "who said it" rather than "what was said."
32. The group should be achieving more than it is.
33. The chairman should give the members guidance.
34. The chairman puts suggestions by members into operation.

Instructions: Using the same agreement–disagreement scale, mark the following statements as you would describe *other members* at department meetings.

35. Assume responsibility for setting group goals.
36. Submit to the chairman when disagreements arise.
37. Reluctant to sacrifice ideas so that group may agree.
38. Act the role that is expected of them.
39. Feel at ease when talking with the chairman.
40. Behavior does not reflect their true feelings.
41. Reluctant in pushing their ideas.
42. Can approach the chairman with ease.
43. Have influence with the chairman.
44. Withdraw from involvement with chairman when disagreements arise.
45. Accept influence from other group members.

Instructions: Using the same agreement–disagreement scale, mark the following statements as you would describe *your own role* at department meetings.

46. Assume responsibility for setting group goals.
47. Submit to the chairman when disagreements arise.
48. Feel at ease when talking with the chairman.
49. Behavior does not reflect my true feelings.
50. Rebel against the chairman when disagreements arise.
51. Reluctant in pushing ideas.
52. Want to actively participate in meetings.
53. Can approach the chairman with ease.
54. Have influence with the chairman.
55. Withdraw from involvement with chairman when disagreements arise.
56. Accept influence from other group members.
57. Enjoy the group meetings.
58. I attended the last group meeting.   Yes _____ No _____
59. I submitted _____ topics for the agenda for the last meeting I attended.
60. I estimate that the last group meeting I attended lasted _____ hours.
61. I have attended approximately _____ group meetings during the past 12 months.
62. I estimate that the chairman talked about _____% of the time during the last group meeting I attended.
63. I estimate that I talked about _____% of the time during the last group meeting I attended.

64. The problem areas which need discussion at the next group meeting are:

    1. _____ 2. _____ 3. _____ Don't know. _____

Instructions: In this section, you are asked to judge the meaning of the concept Group Meeting (as it relates to the _____ Department) in terms of each of the seven scales beneath it. Check one blank for each of the seven scales that best describes the meaning of the concept:

_____ DEPARTMENT GROUP MEETINGS

65. good	:____:____:____:____:____:____:____:	bad
66. weak	:____:____:____:____:____:____:____:	strong
67. active	:____:____:____:____:____:____:____:	passive
68. pleasant	:____:____:____:____:____:____:____:	unpleasant
69. deep	:____:____:____:____:____:____:____:	shallow
70. relaxed	:____:____:____:____:____:____:____:	tense
71. valuable	:____:____:____:____:____:____:____:	worthless

Individualized Trust Scale

Individualized trust is "a *process* of holding certain relevant, favorable *perceptions* of another person which engender certain types of *dependent behaviors* in a *risky situation* where the expected outcomes that are dependent upon that other person(s) are *not known* with certainty" (Wheeless & Grotz, 1977, p. 251). The Individualized Trust Scale (ITS) differs from the Interpersonal Trust Scale (Rotter, 1967) in that the ITS focuses on a specific person rather than trust in other people in general.

Wheeless and Grotz (1977) chose many of the 15 semantic differential items from two source credibility scales: Berlo, Lemert, and Mertz's (1969–1970) (items under Safety–Trustworthiness) and McCroskey's (1966) (items under Character). Factor analysis revealed one dimension that accounted for 59% of the variance. All 15 items had primary loadings of .56 or higher. The ITS uses 7-point semantic differential scales and takes about 1 minute to complete.

RELIABILITY

Wheeless and Grotz (1977) reported a split-half reliability of .92 for the ITS and Wheeless (1978) reported a reliability of .97 for a 14-item version. Van Lear and Trujillo (1986) chose four items from the ITS and reported an alpha of .82. Snavely (1981) reported an alpha of .95 and Buller, Strzyzewski, and Comstock (1991) an alpha of .72 for the ITS. Evidence of test–retest reliability is lacking.

VALIDITY

Wheeless and Grotz (1977) performed the first validity studies. They expected and found that (a) individualized trust and generalized trust were unrelated, (b) individualized trust was related to control and conscious intent to self-disclose, and (c) persons high and low in individualized trust differed in amount of self-disclosure to the target person. These findings

Profile by Rebecca R. Rubin.

were replicated by Wheeless (1978), who also found a strong relationship between self-disclosure, individualized trust, and interpersonal solidarity. And Wheeless and Andersen (1978) found that trust, as predicted, was related to self-disclosure, acquaintance time, relationship type, and solidarity.

Conceptually, given consistently positive interactions, trust should increase over time. Van Lear and Trujillo (1986) found just that. Over a 4-week period, trust increased and uncertainty decreased as a function of time. Snavely (1981) found that trust was related to other person perception measures and differed across styles and contexts of communication.

COMMENTS

The ITS has a strong conceptual base and evidence suggests that it is valid and reliable. If trust of a particular person is required in a research investigation, this scale should receive consideration. However, the ITS has not been used in a significant number of research investigations since its conception, so information on criterion-related and content validity is sparse.

LOCATION

Wheeless, L. R., & Grotz, J. (1977). The measurement of trust and its relationship to self-disclosure. *Human Communication Research, 3,* 250–257.

REFERENCES

Berlo, D. K., Lemert, J. B., & Mertz, R. J. (1970). Dimensions for evaluating the acceptability of message sources. *Public Opinion Quarterly, 33,* 563–576.
Buller, D. B., Strzyzewski, K. D., & Comstock, J. (1991). Interpersonal deception: I. Deceivers' reactions to receivers' suspicions and probing. *Communication Monographs, 58,* 1–24.
McCroskey, J. C. (1966). Scales for the measurment of ethos. *Speech Monographs, 33,* 65–72.
Rotter, J. B. (1967). A new scale for the measurement of interpersonal trust. *Journal of Personality, 35,* 651–665.
Snavely, W. B. (1981). The impact of social style upon person perception in primary relationships. *Communication Quarterly, 29,* 132–143.
Van Lear, C. A., Jr., & Trujillo, N. (1986). On becoming acquainted: A longitudinal study of social judgement processes. *Journal of Social and Personal Relationships, 3,* 375–392.
Wheeless, L. R. (1978). A follow-up study of the relationships among trust, disclosure, and interpersonal solidarity. *Human Communication Research, 4,* 143–157.

Wheeless, L. R., & Andersen, J. F. (1978, April). *An empirical test of social penetration and indices of its critical components*. Paper presented at the meeting of the International Communication Association, Chicago.

Individualized Trust Scale*

Instructions: On the scales that follow, please indicate your reaction to _____ _____. Place an "X" in the space between the colons that represents your immediate "feelings" about this person. Check in the direction of the end of the scale that seems to be most characteristic of this person. Mark only one "X" for each scale and please complete all scales.

```
                  Trustworthy :___:___:___:___:___:___:___: Untrustworthy
      Distrustful of this person :___:___:___:___:___:___:___: Trustful of this person
                  Confidential :___:___:___:___:___:___:___: Divulging
                    Exploitive :___:___:___:___:___:___:___: Benevolent
                          Safe :___:___:___:___:___:___:___: Dangerous
                      Deceptive :___:___:___:___:___:___:___: Candid
                  Not deceitful :___:___:___:___:___:___:___: Deceitful
                         Tricky :___:___:___:___:___:___:___: Straightforward
                     Respectful :___:___:___:___:___:___:___: Disrespectful
                  Inconsiderate :___:___:___:___:___:___:___: Considerate
                         Honest :___:___:___:___:___:___:___: Dishonest
                     Unreliable :___:___:___:___:___:___:___: Reliable
                       Faithful :___:___:___:___:___:___:___: Unfaithful
                       Insincere :___:___:___:___:___:___:___: Sincere
                        Careful :___:___:___:___:___:___:___: Careless
```

Note. Score 1–7, with 7 indicating most positive (high trust), for each item before summing.

Interaction Involvement Scale

Cegala (1981) conceptualized interaction involvement as the degree to which people are engaged, cognitively and behaviorally, in their conversations with others. Involved interactants are aware of the demands of the interaction and respond to others appropriately, while the uninvolved are preoccupied with their own thoughts and concerns rather than their partner's.

Cegala (1981) originally designed the Interaction Involvement Scale (IIS) to measure Erving Goffman's concepts of perceptiveness (being aware of message meanings) and attentiveness (hearing and observing), but Cegala's factor analysis revealed a third dimension, Responsiveness. Originally termed "other-oriented perceptiveness," Responsiveness refers to a person's certainty about how to respond to others during a conversation (Cegala, Savage, Brunner, & Conrad, 1982).

Respondents mark 7-point Likert-type responses, ranging from *not at all like me* (1) to *very much like me* (7), for each of the 18 IIS items. The scale takes less than 6 minutes to complete. Reverse coding is required for 12 items. Both trait and state versions of this scale exist. The most recently revised trait version is reported here because most of the research identified below used the trait version. The state version, used immediately following a conversation to tap involvement in that particular interaction, is available from Donald Cegala. In addition, A. Rubin, Perse, and Taylor (1988) and Perse (1990) adapted some IIS attentiveness items to measure audience involvement with the media, and Allen (1991) adapted the IIS for small group interaction.

RELIABILITY

Test–retest reliability for the trait IIS appears to be very good. Cegala et al. (1982) reported test–retest reliability was .81 after a 6-week delay. R. Rubin and Graham (1988) reported test–retest reliability was .61 after 1 year for a 15-item trait version (the individual scales ranged from .56 to .58).

The IIS also appears to be internally consistent. Alphas for the Responsiveness subscale have ranged from .69 (Duran & Kelly, 1988) to .86 (Cegala,

Profile by Rebecca B. Rubin.

1981), alphas for the Perceptiveness subscale have ranged from .63 (R. Rubin & Graham, 1988) to .88 (Cegala, 1981), and alphas for the Attentiveness subscale have ranged from .64 (Duran & Kelly, 1988) to .87 (Cegala, 1981). Overall alphas have ranged from .83 (Chen, 1989) to .90 (Cegala, 1981; Cegala et al., 1982).

VALIDITY

The evidence for concurrent validity is strong. Research has found attentiveness (a) negatively correlated with neuroticism (Cegala et al., 1982), (b) positively correlated with self-disclosure intent and honesty (Chen, 1989), and (c) positively correlated with social experience (Duran & Kelly, 1988). Responsiveness is (a) positively correlated with sociability and negatively correlated with neuroticism, social anxiety, and communication apprehension in interpersonal contexts (Cegala et al., 1982), (b) negatively correlated with social anxiety and positively correlated with adaptability and self-disclosure intent and honesty (Chen, 1989), (c) positively correlated with social confirmation and appropriate disclosure (Duran & Kelly, 1988), and (d) higher in nondepressed persons (Segrin, 1992). Perceptiveness is (a) positively correlated with communication competence (Cegala et al., 1982), (b) positively correlated with self-consciousness and self-disclosure intent (Chen, 1989), and (c) positively correlated with social composure and social experience (Duran & Kelly, 1988). In addition, attentiveness, responsiveness, and perceptiveness are positively correlated with credibility (expertise, trustworthiness, and dynamism) and with communication satisfaction, appropriateness, and effectiveness (Onyekwere, Rubin, & Infante, 1991). The overall scale is related negatively to communication apprehension and positively to self-reported communication competence (Rubin & Graham, 1988). Also, Street and Wiemann (1988) found that health care satisfaction was significantly related to how involved the patients perceived their physician to be.

Factor analysis has been used to examine the stability of the interaction involvement dimensions. Cegala (1981) originally found three dimensions, and this was confirmed in a later study employing 1802 subjects (Cegala et al., 1982). However, four of the items did not pass a .60/.40 rule for inclusion (five did not pass a .50/.30 rule) yet were kept in the scale. Downs (1985) found that an unrotated factor analysis produced a strong single factor, and orthogonal rotation forced the multifactor pattern reported by Cegala. Downs also concluded that interaction involvement is a significant, but not strong, predictor of social style, in that it accounted for less than 5% of the variance.

Cegala's more recent work has focused on construct validation, examining various verbal and nonverbal behaviors of those high and low in interaction involvement. He found, for instance, that responsiveness is a significant predictor of nonverbal behavior (Cegala et al., 1982). In particular, there are differences between highs and lows on hand gestures and eye gaze but not on body movements (Cegala & Sillars, 1989). In verbal conversation, the highly involved have higher scores on ego strength and positive affect, and they recall more information about conversations than do the low involved, who are perceived as more angry and tired (Cegala, 1984). Cegala (1989) found that low-involved interactants use less immediate language and fewer relational pronouns and speak with less certainty than do highly involved interactants. In addition, Cegala, Wall, and Rippey (1987) found significant differences between high- and low-involved task group members on four of the six interaction continua measured via SYMLOG.

Perhaps the most important work on the conversational styles of high and low involvement was conducted by Villaume and Cegala (1988), who found that low-involved communicators use a text-based style of conversation and play off the surface structure of the partner's last utterance. In contrast, high-involved people use a meaning-based conversational style, reflecting more substantive topic development and rational goal pursuit. Villaume, Jackson, and Goldsmith Schouten (1989) reported additional support for these contrasting styles in terms of issue–event extensions of conversational topics, and Villaume (1988) found evidence for the contrasting styles in more global segments of discourse as well. Overall, these results are interpreted as reflecting the relative uncertainty of low-involved communicators.

COMMENTS

The IIS appears to be a useful scale for measuring a general tendency toward, or the state of, involvement during interpersonal interaction. There are both cognitive and behavioral items in the scale, which is probably why the scale is related to both cognitive and behavioral predispositions. Reliability and validity data are good. Almost all studies have tested the scale exclusively on college students. One concern, however, is the double loading of items on two of the scale's dimensions when the items are factor-analyzed. To correct for this, the author has reworded the items for clarity and has provided the revised version that appears below. Future research should provide factor analysis information about the dimensions found in this new scale version.

LOCATION

Allen, T. (1991). Effects of metaknowledge on talk duration and interaction involvement in small group decision-making. *Communication Research Reports*, 8, 1–7.

Cegala, D. J. (1981). Interaction involvement: A cognitive dimension of communicative competence. *Communication Education*, 30, 109–121.

REFERENCES

Cegala, D. J. (1984). Affective and cognitive manifestations of interaction involvement during unstructured and competitive interactions. *Communication Monographs*, 51, 320–338.

Cegala, D. J. (1989). A study of selected linguistic components of involvement in interaction. *Western Journal of Speech Communication*, 53, 311–326.

Cegala, D. J., Savage, G. T., Brunner, C. C., & Conrad, A. B. (1982). An elaboration of the meaning of interaction involvement: Toward the development of a theoretical concept. *Communication Monographs*, 49, 229–248.

Cegala, D. J., & Sillars, A. L. (1989). Further examination of nonverbal manifestations of interaction involvement. *Communication Reports*, 2, 39–47.

Cegala, D. J., Wall, V. D., & Rippey, G. (1987). An investigation of interaction involvement and the dimensions of SYMLOG: Perceived communication behaviors of persons in task-oriented groups. *Central States Speech Journal*, 38, 81–93.

Chen, G-M. (1989). Relationships of the dimensions of intercultural communication competence. *Communication Quarterly*, 37, 118–133.

Downs, V. C. (1985). Interaction involvement as a predictor of perceived social style: An empirical test of dialogic communication assumptions. *Communication Research Reports*, 2, 62–67.

Duran, R. L., & Kelly, L. (1988). An investigation into the cognitive domain of competence: II. The relationship between communicative competence and interaction involvement. *Communication Research Reports*, 5, 91–96.

Onyekwere, E. O., Rubin, R. B., & Infante, D. A. (1991). Interpersonal perception and communication satisfaction as a function of argumentativeness and ego-involvement. *Communication Quarterly*, 39, 35–47.

Perse, E. M. (1990). Involvement with local television news: Cognitive and emotional dimensions. *Human Communication Research*, 16, 556–581.

Rubin, A. M., Perse, E. M., & Taylor, D. S. (1988). A methodological examination of cultivation. *Communication Research*, 15, 107–134.

Rubin, R. B., & Graham, E. E. (1988). Communication correlates of college success: An exploratory investigation. *Communication Education*, 37, 14–27.

Segrin, C. (1992). Specifying the nature of social skill deficits associated with depression. *Human Communication Research*, 19, 89–123.

Street, R. L., Jr., & Wiemann, J. M. (1988). Differences in how physicians and patients perceive physicians' relational communication. *Southern Speech Communication Journal*, 53, 420–440.

Villaume, W. A. (1988). Identify and similarity chains in the conversation of high-involved and low-involved speakers: Evidence of integrated discourse strategies. *Western Journal of Speech Communication, 52*, 185–202.

Villaume, W. A., & Cegala, D. J. (1988). Interaction involvement and discourse strategies: The patterned usage of cohesive devices in conversation. *Communication Monographs, 55*, 22–40.

Villaume, W. A., Jackson, J., & Goldsmith Schouten, T. (1989). Issue–event extensions and interaction involvement: Text-based and meaning-based discourse strategies. *Human Communication Research, 15*, 407–427.

Interaction Involvement Scale*

Instructions: This questionnaire is designed to provide information about how people communicate. There are no right or wrong answers to any of the items. You only need to indicate the extent to which you feel each item describes *your own behavior*.

In responding to some of the items, you might say, "sometimes I do that and sometimes I don't." You should respond to each item in a way that best describes your typical manner of communication—how you behave in most situations. If you cannot decide how a particular item applies to you, circle the "not sure" alternative. However, please be sure to respond to all of the items.

Circle the one alternative for each item that best characterizes your communication in general:

| Not at all like me | Not like me | Somewhat unlike me | Not sure | Somewhat like me | Like me | Very much like me |

[Editors' note: The above scale appears after each item.]

1. I am keenly aware of how others perceive me during my conversations.
2. My mind wanders during conversations and I often miss parts of what is going on.
3. Often in conversations I'm not sure what to say, I can't seem to find the appropriate lines.
4. I am very observant of others' reactions while I'm speaking.
5. During conversations I listen carefully to others and obtain as much information as I can.
6. Often in conversations I'm not sure what my role is, I'm not sure how I'm expected to relate to others.
7. Often in conversations I will pretend to be listening, when in fact I was thinking of something else.

---

8. Often during conversations I feel like I know what should be said (like accepting a compliment, or asking a question), but I hesitate to do so.

9. Sometimes during conversations I'm not sure what the other really means or intends by certain comments.

10. I carefully observe how the other is responding to me during a conversation.

11. Often I feel withdrawn or distant during conversations.

12. Often in conversations I'm not sure what others' needs are (e.g., a compliment, reassurance, etc.) until it is too late to respond appropriately.

13. I feel confident during my conversations, I am sure of what to say and do.

14. Often I'm preoccupied in my conversations and do not pay complete attention to others.

15. Often I feel sort of "unplugged" during conversations, I am uncertain of my role, others' motives, and what is happening.

16. In my conversations I often do not accurately perceive others' intentions or motivations.

17. In conversations I am very perceptive to the meaning of my partner's behavior in relation to myself and the situation.

18. Often during my conversation I can't think of what to say, I just don't react quickly enough.

Note. Items 2, 3, 6, 7, 8, 9, 11, 12, 14, 15, 16, and 18 are reverse-coded.

Perceptiveness items are 1, 9, 16, and 17. Attentiveness items are 2, 4, 5, 7, 10, and 14. Responsiveness items are 3, 6, 8, 11, 12, 13, 15, and 18.

International Communication Association Audit

The Organizational Communication Division of the International Communication Association (ICA) devoted more than 5 years (1971–1976) to the
development of the ICA Audit and an additional 3 years to refining the
methods (1976–1979). Many members worked on its original development
(Downs, 1988; Goldhaber & Rogers, 1979). The ICA Audit is a package of
instruments used in the assessment of employees' perceptions of communication processes in their organization. It has been used extensively in research and consulting in the years since its development.

The total assessment package includes a standardized survey questionnaire, interview guides, observations, network analysis, critical incidents,
and a communication diary. This review only focuses on the survey questionnaire, which was very unique at the time of its development. The ICA
Audit survey questionnaire contains 122 questions divided into eight major
sections: (a) amount of *information* desired and actually *received* about a series
of work related topics, (b) amount of *information* desired and actually *sent*
about a series of work related topics, (c) amount of *follow-up* by people now
and amount needed, (d) amount of information received and desired from
sources of information, (e) *timeliness* of information, (f) *organizational communication relationships*, (g) satisfaction with *organizational outcomes*, and (h)
amount of information received and desired from *channels* of information.
Scales a, b, c, d, and h provide a measure of employees' need for various
communication functions by calculating a difference score—subtracting the
amount of communication currently sent or received from the amount desired.

In a factor analysis of data from more than 1,500 subjects, DeWine
and James (1988) found three dimensions of the first scale, Information
Received: Organizational Performance, Personal Performance, and Policies
and Benefits. These factors were similar to those previously identified (Daly,
Falcione, & Damhorst, 1979; Daniels & Spiker, 1983) and referred to types
of information an employee may receive within the organizational context.
This factor structure suggested that some of the items relate to information

Profile by Sue DeWine.

about how the organization as a whole performs, some relate to information about individual performance, and some focus on information relative to policies, procedures, and benefits that exist within the organization.

The second scale, Information Sent, includes items that are oriented toward upward communication in the form of reports, complaints, and requests for more information. Items in this section of the ICA Audit loaded onto one factor, suggesting that all the items were measuring the same construct (DeWine & James, 1988). The third scale, Follow-up, also resulted in a one-factor structure.

The fourth scale, Sources, lists various sources from which information can be received. It gives employees an opportunity to indicate how much information they would like to receive and are currently receiving from each of these sources. For example, it includes information from individuals within one's unit, coworkers, departmental meetings, formal management presentations, and the grapevine. According to the factor structure, these items grouped into (a) information from organizational hierarchy sources and (b) information from peer–subordinate sources (DeWine & James, 1988).

The fifth scale, Timeliness, resulted in two factors: Management, and Peer and Subordinate (DeWine & James, 1988). Timeliness items deal with how timely the information is when it reaches the employee. Clearly the factors indicate how timely one's colleagues are versus how timely one's superiors are.

The sixth scale, Organizational Communication Relationships, examines individuals' perceptions of the quality of relationships they have with coworkers and various other people in the organization. This scale factored into four dimensions: Supervisor, Top Management, Coworkers, and Personal Influence (how much impact employees perceive they have on decision making and policymaking in the organization) (Chua & DeWine, 1982; Daniels & Spiker, 1983; DeWine & James, 1988).

The seventh scale, Organizational Outcomes, had two factors: Organizational Effectiveness and Personal Achievement. These items focus on the outcomes of the individual's own personal efforts as well as organizational outcomes.

The eighth scale, Channels, had five factors: Media, Phone/Memos, Face-to-Face, Publications, and Bulletin Board Channels (DeWine & James, 1988). This scale is often adapted to the individual organization being audited; the organization lists specific channels (e.g., names of the in-house newsletters and external publications) present in that environment.

One intention of the developers of the ICA Audit was to increase the instrument's standardization so that the resulting information from different organizations could be compared (Goldhaber & Rogers, 1979); this would increase the researcher's ability to communicate results to the client. However, discussion of the development of recommendations to clients by the original authors is unclear and vague. Thus, comparability and consistency are unlikely across different organizations. Although guidelines do exist for the statistical analysis of the data from the survey instrument (Goldhaber, 1986; Goldhaber & Rogers, 1979; Porter, 1979), there are no sources that discuss how the audit team creates recommendations from the combined data of the interviews, communication experience form, and survey results. Yet there is one exception. A procedure for reporting results has been detailed in a recent publication by DeWine and James (1988). Additionally, a follow-up study on the impact of the audit on organizations suggested that a number of items in the ICA Audit should be eliminated (DeWine, James, & Wallence, 1985). This revision allows for a stronger internal structure of the survey as well as reduction in time needed to administer the audit. Normally the instrument takes about 30 minutes to complete.

DeWine and Pearson (1985b), after a review of 180 journals (including the nine major ones in speech communication) during a 5-year period, determined the most frequently used self-report instruments. The ICA Audit was one of the five most frequently used. Of the eight individual scales in the ICA Audit, three scales were used most frequently: Organizational Communication Relationships, Organizational Outcomes (which measures satisfaction with the job), and Information Received. The advantages of the ICA Audit are well documented (Dennis, Goldhaber, & Yates, 1978; Falcione, Goldhaber, Porter, & Rogers, 1979; Goldhaber, Yates, Porter, & Lesniak, 1978) with numerous authors providing suggestions and improvements (Brooks, Callicoat, & Siegerdt, 1979; Downs, Clampitt, & Laird, 1981; Falcione et al., 1979).

Six studies, using the ICA data bank, reported using the Relationship scale, the Outcome scale, and the Information Received scale. Without exception, the respondents were organizational employees (Gorden, Tengler, & Infante, 1982; Infante & Gorden, 1981; Murray, 1983; Spiker & Daniels, 1981). Frone and Major (1988) modified sections of the ICA Audit to measure communication quality and satisfaction as they relate to employee involvement. The adapted items assess the perceived quality (i.e., timeliness, accuracy, and usefulness of communication) of information received from subordinates, superiors, coworkers, and administration. Regression analysis suggested that job involvement moderated the relationship between perceived communication quality and job satisfaction when immediate supervisors, subordinates, and coworkers were the sources of information.

RELIABILITY

Over the past decade, the ICA Audit has consistently received high internal reliability scores. DeWine and Pearson (1985a) reported coefficient alphas for the relationship scale averaged .90 and those for the organizational outcome scale averaged .76. Below is a comparison of reliability scores derived from a national data bank of over 4,600 subjects (Porter, 1979) and a regional data bank of over 1,500 subjects (DeWine & James, 1988).

Scale names	Coefficient alphas	
	DeWine & James (1988)	Porter (1979)
Total Instrument	.97	NA
Information Received—Current	.89	.86
Information Received—Needed	.93	.88
Sending Information—Current	.81	.80
Sending Information—Needed	.89	.63
Follow-up—Current	.80	.80
Follow-up—Needed	.84	.57
Sources—Current	.79	.79
Sources—Needed	.85	.77
Timeliness	.73	.46
Relationships	.94	.90
Outcomes	.93	.88
Channels	.89	NA

Other studies testing various parts of this scale with other outcome variables also reported high internal consistency. For example, Shockley-Zalabak and Morley (1989) used portions of the ICA Audit scale to test the relationship between organizational culture, individual values, organizational communication activity, and perceptions of organizational outcome. They reported a reliability of .95 on the Satisfaction scale, .77 on Sending Information, and .89 on different scores for the Receiving Information scale. Other researchers have used portions of the scales to identify information adequacy and communication relationships (McDowell, 1985) and to do follow-up data analysis on data that are included in the national data bank (Alesse et al., 1981).

VALIDITY

In the original work on the audit, the designers tested the validity of the audit by measuring various scales against outcome variables. The claim was made that this was a form of validity testing whether or not each of these communication variables had some relationship to organizational outcomes

(Goldhaber & Rogers, 1979). The following were the results of the validity tests correlating each of the communication variables with the Organizational Outcome Scale: Information Received, −.69; Information Desired, −.07; Sending Information (Sent), −.56; Sending Information (Desired), −.10; Sources (Received), −.63; Sources (Desired), −.03; and Organizational Communication Relationships, −.70.

Finally, ability of items to significantly discriminate between the top and bottom 17% of the respondents resulted in the following five scales accurately discriminating 100% of the cases: Information Received, Information Desired, Information Sent, Information Desired to Send, and Organizational Outcomes (Goldhaber & Rogers, 1979). Information Received discriminated between the top and bottom 17% of the respondents for 78% of the cases and Information Desired resulted in 89% accuracy.

While the original authors of the audit tested validity, others have challenged the methods used. Greenbaum, DeWine, and Downs (1987) suggested that confusion has arisen over definitions of validity. For example, whereas predictive validity refers to a measure's ability to predict a respondent's behavior, ICA Audit researchers defined predictive validity as "the correlation between two portions of a self report instrument" and argued that "the instrument had predictive validity because a variety of satisfaction measures were related to self reports of organizational outcome variables in the same instrument" (Greenbaum et al., 1987, p. 136). It would be useful to measure the predictive validity of the audit by testing the self-report instrument against actual organizational behavior.

COMMENTS

The ICA Audit still remains one of the best sources of information about organizational relationships and the kind of information that moves throughout an organization. It has an applied and practical use as well as a research function. At the time these scales were developed, they were the single most significant contribution to the field of organizational communication. The fact that they involved a large number of researchers over a long period is impressive. The scales have been used in a variety of contexts across many types of organizations. Over 30 different organizations have been audited and data stored in a regional data bank at Ohio University.

The survey instruments are not often used in isolation but usually in conjunction with in-depth interviews, network analyses, or communication diaries. While there has been widespread usage of these instruments, there are some shortcomings in terms of length and ambiguity of questions. Downs (1988) pointed out that "the problem with some questions is not that the

analysts can not generate possible interpretations but rather that these interpretations may not be faithful to the meanings intended by the respondents"
(p. 110). He also concluded, however, that it "continues to be a viable tool
for individual auditors and as such it merits our attention" (p. 111). DeWine
and James (1988) attempted to answer criticisms of the ICA Audit and concluded: "It does present an organization's generalized and collective view
of its communication climate that may or may not be parallel with the views
of top management" (p. 158). They proposed modification of some of the
scale items and of the structures of the scales themselves. "With the modified version of these instruments and procedures we assert that its usefulness will be enhanced and its administration streamlined" (DeWine & James,
1988, p. 159).

Researchers interested in using the audit instruments should examine
some of the suggested modifications and should be scoring the instruments
according to the subscales indicated by the factor analyses. If anything, these
scales will provide more information than desired or easily analyzed. In that
sense, they remain one of the most comprehensive measures of organizational
communication.

LOCATION

Downs, C. W. (1988). *Communication audits.* Glenview, IL: Scott Foresman.
Goldhaber, G. (1986). *Organizational communication* (4th ed.). Dubuque, IA: Wil-
    liam C. Brown.

REFERENCES

Alesse, B., Colten, L., Deutschman, M., Gordon, A., Klein, J., Mitchell, J., Palmer,
    M., & Williams, V. (1981, May). *Information discrepancy as a predictor of orga-
    nizational satisfaction.* Paper presented at the meeting of the International
    Communication Association, Minneapolis.
Brooks, K., Callicoat, J., & Siegerdt, G. (1979). The ICA Communication Audit
    and perceived communication effectiveness changes in 16 audited organiza-
    tions. *Human Communication Research, 5,* 130–137.
Chua, B., & DeWine, S. (1982, November). *A study of cultures: Communication satis-
    faction and job satisfaction of Singapore workers.* Paper presented at the meeting
    of Speech Communication Association, Louisville, KY.
Daly, J., Falcione, R., & Damhorst, M. (1979, May). *Communication correlates of re-
    lational and organizational satisfaction: An audit based investigation.* Paper pre-
    sented at the meeting of the International Communication Association, Phila-
    delphia.
Daniels, T., & Spiker, B. (1983). Social exchange and the relationship between

information adequacy and relational satisfaction. *Western Journal of Speech Communication*, 47, 118–137.

Dennis III, H., Goldhaber, G., & Yates, M. (1978). Organizational communication theory and research: An overview of research methods. *Communication Yearbook*, 2, 243–269.

DeWine, S., & James, A. C. (1988). Examining the Communication Audit: Assessment and modification. *Management Communication Quarterly*, 2, 144–168.

DeWine, S., James, A.C., & Wallence, W. (1985, May). *Validation of organizational communication audit instruments.* Paper presented at the meeting of the International Communication Association, Honolulu.

DeWine, S., & Pearson, J. C. (1985a, May). *The most frequently used self report instruments in communication.* Paper presented at the International Communication Association, Honolulu.

DeWine, S., & Pearson, J. C. (1985b, May). *State of the art: Self report paper and pencil instruments reported in communication journals.* Paper presented at the International Communication Association, Honolulu.

Downs, C., Clampitt, P., & Laird, A. (1981, May). *Critique of the ICA Communication Audit.* Paper presented at the meeting of the International Communication Association, Minneapolis.

Falcione, R., Goldhaber, G., Porter, P., & Rogers, D. (1979, November). *The future of the ICA Communication Audit.* Paper presented at the meeting of the International Communication Association, Philadelphia.

Frone, M. R., & Major, B. (1988). Communication quality and job satisfaction among managerial nurses. *Group and Organization Studies*, 13, 332–347.

Goldhaber, G., & Rogers, D. (1979). *Auditing organization communication systems: The ICA Communication Audit.* Dubuque, IA: Kendall Hunt.

Goldhaber, G., Yates, M., Porter, D. T., & Lesniak, R. (1978). Organizational communication: 1978. *Human Communication Research*, 5, 76–96.

Gorden, W. I., Tengler, C. D., & Infante, D. A. (1982). Women's clothing predispositions as predictors of dress at work, job satisfaction, and career advancement. *Southern Speech Communication Journal*, 47, 422–434.

Greenbaum, H. H., DeWine, S., Downs, C. W. (1987). Management and organizational communication measurement: A call for review and evaluation. *Management Communication Quarterly*, 1, 129–144.

Infante, D. A., & Gorden, W. I. (1981). Similarities and differences in the communicator styles of superiors and subordinates: Relations to subordinate satisfaction. *Communication Quarterly*, 30, 67–71.

McDowell, E. (1985, November). *Faculty members' perceptions of information adequacy and communication relationships in their world of work.* Paper presented at the annual meeting of the Speech Communication Association, Denver.

Murray, E. (1983). Channels to the top: An exploration of sex role and information source. *Communication Quarterly*, 31, 156-166.

Porter, T. (1979, May). *The ICA Communication Audit: 1979 norms. An instrument documentation for 17 audits using the survey (1974–1979).* Paper presented at the meeting International Communication Association, Philadelphia.

Shockley-Zalabak, P., & Morley, D. D. (1989). Adhering to organizational culture: What does it mean? Why does it matter? *Group and Organization Studies, 14*, 483–500

Spiker, B., & Daniels, T. (1981). Information adequacy and communication relationships: An empirical examination of 18 organizations. *Western Journal of Speech Communication, 45*, 342–354.

International Communication Association Audit*

A
Receiving Information from Others

Instructions: For each topic listed on the following pages, mark your responses on the answer sheet that best indicates: (1) the amount of information you are receiving on that topic and (2) the amount of information you need to receive on that topic in order to do your job.

[Editors' note: Two Likert-type scales appear to the right of each item. The first is headed, "This is the amount of information I receive now," the second, "This is the amount of information I need to receive." Each scale has a range of 1 to 5, including *very little* (1), *little* (2), *some* (3), *great* (4), and *very great* (5). The respondent circles a number from each scale for each item.]

Topic area
How well I am doing in my job
My job duties
Organizational policies
Pay and benefits
How technological changes affect my job
Mistakes and failures of my organization
How I am being judged
How my job-related problems are being handled
How organization decisions are made that affect my job
Promotion and advancement opportunities in my organization
Important new product, service or program developments in my organization
How my job relates to the total operation of my organization
Specific problems faced by management.

---

*Reprinted from an International Communication Association document. In the public domain.

B
Sending Information to Others

Instructions: For each topic listed on the following pages, mark your responses on the answer sheet that best indicates: (1) the amount of information you are sending on that topic and (2) the amount of information you need to send on that topic in order to do your job.

[Editors' note: Two Likert-type scales appear to the right of each item. The first is headed, "This is the amount of information I send now," the second, "This is the amount of information I need to send now." Each scale has a range of 1 to 5, including *very little* (1), *little* (2), *some* (3), *great* (4), and *very great* (5). The respondent circles a number from each scale for each item.]

<u>Topic area</u>
Reporting what I am doing in my job
Reporting what I think my job requires me to do
Reporting job-related problems
Complaining about my job and/or working conditions
Requesting information necessary to do my job
Evaluating the performance of my immediate supervisor
Asking for clearer work

C
Follow-Up on Information Sent

Instructions: Indicate the amount of action or follow-up that is and needs to be taken on information you send to the following:

[Editors' note: Two Likert-type scales appear to the right of each item. The first is headed, "This is the amount of follow-up now," the second, "This is the amount of follow-up needed." Each scale has a range of 1 to 5, including *very little* (1), *little* (2), *some* (3), *great* (4), and *very great* (5). The respondent circles a number from each scale for each item.]

<u>Topic area</u>
Subordinates
Co-workers
Immediate supervisor
Middle management
Top management

D
Sources of Information

Instructions: You not only receive various kinds of information, but can receive such information from various sources within the organization. For each source listed below, mark your response on the answer sheet that indicates: (1) the amount of information you are receiving from that source and (2) the amount of information you need to receive from that source in order to do your job.

[Editors' note: Two Likert-type scales appear to the right of each item. The first is headed, "This is the amount of information I receive now," the second, "This is the amount of information I need to receive." Each scale has a range of 1 to 5, including *very little* (1), *little* (2), *some* (3), *great* (4), and *very great* (5). The respondent circles a number from each scale for each item.]

Sources of information
Subordinates (if applicable)
Co-workers in my own unit or department in my organization
Individuals in other units, departments in my organization
Immediate supervisor
Department meetings
Middle management
Formal management presentations
Top management
The "grapevine"

E
Timeliness of Information
Received from Key Sources

Instructions: Indicate the extent to which information from the following sources is usually timely (you get information when you need it—not too early, not too late).

[Editors' note: A Likert-type scale appears to the right of each item. The scale has a range of 1 to 5, including *very little* (1), *little* (2), *some* (3), *great* (4), and *very great* (5). The respondent circles a number from the scale for each item.]

Sources of information
Subordinates (if applicable)

Coworkers
Immediate supervisor
Middle management
Top management
"Grapevine"

F
Organizational Communication Relationships

Instructions: A variety of communicative relationships exist in organizations such as your own. Employees exchange messages regularly with supervisors, subordinates, coworkers, etc. Considering your relationships with others in your organization, please mark your response on the answer sheet.

[Editors' note: A Likert-type scale appears to the right of each item. The scale has a range of 1 to 5, including *very little* (1), *little* (2), *some* (3), *great* (4), and *very great* (5). The respondent circles a number from the scale for each item.]

Relationship
I trust my coworkers
My coworkers get along with each other
My relationship with my coworkers is satisfying
I trust my immediate supervisor
My immediate supervisor is honest with me
My immediate supervisor listens to me
I am free to disagree with my immediate supervisor
I can tell my immediate supervisor when things are going wrong
My immediate supervisor praises me for a good job
My immediate supervisor is friendly with his/her subordinates
My immediate supervisor understands my job needs
My relationship with my immediate supervisor is satisfying
I trust top management
Top management is sincere in its efforts to communicate with employees
My relationship with top management is satisfying
My organization encourages differences of opinion
I have a say in decisions that affect my job
I influence operations in my unit or department
I have a part in accomplishing my organization's goals

G
Organizational Outcomes

Instructions: One of the most important outcomes of working in an organization is the satisfaction one gets or fails to receive through working there. Such satisfaction can relate to the job, one's immediate supervisor, or the organization as a whole. Please mark your response on the answer sheet to indicate the extent to which you are satisfied with:

[Editors' note: A Likert-type scale appears to the right of each item. The scale has a range of 1 to 5, including *very little* (1), *little* (2), *some* (3), *great* (4), and *very great* (5). The respondent circles a number from the scale for each item.]

Outcome
My job
My pay
My progress in my organization up to this point in time
My chances for getting ahead in my organization
My opportunity to "make a difference"—to contribute to the overall success of my organization
My organization's system for recognizing and rewarding outstanding performance
My organization's concern for its members welfare
My organization's overall communicative efforts
Working in my organization
My organization, as compared to other such
My organization's overall efficiency of operation
The overall quality of my organization's product or service
My organization's achievement of its goals and objectives

H
Channels of Information

Instructions: Listed below are a variety of channels through which messages are transmitted. Please indicate on the answer sheet (1) the amount of information you now receive through that channel, and (2) the amount you need to receive through that channel.

[Editors' note: Two Likert-type scales appear to the right of each item. The first is headed, "This is the amount of information I receive now," the second, "This is the amount of information I need to receive." Each scale has a range of 1 to 5, including *very little* (1), *little* (2), *some* (3), *great* (4), and *very great* (5). The respondent circles a number from each scale for each item.]

<u>Channels</u>
Face to face
Written memos, letters, and notices
Bulletin boards
Corporate newsletter
Plant newsletter
Procedural manual
Home mailings
Pay envelope stuffers
Communication committee minutes
Safety steering committee minutes
Shift briefings
Meeting with supervisor
Meeting with divisional management
Meeting with plant management
Departmental safety meetings

Interpersonal Attraction Scale

McCroskey and McCain (1974) conceptualized interpersonal attraction as a multidimensional construct. Prior research suggested that interpersonal attraction was characterized by three dimensions: (a) a liking or social dimension; (b) a task or respect dimension; and (c) a physical dimension. The authors concluded that perceptions of attraction were responsible for both increased communication and interpersonal influence.

McCroskey and McCain (1974) created the Interpersonal Attraction Scale (IAS) by first generating 30 items thought to measure the Social, Task, and Physical dimensions of attraction. Next, 215 undergraduate students completed the questionnaire with an acquaintance in mind. A series of factor analyses revealed a 15-item, three-factor solution accounting for 49% of the total variance. The three factors were: Social Attraction, Task Attraction, and Physical Attraction. The authors suggested that these subscales are related but are independent of one other.

The IAS was designed as a self-report measure. Respondents report their attraction toward another by using Likert scales ranging from *strongly disagree* (1) to *strongly agree* (7). The scale takes less than 10 minutes to complete.

RELIABILITY

McCroskey and McCain (1974) reported internal reliabilities for the 15-item scale as follows: Social Attraction, .84; Task Attraction, .81; and Physical Attraction, .86. Various researchers have reported similar results (Ayres, 1989; Brandt, 1979; Duran & Kelly, 1988; Wheeless, Frymier, & Thompson, 1992). Split-half reliability was reported as .90 for Social, .87 for Task, and .92 for Physical Attraction (McCroskey, Richmond, Daly, & Cox, 1975).

VALIDITY

The IAS has been used rather extensively across the communication discipline and to a lesser extent in related fields. Attraction has been positively

Profile by Elizabeth E. Graham.

associated with a host of communication behaviors and perceptions, providing ample evidence of construct validity. For example, some researchers reported a positive relationship between attraction and interpersonal competence (Brandt, 1979; Canary & Spitzberg, 1987; Duran & Kelly, 1988; Johnson, 1992), while others investigated the role of attraction in initial interactions (Clatterbuck, 1979; Sunnafrank, 1990).

Burgoon and associates studied the impact of nonverbal behavior on perceptions of attraction. Burgoon, Coker, and Coker (1986) reported that differential gaze behavior (constant, normal, and aversion) resulted in different levels of perceived attraction. Conversational involvement (Burgoon, Newton, Walther, & Baesler, 1989) and immediacy (Burgoon & Hale, 1988) were also linked to perceptions of attraction. Still others reported on the negative consequences of reticence and apprehension on perceptions of attraction (Ayres, 1989; Burgoon & Koper, 1984; Hawkins & Stewart, 1991; McCroskey et al., 1975; Richmond, 1978) and on the positive relationship between attraction and cognitive complexity (Powers, Jordan, Gurley, & Lindstrom, 1986).

Interpersonal attraction was investigated in a variety of contexts. For example, Rubin and McHugh (1987) noted that people can become socially attracted to TV characters. In the organizational context, Wheeless and Reichel (1990) reported that supervisor versatility, assertiveness, and responsiveness led to subordinates' perceptions of their task attractiveness. Also, Andersen and Kibler (1978) found evidence that physical and social attractiveness influences voter preferences.

COMMENTS

The IAS has received a generous amount of attention in the literature, yet some studies question the factor structure of the scale. For example, Hill and Courtright (1981) conducted a factor analysis and found that the IAS was unidimensional rather than multidimensional. Warfel (1984) also concluded that the items on the Attraction scale did not load as expected. Users of the IAS should factor-analyze the scale and employ the resulting subscales rather than rely on the factor structure originally provided by the authors.

Tardy (1988) summarized many of the strengths and weaknesses of attraction measures and concluded that the IAS "may be too general to actually detect differences among individuals who have known each other for a long period of time. In other words, items may have a ceiling over which increased attraction cannot be measured" (p. 272). For this reason, as well as to increase the reliability of the IAS, McCroskey and Richmond (1979) substantially modified the McCroskey and McCain (1974) measure. The new version of the scale is a 38-item instrument that employs a seven-interval response option.

Taking into account all the studies that have used the IAS, it is reasonable to conclude that this measure is reliable and valid. There is a great amount of support for the construct validity of this measure, yet there is not nearly as much evidence of concurrent or criterion-related validity. Future research should provide information concerning other forms of validity.

LOCATION

McCroskey, J. C., & McCain, T. A. (1974). The measurement of interpersonal attraction. *Speech Monographs, 41*, 261-266.

REFERENCES

Andersen, P. A., & Kibler, R. J. (1978). Candidate valence as a predictor of voter preference. *Human Communication Research, 5*, 4–14.

Ayres, J. (1989). The impact of communication apprehension and interaction structure on initial interactions. *Communication Monographs, 56*, 75–88.

Brandt, D. R. (1979). On linking social performance with social competence: Some relations between communication style and attributions of interpersonal attractiveness and effectiveness. *Human Communication Research, 5*, 223–237.

Burgoon, J. K., Coker, D. A., & Coker, R. A. (1986). Communicative effects of gaze behavior: A test of two contrasting explanations. *Human Communication Research, 12*, 495–524.

Burgoon, J. K., & Hale, J. L. (1988). Nonverbal expectancy violations: Model elaboration and application to immediacy behaviors. *Communication Monographs, 55*, 58–79.

Burgoon, J. K., & Koper, R. J. (1984). Nonverbal and relational communication associated with reticence. *Human Communication Research, 10*, 601–626.

Burgoon, J. K., Newton, D. A., Walther, J. B., & Baesler, E. J. (1989). Nonverbal expectancy violations and conversational involvement. *Journal of Nonverbal Behavior, 13*, 97–119.

Canary, D. J., & Spitzberg, B. H. (1987). Appropriateness and effectiveness perceptions of conflict strategies. *Human Communication Research, 14*, 93–118.

Clatterbuck, G. W. (1979). Attributional confidence and uncertainty in initial interaction. *Human Communication Research, 5*, 147–157.

Duran, R. L., & Kelly, L. (1988). The influence of communicative competence on perceived task, social, and physical attraction. *Communication Quarterly, 36*, 41–49.

Hawkins, K., & Stewart, R. A. (1991). Effects of communication apprehension on perceptions of leadership and intragroup attraction in small task-oriented groups. *Southern Communication Journal, 57*, 1–10.

Hill, S. E. K., & Courtright, J. A. (1981). Perceived empathy: Its relationship to selected interpersonal variables and student's interpersonal laboratory performance. *Western Journal of Speech Communication, 45*, 213–226.

Johnson, G. M. (1992). Subordinate perceptions of superior's communication competence and task attraction related to superior's use of compliance-gaining tactics. *Western Journal of Communication*, *56*, 54–67.

McCroskey, J. C., & Richmond, V. P. (1979, May). *The reliability and validity of scales for the measurement of interpersonal attraction and homophily*. Paper presented at the meeting of the Eastern Communication Association, Philadelphia.

McCroskey, J. C., Richmond, V. P., Daly, J. A., & Cox, B. G. (1975). The effects of communication apprehension on interpersonal attraction. *Human Communication Research*, *2*, 51–65.

Powers, W. G., Jordan, W. J., Gurley, K., & Lindstrom, E. (1986). Attributions toward cognitively complex sources based upon message samples. *Communication Research Reports*, *3*, 110–114.

Richmond, V. P. (1978). The relationship between trait and state communication apprehension and interpersonal perceptions during acquaintance stages. *Human Communication Research*, *4*, 338–349.

Rubin, R. B., & McHugh, M. P. (1987). Development of parasocial interaction relationships. *Journal of Broadcasting and Electronic Media*, *31*, 279–292.

Sunnafrank, M. (1990). Predicted outcome value and uncertainty reduction theories: A test of competing perspectives. *Human Communication Research*, *17*, 76–103.

Tardy, C. H. (1988). Interpersonal evaluations: Measuring attraction and trust. In C. H. Tardy (Ed.), *A handbook for the study of human communication: Methods and instruments for observing, measuring, and assessing communication processes* (pp. 269–283). Norwood, NJ: Ablex.

Warfel, K. A. (1984). Gender schemas and perceptions of speech style. *Communication Monographs*, *51*, 253–267.

Wheeless, L. R., Frymier, A. B., & Thompson, C. A. (1992). A comparison of verbal output and receptivity in relation to attraction and communication satisfaction in interpersonal relationships. *Communication Quarterly*, *40*, 102–115.

Wheeless, L. R., & Reichel, L. S. (1990). A reinforcement model of the relationships of supervisors' general communication styles and conflict management styles to task attraction. *Communication Quarterly*, *38*, 372–387.

Interpersonal Attraction Scale*

Instructions: Please indicate the degree to which you agree or disagree with the following statements as they apply to _____. Use the following scale and write one number before each statement to indicate your feelings.

7 = Strongly agree
6 = Moderately agree
5 = Slightly agree
4 = Undecided
3 = Slightly disagree
2 = Moderately disagree
1 = Strongly disagree

Social Attraction
1. I think he (she) could be a friend of mine.
2. It would be difficult to meet and talk with him (her).
3. He (she) just wouldn't fit into my circle of friends.
4. We could never establish a personal friendship with each other.
5. I would like to have a friendly chat with him (her).

Physical Attraction
6. I think he (she) is quite handsome (pretty).
7. He (she) is very sexy looking.
8. I find him (her) very attractive physically.
9. I don't like the way he (she) looks.
10. He (she) is somewhat ugly.

Task Attraction
11. He (she) is a typical goof-off when assigned a job to do.
12. I have confidence in his (her) ability to get the job done.
13. If I wanted to get things done, I could probably depend on him (her).
14. I couldn't get anything accomplished with him (her).
15. He (she) would be a poor problem solver.

Note. Items 2, 3, 4, 9, 10, 11, 14, and 15 are reverse-coded. Items should be randomly arranged and dimension labels removed before administration.

Interpersonal Communication Motives Scale

In an effort to understand why people communicate with one another, R. Rubin, Perse, and Barbato (1988) developed the Interpersonal Communication Motives (ICM) scale. These researchers drew on a rich tradition of interpersonal functional approaches as well as the mass media uses and gratifications perspective to ascertain the reasons or motives individuals have for communicating with others.

To begin scale development, 85 college students completed a 1-day diary detailing their communication behaviors, indicating where, when, and to whom they communicated; what was talked about; which medium was used; and the reason for entering into the conversation (R. Rubin et al., 1988). Trained coders analyzed the diaries, and the communication events were classified into one of 18 functional categories that were derived from the literature. Next, five statements from each of the 18 categories were cast in a 90-item scale and 32 students were asked to indicate the extent to which the 90 items represented reasons for why they talk to other people. In focus groups, they assessed the items for difficulty level and clarity and provided additional motives for communicating. The resulting 60-item scale consisted of 4 items representing 15 interpersonal communication functions: caring, relaxation, companionship, habit, passing time, entertainment, social interaction, arousal, information, escape, self-learning, convenience, social norms, control, and emotional expression.

Questionnaires were then administered to 504 respondents, representing a wide array of ages and educational backgrounds, from the Midwest (R. Rubin et al., 1988). A series of factor analyses revealed a 28-item, six-factor instrument that accounted for 62% of the total variance. The six factors were Pleasure, Affection, Inclusion, Escape, Relaxation, and Control. Pleasure reflects an entertainment, exciting, fun-loving motive for communicating. Affection refers to communicating for the purpose of social ritual and showing appreciation and concern for others. Inclusion is a need to be with and share feelings with others. Escape taps a need to escape other activities through communicating. Relaxation reflects the need to commu-

Profile by Elizabeth E. Graham.

211

nicate for the purpose of resting and unwinding. Control represents communicating for instrumental compliance-gaining reasons.

Participants assess how much the ICM scale reasons are like their own motives for engaging in interpersonal communication by responding to 28 items using a Likert-type scale that ranges from *not at all* (1) to *exactly* (5). Although the 28-item measure is preferable, an 18-item scale consisting of the first three items in each factor yields similar results. The 28-item measure takes less than 10 minutes to complete.

RELIABILITY

Cronbach alphas for the 28-item ICM were as follows: Pleasure, .89; Affection, .85; Inclusion, .84; Escape, .77; Relaxation, .81; and Control, .75 (R. Rubin et al., 1988). The 18-item ICM produced reliabilities ranging from .66 to .88 (Graham, Barbato, & Perse, 1993; A. Rubin & Rubin, 1989). Hosman (1991) and Downs and Javidi (1990) reported similar reliabilities, which indicates that the abbreviated ICM measure can be used with confidence.

VALIDITY

R. Rubin et al. (1988) provided evidence of construct validity by examining variables that should be theoretically related to interpersonal communication motives: communication apprehension, communication satisfaction, gender, age, and education. Correlations indicated that younger people communicate for pleasure, inclusion, control, and escape and older people communicate to show affection. Women were more inclined to communicate for pleasure, affection, inclusion, and relaxation than were men. Education was positively related to control and negatively related to the inclusion motive. Furthermore, regression analysis revealed that gender, communication apprehension, pleasure, affection, relaxation, and escape motives contributed significantly to higher levels of general communication satisfaction.

Since the introduction of the ICM, others have provided additional support for the ICM factor structure (Downs & Javidi, 1990; Hosman, 1991; Javidi, Long, Long, & Javidi, 1990). Motives for communicating have been linked to gender (Barbato & Perse, 1992; Javidi et al., 1990; R. Rubin et al., 1988), age (Barbato & Perse, 1992; Downs & Javidi, 1990; Javidi et al., 1990; R. Rubin et al., 1988), communication apprehension (R. Rubin et al., 1988), level of loneliness (Downs & Javidi, 1990; Hosman, 1991), contextual age (Barbato & Perse, 1992; R. Rubin & Rubin, 1992), locus of control (R. Rubin & Rubin, 1992), general communication satisfaction (R. Rubin et al., 1988), and who people speak to and what they talk about (Graham et al., 1993).

Additional research by Hosman (1991) indicated that the pleasure and affection motives were negatively correlated with the need for seclusion and positively correlated with need for intimacy. Conversational sensitivity was positively related to pleasure, affection, and relaxation motives. Furthermore, loneliness was found to be inversely related to the pleasure and affection motives. However, these results conflict with the results reported by Downs and Javidi (1990). Likewise, A. Rubin and Rubin (1989) highlighted the versatility of the ICM. Their results suggested that people have motives for engaging in personal communication similar to those for using their video-cassette recorders. For example, people are motivated to control others in much the same way that they are motivated to control their time by video-taping and storing tapes for later use. Indeed, "communication needs appear to transcend communication channels or contexts" (A. Rubin & Rubin, 1989, p. 107).

Three studies provided additional evidence of construct validity. Hosman (1991) tested the Interpersonal Motive factors with factor analysis; pleasure and affection items loaded on one factor rather than on two separate factors. Downs and Javidi (1990), however, found the six-motive factor structure of the ICM. In addition, R. Rubin, Fernandez-Collado, and Hernandez-Sampieri (1992) reported that five of the six factors were confirmed in a sample of Mexican subjects.

COMMENTS

Although the ICM scale is relatively new, it does offer promise as a means of assessing why people engage in conversations with others. The reliability and validity information amassed so far leads to the conclusion that the ICM is a stable measure that discriminates among other variables in expected ways.

LOCATION

Rubin, R. B., Perse, E. M., & Barbato, C. A. (1988). Conceptualization and measurement of interpersonal communication motives. *Human Communication Research, 14*, 602–628.

REFERENCES

Barbato, C. A., & Perse, E. M. (1992). Interpersonal communication motives and the life position of elders. *Communication Research, 19,* 516–531.

Downs, V. C., & Javidi, M. (1990). Linking communication motives to loneliness in the lives of older adults: An empirical test of interpersonal needs and gratifications. *Journal of Applied Communication Research, 18,* 32–48.

Graham, E. E., Barbato, C. A., & Perse, E. M. (1993). The interpersonal communication motives model. *Communication Quarterly, 41,* 172–186.

Hosman, L. A. (1991). The relationships among need for privacy, loneliness, conversational sensitivity, and interpersonal communication motives. *Communication Reports, 4,* 73–80.

Javidi, M., Long, L. W., Long, P. N., & Javidi, A. (1990, November). *An examination of interpersonal communication motives across age groups.* Paper presented at the annual meeting of the Speech Communication Association, Chicago.

Rubin, A. M., & Rubin, R. B. (1989). Social and psychological antecedents of VCR use. In M. R. Levy (Ed.), *The VCR age: Home video and mass communication* (pp. 92–111). Newbury Park, CA: Sage.

Rubin, R. B., Fernandez-Collado, C., & Hernandez-Sampieri, R. (1992). A cross-cultural examination of interpersonal communication motives in Mexico and the United States. *International Journal of Intercultural Relations, 16,* 145–157.

Rubin, R. B., & Rubin, A. M. (1992). Antecedents of interpersonal communication motivation. *Communication Quarterly, 40,* 305–317.

Interpersonal Communication Motives*

Instructions: Here are several reasons people give for why they talk to other people. For each statement, please circle the number that best expresses your own reasons for talking to others.

If the reason is EXACTLY like your own reason, circle a 5.
If the reason is A LOT like your own reason, circle a 4.
If the reason is SOMEWHAT like your own reason, circle a 3.
If the reason is NOT MUCH like your own reason, circle a 2.
If the reason is NOT AT ALL like your own reason, circle a 1.

[Editors' note: An example of the response categories is presented with the first item.]

---

*Copyright 1988 by Sage Publications, Inc. Reprinted by permission.

"I talk to people . . ."

Pleasure

	Exactly	A lot	Somewhat	Not much	Not at all
	5	4	3	2	1

1. Because it's fun
2. Because it's exciting
3. To have a good time
4. Because it's thrilling
5. Because it's stimulating
6. Because it's entertaining
7. Because I enjoy it
8. Because it peps me up

Affection

9. To help others
10. To let others know I care about their feelings
11. To thank them
12. To show others encouragement
13. Because I'm concerned about them

Inclusion

14. Because I need someone to talk to or be with
15. Because I just need to talk about my problems sometimes
16. Because it makes me feel less lonely
17. Because it's reassuring to know someone is there

Escape

18. To put off something I should be doing
19. To get away from what I am doing
20. Because I have nothing better to do
21. To get away from pressures and responsibilities

Relaxation

22. Because it relaxes me
23. Because it allows me to unwind

24. Because it's a pleasant
    rest
25. Because it makes me
    feel less tense

Control
26. Because I want some-
    one to do something
    for me
27. To tell others what
    to do
28. To get something I
    don't have

Note. The 18-item form comprises the first three items in each subscale; each subscale score may be computed by summing those three items. If the 28-item scale is used, however, it is necessary to compute mean scores for each subscale to standardize the measures.

Items are grouped by category. When administered, they should be arranged randomly.

Interpersonal Communication Satisfaction Inventory

Hecht (1978b) conceptualized communication satisfaction as the positive reinforcement provided by a communication event that fulfills positive expectations, and he employed a behavioral perspective to view satisfaction as a communication outcome. Hecht's discriminitive fulfillment approach says that past experiences, given one's own behavior, influence expectations of another's behavior. The fulfillment of these expectations through interaction results in communication satisfaction (Hecht, 1978a).

The Interpersonal Communication Satisfaction Inventory (Com-Sat), a unidimensional self-report instrument, was developed in a series of stages. First, items were generated from questionnaires and interviews that assessed conversational satisfaction–dissatisfaction in actual and recalled conversations with a friend, acquaintance, or stranger (Hecht, 1978a). Second, through item analysis, the number of items was reduced to 93 and pretested. Third, 60 items were reduced to 19, which were the factor-analyzed. Prior to rotation, all items had their highest loading on the first factor. After rotation, three factors emerged, but no clear factor structure was evident. Furthermore, the correlations among the factors were especially high (+.30), casting doubt on the independence of the factors. Consequently, Hecht (1978a) suggested that "attention should be focused on the entire inventory and not limited to those items loading on the factors" (p. 260). Thus, the inventory is conceived as a general measure of communication satisfaction that is useful for assessing satisfaction after actual as well as recalled conversations with friends, acquaintances, and strangers.

Participants assess their own satisfaction by responding to the 19 items using Likert scales that range from *strongly agree* (7) to *strongly disagree* (1); responses to these items are summed. Hecht (1978a) also provided a more condensed version of the satisfaction inventory (16 items). Each inventory requires about 5 minutes to complete. Some researchers modified the original inventory so that satisfaction could be assessed between superiors and subordinates (Lamude, Daniels, & Graham, 1988), police officers and citizens (Glauser & Tullar, 1985), and physicians and patients (Buller & Buller,

Profile by Elizabeth E. Graham.

217

1987; Burgoon, Birk, & Hall, 1991). Also, researchers modified the Com-Sat Inventory to assess satisfaction with communication in general (Rubin, Perse, & Barbato, 1988; Rubin & Rubin, 1989). Hecht and Ribeau (1984) presented versions for use with white American, African American, and Mexican American populations. Although Hecht originally intended the Com-Sat Inventory to be a self-report measure, other-report formats have also been successfully used (Zakahi, 1985).

RELIABILITY

Hecht (1978a) reported split-half reliability coefficients for the 19-item inventory of .97 for the actual conversation treatment group, .90 for the re-called conversation, .93 when satisfaction was assessed for friends, .97 for acquaintances, and .96 for strangers. Similar reliabilities were reported for the 16-item instrument (Wheeless, Frymier, & Thompson, 1992).

Various researchers employed the Com-Sat Inventory and reported coefficient alphas ranging from .72 to .93 (Buerkel-Rothfuss & Bell, 1987; Daly, Bell, Glenn, & Lawrence, 1985; Duran & Zakahi, 1987; Hecht & Marston, 1987; Newton & Burgoon, 1990; VanLear, 1991). Even when the inventory was modified, sufficient reliability was found.

VALIDITY

Hecht (1978b) provided evidence of content and convergent validity for the Com-Sat Inventory. First, 253 items were derived from critical-incident techniques, communication experts, and communication satisfaction litera-ture. The representativeness of the data collection techniques employed and the flexibility of the inventory (the inventory may be used in actual and recalled conversations with friends, acquaintances, and strangers) contrib-ute to the content validity of the Com-Sat Inventory. Convergent validity was established by correlating Com-Sat with the Faces Scale (Kunin, 1955). The correlations were high and statistically significant, providing evidence of concurrent validity.

The Com-Sat Inventory has been used rather extensively across the communication discipline and to a lesser extent in related fields such as health and psychology. Communication satisfaction has been positively associated with a host of communication behaviors and perceptions such as interpersonal competence (Onyekwere, Rubin, & Infante, 1991; Spitzberg, 1991), relationship intimacy and duration (Hecht, 1984b), integrative con-flict strategies (Canary & Cupach, 1988), affinity seeking–seeking com-petence (Buerkel-Rothfuss & Bell, 1987), use of supportive tactics during disagreements (Newton & Burgoon, 1990), social influence (Hecht, 1984a), interethnic communication effectiveness (Hecht, Larkey, & Johnson, 1992), and an orientation and concern for others (Duran & Zakahi, 1987; Spitzberg & Hecht, 1984).

Communication satisfaction has been investigated in many contexts. For example, Prisbell (1985), interested in classroom communication, concluded that instructors who help students feel good about themselves and provide a safe and certain environment contribute to the communication satisfaction of their students. Furthermore, communication satisfaction is positively related to classroom learning and course and instructor evaluations. The extensive and varied use of the Com-Sat Inventory suggests that satisfaction is a salient concern in the communication discipline.

COMMENTS

Although the Com-Sat Inventory is widely used, only one article (Hecht, 1984b) has purposefully reviewed or investigated the validity of the instrument since the measure was first introduced in 1978. This is not to suggest that the measure lacks validity; one need only look at the many correlational studies that employed the measure to realize the presence of many forms of validity. However, periodic investigation of important measures is necessary in view of changes in society as well as advances in statistical procedures. Regardless, because there are still few other criterion or outcome variables identified in the literature, the Com-Sat Inventory will likely be chosen for research in the future.

LOCATION

Hecht, M. L. (1978a). The conceptualization and measurement of interpersonal communication satisfaction. *Human Communication Research, 4,* 253–264.

REFERENCES

Buerkel-Rothfuss, N. L., & Bell, R. A. (1987). Validity of the affinity-seeking instrument. *Communication Research Reports, 4,* 24–30.

Buller, M. K., & Buller, D. B. (1987). Physicians' communication style and patient satisfaction. *Journal of Health and Social Behavior, 28,* 375–388.

Burgoon, M., Birk, T. S., & Hall, J. R. (1991). Compliance and satisfaction with physician-patient communication: An expectancy theory interpretation of gender differences. *Human Communication Research, 18,* 177–208.

Canary, D. J., & Cupach, W. R. (1988). Relational and episodic characteristics associated with conflict tactics. *Journal of Social and Personal Relationships, 5*, 305–325.

Daly, J. A., Bell, R. A., Glenn, P. J., & Lawrence, S. (1985). Conceptualizing conversational complexity. *Human Communication Research, 12*, 30–53.

Duran, R. L., & Zakahi, W. R. (1987). Communication performance and communication satisfaction: What do we teach our students? *Communication Education, 36*, 13–22.

Glauser, M. J., & Tullar, W. L. (1985). Citizen satisfaction with police officer/citizen interaction: Implications for the changing role of police organizations. *Journal of Applied Psychology, 70*, 514–527.

Hecht, M. L. (1978b). Measures of communication satisfaction. *Human Communication Research, 4*, 350–368.

Hecht, M. L. (1984a). Persuasive efficacy: A study of the relationship among type and degree of change, message strategies and satisfying communication. *Western Journal of Speech Communication, 48*, 373–389.

Hecht, M. L. (1984b). Satisfying communication and relational labels: Intimacy and length of relationship as perceptual frames of naturalistic conversations. *Western Journal of Speech Communication, 48*, 201–216.

Hecht, M. L., Larkey, L. K., & Johnson, J. N. (1992). African American and European American perceptions of problematic issues in interethnic communication effectiveness. *Human Communication Research, 19*, 209–236.

Hecht, M. L., & Marston, P. J. (1987). Communication satisfaction and the temporal development of conversations. *Communication Research Reports, 4*, 60–65.

Hecht, M. L., & Ribeau, S. (1984). Ethnic communication: A comparative analysis of satisfying communication. *International Journal of Intercultural Relations, 8*, 135–151.

Kunin, T. (1955). The construction of a new type of attitude measure. *Personnel Psychology, 8*, 65–77.

Lamude, K. G., Daniels, T. D., & Graham, E. E. (1988). The paradoxical influence of sex on communication rules coorientation and communication satisfaction in superior-subordinate relationships. *Western Journal of Speech Communication, 52*, 122–134.

Newton, D. A., & Burgoon, J. K. (1990). The use and consequences of verbal influence strategies during interpersonal disagreements. *Human Communication Research, 16*, 477–518.

Onyekwere, E. O., Rubin, R. B., & Infante, D. A. (1991). Interpersonal perception and communication satisfaction as a function of argumentativeness and ego-involvement. *Communication Quarterly, 39*, 35–47.

Prisbell, M. (1985). Interpersonal perception variables and communication satisfaction in the classroom. *Communication Research Reports, 2*, 90–96.

Rubin, R. B., Perse, E. M., & Barbato, C. A. (1988). Conceptualization and measurement of interpersonal communication motives. *Human Communication Research, 14*, 602–628.

Rubin, R. B., & Rubin, A. M. (1989). Communication apprehension and satisfaction in interpersonal relationships. *Communication Research Reports, 6*, 13–20.

Spitzberg, B. H. (1991). An examination of trait measures of interpersonal competence. *Communication Reports, 4,* 22–29.

Spitzberg, B. H., & Hecht, M. L. (1984). A component model of relational competence. *Human Communication Research, 10,* 575–599.

VanLear, C. A. (1991). Testing a cyclical model of communicative openness in relationship development: Two longitudinal studies. *Communication Monographs, 58,* 337–361.

Wheeless, L. R., Frymier, A. B., & Thompson, C. A. (1992). A comparison of verbal output and receptivity in relation to attraction and communication satisfaction in interpersonal relationships. *Communication Quarterly, 40,* 102–115.

Zakahi, W. R. (1985). The relationship of assertiveness to communicative competence and communication satisfaction: A dyadic assessment. *Communication Research Reports, 2,* 36–40.

Interpersonal Communication Satisfaction Inventory*

(For use with actual conversations)

Instructions: The purpose of this questionnaire is to investigate your reactions to the conversation you just had. Please indicate the degree to which you agree or disagree that each statement describes this conversation. The 4 or middle position on the scale represents "undecided" or "neutral," then moving out from the center, "slight" agreement or disagreement, then "moderate," then "strong" agreement or disagreement. For example, if you strongly agree with the following statement you would circle 1.

The other person moved around a lot.

Agree : 1 : 2 : 3 : 4 : 5 : 6 : 7 : Disagree

1. The other person let me know that I was communicating effectively.
2. Nothing was accomplished.
3. I would like to have another conversation like this one.
4. The other person genuinely wanted to get to know me.
5. I was very *dis*satisfied with the conversation.
6. I had something else to do.
7. I felt that during the conversation I was able to present myself as I wanted the other person to view me.
8. The other person showed me that he/she understood what I said.
9. I was very satisfied with the conversation.
10. The other person expressed a lot of interest in what I had to say.

11. I did *not* enjoy the conversation.
12. The other person did *not* provide support for what he/she was saying.
13. I felt I could talk about anything with the other person.
14. We each got to say what we wanted.
15. I felt that we could laugh easily together.
16. The conversation flowed smoothly.
17. The other person changed the topic when his/her feelings were brought into the conversation.
18. The other person frequently said things which added little to the conversation.
19. We talked about something I was *not* interested in.

Note. Items 6, 8, and 17 are not included in the 16-item version.

For Items 1, 3, 4, 7, 8, 9, 10, 13, 14, 15, and 16: *strongly agree* = 7; *moderately agree* = 6; *slightly agree* = 5; *neutral* = 4; *slightly disagree* = 3; *moderately disagree* = 2; *strongly disagree* = 1.

For Items 2, 5, 6, 11, 12, 17, 18, and 19: *strongly agree* = 1; *moderately agree* = 2; *slightly agree* = 3; *neutral* = 4; *slightly disagree* = 5; *moderately disagree* = 6; *strongly disagree* = 7.

Interpersonal Solidarity Scale

Interpersonal solidarity is a feeling of closeness between people that develops as a result of shared sentiments, similarities, and intimate behaviors (Wheeless, 1976). Conceptually, people with strong solidarity feelings should also trust, like, and self-disclose to one another.

The first version of the Interpersonal Solidarity Scale (ISS) consisted of 10 items, 9 of which formed a unidimensional scale with high internal consistency (Wheeless, 1976). Closeness items were added to improve the scale's content validity and the resulting 20-item Likert-type scale was factor-analyzed (Wheeless, 1978). The scale appeared to be unidimensional and reliable. Respondents use 7-point Likert-type scales ranging from *strongly agree* to *strongly disagree* and take less than 3 minutes to complete the 20 items. The scale has been adapted to measure group solidarity (Wheeless, Wheeless, & Dickson-Markman, 1978) and teacher solidarity (Andriate, 1982; Sorensen, 1989).

RELIABILITY

Reliability information is sparse; however, the scale appears internally consistent. Wheeless reported split-half reliabilities of .96 (Wheeless, 1978) and .94 (Wheeless, Wheeless, & Baus, 1984). And Bell and Healey (1992) reported an alpha of .90 for a 19-item scale.

VALIDITY

There is sufficient evidence of concurrent and criterion-related validity. Wheeless (1978) predicted and found a strong relationship between self-disclosure, individualized trust, and interpersonal solidarity. Solidarity was higher when people were evaluating close, rather than distant, relationships. He suggested that trustworthiness and self-disclosure might be components of interpersonal solidarity.

Downs (1988) and Eggert and Parks (1987) used the early edition of

Profile by Rebecca B. Rubin.

the scale and found predicted relationships between solidarity and (a) self-disclosure in grandparents and grandchildren and (b) attraction to and expressed support from a dating partner's network. Solidarity also differed among beginning, developed, and terminating stages of relationships in an inverted U-shape manner (Wheeless et al., 1984). Bell and Healey (1992) found solidarity correlated with idioms used by friends.

COMMENTS

Interpersonal solidarity is becoming increasingly more important in interpersonal relationship research, and this scale will help provide an index of how close relationships are. Research using this instrument has been scant, but the results are consistent that interpersonal solidarity as measured here is correlated with related constructs in the expected direction. Future studies should provide additional evidence of internal consistency.

LOCATION

Wheeless, L. R. (1978). A follow-up study of the relationships among trust, disclosure, and interpersonal solidarity. *Human Communication Research*, 4, 143–157.

REFERENCES

Andriate, G. S. (1982). Teacher communication and student learning: The effects of perceived solidarity with instructor and student anxiety proneness. *Communication Yearbook*, 6, 792–810.

Bell, R. A., & Healey, J. G. (1992). Idiomatic communication and interpersonal solidarity in friends' relational cultures. *Human Communication Research*, 18, 307–335.

Downs, V. C. (1988). Grandparents and grandchildren: The relationship between self-disclosure and solidarity in an intergenerational relationship. *Communication Research Reports*, 5, 173–179.

Eggert, L. L., & Parks, M. R. (1987). Communication network involvement in adolescents' friendships and romantic relationships. *Communication Yearbook*, 10, 283–322.

Sorensen, G. (1989). The relationships among teachers' self-disclosure statements, students' perceptions, and affective learning. *Communication Education*, 38, 259–276.

Wheeless, L. R. (1976). Self-disclosure and interpersonal solidarity: Measurement, validation, and relationships. *Human Communication Research*, 3, 47–61.

Wheeless, L. R., Wheeless, V. E., & Baus, R. (1984). Sexual communication satisfaction, communication satisfaction, and solidarity in the developmental stages of intimate relationships. *Western Journal of Speech Communication, 48,* 217–230.

Wheeless, L. R., Wheeless, V. E., & Dickson-Markman, F. (1978). Research note: The relations among social and task perceptions in small groups. *Small Group Behavior, 13,* 373–384.

Interpersonal Solidarity Scale*

Instructions: Please mark these scales to indicate how you relate to _____. Please mark the following statements to indicate whether you: (7) strongly agree; (6) agree; (5) moderately agree; (4) are undecided; (3) moderately disagree; (2) disagree; or (1) strongly disagree. Record the number of your response in the space provided beside each statement.

1. We are very close to each other.
2. This person has a great deal of influence over my behavior.
3. I trust this person completely.
4. We feel very differently about most things.
5. I willingly disclose a great deal of positive and negative things about myself, honestly, and fully (in depth) to this person.
6. We do *not* really understand each other.
7. This person willingly discloses a great deal of positive and negative things about him/herself, honestly and fully (in depth) to me.
8. I distrust this person.
9. I like this person much more than most people I know.
10. I seldom interact/communicate with this person.
11. I love this person.
12. I understand this person and who s/he really is.
13. I dislike this person.
14. I interact/communicate with this person much more than with most people I know.
15. We are not very close at all.
16. We share a lot in common.
17. We do a lot of helpful things for each other.
18. I have little in common with this person.
19. I feel very close to this person.
20. We share some private way(s) of communicating with each other.

Note. Items 4, 6, 8, 10, 13, 15, and 18 are reverse-coded before items are summed.

Mean World Index

The Mean World Index (MWI) comes from the media cultivation literature that assumes that enculturation is the primary function of TV in society. Two principal assumptions form the basis of cultivation research: (a) TV messages are uniform (i.e., TV presents a common symbolic, cultural portrait so that differences between information and entertainment content are irrelevant) and (b) viewers are nonselective, habitual users of TV (Gerbner & Gross, 1976).

Cultivation research uses two methods of analysis. First, a message-system analysis examines the patterns of TV content. It seeks to ascertain "television answers" that show how TV presents content such as the depiction of violence and the portrayal of gender and occupational roles. Second, cultivation analysis considers the social reality beliefs of people. It is assumed that heavy viewers of TV form their beliefs from watching the medium, and that the beliefs and outlooks of heavy and light TV viewers differ.

Gerbner and colleagues (Gerbner et al., 1977; Gerbner, Gross, Jackson-Beeck, Jeffries-Fox, & Signorielli, 1978) used the MWI, representing perceptions of mistrust and alienation. The MWI considers whether people can be trusted, are fair, and are altruistic. It comes from the National Opinion Research Center's General Social Surveys, which extracted the items from the five-item Faith-in-People Scale (Rosenberg, 1957). As compared with light viewers, Gerbner and associates have reported that heavy viewers feel that people cannot be trusted and take advantage of others (Gerbner et al., 1977, 1978). The three questions are usually asked by interviewers or can be self-administered and take less than 2 minutes to complete.

RELIABILITY

Gerbner and associates (e.g., Gerbner & Gross, 1976; Gerbner et al., 1977; Gerbner et al., 1978) did not report the reliability of the MWI. Rosenberg (1957) reported a Guttman reproducibility coefficient of .92 for his five-item Faith-in-People Scale, and a .90 Guttman coefficient for a four-item version, which includes the three MWI items. Gerbner, Gross, Morgan, and

Profile by Alan M. Rubin.

226

Signorielli (1980) reported an alpha of .68 for the three-item MWI, which they called the Interpersonal Mistrust Scale. Morgan (1986) found a .66 alpha for the MWI. Hawkins and Pingree (1981) found that six items (i.e., three positively and three negatively worded ones) divided into Positive ("nice") and Negative ("mean") factors for Australian children. Therefore, they used only the three MWI items (mean intercorrelation = .22). Pingree (1983) observed a single factor and an average .20 intercorrelation among the six mean-world (i.e., interpersonal mistrust) items. Rubin, Perse, and Taylor (1988) reported a .91 Cronbach alpha for a nine-item Faith-in-Others Scale that included positively phrased variants of the three faith-in-people/mean-world items.

VALIDITY

Rosenberg (1957) reported content validity (via the use of expert judges) for his Faith-in-People Scale along with extensive development of its five items. The remaining evidence for criterion-related and concurrent validity is mixed. Gerbner et al. (1980) reported a correlation of .12 between overall TV viewing and the MWI, which dropped to .04 after controlling for eight demographic and individual characteristics. Using a six-item version of the scale, Pingree (1983) found a .04 correlation between total TV viewing and the MWI. When applying items from the Anomie Scale (Srole, 1956), Gerbner et al. (1978) found that heavy viewers are more likely than light viewers to feel that society's outlook and condition are gloomy (gammas ranged from .18 to .22), although relationships were not significant for all gender and education controls. Wober (1978) used one mean-world and one social-perceptions item to construct a security scale and found no differences between heavy and light viewers in Britain.

COMMENTS

Some have questioned the theoretical assumptions of cultivation research and the reliability and validity of measurement. For example, investigators differ about definitions of heavy and light TV viewers (e.g., Gerbner et al., 1978; Gerbner et al., 1980). Significant relationships (e.g., correlation and gamma) are usually small in magnitude, although often consistent. Some have argued that relationships are further reduced or erased when various demographic and individual controls are introduced (e.g., Hirsch, 1980; Hughes, 1980). Refer to the Cultivation Index profile for further cultivation explanation and comments.

LOCATION

Gerbner, G., Gross, L., Eleey, M. F., Jackson-Beeck, M., Jeffries-Fox, S., & Signorielli, N. (1977). TV violence profile no. 8: The highlights. *Journal of Communication, 27*(2), 171–180.

Rosenberg, M. (1957). *Occupations and values.* Glencoe, IL: Free Press.

REFERENCES

Gerbner, G., & Gross, L. (1976). Living with television: The violence profile. *Journal of Communication, 26*(2), 173–199.

Gerbner, G., Gross, L., Jackson-Beeck, M., Jeffries-Fox, S., & Signorielli, N. (1978). Cultural indicators: Violence profile no. 9. *Journal of Communication, 28*(3), 176–207.

Gerbner, G., Gross, L., Morgan, M., & Signorielli, N. (1980). The "mainstreaming" of America: Violence profile no. 11. *Journal of Communication, 30*(3) 10–29.

Hawkins, R. P., & Pingree, S. (1981). Uniform messages and habitual viewing: Unnecessary assumptions in social reality effects. *Human Communication Research, 7*, 291–301.

Hirsch, P. M. (1980). The "scary world" of the nonviewer and other anomalies: A reanalysis of Gerbner et al.'s findings on cultivation analysis, part I. *Communication Research, 7*, 403–456.

Hughes, M. (1980). The fruits of cultivation analysis: A reexamination of some effects of television watching. *Public Opinion Quarterlv, 44*, 287–302.

Morgan, M. (1986). Television and the erosion of regional diversity. *Journal of Broadcasting and Electronic Media, 30*, 123–139.

Pingree, S. (1983). Children's cognitive processes in constructing social reality. *Journalism Quarterly, 60*, 415–422.

Rubin, A. M., Perse, E. M., & Taylor, D. S. (1988). A methodological examination of cultivation. *Communication Research, 15*, 107–134.

Srole, L. (1956). Social integration and certain corollaries: An exploratory study. *American Sociological Review, 21*, 709–716.

Wober, J. M. (1978). Televised violence and paranoid perceptions: The view from Great Britain. *Public Opinion Quarterly, 42*, 315–321.

Mean World Index*

Instructions: Instructions were not provided, but, when self-administered, respondents are asked to read each statement and to select one of the two alternatives presented in each item.

1. Do you think that most people would try to take advantage of you if they get a chance or would try to be fair?
2. Generally speaking, would you say that most people can be trusted or that you can't be too careful in dealing with people?
3. Would you say that most of the time people try to be helpful, or that they are mostly just looking out for themselves?

Note. "Try to take advantage," "can't be too careful," and "out for themselves" are the TV answers for the respective questions.

Mentoring and
Communication Support Scale

Mentoring is a communication support system designed to enhance both the individual's and the organization's success. Traditionally, this support was given by an older, more experienced organizational member to a less experienced protege to facilitate greater career success for the novice. Mentoring is now a popular organizational strategy to make certain that women and minorities have access to career development. Shapiro, Haseltine, and Rowe (1978) advanced the theory that mentoring behaviors were aspects of patronage ranging from mentor to peer–pal. Hill, Bahniuk, Dobos, and Rouner (1989) developed this instrument as a means of assessing the full range of mentoring behaviors.

The Mentoring and Communication Support Scale has undergone revisions as it has been used with different populations. Currently it has 15 items that are responded to using a Likert scale ranging from *strongly agree* (5) to *strongly disagree* (1). Several factor analyses indicate that the items group into four factors: (a) Collegial Task Support contains four items that reflect a reciprocal collaborative relationship focused on sharing and exchanging work assignments and ideas; (b) Career Mentoring contains four items that represent a personal and intense patronage relationship with someone of higher rank; (c) Coaching Mentoring contains three items that represent a focus on teaching the rules and goals of the organization and/or profession, including organizational politics; and (d) Collegial Social Support contains four items that measure a reciprocal friendship relationship focused on sharing and exchanging personal problems and confidences.

RELIABILITY

Hill et al. (1989) reported sufficiently high Cronbach alphas. They ranged from .75 to .89 for management respondents and from .76 to .84 for a general population.

Profile by Cal W. Downs, with assistance from S. E. K. Hill, M. H. Bahniuk, and D. Rouner.

230

VALIDITY

Hill et al. (1989) presented some initial information about the scale's criterion-related validity. All four factors correlated positively with satisfaction with promotions and fast-track mobility. Collegial Social Mentoring and Collegial Task Mentoring correlated positively, but Coaching and Career Mentoring were not correlated with job satisfaction.

Construct validity is indicated by some stability of factors across three different sample groups: 224 professors, 258 managers and professionals, and 418 telephone respondents from a survey of the general population (Hill et al., 1989). For the academic sample, the factors were (a) Paternalistic Mentoring, (b) Collegial Task Mentoring, and (c) Collegial Social Mentoring. Teacher–Coach Mentoring was added to this list by the management sample; the factor had been embedded in the Paternalistic Mentoring factor in the previous study. With the general population sample, three factors appeared again. In this instance, Collegial Task Mentoring and Collegial Social Mentoring collapsed into one factor indicating peer support.

The four-factor solution with the managers accounted for 92% of the variance, and interfactor correlations ranged from .33 to .50 with an average correlation of .40. With the general population sample, the three factors accounted for 97% of the common variance, and the interfactor correlations ranged from .47 to .54. The current structure is based on data from managers and professionals (Bahniuk, Dobos, & Hill, 1990; Dobos, Hill, & Bahniuk, 1991a) and a third study of all occupational groups (Dobos, Hill, & Bahniuk, 1991b).

COMMENTS

Although most previous research has investigated only paternalistic mentoring, the Mentoring and Communication Support Scale allows for the delineation of the various types of mentoring and communication support behaviors. The instrument has the potential for enriching studies involving minorities and women. Hill, Bahniuk, and Dobos have already begun to investigate the differential effects of types of mentoring behaviors on success and career development for men and women. Their research shows that men with mentors have the highest success scores; next most successful are men without mentors, women with mentors, and women without mentors (Hill, Bahniuk, & Dobos, 1989). Dobos et al. (1991b) have also developed the Home Support Instrument to be used jointly with the mentoring instrument.

This instrument provides possibilities for linking the mentoring process to all kinds of communication dimensions and to organizational outcomes such as commitment and satisfaction. As a self-administered questionnaire that takes only 5 minutes to complete, it can easily be administered along with instruments measuring other variables.

LOCATION

Hill, S. E. K., Bahniuk, M. H., Dobos, J., & Rouner, D. (1989). Mentoring and other communication support in the academic setting. *Group and Organization Studies, 14,* 355–368.

REFERENCES

Bahniuk, M. H., Dobos, J., & Hill, S. E. K. (1990). The impact of mentoring, collegial support, and information adequacy on career success: A replication. *Journal of Social Behavior and Personality, 5,* 431–451.

Dobos, J., Hill, S. E. K., & Bahniuk, M. H. (1991a). Power-gaining communication strategies and career success. *Southern Communication Journal, 57,* 35–48.

Dobos, J., Hill, S. E. K., & Bahniuk, M. H. (1991b, November). *The relationship of home and work power gaining communication strategies to career success for mean and women.* Paper presented at the meeting of the Speech Communication Association, Atlanta.

Hill, S. E. K., Bahniuk, M. H., & Dobos, J. (1989). The impact of mentoring and collegial support on faculty success: An analysis of support behavior, information adequacy, and communication apprehension. *Communication Education, 38,* 15–33.

Shapiro, E. C., Haseltine, F. P., & Rowe, M. P. (1978). Moving up: Role models, mentors, and the patron system. *Sloan Management Review, 19,* 51–58.

Mentoring and Communication Support Scale*

Instructions: We would like to focus on some specific activities in which you may have participated. For the following situations, please indicate *whether or not* you agree that you have engaged in the following activities. Circle the number which best describes your feelings.

5 = Strongly agree
4 = Agree
3 = Neither
2 = Disagree
1 = Strongly disagree

---

1. Someone of higher rank has placed me in important assignments or positions.
2. Someone of higher rank frequently devotes extra time and consideration to me.
3. Someone of higher rank has shown a parental-like interest in me and my career.
4. I receive special attention from someone in a higher position.
5. I have had an associate teach me the informal rules of my organization.
6. I have had an associate teach me strategies for influencing group or departmental meetings.
7. I have been coached about office politics.
8. My associates and I are friends as well as coworkers.
9. My associates and I frequently listen to each other's personal problems.
10. My associates and I share confidences with each other.
11. My associates and I frequently exchange constructive criticism.
12. My associates and I assist each other in accomplishing assigned tasks.
13. My associates and I frequently exchange compliments and positive evaluations.
14. I work jointly on major projects or cases with my associates.
15. I frequently exchange ideas with my associates.

Note. Items 1–4 are Career Mentoring, Items 5–7 are Coaching, Items 8–11 are Collegial Social, and Items 12–15 are Collegial Task.

News Credibility Scale

Credibility has been widely researched in the news media sector of the communication field. Measures ranged from the unidimensional Roper-like questions of Westley and Severin (1964) to multidimensional measures of Markham (1968). Westley and Severin simply asked their respondents one question: "As between television, radio and the newspapers, which one do you feel gives the most accurate and truthful news?" (p. 326). Markham, on the other hand, had college students evaluate the credibility of videotaped newscasters on 55 semantic differential items. He identified three primary credibility factors: Reliable–Logical, Showmanship, and Trustworthiness. Regardless of dimensionality, one common element of this early research is that validity and reliability of measures are rarely discussed.

Other researchers used Markham's (1968) items, or those from Berlo, Lemert, and Mertz (1970), McCroskey (1966), and others, subjecting the many items to factor analysis, and producing various dimensions of credibility. For example, McCroskey and Jenson (1975) factor-analyzed responses to 46 semantic differential items and identified five news-credibility factors: Competence, Character, Sociability, Composure, and Extroversion.

Gaziano and McGrath (1986) created a more recent measure of media credibility for the American Society of Newspaper Editors (ASNE). In a national ASNE-sponsored survey of 1,002 adults age 18 and older living in the contiguous United States, respondents rated both their daily newspapers and TV news on 5-point bipolar-statement scales. Gaziano and McGrath factor-analyzed responses to 16 items about attitudes toward newspapers and TV and located two factors: Credibility, with 12 items (e.g., fair–unfair); and Social Concerns, with 3 items (e.g., moral–immoral).

Our focus here is on the 12-item Credibility dimension. The Newspaper Credibility factor explained 37% of the total variance, whereas the first TV Credibility factor explained 38% of the total variance (Gaziano & McGrath, 1986). Based on this scale, news media credibility consists of "fairness, (un)bias, telling the whole story, accuracy, respect for privacy, watching out after people's interest, concern for community well-being, separation of fact and opinion, trustworthiness, concern for public interest, factuality, and reporter training level" (Andsager, 1990, p. 487). The News Credibility Scale takes less than 5 minutes to complete.

Profile by Alan M. Rubin.

RELIABILITY

Gaziano and McGrath (1986) did not report reliability. However, Rimmer and Weaver (1987), in their secondary analysis of the ASNE data, reported a .90 Cronbach alpha for the 12-item credibility index for both newspapers and TV. Newhagen and Nass (1989) also conducted a secondary analysis, separating perceptions of TV and newspaper credibility. Their principal-components analysis of all 16 items located 9 acceptable items for TV credibility (i.e., factual, accurate, fair, unbiased, tells the whole story, can be trusted, concerned mainly about the public interest, concerned about the community's well-being, and separates facts from opinions) and 10 items for newspaper credibility (i.e., the prior 9 items plus reporters are well trained). They reported Cronbach alphas of .91 for TV and .92 for newspaper credibility.

Meyer (1988) questioned the reliability and validity of the Gaziano and McGrath measure. He used three versions of their instrument (i.e., the original, one with the semantic differential items in positive polarity, and one with the items in random polarity) in a replication with college students and community residents. He dropped items not critical to Gaziano and McGrath's Believability dimension and factor-analyzed 13 of the original 16 items. Two of the items cross-loaded, but the remaining 11 produced two factors: Believability and Alienation. Meyer reported Cronbach alphas of .72 for the four-item Alienation measure and .84 for the seven-item Credibility scale. Because he regarded this to be a "bulky" scale, Meyer deleted two items, leaving a five-item News Credibility scale with a Cronbach alpha of .83 (i.e., fair, unbiased, tells the whole story, accurate, and can be trusted).

VALIDITY

Although they did not state it as their intent, Gaziano and McGrath (1986) supported the construct validity of the Credibility measure by finding that credibility scores were related to the choice of which medium (newspapers or TV) one would believe in light of conflicting stories. Newhagen and Nass (1989) also noted the ability of the measure to discriminate between newspaper credibility and TV credibility. They based this distinction of newspaper and TV credibility on newspapers being perceived on an institutional level and TV on an individual level of personalities.

One might expect credibility to lead to more frequent use of a selected medium. In their secondary analysis of the ASNE data, though, Rimmer and Weaver (1987) found that frequency of media exposure did not relate to media credibility. They did note that media choice or preference showed "some weak associations with the credibility measures" (p. 36). They suggested the need to separate measures of frequency and measures of media preference or media reliance.

Meyer (1988) criticized the lack of face validity and the absence of theory in the Gaziano and McGrath (1986) measures. He noted how "response set can create an artifact when a concept as subtle as newspaper credibility is measured" (Meyer, 1988, p. 571). Following his replication of Gaziano and McGrath (noted above), Meyer suggested that all five of his remaining credibility items made "closely equivalent contributions to the additive index" (p. 573) and that the five-item scale had face validity because each item reflected "believability."

COMMENTS

Conceptualization and measurement are problems for the credibility concept. Differences exist about the dimensions of credibility to tap, credibility sources or stimuli, defining the nature of sources, and whether credibility should be measured from the perspective of the receiver's perceptions or from characteristics of the source. Such differences in the nature and scope of definition and measurement lead to rampant factor analyzing of data and limit generalizability. Rimmer and Weaver (1987) also argued that affective or attitudinal media-use measures can confound relationships with media credibility perceptions.

Most research to date, though, supports at least some variation of the News Credibility Scale (Gaziano & McGrath, 1986). We should note, however, that "concerned about the community's well-being" did not load highly on the newspaper Credibility factor, and "has well-trained reporters" did not load highly on the TV news Credibility factor for the Gaziano and McGrath scale.

LOCATION

Gaziano, C., & McGrath, K. (1986). Measuring the concept of credibility. *Journalism Quarterly, 63*, 451–462.

REFERENCES

Andsager, J. L. (1990). Perceptions of credibility of male and female syndicated political columnists. *Journalism Quarterly, 67*, 485–491.

Berlo, D. K., Lemert, J. B., & Mertz, R. J. (1970). Dimensions for evaluating the acceptability of message sources. *Public Opinion Quarterly, 33*, 563–576.

Markham, D. (1968). The dimensions of source credibility of television newscasters. *Journal of Communication, 18*, 57–64.

McCroskey, J. C. (1966). Scales for the measurement of ethos. *Speech Monographs*, *33*, 65–72.

McCroskey, J. C., & Jenson, T. A. (1975). Image of mass media news sources. *Journal of Broadcasting*, *19*, 169–180.

Meyer, P. (1988). Defining and measuring credibility of newspapers: Developing an index. *Journalism Quarterly*, *65*, 567–574, 588.

Newhagen, J., & Nass, C. (1989). Differential criteria for evaluating credibility of newspapers and TV news. *Journalism Quarterly*, *66*, 277–284.

Rimmer, T., & Weaver, D. (1987). Different questions, different answers? Media use and media credibility. *Journalism Quarterly*, *64*, 28–36, 44.

Westley, B. H., & Severin, W. J. (1964). Some correlates of media credibility. *Journalism Quarterly*, *41*, 325–335.

News Credibility Scale*

Instructions: We'd like you to think about the *daily newspaper* you are the most familiar with. Please circle the number between each pair (of words and phrases with opposite meanings) that best represents how you feel about the daily newspaper you have in mind.

Is fair	5	4	3	2	1	Is unfair
Is biased	5	4	3	2	1	Is unbiased
Tells the whole story	5	4	3	2	1	Doesn't tell the whole story
Is accurate	5	4	3	2	1	Is inaccurate
Invades people's privacy	5	4	3	2	1	Respects people's privacy
Does watch after readers' interests	5	4	3	2	1	Does not watch after readers' interests
Is concerned about the community's well-being	5	4	3	2	1	Is not concerned about the community's well-being
Does separate fact and opinion	5	4	3	2	1	Does not separate fact and opinion
Can be trusted	5	4	3	2	1	Cannot be trusted
Is concerned about the public interest	5	4	3	2	1	Is concerned about making profits
Is factual	5	4	3	2	1	Is opinionated
Has well-trained reporters	5	4	3	2	1	Has poorly-trained reporters

Note. The instructions were repeated for *TV news*. For TV news, the sixth item reads "viewers' interests." The second and fifth items are reverse-coded.

Nonverbal Immediacy
Behaviors Instrument

Richmond, Gorham, and McCroskey (1987) constructed a specific, behavioral, low-inference measure of the construct of immediacy. Relying heavily on the 15-item Behavioral Indicants of Immediacy Scale developed by Andersen (1979), the revised 14-item Likert-type scale measures actual nonverbal behaviors that a teacher might use while lecturing in front of the class. Consistent with Mehrabian's (1967, 1981) conceptualization of immediacy, the Nonverbal Immediacy Behaviors (NIB) Instrument assesses students' perceptions of a teacher's physical or psychological closeness by identifying behaviors of approach–avoidance (e.g., eye contact, proximity, gestures, open-body position, and movement).

Students report their perceptions of their teacher's nonverbal immediacy by indicating, first of all, whether the teacher engages in the specified behavior. If the response is yes, students are asked to indicate how frequently their teacher did so; responses range from *rarely* (1) to *very often* (4). Frequency of use score is set at 0 for those students who did not perceive their teacher using the specific behavior described. The instrument takes less than 3 minutes to complete.

RELIABILITY

The NIB Instrument has an estimated reliability ranging from .73 to .89 (Christophel, 1990; Gorham, 1988; Gorham & Zakahi, 1990; Richmond et al., 1987). The lower estimates reflect data obtained from teacher self-reports, whereas the higher reliability estimates relied on student reports of their teacher's immediacy behaviors.

VALIDITY

Numerous studies support the concurrent validity of the NIB Instrument. The items on this instrument consistently result in a single-factor solution

Profile by Patricia Kearney.

when analyzed with items from the Verbal Immediacy Scale developed by Gorham (1988). Moreover, the summed scores across both instruments correlate highly and positively. These results have been confirmed over and over again (Christophel, 1990; Gorham, 1988; Gorham & Zakahi, 1990; Richmond et al., 1987). Finally, both teacher self-reports and students' reports of their teacher's level of immediacy correlate at .70 (Gorham & Zakahi, 1990).

In terms of the instrument's construct validity, there is a great deal of evidence to support a moderate to substantial relationship between NIB and affective and/or cognitive learning Christophel, 1990; Gorham, 1988; Gorham & Zakahi, 1990; Richmond et al., 1987; Sanders & Wiseman, 1990).

COMMENTS

Andersen (1979) also provided the Generalized Immediacy Scale to assess teachers' nonverbal immediacy, and it is included in this volume. Unlike the Richmond et al. (1987) low-inference assessment of immediacy, however, Andersen's scale measures a more gestalt, high-inference perception of another's level of immediacy. Both instruments are reliable, valid indicators of immediacy.

The decision to use a low- versus a high-inference scale is based on several factors. First, recall data may be more accurately obtained with a global, high-inference assessment, particularly if students are recalling their teacher's nonverbal behaviors from past semesters. Second, infrequent interface with the targeted teacher (e.g., beginning of the semester or class meets occasionally) may require high-inference assessment. Third, prescribing specific teacher behaviors for training and instruction should mandate a low-inference measure. Fourth, identifying the relative contributions of each behavior toward outcome variables (such as affect and cognitive learning) would require a low-inference assessment.

LOCATION

Christophel, D. (1990). The relationships among teacher immediacy behaviors, student motivation, and learning. *Communication Education, 39*, 323–340.

Richmond, V. P., Gorham, J. S., & McCroskey, J. C. (1987). The relationship between selected immediacy behaviors and cognitive learning. *Communication Yearbook, 10*, 574–590.

REFERENCES

Andersen, J. F. (1979). Teacher immediacy as a predictor of teaching effectiveness. *Communication Yearbook, 3,* 543–559.

Gorham, J. (1988). The relationship between verbal teacher immediacy behaviors and student learning. *Communication Education, 37,* 40–53.

Gorham, J., & Zakahi, W. R. (1990). A comparison of teacher and student perceptions of immediacy and learning: Monitoring process and product. *Communication Education, 39,* 354–368.

Mehrabian, A. (1967). Attitudes inferred from nonimmediacy of verbal communication. *Journal of Verbal Learning and Verbal Behavior, 6,* 294–295.

Mehrabian, A. (1981). *Silent messages: Implicit communication of emotions and attitudes* (2nd ed.). Belmont, CA: Wadsworth.

Sanders, J. A., & Wiseman, R. L. (1990). The effects of verbal and nonverbal teacher immediacy on perceived cognitive, affective, and behavioral learning in the multicultural classroom. *Communication Education, 39,* 341–353.

Nonverbal Immediacy Behaviors Instrument*

Instructions: Below is a series of descriptions of things some teachers have been observed doing in some classes. Please respond to the items *in terms of the class you are taking now.* For each item, please indicate on a scale of 0–4 how often your teacher in that class engages in those behaviors. Use this scale: never = 0, rarely = 1, occasionally = 2, often = 3, and very often = 4.

1. Sits behind desk while teaching.
2. Gestures while talking to the class.
3. Uses monotone/dull voice when talking to the class.
4. Looks at the class while talking.
5. Smiles at the class while talking.
6. Has a very tense body position while talking to the class.
7. Touches students in the class.
8. Moves around the classroom while teaching.
9. Sits on a desk or in a chair while teaching.
10. Looks at board or notes while talking to the class.
11. Stands behind podium or desk while teaching.
12. Has a very relaxed body position while talking to the class.
13. Smiles at individual students in the class.
14. Uses a variety of vocal expressions when talking to the class.

Note. Instructions may vary with a different target teacher by inserting instead: *in terms of the class you take immediately preceding this class.* In this way, the diversity and sample size of target teacher increases dramatically.

Items 1, 3, 6, 9, 10, and 11 are presumed to be *non*immediate. They are reverse-coded before summing.

Organizational Communication Conflict Instrument

Putnam and Wilson (1982) developed the Organizational Communication Conflict Instrument (OCCI) as a reaction against what they perceived as weaknesses in the study of conflict at that time. For example, they felt that (a) many of the approaches were value laden, (b) the styles of conflict resolution were often characterized by low reliabilities, (c) even the nature of conflict was often undefined, and (d) investigations of conflict were often plagued by both conceptual and methodological problems. Particularly, they felt that the role of communication was relatively unattended. Consequently, they set out to develop an instrument focusing on concrete communicative behaviors assuming (a) "conflict strategies are those communicative behaviors, both verbal and nonverbal, that provide a means for handling conflict" and (b) use of "a particular conflict strategy is largely governed by situational rather than personality constraints" (Putnam & Wilson, 1982, p. 633). The instrument was, therefore, designed to assess choices about strategies in the management of conflict across organizational contexts.

In the first stage of instrument development, 65 items were created to tap the concrete verbal and nonverbal behaviors associated with the communication dimensions of Blake and Mouton's (1964) five conflict orientations. Form A contained 30 of the 65 items, but this form was rejected when it did not meet "standards of discriminatory power, item consistency, and internal reliability" (Putnam & Wilson, 1982, p. 635). Form B was developed using the 10 best items from Form A plus 25 other items. Using a 7-point Likert scale, 360 respondents chose the communicative behaviors they would use in a specific type of organizational conflict. Principal-components factor analysis with a varimax rotation yielded a three-factor solution; Putnam and Wilson labeled these nonconfrontation strategies (12 items), solution-oriented strategies (11 items), and control strategies (7 items). These factors accounted for 58% of the variance. Two additional factors were identified, but they accounted for only 9% of the variance and were deemed insignificant. Although Form C was designed to reduce the social desirability bias of the nonconfrontation scales, Form B is the most widely used.

Profile by Cal W. Downs.

Form B contains 30 items and respondents indicate on a 7-point Likert-type scale how often they use a particular strategy:

Nonconfrontation strategies avoid disagreements, downplay controversies, or approach conflict indirectly; they are a combination of what Blake and Mouton (1964) would call "avoidance" and "smoothing," or moving away from the opposition.

Solutions-oriented strategies use compromise as well as a search for innovation; they move toward the opposition.

"*Control strategies* manage conflict by arguing persistently for their positions and using nonverbal messages to emphasize demands" (Wilson & Waltman, 1988, p. 369); they move against the opposition.

Total strategy scores are obtained by summing across the items for each particular strategy. Because 1 represents *always* and 7 represents *never*, low scores represent most frequent use.

Putnam and Wilson (1982) reported normative data obtained from 360 respondents from business and a university. The mean nonconfrontation score was 55 (*SD* = 17.7) and the range was 10 to 84, the mean solution-oriented score was 36 (*SD* = 10.1) and the range was 16 to 73, and the mean control score was 32 (*SD* = 8.7) and the range was 10 to 49.

RELIABILITY

Initial examinations of the reliability of the OCCI are quite positive. Wilson and Waltman (1988) reported alpha coefficients ranging from .70 to .93 for the subscales. Most coefficients were above .80, which is very favorable. The Control subscale often had the lowest internal consistency levels (e.g., Chua & Gudykunst, 1987).

Wilson and Waltman (1988) (obtained test–retest coefficients of the OCCI from 39 undergraduates across four situations: Solution–Orientation, .54; Control, .70; and Nonconfrontation, .75. They claimed that these reliabilities are as good as any obtained for other frequently used measures of conflict.

VALIDITY

Content validity assesses how adequately the OCCI samples communication strategies used to manage organizational conflict. Wilson and Waltman (1988) noted that (a) considerable variation in the abstraction level was used to describe behaviors and (b) the items do not reflect some tactics reported in open-ended surveys. Nevertheless, the items do focus on communication and reflect all five of the conflict styles described by Blake and Mouton (1964).

In their review of the construct validity of the OCCI, Wilson and Waltman (1988) reported several studies comparing the OCCI to other conflict instruments. They concluded that the "OCCI generally shows the expected pattern of correlations with other conflict instruments, but degree of convergence is moderate, reflecting different conceptions of the same style across instruments" (p. 373). In particular, they argued for the separation of collaboration and compromise on conceptual grounds, whereas the OCCI includes both under solution orientation.

No study has been reported on the predictive validity of the OCCI.

COMMENT

The OCCI has several strengths. First, its reliabilities are as good as those for other conflict instruments and, in fact, are better than most. Second, its emphasis on communication behaviors in particular situations separates it from instruments that measure style. This characteristic has great appeal for communication researchers. Third, the instrument has great potential as a training tool for getting people to think about strategies for measuring conflict. However, users should be careful that a social desirability bias may be associated with some items. Perhaps additional scale refinements are called for.

Another important strength is that the OCCI has been so usable that an important body of literature has already amassed in its behalf. Researchers have contrasted use of strategies (a) in vertical communication versus horizontal communication in organizations, (b) about different conflict topics, (c) in different levels of conflict, (d) in relation to customer satisfaction, (e) in relation to rhetorical sensitivity, (f) in relation to gender, and (g) in different cultural contexts. For example, Joe Scudder at Indiana University has had it translated into Japanese and is developing a comparison of data from national and cross-cultural samples, including factor comparisons across a wide group of participants. Ross (1989) has contrasted styles in the United States and in Great Britain.

LOCATION

Putnam, L. L., & Wilson, C. E. (1982). Communicative strategies in organizational conflicts: Reliability and validity of a measurement scale. *Communication Yearbook, 6,* 629–652.

REFERENCES

Blake, R. R., & Mouton, J. S. (1964). *The managerial grid*. Houston, TX: Gulf.
Chua, E. G., & Gudykunst, W. G. (1987). Conflict resolutions styles in low and high context cultures. *Communication Research Reports, 4*, 32–37.
Ross, R. G. (1989, November). *A question of style: A comparison between the United States and British conflict management styles*. Paper presented at the annual meeting of the Speech Communication Association, San Francisco.
Wilson, S. R., & Waltman, M. (1988). Assessing the Putnam–Wilson Organizational Communication Conflict Instrument. *Management Communication Quarterly, 1*, 367–388.

Organizational Communication Conflict Instrument*: Form B

Instructions: Think of disagreements you have encountered in a particular task situation with your immediate supervisor. Then indicate below how frequently you engage in each of the described behaviors. For each item select the number that represents the behavior you are *most likely* to exhibit. There are no right or wrong answers. Please respond to all items on the scale. The alternative responses (1–7) are:

Always	Very often	Often	Sometimes	Seldom	Very seldom	Never
1	2	3	4	5	6	7

1. I blend my ideas with others to create new alternatives for resolving a conflict.
2. I shy away from topics that are sources of disputes.
3. I make my opinion known in a disagreement with my supervisor.
4. I suggest solutions which combine a variety of viewpoints.
5. I steer clear of disagreeable situations.
6. I give in a little on my ideas when my supervisor also gives in.
7. I avoid my supervisor when I suspect that he or she wants to discuss a disagreement.
8. I integrate arguments into a new solution from issues raised in a dispute with my supervisor.
9. I will go 50–50 to reach a settlement with my supervisor.
10. I raise my voice when I'm trying to get my supervisor to accept my position.

11. I offer creative solutions in discussions of disagreements.
12. I keep quiet about my views in order to avoid disagreements.
13. I give in if my supervisor will meet me halfway.
14. I downplay the importance of a disagreement.
15. I reduce disagreements by making them seem insignificant.
16. I meet my supervisor at a midpoint in our differences.
17. I assert my opinion forcefully.
18. I dominate arguments until my supervisor understands my position.
19. I suggest we work together to create solutions to disagreements.
20. I try to use my supervisor's ideas to generate solutions to problems.
21. I offer trade-offs to reach solutions in a disagreement.
22. I argue insistently for my stance.
23. I withdraw when my supervisor confronts me about a controversial issue.
24. I side-step disagreements when they arise.
25. I try to smooth over disagreements by making them appear unimportant.
26. I insist my position be accepted during a disagreement with my supervisor.
27. I make our differences seem less serious.
28. I hold my tongue rather than argue with my supervisor.
29. I ease conflict by claiming our differences are trivial.
30. I stand firm in expressing my viewpoints during a disagreement with my supervisor.

Note. Items 2, 5, 7, 12, 14, 15, 23, 24, 25, 27, 28, and 29 are nonconfrontation strategies. Solution-oriented strategies contain Collaboration (Items 1, 4, 8, 11, 19, and 20) and Compromise (Items 6, 9, 13, 16, and 21) items. Items 3, 10, 17, 18, 22, 26, and 30 are control strategies.

Organizational
Communication Development
Audit Questionnaire

Wiio's (1975) development of the Organizational Communication Development (OCD) Audit Questionnaire has been thorough, involving (a) research over a 10-year period, (b) thousands of subjects in Finnish organizations, and (c) several scale revisions. Working at the Helsinki Institute for Business Economics, Wiio developed the LTT Communication Audit (using the Finnish initials for the Institute). The original objectives were to develop a "cheap and fast" means of assessing the communication climate in organizations, to give a rough measure of communication and job satisfaction, and to give an indication about possible bottlenecks in organizational communication. After a pilot study involving more than 1,500 subjects, the audit procedures were refined and standardized to measure demographic backgrounds, access to information, levels of satisfaction, satisfaction with communication, information adequacy, organizational climate, and information quality. This instrument was then used to audit communication in 230 organizations involving approximately 6,000 subjects. This experience led Wiio to develop a new instrument, the OCD Audit Questionnaire (Wiio, 1977). The principal change involved removing items that proved redundant through factor analysis and regression analysis. Since the 1970s, a number of refinements were made in the instrument. The description given here is based on that presented in *Information Strategies* (Goldhaber, Dennis, Richetto, & Wiio, 1979).

With 76 items, the OCD Questionnaire is of medium length and can be completed in less than 30 minutes. There are 63 primary items and 10 demographic items. The scale for each item is a 5-point Likert scale assessing (a) how satisfied one is, (b) how much one gets from a communication dimension, or (c) how much one would like to get from a communication dimension. This allows answering the same item on the "how much do I get" scale and the "how much would I like" scale so that the difference becomes the measure of the level of satisfaction. For example, Items 11 to 20 and 21 to 30 are identical, but one group is scaled for "how much would you like?" and the other group is scaled for "how much do you get?" The

Profile by Cal W. Downs.

dimensions include Organization and Person Code (1–6), Overall Communication Satisfaction (7), Reactions to Media (8–10), Amount of Information Received from Different Sources Now (11–20), Wanted Amount of Information from Different Sources (21–30), Amount of Information Currently Received about Different Types of Information (31–38), Amount of Information Desired about Types of Information (39–46), Interunit Areas for Improved Communication (47–52), Rating of Worst Defects in Organization's Communication (53–63), Levels of Satisfaction (64–69), and Demographic Data (70–79).

The OCD Audit Questionnaire is one of the most thoroughly worked out instruments for organizations. There is a problem, however, in that the OCD Audit Questionnaire is a refined version of the LTT Audit, and most of the statistical analyses reported are for the LTT or preliminary versions. Nevertheless, Wiio has been most generous in publishing background data including factor analyses, regressions, and norms that were obtained in Finland for the LTT version. What is not always clear, however, is how the OCD version was generated from the LTT. Without explaining the details, Wiio suggests that (a) some LTT items proved redundant because several items measured more or less the same thing as shown by factor analysis and regression analysis, (b) the 22 satisfaction items from the LTT were reduced to 6 in the OCD, and (c) very little difference exists between the immediate superior and other superiors as information sources. Therefore, superiors are combined in the OCD.

RELIABILITY AND VALIDITY

Specific data about the reliability and validity of the instrument have not been reported. However, the development of the instruments as described above indicate that Wiio has carefully weeded out redundant items and has used factor analysis to determine which items to keep.

COMMENTS

The instrument was developed in Finland and has been used there extensively. Whereas norms from the 1970s may be somewhat dated, further research and testing in other countries are warranted. A quick review of the items indicates that they could be used generally, and they certainly have been shown to apply to many different kinds of organizations. Furthermore, the manner in which the items are phrased sometimes seems to be more direct than those items in other instruments (e.g., Item 63).

The OCD Audit Questionnaire has been used extensively by Wiio to investigate (a) the relationship between communication and satisfaction and (b) the communication contingencies necessary for success in different types of organizations. He is an ardent proponent of the idea that organizational communication is situational.

One of the most interesting uses of the OCD Audit Questionnaire is Wiio's development of workshop delphi techniques. While most instruments are answered individually, and Wiio uses it that way, he also has small groups fill out the instrument together. Through discussion, the group must come to enough consensus to fill out only one form for the group. It is a time-consuming process, but Wiio advocates it as one of the best ways of getting insights into one's organization.

Finally, the OCD Questionnaire is a relatively quick, simple way of obtaining a lot of data about the organization. On the other hand, the amount of coverage of organizational phenomena seems limited when compared to the ICA Audit or even to Wiio's original LTT instrument.

LOCATION

Wiio, O. A. (1975). *Systems of information, communication, and organization*. Helsinki: Helsinki Research Institute for Business Economics.
Wiio, O. A. (1977). *Organizational communication and its development*. Helsinki: Viestintainstituutti (Institute for Human Communication).

REFERENCES

Goldhaber, G. M., Dennis, H. S., Richetto, G. M., & Wiio, O. A. (1979). The OCD Audit system. In G. M. Goldhaber (Ed.), *Information strategies: New pathways to corporate power* (pp. 251–269). Englewood Cliffs: Prentice Hall.

Organizational Communication Development Audit Questionnaire*

Instructions: The purpose of this questionnaire is to ascertain opinions of personnel concerning internal communication in your company. We ask your *personal* opinion about some problems connected with internal communication and interpersonal relations.

How to answer:
1. Please put an X in the appropriate box.
2. We'd like your opinion according to the scales below. Please write only one X for each scale in the box which you feel is closest to your opinion about the matter in hand.

Example:

Question ↓	Scale → Opinion ↓	Very or entirely	Quite	I cannot tell	Quite	Very or entirely	Scale ← Opinion ↓
Do you read bulletins?	OFTEN						SELDOM
Your answer→ could be	If you read bulletins very often mark:						
					X		
	If you read bulletins quite seldom, mark:						
					X		

3. Please use the whole scale, including the extremes. Avoid the middle or "I cannot say" if possible; only in cases where you feel that it is impossible to give any other choice should you give such an answer.
4. Answer all the questions. Correct any errors by erasing out the whole box.
5. Other scales will be explained as they appear. Please put an X into the appropriate box.
6. The numbers before the questions are used for statistical purposes; pay no attention to them.

    Your answers are *completely confidential*. The questionnaire is anonymous; you need not sign it. In the research reports, it is impossible to recognize individual answers.
    Please take careful note of the direction of the scale.

[Editors' note: For Questions 1 and 10, the scale ranges from *very dissatisfied* (1) to *very satisfied* (5), with 5 boxes separating the bipolar anchors. For Question 2, the scale anchors are *very seldom* (1) and *very often* (5). For Questions 3–7, the anchors are *very little* (1) and *very much* (5).]

1. Are you satisfied or dissatisfied with communication and the availability of information in your organization.

    7
2. Do you read:

    8 Bulletin boards?

    9 Circular letters and other written materials?

    10 Newsletters and house organ?

3. How much information about your work and organization do you get now from:

    11 Superiors and management?

    12 Shop stewards and liaison persons?

    13 Fellow employees?

    14 Bulletin boards?

    15 Newsletters and house organ?

    16 Joint committees?

    17 Meetings and negotiations?

    18 Rumors?

    19 Circular letters and other written material?

    20 Newspapers and other mass media?

4. How much information about your work and organization would you like to get from?

    21 Superiors and management?

    22 Shop stewards and liaison persons?

    23 Fellow employees?

    24 Bulletin boards?

    25 Newsletters and house organ?

    26 Joint committees?

    27 Meetings and negotiations?

    28 Rumors?

    29 Circular letters and other written material?

    30 Newspapers and other mass media?

5. This is the amount of information I receive now about the following job items:

    31 Economic situation of the organization

    32 Employment situation of the organization

    33 My own work

    34 Changes in production

    35 Training and courses

    36 Social welfare in the organization

    37 Sales of our products

    38 Expansions and other large investments of our organization

6. This is the amount of information I should like to receive about the following job items:

    39 Economic situation of the organization

    40 Employment situation of the organization

    41 My own work

    42 Changes in production

43 Training and courses
44 Social welfare in the organization
45 Sales of our products
46 Expansions and other large investments of our organization
7. I should like to see improved communication:
   47 from personnel to superiors and management
   48 From superiors and management to personnel
   49 With my own superior
   50 Among fellow employees
   51 Between shop stewards or liaison person and personnel
   52 Between joint committees and personnel
8. Somewhere else (where?):
9. We should like you to select from the following list at least one but not more than three (one, two, or three) items about the worst defects in communication of your organization.
   53 ___ Information is not readily available.
   54 ___ Information reaches me too late.
   55 ___ Information is not reliable and accurate.
   56 ___ Information is often useless and not important.
   57 ___ The language in information material is often difficult.
   58 ___ I get too much information.
   59 ___ Information does not reach me.
   60 ___ Management conceals important information.
   61 ___ Management does not know what the employees think and feel
   62 ___ I cannot express my opinions freely in my organization.
   63 ___ My opinions do not count and nobody listens to what I say.
   Are there other defects in communication? What?
10. Are you dissatisfied or satisfied with the following aspect of your job?
   64 Supervision of work?
   65 Chances for promotion and advancement?
   66 Wages and salary?
   67 Social benefits?
   68 My work in this organization?
   69 Participation, my possibilities to influence matters concerning my work?

Background information: Finally, we should like to have some background information for statistical purposes. The questions are very general and the answers will not identify you. We do not want your name:
11. 70 What is your sex?
       1 ___ Male
       2 ___ Female

12. 71 How old are you?
    1 ___ under 35 years
    2 ___ over 35 years
13. 72 How long have you worked with this organization?
    1 ___ under one year
    2 ___ over one year
14. 73 What is your classification?
    1 ___ hourly
    2 ___ other
15. 74 What is the last level you have completed in school?
    1 ___ high school or less
    2 ___ more than high school
16. 75 Do you supervise the activities of at least one full-time employee in your organization?
    1 ___ yes
    2 ___ no
17. 76 Think about a regular working day. How many people do you regularly communicate with on your job (about any subject at all)?
    1 ___ 0-3 persons
    2 ___ 4 persons or more
18. 77 Are you a union member?
    1 ___ yes
    2 ___ no
19. 78–79 What is your department (or equivalent)?

Thank you for your valuable help.

Note. The OCD Audit Questionnaire may be used without permission for research purposes by scientific institutions.

Organizational Communication Scale

Roberts and O'Reilly (1974) developed an instrument designed to measure "communication variables in organizations" (p. 321). The Organizational Communication Scale (OCS) is composed of 35 items measuring 16 dimensions of organizational communication. Roberts and O'Reilly (1974) first started with 189 Likert-type items administered to 70 graduate students, "all of whom had prior work experience. These students were asked to respond to the questions based on their experience in some past or current job, considering their communication behavior in a typical work week" (p. 322). Items with high intercorrelations (with items ostensibly measuring the same facets) and low correlations with the rest of the items were retained.

A 60-item scale was submitted to further testing. A variety of subject populations were used, including mental health workers, health care delivery teams, graduate business students, managers, military personnel, emergency room personnel, and financial institutions in the United Kingdom. A series of data reduction steps was implemented including V-type cluster analysis, principal-components analysis, and various reliability and validity tests. The result was a 16-dimension, 35-item scale.

The first eight dimensions are composed of 21 items: (a) Trust of Subordinate for Supervisor (3 items), (b) Influence of Superior (3 items), (c) Importance of Upward Mobility to the Subordinate (2 items), (d) Desire for Interaction (3 items), (e) Accuracy (3 items), (f) Summarization (3 items), (g) Gatekeeping (3 items), and (h) Overload (1 item). Each item is scored on a 7-point Likert scale. Three additional dimensions (9 items) ask respondents to indicate percentage of time they engage in that communication activity: (i) Directionality of Information—Upward (3 items), (j) Directionality—Downward (3 items), and (k) Directionality—Lateral (3 items). Four additional items ask respondents to indicate the percentage of time spent

Profile by Sue DeWine.

254

using the following modes of communication: written, face-to-face, tele-phone, and other. The 13th dimension (1 item) indicates degree of satisfac-tion with communication in the organization and is a variation of the Gen-eral Motors Faces Scale. Roberts and O'Reilly (1974) considered three of the dimensions to be noncommunication (Trust, Mobility, and Influence) yet closely related to communication variables.

Researchers have used OCS items to test a number of different vari-ables and hypotheses. Harrison (1985) tested the relationship between level of participation in decision making with desire to interact with a superior. Muchinsky (1977b) reported a strong relationship between communica-tion behaviors of superiors–subordinates and organizational climate and job satisfaction. Two researchers tested for differences between organic and more mechanistic departments on desire for interaction and degree of lateral communication (Gillen & Carroll, 1985). O'Reilly (1978) conducted a series of field and laboratory studies to determine consequences of in-tentional distortion of information by senders in organizational commu-nication networks. He used items assessing trust, influence, and mobility aspirations. Adams (1978) used the instrument to test for differences be-tween minority and majority managers. Roberts, Cerruti, and O'Reilly (1976) also used the instrument to measure the impact of a specific inter-vention activity for emergency room personnel and their attitudes toward work.

Roberts and O'Reilly (1979) used the OCS to measure differences in the communication behavior of isolates and participants in organizations. Various subscales allowed them to conclude that isolates tended to deliber-ately withhold information from others and participants were associated with perceptions of increased information and greater overall satisfaction with communication in the organization. In another study, O'Reilly and Rob-erts (1978) utilized the mobility aspirations and influence scales as mod-erators of consideration and initiating structure.

RELIABILITY

In O'Reilly and Roberts's (1978) research, test–retest reliabilities for the 10 indexes and 6 individual items resulted in nine "reasonable" reliabil-ities. The lowest reliabilities were .35 and .37 for two different samples on the summarization scale. The other scales ranged from an average of .49 to .87.

Coefficient alpha reliability was relatively high in both the original study and in Muchinsky's (1977a) replication study. The following is a comparison of those reliabilities for each scale:

Scale item	Roberts & O'Reilly (1979)	Muchinsky (1977a) Sample 1	Muchinsky (1977a) Sample 2
Trust	.68	.84	.82
Influence	.69	.67	.70
Mobility	.82	.93	.93
Desire—interaction	.68	.62	.62
Direction—up	.65	.64	.54
Direction—down	.84	.87	.83
Direction—lateral	.71	.76	.76
Accuracy	.62	.61	.46
Summarization	.73	.82	.74
Gatekeeping	.53	.40	.51
Overload	—	.64	.70

Other studies have demonstrated high reliability as well. Harrison (1985) used the OCS trust items to test for a relationship between participative decision making and superior–subordinate communication behavior. She reported a reliability of .84 for the three items measuring trust. Yeager (1978) also conducted a replication study testing reliability and validity of the OCS. Data were collected from 2,700 employees of a soft goods company. Yeager reported a factor structure similar to the original one identified by Roberts and O'Reilly (1974): "An eyeball comparison of these matrices suggests that they are identical (to original study), or nearly so, and statistical analysis confirms this general impression" (Yeager, 1978, p. 1321). Cronbach alphas were Trust, .86; Mobility, .77; and Influence, .61. Adams (1978) reported the following alphas for the same three subscales: Trust, .57; Influence, .76; and Mobility, .90.

VALIDITY

There has not been an extensive amount of validity work on this instrument. In the original research, Roberts and O'Reilly (1974) suggested that "the difficulty in obtaining objective criterion measures and their potential inappropriateness once obtained warrant consideration of more indirect validity assessments" (p. 323). Consequently, they tested for construct validity through the use of the cluster analysis (reported earlier), which indicated "that even similar appearing facets such as trust and influence, or interaction and desire for interaction, can be successfully differentiated from each other" (p. 324). By having respondents indicate confusing questions, the researchers attempted to establish face validity. Finally, a limited attempt at convergent–discriminant validity was made by generating intercorrelations of the nine communication and three noncommunication dimensions with other similar and dissimilar measures such as job satisfaction, supervisor's leadership style, and organizational commitment.

Another study examined the construct validity of the OCS. Muchinsky (1977a) factor-analyzed the OCS items (with one additional trust item added), which produced seven factors that were almost identical to those in the original study and an eighth factor (Accuracy) that was unique to only one of Muchinsky's samples. Muchinsky concluded, "In general, these results are quite supportive of the research reported by Roberts and O'Reilly. However, two other factors are broad both in terms of the numbers of items comprising the factors and the divergence of their content" (p. 186). Muchinsky's research identified differences in the first factor (Motivation to Interact with Superior) and the seventh factor (Directionality—Downward/Lateral). The similarity of the factor structures for the original study and two replication studies (Muchinsky, 1977a; Yeager, 1978) would suggest evidence of construct validity. In the final analysis, while this instrument has been tested over a wide variety of organizations, there need to be more attempts to test whether it truly measures what it claims to measure.

COMMENTS

The contrast in factor structures between Roberts and O'Reilly's (1974) original work and Muchinsky's (1977a) validity and reliability study on the instrument suggests that the dimension of communication directionality may be contingent upon factors such as communication content and purpose. Muchinsky's factor structure implies that the original instrument may need to be further subdivided in this area of the scale. In addition, the factor labeled Motivation to Interact with Superior included a variety of items from the original study and may need close scrutiny.

Muchinsky (1977b) pointed out a missing element in the OCS. Whereas the OCS does not include any items related to communication between departments or units within the organization, Muchinsky suggested that a more appropriate name for the instrument might be Individual Communication in Organizations. The notion that organizational communication must include structural organization elements like departments, as well as individuals, is a valid argument. Too much organizational communication research focuses only on individual behavior in the organizational context. Certainly the complexity of inner relationships and the actual structure of groups in organizations creates a much more complicated web of communication than does a group of individual behaviors. That is what makes organizational research different from interpersonal research.

The OCS appears to be reliable and to be valid across an amazing variety of organizational types. As suggested by Yeager (1978), "these scales will replicate in substantially different organizations" (p. 1324).

LOCATION

Roberts, K. H., & O'Reilly, C. A. (1974). Measuring organizational communication. *Journal of Applied Psychology, 59*, 321–326.

REFERENCES

Adams, E. F. (1978). A multivariate study of subordinate perceptions of and attitudes toward minority and majority managers. *Journal of Applied Psychology, 63*, 277–288.

Gillen, D. J., & Carroll, S. J. (1985). Relationship of managerial ability to unit effectiveness in more organic versus more mechanistic departments. *Journal of Management Studies, 22*, 668–676.

Harrison, T. M. (1985). Communication and participative decision making: An exploratory study. *Personnel Psychology, 38*, 93–116.

Muchinsky, P. M. (1977a). An intraorganizational analysis of the Roberts and O'Reilly Organizational Communication Questionnaire. *Journal of Applied Psychology, 62*, 184–188.

Muchinsky, P. M. (1977b). Organizational communication: Relationships to organizational climate and job satisfaction. *Academy of Management Journal, 20*, 592–607.

O'Reilly, C. A. (1978). The intentional distortion of information in organizational communication: A laboratory and field investigation. *Human Relations, 31*, 173–193.

O'Reilly, C. A., & Roberts, K. H. (1978). Supervisor influence and subordinate mobility aspirations as moderators of consideration and initiating structure. *Journal of Applied Psychology, 63*, 96–102.

Roberts, K. H., Cerruti, N. L., & O'Reilly, C. A. (1976). Changing perceptions of organizational communication: Can short-term intervention help? *Nursing Research, 25*, 197–200.

Roberts, K. H., & O'Reilly, C. A. (1979). Some correlates of communication roles in organizations. *Academy of Management Journal, 22*, 42–57.

Yeager, S. J. (1978). Measurement of independent variables which affect communication: A replication of Roberts and O'Reilly. *Psychological Reports, 43*, 1319–1324.

Organizational Communication Scale*

Instructions: This is a series of questions about how people communicate at work. *Imagine a typical week at work*, and answer the questions accordingly. Please attempt to answer all the questions.

Please indicate the degree of your agreement with each statement by checking one of the seven alternatives below each statement.

1. Do you have subordinates working for you?   Yes _____ No _____
2. How free do you feel to discuss with your *immediate superior* the problems and difficulties you have in your job without jeopardizing your position or having it "held against you" later in this organization?

    Completely free   1   2   3   4   5   6   7   Very cautious

3. How often is your *immediate superior* successful in overcoming restrictions (such as regulations or quotas) in getting you the things you need in your job (such as equipment, personnel, etc.)?

    Always successful   1   2   3   4   5   6   7   Never successful

4. *Immediate superiors* at times must make decisions which seem to be against the interests of their subordinates. When this happens to you as a subordinate, how much trust do you have that your *immediate superior's* decision was justified by other considerations?

    Trust completely   1   2   3   4   5   6   7   Feel very distrustful

5. In general, how much do you feel that your *immediate superior* can do to further your career in this organization?

    Much   1   2   3   4   5   6   7   Little

6. How much weight would your immediate superior's recommendation have in any decision which would affect your standing in this organization, such as promotions, transfers, etc.?

    Very important   1   2   3   4   5   6   7   Very unimportant

7. As part of your present job plans, do you want a promotion to a higher position at some point in the future?

    Content as I am   1   2   3   4   5   6   7   Very much want a promotion

8. How important is it for you to progress upward?

    Very important   1   2   3   4   5   6   7   Very unimportant

---

*Copyright 1974 by the American Psychological Association. Reprinted by permission.

9. To what extent do you have confidence and trust in your *immediate superior* regarding his/her general fairness?

Have little con-   1 2 3 4 5 6 7   Have complete confidence or trust   fidence and trust

10. While working, what percentage of the time do you spend interacting with:

Immediate superiors   _____ %
Subordinates   _____ %
Peers (others at same job level)   _____ %

                                   _____
                                   100 %

11. Of the total time you engage in communications while on the job, about what percentage of the time do you use the following methods to communicate:

Written   _____ %
Face-to-face   _____ %
Telephone   _____ %
Other (specify)   _____ %

                   _____
                   100 %

[Editors' note: Use the following response option for each part of the next question:

Completely   1 2 3 4 5 6 7   Completely
accurate   inaccurate]

12. When receiving information from the sources listed below, how accurate would you estimate it usually is:

a. *immediate superiors*:
b. *subordinates*:
c. *peers* (others at your job level):

13. How often do you find the amount of available information hinders rather than helps your performance in this organization?

Almost never have   1 2 3 4 5 6 7   Have too much
too much information   information fairly
                                           often

14. Do you feel that you receive more information than you can efficiently use in this organization?

Always   1 2 3 4 5 6 7   Never

15. Of the total time you spend *receiving* information at work, what percentage comes from:

Immediate superiors	____ %
Subordinates	____ %
Peers (others at same job level)	____ %

100 %

16. Of the total time you spend *sending* information at work, what percentage goes to:

Immediate superiors	____ %
Subordinates	____ %
Peers (others at same job level)	____ %

100 %

[Editors' note: Use the following response option for the next three questions:

Always   1   2   3   4   5   6   7   Never]

17. When transmitting information to *immediate superiors* in this organization, how often do you summarize by emphasizing those aspects which are important and minimizing those aspects which are unimportant?

18. When transmitting information to *subordinates* in this organization, how often do you summarize by emphasizing those aspects which are important and minimizing those aspects which are unimportant?

19. When transmitting information to *peers* (others at your job level), how often do you summarize by emphasizing those aspects which are important and minimizing those aspects which are unimportant?

[Editors' note: Use the following response option for each part of the next question:

All   1   2   3   4   5   6   7   None]

20. Of the total amount of information you receive at work, how much do you pass on to:

a. *immediate superiors*:

b. *subordinates*:

c. *peers* (others at your own job level):

[Editors' note: Use the following response option for each part of the next question:

Very desirable   1   2   3   4   5   6   7   Completely undesirable]

21. How desirable do you feel it is in your department to interact frequently with:

   a. *immediate superiors*:
   b. *subordinates*:
   c. *peers* (others at your own job level):

22. Are there forces that cause you to distort information you send upward in this organization?

   Virtually no forces 1 2 3 4 5 6 7 Powerful forces to
   to distort   distort

23. Put a check under the face that expresses how you feel about *communications* in *general*, including the amount of information you receive, interaction with your immediate superior and others, the accuracy of information available, etc.

___   ___   ___   ___   ___   ___   ___

Organizational Culture Survey

Organizational culture is composed of the rules, assumptions, beliefs, rituals, myths, and values that

> a group has invented, discovered or developed in learning to cope with its problems of external adaptation and internal integration, and that have worked well enough to be considered valid and therefore to be taught to new members as the correct way to perceive, think, and feel in relation to those problems. (Schein, 1985, p. 3)

The culture metaphor has been adopted by scholars from many disciplines as a means of understanding organizational complexities, and the result has been a plethora of definitions of culture and great variance in methodologies for studying it. Communication scholars have been particularly interested in how symbols both create and reflect the culture. Most studies to date have used ethnographic observation, content analysis of narratives, and interviews to understand the "culture" that is unique for each organization.

The task that Glaser, Zamanou, and Hacker (1987) set for themselves in operationalizing culture with a standardized questionnaire is not universally acceptable. Nevertheless, they argued that it is time to operationalize the concept and to ground the conceptual and theoretical literature in empirical data: "If organizational cultures are created through symbol, ideology, belief, ritual and myth, then categories are now needed to establish themes and patterns around which stories are told, legends are built, and beliefs are developed" (Glaser et al., 1987, p. 174).

Originally, 62 items were developed from themes obtained from open-ended critical incident interviews and a comprehensive literature review (Glaser et al., 1987). These items were then grouped into five subscales, and the total questionnaire was given to 267 members of an organization. Through analysis of interitem correlations, Cronbach alphas, and multiple correlations among subscale items, weak items were deleted. The new revised questionnaire contained 31 items; it was administered to 138 members of a manufacturing company and 195 members of a government agency. Interitem correlations exceed .34 for all but three items. Principal-components factor analysis yielded a six-factor solution with eigenvalues above 1.0 and no item that loaded less than .56.

Profile by Cal W. Downs.

The current Organizational Culture Survey (OCS) contains 36 items; respondents use a Likert-type scale that ranges from *to a very little extent* (1) to *to a very great extent* (5). These items are grouped into the following six subscales:

1. Teamwork: coordination of effort, honesty, support, conflict resolution, teamwork, concern, and cooperation; a feeling of open group communication.
2. Morale: good working relationship, respect for workers, fairness, family, trust, and organizational character.
3. Information Flow: sufficient information to do one's job, communication about changes, and contact with other work areas.
4. Involvement: input of ideas and participation in decision making; thoughts and ideas count and workers are encouraged by management to offer them.
5. Supervision: employees reporting on the amount, valence, and clarity of their immediate supervisor's feedback about their work performance.
6. Meetings: how productive and democratic meetings are.

RELIABILITY

Glaser et al. (1987) reported Cronbach alphas for the subscales ranging from .63 to .91, which is acceptable. Each subscale was further researched through interitem correlations, and those with a minimal relationship were dropped. Test–retest reliability was computed for 35 subjects, using both paired comparison t tests and Pearson product–moment correlations. Both analyses indicated satisfactory reliability for the subscales even though the one subscale was considerably lower than the others.

VALIDITY

Glaser et al. (1987) used the OCS in conjunction with observation and 45-minute critical-incident interviews. The interviews were coded in conjunction with the six factors of the scale, and this analysis reinforced the description of the organization's culture that emerged from the analysis of the scale data. This "illustrated qualitatively why employees believed as they did" (Zamanou & Glaser, 1989, p. 190).

COMMENTS

First, because the six subscales have names similar to the names of complete instruments, more work needs to be done to determine how the OCS Teamwork dimension might relate to a score on a Team instrument or how the Morale dimension might relate to a Morale instrument. This would provide greater insights about the validity of the subscales.

Second, the OCS can best be used in conjunction with other methodologies in assessing culture. Because culture is such an abstract metaphor for characterizing an organization, the potential categories for measuring it are limitless. In one sense, any characteristic one measures about an organization may be an aspect of culture. Therefore, having only six subscales may be limiting. However, the authors never intended for this to be exhaustive, noting that additional culture dimensions most likely will be forthcoming in research (Glaser et al., 1987).

Glaser et al. (1987) did identify their dimensions as central foci for any organizational culture. Furthermore, they suggested that the OCS be used jointly with other methods of collecting data to capture the nature of culture through methodological triangulation. Many of their studies used it that way.

Third, the six culture dimensions also seem to purport a set of values that organizations should follow. This is perhaps a liability for all standardized questionnaires. However, it might be desirable for researchers to assess the degree to which the items actually state the "ideal" value for their organization. Kilmann (1984) used this procedure in mapping out culture gaps in the organization.

Fourth, the OCS must be seen as but one means of assessing culture. Mohan (1990) listed three types of cultural penetration: sociological, historical, and psychological. The OCS best addresses the sociological. A longitudinal study with it can also tap the historical somewhat, as Zamanou and Glaser (1989) suggested. However, the psychological (i.e., the consistency or homogeneity in interpretation of shared meanings) is not specifically addressed by this instrument. Nor does it address symbolic activities of myths, rites, and rituals, which some scholars equate with culture. Nevertheless, the refinement that has gone into preparation of this instrument is admirable. It is short, easy to use, addresses some of the major components of organizations, and should have utility for organizational research.

LOCATION

Glaser, S. R., Zamanou, S., & Hacker, K. (1987). Measuring and interpreting organizational culture. *Management Communication Quarterly, 1*, 173–198.

REFERENCES

Kilmann, R. (1984). *Beyond the quick fix: Managing five tracks to organizational success*. San Francisco: Jossey-Bass.

Mohan, M. L. (1990, August). *Interfacing theory and method in creating a model of organizational culture.* Paper presented at the annual meeting of the Academy of Management, San Francisco.

Schein, E. H. (1985). *Organizational culture and leadership.* San Francisco: Jossey-Bass.

Zamanou, S., & Glaser, S. R. (1989, May). *Managing organizational culture.* Paper presented at the annual meeting of the International Communication Association, San Francisco.

Organizational Culture Survey*

Instructions: Circle the number that represents the extent to which the following statements apply to you:

To a very little extent	To a little extent	To some extent	To a great extent	To a very great extent
1	2	3	4	5

1. People I work with are direct and honest with each other.
2. People I work with accept criticism without becoming defensive.
3. People I work with resolve disagreements cooperatively.
4. People I work with function as a team.
5. People I work with are cooperative and considerate.
6. People I work with constructively confront problems.
7. People I work with are good listeners.
8. People I work with are concerned about each other.
9. Labor and management have a productive working relationship.
10. This organization motivates me to put out my best efforts.
11. This organization respects its workers.
12. This organization treats people in a consistent and fair manner.
13. Working here feels like being part of a family.
14. There is an atmosphere of trust in this organization.
15. This organization motivates people to be efficient and productive.
16. I get enough information to understand the big picture here.
17. When changes are made the reasons why are made clear.
18. I know what's happening in work sections outside of my own.
19. I get the information I need to do my job well.
20. I have a say in decisions that affect my work.
21. I am asked to make suggestions about how to do my job better.
22. This organization values the ideas of workers at every level.
23. My opinions count in this organization.

24. Job requirements are made clear by my supervisor.
25. When I do a good job my supervisor tells me.
26. My supervisor takes criticism well.
27. My supervisor delegates responsibility.
28. My supervisor is approachable.
29. My supervisor gives me criticism in a positive manner.
30. My supervisor is a good listener.
31. My supervisor tells me how I'm doing.
32. Decisions made at meetings get put into action.
33. Everyone takes part in discussions at meetings.
34. Our discussions in meetings stay on track.
35. Time in meetings is time well spent.
36. Meetings tap the creative potential of the people present.

Note. Items for the six dimensions are summed: Teamwork, 1–8; Morale, 9–15; Information Flow, 16–19; Involvement, 20–23; Supervision, 24–31; Meetings, 32–36.

Organizational
Identification Questionnaire

Cheney's work on organizational identification falls within the thrust of scholarship that investigates individuals' linkages with an organization. Cheney characterized identification as "an active process by which individuals link themselves to elements in the social scene" (p. 342). This link is what many other scholars have termed organizational commitment. For example, Cook and Wall (1980) listed identification as one factor of organizational commitment. Mowday, Porter, and Steers (1982) used identification in their definition of organizational commitment: "the relative strength of an individual's identification with and involvement in a particular organization" (p. 27).

Originally piloted with 30 items, the current version of the Organizational Identification Questionnaire (OIQ) contains 25 items, which are scored on a 7-point Likert scale ranging from *very strong agreement* (7) to *very strong disagreement* (1). Respondents require about 10 minutes to complete it.

The OIQ "was designed to reflect three identifiable, but not analytically distinct 'components' of organizational identification isolated by Patchen (1970): membership, loyalty, and similarity" (Cheney, 1983, p. 349). Membership is reflected in items such as "I often describe myself to others by saying, 'I work for _____'" and "I find it easy to identify with _____." Loyalty is reflected in items such as "I would probably continue working for _____ even if I didn't need the money" and "I feel very little loyalty to _____." Two items that indicate similarity are "In general, the people employed by _____ are working toward the same goals" and "I have a lot in common with others employed by _____." Cheney argued that the three components are not "analytically distinct," and a unidimensional composite score should be used to measure identification. This conclusion was reached when the original pilot study yielded a single-factor solution accounting for 73% of the variance. After the number of items was reduced to 25, the single-factor solution accounted for 86% of the variance. In a later factor analysis of the 25-item version, Potvin (1991/1992) discovered a three-factor solution, with the first factor being composed of seven items, which accounted for 50% of the variance. Each of the other factors accounted

Profile by Cal W. Downs.

for only 4% of the variance, so she also used the composite score for her analysis.

RELIABILITY

Although there have been no test–retest measures of reliability, there are three indications of the instrument's reliability. First, Cheney's (1983) pilot study enabled him to discard irrelevant or ambiguous items and to reduce the number of items from 30 to 25.

Second, the internal reliability for the instrument has been consistently high. Cheney (1983) reported a Cronbach alpha of .94, and Potvin (1991/1992) reported an alpha of .96 across respondents in three different organizations.

Third, Potvin (1991/1992) compared four different commitment instruments while using the same sample, and the alpha was higher for the OIQ than for the instruments created by Mowday, Porter, and Steers (1979) (.90), Hrebiniak and Alutto (1972) (.90), and Cook and Wall (1980) (.83).

VALIDITY

Content validity was affirmed by Cheney (1983) after he solicited comments about items from respondents (Barge & Schlueter, 1988). Furthermore, Cheney found that responses to the question "Do you identify with this organization?" closely paralleled 14 of the 25 items. Potvin (1991/1992) found the composite score for the OIQ to have high Pearson correlations with composite scores for instruments measuring organizational commitment developed by Mowday et al. (1979) (.86) and Cook and Wall (1980) (.82).

Barge and Schlueter (1988) reported "partial support for the predictive validity of the OIQ" (p. 124) because Cheney's research supported his assumption that people high in organizational identification would be less likely to engage in job search behaviors. This was addressed directly by Potvin (1991/1992), who found a significant negative Pearson correlation between the composite OIQ and Job Search Intentions. Discriminant validity has not been convincingly established by research with the OIQ so far.

COMMENTS

Because the OIQ contains only 25 items, it is easy to use and has been found to be generally consistent with other instruments that measure identification and organizational commitment. It correlates well with the Organizational Commitment Questionnaire by Mowday et al. (1979), which has been the instrument most often used for measuring organizational commitment. Nevertheless, both commitment instruments (Cook & Wall, 1980; Mowday et al., 1979) have short, nine-item versions, which would make them appealing additions to other questionnaires for studies of the relationships among variables. Both Cheney (1983) and Potvin (1991/1992) indicated that the instrument might be shortened without serious damage.

Currently, little normative data are available for the OIQ. Also, care should be taken when comparing results across studies using the different commitment instruments because although they are similar, they also have important differences in the way that identification or commitment is conceptualized. Barge and Schlueter (1988) pointed to one important difference that sets the OIQ apart from the others. The Organizational Commitment Questionnaire and the Organizational Commitment Instrument (Cook & Wall, 1980) identification scales incorporate exertion of effort into their measures, while Cheney's (1983) OIQ does not. This is not surprising, because Cheney based his concept on Kenneth Burke's notion of identification as consubstantiality, the sharing of substance. Identification as shared substances does not necessarily entail heightened effort but merely requires similarity between two entities, the individual and the organization.

LOCATION

Cheney, G. (1983). On the various and changing meanings of organizational membership: Field study of organizational identification. *Communication Monographs*, 50, 342–362.

REFERENCES

Barge, J., & Schlueter, D. (1988). A critical evaluation of organizational commitment and identification. *Management Communication Quarterly*, 2, 116–133.

Cook, J., & Wall, T. (1980). New work attitude measures of trust, organizational commitment and personal need non-fulfillment. *Journal of Occupational Psychology*, 53, 39–52.

Hrebiniak, L. G., & Alutto, J. A. (1972). Personal and role-related factors in the development of organizational commitment. *Administrative Science Quarterly*, 17, 555–573.

Mowday, R., Porter, L., & Steers, R. (1979). The measurement of organizational commitment. *Journal of Vocational Behavior*, 14, 224–247.

Mowday, R. T., Porter, L. W., & Steers, R. M. (1982). *Employee–organization link-

ages: The psychology of commitment, absenteeism, and turnover. New York: Academic Press.

Potvin, T. C. (1992). Employee organizational commitment: An examination of its relationship to communication satisfaction and an evaluation of questionnaires designed to measure the construct (Doctoral dissertation, University of Kansas, 1991). *Dissertation Abstracts International, 52,* 4147A.

Organizational Identification Questionnaire*

Instructions: Think of your role as an employee of <u>Organization</u>. For each item below select the answer that best represents your belief about or attitude toward <u>Organization</u>. Please respond to all items. The alternative responses are:

YES!	I agree *very strongly* with the statement.
YES	I agree *strongly* with the statement.
yes	I agree with the statement.
?	I neither agree nor disagree with the statement.
no	I disagree with the statement.
NO	I disagree *strongly* with the statement.
NO!	I disagree *very strongly* with the statement.

After reading each item carefully, please circle your response.

[Editors' note: The scale appears after each statement.]

1. I would probably continue working for _____ even if I didn't need the money.
2. In general, the people employed by _____ are working toward the same goals.
3. I am very proud to be an employee of _____.
4. _____'s image in the community represents me as well.
5. I often describe myself to others by saying, "I work for _____" or "I am from _____."
6. I try to make on-the-job decisions by considering the consequences of my actions for _____.
7. We at _____ are different from others in our field.
8. I am glad I chose to work for _____ rather than another company.
9. I talk up _____ to my friends as a great company to work for.
10. In general, I view _____'s problems as my own.
11. I am willing to put in a great deal of effort beyond that normally expected in order to help _____ be successful.

12. I become irritated when I hear others outside _____ criticize the company.
13. I have warm feelings toward _____ as a place to work.
14. I would be quite willing to spend the rest of my career with _____.
15. I feel that _____ cares about me.
16. The record of _____ is an example of what dedicated people can achieve.
17. I have a lot in common with others employed by _____.
18. I find it difficult to agree with _____'s policies on important matters relating to me.
19. My association with _____ is only a small part of who I am.
20. I like to tell others about projects that _____ is working on.
21. I find that my values and the values of _____ are very similar.
22. I feel very little loyalty to _____.
23. I would describe _____ as a large "family" in which most members feel a sense of belonging.
24. I find it easy to identify with _____.
25. I really care about the fate of _____.

Note. Items 18, 19, and 22 are reverse-scored.

Parasocial Interaction Scale

Parasocial interaction (PSI) is a relationship of friendship or intimacy by a media consumer with a remote media "persona" (Horton & Wohl, 1956). It is based on affective ties of audience members with media personalities (Levy, 1979). PSI is a case of media interaction or involvement that "may take many forms including seeking guidance from a media persona, seeing media personalities as friends, imagining being part of a favorite program's social world, and desiring to meet media performers" (A. Rubin, Perse, & Powell, 1985, pp. 156–157).

Media personae such as TV personalities use conversational style and gestures within informal settings that mirror interpersonal communication and invite interactive responses (A. Rubin et al., 1985). The persona anticipates audience responses and adjusts his/her behavior accordingly, and the consumer responds to the persona in "something more than mere observation" (Rosengren & Windahl, 1972, p. 181). PSI parallels interpersonal interaction so that a sense of intimacy and self-disclosure should follow from increased and regular interaction. Other components of PSI include friendliness, companionship, knowing, showing interest in, and identification with the persona (Levy, 1979; Nordlund, 1978; Rosengren & Windahl, 1972).

Early writings and some prior research (e.g., Horton & Wohl, 1956; Levy, 1979; Miller, 1983, 1984) provided guidance in A. Rubin et al.'s (1985) generation of 29 items about persona, program, and audience features that represent PSI. The items were oriented to one's favorite local TV news program, news personality, the news team, and perceptions and dispositions about a favorite newscaster.

The PSI Scale contains elements of empathy, perceived similarity, and physical attraction. Horton and Wohl (1956) suggested such elements to be reminiscent of face-to-face interpersonal interaction. A. Rubin et al. (1985) stated that PSI appears to "stem from an active bonding with a persona who is perceived as real and similar" (p. 175), rather than from a perceived state of deficiency such as loneliness.

The original 20-item PSI Scale for local TV news is reported here (A. Rubin et al., 1985). Others have adapted the statements for "favorite TV personality" (Conway & Rubin, 1991; R. Rubin & McHugh, 1987),

Profile by Alan M. Rubin.

for "favorite soap opera character" (Perse & R. Rubin, 1989; A. Rubin & Perse, 1987), for "TV shopping personality" (Grant, Guthrie, & Ball-Rokeach, 1991), and for "favorite characters from a just-watched TV program" (Auter, 1992). Respondents report their agreement with each statement on 5-point Likert scales ranging from *strongly disagree* (1) to *strongly agree* (5). The PSI Scale takes about 5 minutes to complete.

RELIABILITY

The Cronbach alpha for the 29-item scale was .95 (A. Rubin et al., 1985). Through item analysis, the authors eliminated nonsalient and redundant items, reducing the measure to a 20-item PSI Scale with a mean score of 2.70 and a .93 Cronbach alpha. Factor analysis confirmed a single-factor solution explaining 46% of the total variance.

Subsequent research adapted the PSI Scale to other settings. R. Rubin and McHugh (1987) adapted the scale (Cronbach alpha = .88) to favorite TV personality. Auter (1992) forced a parasocial choice with a favorite character on an experimental treatment videotape of a TV program and reported a .81 Cronbach alpha. A. Rubin and Perse (1987) reduced the 20-item scale to 10 items that accounted for 51% of the total variance and correlated highly with the original scale (r = .96). The 10-item scale, adapted for soap opera involvement, had a .88 Cronbach alpha. The 10-item version was used in other research addressing favorite soap opera characters (alpha = .85) (Perse & Rubin, 1989), local TV news involvement (alpha = .91) (Perse, 1990), and favorite TV personality (alpha = .90) (Conway & Rubin, 1991). Grant et al. (1991) used a 14-item version for their TV shopping dependency research (alpha = .91).

VALIDITY

PSI should reflect goal-directed and involved perceptions and behavior. Canonical correlation and multiple regression analyses supported the goal-directed nature of the concept, linking PSI to perceived TV news realism and affinity and to informational news-viewing motivation (A. Rubin et al., 1985). PSI correlated with news affinity (r = .61) and perceived news realism (r = .47). R. Rubin and McHugh (1987) found PSI to relate significantly to the Social (r = .35) and Task (r = .33) dimensions of interpersonal attraction and to perceived relationship importance (r = .52). In their path model, PSI directly predicted perceived relationship importance and mediated the role of social and task attraction in predicting relationship importance. PSI also has correlated with cognitive and emotional involvement with

TV news (Perse, 1990) and soap operas (A. Rubin & Perse, 1987). In an experimental treatment of direct address on edited versions of the *Burns and Allen* TV program, Auter (1992) supported the construct validity of the PSI Scale by finding PSI to be altered by the program context.

COMMENTS

Investigators have usually treated PSI as an outcome of interaction potential and media behavior (e.g., Rosengren & Windahl, 1972). Levy (1979) suggested that the causal direction is from exposure to PSI, but that those who find these relationships gratifying then increase their exposure to expand their contact with a persona. PSI has been treated as an outcome of news (A. Rubin et al., 1985), soap opera (A. Rubin & Perse, 1987), and comedy viewing (Auter, 1992). It also has been studied as an affective mediator of or antecedent to perceived relationship importance (R. Rubin & McHugh, 1987), satisfaction with soap operas (Perse & A. Rubin, 1988), news involvement (Perse, 1990), TV viewing motivation (Conway & Rubin, 1991), and TV shopping dependency and exposure (Grant et al., 1991). Test–retest reliability needs to be assessed to determine instrument stability.

LOCATION

Rubin, A. M., Perse, E. M., & Powell, R. A. (1985). Loneliness, parasocial interaction, and local television news viewing. *Human Communication Research, 12,* 155–180.

REFERENCES

Auter, P. J. (1992). TV that talks back: An experimental validation of a parasocial interaction scale. *Journal of Broadcasting and Electronic Media, 36,* 173–181.
Conway, J. C., & Rubin, A. M. (1991). Psychological predictors of television viewing motivation. *Communication Research, 18,* 443–463.
Grant, A. E., Guthrie, K. K., & Ball-Rokeach, S. J. (1991). Television shopping: A media system dependency perspective. *Communication Research, 18,* 773–798.
Horton, D., & Wohl, R. R. (1956). Mass communication and para-social interaction: Observations on intimacy at a distance. *Psychiatry, 19,* 215–229.
Levy, M. R. (1979). Watching TV news as para-social interaction. *Journal of Broadcasting, 23,* 69–80.
Miller, R. V. (1984). A descriptive study of television usage among older Americans: Refining the parasocial concept (Doctoral dissertation, Pennsylvania

State University, University Park, 1983). *Dissertation Abstracts International,* *44*, 2282A.

Nordlund, J-E. (1978). Media interaction. *Communication Research, 5,* 150–175.

Perse, E. M. (1990). Media involvement and local news effects. *Journal of Broadcasting and Electronic Media, 34,* 17–36.

Perse, E. M., & Rubin, A. M. (1988). Audience activity and satisfaction with favorite television soap opera. *Journalism Quarterly, 65,* 368–375.

Perse, E. M., & Rubin, R. B. (1989). Attribution in social and parasocial relationships. *Communication Research, 16,* 59–77.

Rosengren, K. E., & Windahl, S. (1972). Mass media consumption as a functional alternative. In D. McQuail (Ed.), *Sociology of mass communications* (pp. 166–194). Middlesex, England: Penguin.

Rubin, A. M., & Perse, E. M. (1987). Audience activity and soap opera involvement. *Human Communication Research, 14,* 246–268.

Rubin, R. B., & McHugh, M. P. (1987). Development of parasocial interaction relationships. *Journal of Broadcasting and Electronic Media, 31,* 279–292.

Parasocial Interaction Scale*

Instructions: Here are several statements about watching local television news. For each statement, please circle the number that best expresses your own feelings about your favorite local television news program or your favorite local television newscaster. If you *strongly agree* with the statement circle a 5. If you *agree* with it circle a 4. If you *disagree some and agree some* circle a 3. If you *disagree* with it circle a 2. If you *strongly disagree* with the statement circle a 1.

1. The news program shows me what the newscasters are like.
2. When the newscasters joke around with one another it makes the news easier to watch.
3. When my favorite newscaster shows me how he or she feels about the news, it helps me make up my own mind about the news story.
4. I feel sorry for my favorite newscaster when he or she makes a mistake.
5. When I'm watching the newscast, I feel as if I am part of the group.
6. I like to compare my ideas with what my favorite newscaster says.
7. The newscasters make me feel comfortable, as if I am with friends.
8. I see my favorite newscaster as a natural, down-to-earth person.
9. I like hearing the voice of my favorite newscaster in my home.
10. My favorite newscaster keeps me company when the news is on TV.
11. I look forward to watching my favorite newscaster on tonight's news.

---

12. If my favorite newscaster appeared on another TV program, I would watch that program.

13. When my favorite newscaster reports a story, he or she seems to understand the kinds of things I want to know.

14. I sometimes make remarks to my favorite newscaster during the newscast.

15. If there were a story about my favorite newscaster in a newspaper or magazine, I would read it.

16. I miss seeing my favorite newscaster when he or she is on vacation.

17. I would like to meet my favorite newscaster in person.

18. I think my favorite newscaster is like an old friend.

19. I find my favorite newscaster to be attractive.

20. I am not as satisfied when I get my news from a newscaster other than my favorite newscaster.

Note. The 10-item version of the PSI Scale includes Items 4, 7, 8, 11, 12, 13, 15, 16, 17, and 19.

Perceived Homophily Measure

McCroskey, Richmond, and Daly developed the Perceived Homophily Measure (PHM) in 1975. They conceptualized homophily as the degree to which interactants are similar to one another. An underlying assumption of this line of research is that "people's perceptions of other people determine to a major extent whether there is a communication attempt made, and have a major impact on the results of any communication encounter" (McCroskey et al., 1975, p. 323). The authors surveyed the literature to identify the countless ways that people are different and similar to one another. These efforts resulted in 47 items representative of specific components of homophily.

The PHM was further refined in a series of factor-analytic studies (McCroskey et al., 1975). The first study involved subjects who were members of five-person work groups and thus had established relationships and a basis for evaluating one another. The subjects were asked to complete the 47-item homophily instrument as it pertained to two fellow group members and another individual (not a group member) to whom they most often turn for advice ("opinion leaders"). A second study used similar procedures with subjects who did not personally know the people they rated; researchers provided them with minimal information about the other. The result was a 16-item measure that tapped four factors: Attitude, Value, Appearance, and Background.

People self-report their perceptions of their own homophily on a 16-item 7-point semantic differential scale representing the four dimensions of homophily. Items are summed to create subscale scores and each subscale takes less than 1 minute to complete.

RELIABILITY

Elliot (1979) reported a coefficient alpha of .71 for the Background factor and .88 for the Attitude factor. Other researchers reported similar alphas for the Attitude dimension (Gudykunst, 1985; Gudykunst, Yang, & Nishida, 1985). Sorensen and Beatty (1988) reported a .74 reliability for the Value dimension.

Profile by Elizabeth E. Graham.

VALIDITY

McCroskey et al. (1975) provided discriminant validity information on the homophily measure when they reported that same-sex opinion leaders were perceived as more homophilous with their followers than were non-opinion leaders. The authors also assessed the construct validity of the PHM when the original factor structure was repeated with diverse populations and different factor rotations. In addition, scores on the homophily measure were examined in conjunction with scores on a measure of source credibility and interpersonal attraction. Again, the same four factors emerged and they were independent of each other and independent of both the source credibility and the interpersonal attraction measures.

Various researchers have investigated the construct validity of the PHM. For example, Elliot (1979) hypothesized that homophily would be related to learning. He found that a moderate degree of similarity of attitude and background between a teacher and a student was related to perceptions of "positive affect toward that instructor, which in turn carries over to his/her affect toward the course" (p. 601).

Gudykunst et al. (1985) also contributed to the construct validity of the homophily measure by investigating the effects of similarity on uncertainty reduction strategies for different cultures (Japan, Korea, and United States) across three relationship types (acquaintances, friends, and dates). One of their primary findings with respect to homophily suggested that "in dating relationships similarity leads to interactive strategy use and this leads to other self-disclosure that in turn influences attributional confidence" (p. 444). In a similar study, Gudykunst (1985) reported that cultural similarity and type of relationship (acquaintances and friends) influence the uncertainty reduction process.

More recently, Sorensen and Beatty (1988) provided additional evidence of construct validity in their finding that touch approachers who were touched during interviews rated the interviewer higher on Attitude, Value, and Background homophily and higher on Task and Social Attraction than did touch avoiders who were touched.

COMMENTS

This measure has not been used extensively; however, the strength of the validity studies indicates that the scale does measure homophily. Most studies employed only one or two dimensions of the measure. For this reason, McCroskey and Richmond (1979) reevaluated the factor structure of the PHM. They suggested that the Appearance and Morality factors were unstable and cautioned users to use only the Attitude and Background factors. For this reason, only the Attitude and Background subscales are presented here. Future research should provide test–retest reliability information as well as further evidence of criterion-related validity.

LOCATION

McCroskey, J. C., Richmond, V. P., & Daly, J. A. (1975). The development of a measure of perceived homophily in interpersonal communication. *Human Communication Research, 1*, 323–332.

REFERENCES

Elliot, S. (1979). Perceived homophily as a predictor of classroom learning. *Communication Yearbook, 3*, 585–602.
Gudykunst, W. B. (1985). The influence of cultural similarity, type of relationship, and self-monitoring on uncertainty reduction processes. *Communication Monographs, 52*, 203–217.
Gudykunst, W. B., Yang, S. M., & Nishida, T. (1985). A cross-cultural test of uncertainty reduction theory: Comparisons of acquaintances, friends, and dating relationships in Japan, Korea, and the United States. *Human Communication Research, 11*, 407–454.
McCroskey, J. C., & Richmond, V. P. (1979, May). *The reliability and validity of scales for the measurement of interpersonal attraction and homophily.* Paper presented at the meeting of the Eastern Communication Association, Philadelphia.
Sorensen, G., & Beatty, M. J. (1988). The interactive effects of touch and touch avoidance on interpersonal evaluations. *Communication Research Reports, 5*, 84–90.

Perceived Homophily Measure*

Instructions: On the scale below, please indicate your feelings about _____ _____. Circle the number that best represents your feelings. Numbers "1" and "7" indicate a *very strong feeling*. Numbers "2" and "6" indicate a *strong feeling*. Numbers "3" and "5" indicate a *fairly weak feeling*. Number "4" indicates you are *undecided* or *don't know*. Please work quickly. There are no right or wrong answers.

1.	Doesn't think like me	1 2 3 4 5 6 7	Thinks like me
2.	From social class similar to mine	1 2 3 4 5 6 7	From social class different from mine
3.	Behaves like me	1 2 3 4 5 6 7	Doesn't behave like me
4.	Economic situation different from mine	1 2 3 4 5 6 7	Economic situation like mine
5.	Similar to me	1 2 3 4 5 6 7	Different from me
6.	Status like mine	1 2 3 4 5 6 7	Status different from mine
7.	Unlike me	1 2 3 4 5 6 7	Like me
8.	Background different from mine	1 2 3 4 5 6 7	Background similar to mine

Note. Items 2, 3, 5, and 6 are reverse-coded.

Items 1, 3, 5, and 7 are Attitude homophily and 2, 4, 6, and 8 are Background homophily. High scores represent high homophily.

Perceived Realism Scale

Perceived TV realism is a concept that has been widely integrated into media uses and effects research (Potter, 1988). Investigators have considered TV's realism as defined either by the accuracy (i.e., true-to-life depiction) of the messages or as an attitude influenced by individual characteristics of receivers. Perceived realism is rarely treated as an outcome variable (cf. Austin & Myers, 1984; Rubin, 1983). Most studies use realism as a moderator or mediator of TV behaviors and effects.

Greenberg integrated measures of perceived realism into several earlier studies to describe how different samples react to TV messages (e.g., Dervin & Greenberg, 1972; Greenberg, 1974; Greenberg & Dominick, 1969). Greenberg's (1974) three-item scale was used by Rubin (1977, 1979), and has been the basis for versions created in later studies. That scale focuses on how realistic viewers believe television content to be.

Rubin (1981a) expanded Greenberg's (1974) scale to five items that assess how true to life people believe TV is. Adaptations of the Perceived Realism Scale (PRS) have been used to measure perceived realism of TV news and information programs (Perse, 1990; Rubin, 1981b; Rubin, Perse, & Powell, 1985) and of soap operas (Perse, 1986; Rubin & Perse, 1987). The PRS was initially used to describe how various samples, such as racial groups (Dervin & Greenberg, 1972) and age groups (Rubin, 1977), differed in their attitudes toward TV. It also has been related to viewing motives in exploring the meaning of reasons for watching TV (e.g., Greenberg, 1974; Rubin, 1979).

Later uses and gratifications research considered how perceived realism was part of ritualistic and instrumental media-use orientations (Rubin, 1983) and affected viewing of such programs as soap operas (Rubin & Perse, 1987) and 60 Minutes (Rubin, 1981b). Researchers also have used perceived realism as a predictor variable of viewing outcomes such as parasocial interaction with newscasters (Rubin et al., 1985), soap opera cultivation (Perse, 1986), and soap opera involvement (Rubin & Perse, 1987).

The PRS used by Rubin (1981a) is reported in this volume. Respondents report their agreement with each statement using 5-point Likert responses ranging from *strongly disagree* (1) to *srongly agree* (5). Perceived real-

Profile by Elizabeth M. Perse.

ism scores are usually defined as the average of the item scores. The scale takes less than 1 minute to complete. The items are often mingled with other attitudinal statements.

Many studies used adaptations of the scale. Some studies (e.g., Rubin, 1981b) use positively worded Items 2 ("If I see something on *60 Minutes*, I can be sure it really is that way") and 4 ("*60 Minutes* shows life as it really is"). Other studies (e.g., Rubin & Perse, 1987) used a sixth item ("My favorite soap opera lets me understand some of the problems other people have").

RELIABILITY

Three-, four-, five-, and six-item versions of the PRS are internally consistent. A Cronbach alpha of .93 has been reported for the three-item version (Rubin, 1979), four-item alphas range from .74 (Rubin, 1981a) to .83 (Perse, 1986), a five-item alpha is .85 (Rubin et al., 1985), and six-item alphas range from .80 (Perse, 1990) to .87 (Rubin & Perse, 1987). The scale has been used reliably with various samples: children (Rubin, 1979), traditional and nontraditional college students (Austin & Myers, 1984; Perse, 1986; Rubin & Perse, 1987; Rubin et al., 1985), and adults (Perse, 1990; Rubin, 1981a, 1983). Although researchers treat perceived realism as an attitude toward TV, there has been no test of score stability over time.

VALIDITY

Descriptive analyses provide criterion-related validity for the scale. Rubin (1977) found perceived realism to be negatively related to age in a sample of children and adolescents. As children grow older, they not only watch less TV, but believe it to be less realistic. Rubin (1977) suggested that realism declines because older children have more opportunities to experience the world and become less attached to TV.

Other studies observed that perceived realism related to viewing motives in predictable ways. Generally, increased realism accompanies increased motivation to watch TV. Motives that reflect learning and seeking information from TV are most strongly correlated with perceived realism (Rubin, 1979, 1981a, 1983).

Perceived realism's relationships to viewing outcomes support construct validity. Perceived realism was a significant hypothesized contributor to parasocial interaction (Perse, 1990; Rubin & Perse, 1987; Rubin et al., 1985) and cultivation (Perse, 1986). TV and loneliness research also provides evidence of validity. Expecting chronically lonely persons to be apathetic about communication, Perse and Rubin (1990) observed chronic loneliness to be associated with believing news to be less realistic but soap operas to be more realistic. The findings supported research that suggests that the chronically lonely withdraw from social interaction.

COMMENTS

Perceived realism scores vary considerably depending on the focus of the study. Averaged soap opera realism scores range from 1.66 to 1.86 (Perse, 1986; Rubin & Perse, 1987). TV realism is usually somewhat higher, ranging from 1.77 to 2.54 (Rubin, 1979, 1981a, 1983). Perceived realism of news programs has ranged from 3.28 to 3.58 (Perse, 1990; Rubin, 1981b; Rubin et al., 1985).

These differences across program types suggest that perceived realism of TV content may not be a global construct (Potter, 1988). Respondents judge various types of messages differently. Although perceived TV realism has some evidence of construct validity, content-specific adaptations of the scale might be more valid measures of the construct.

Although there is evidence that this scale assesses a single dimension, others have argued that perceived realism is multidimensional (Hawkins, 1977; Potter, 1986). Potter suggested that perceptions of realism can focus on stylistic (e.g., production techniques and casting), thematic, utility (i.e., how well messages transfer to real life), and TV character dimensions.

LOCATION

Rubin, A. M. (1981a). An examination of television viewing motivations. *Communication Research*, 8, 141–165.

REFERENCES

Austin, B. A., & Myers, J. W. (1984). Hearing-impaired viewers of prime-time television. *Journal of Communication*, 34(4), 60–71.

Dervin, B., & Greenberg, B. S. (1972). The communication environment of the urban poor. In F. G. Kline & P. J. Tichenor (Eds.), *Current perspectives in mass communication research* (pp. 195–233). Beverly Hills, CA: Sage.

Greenberg, B. S. (1974). Gratifications of television viewing and their correlates for British children. In J. G. Blumler & E. Katz (Eds.), *The uses of mass communications: Current perspectives on gratifications research* (pp. 71–92). Beverly Hills, CA: Sage.

Greenberg, B. S., & Dominick, J. R. (1969). Racial and social class differences in teen-agers' use of television. *Journal of Broadcasting*, 13, 331–344.

Hawkins, R. P. (1977). The dimensional structure of children's perceptions of television reality. *Communication Research, 4*, 299–320.

Perse, E. M. (1986). Soap opera viewing patterns of college students and cultivation. *Journal of Broadcasting and Electronic Media, 30*, 175–193.

Perse, E. M. (1990). Media involvement and local news effects. *Journal of Broadcasting and Electronic Media, 34*, 17–36.

Perse, E. M., & Rubin, A. M. (1990). Chronic loneliness and television use. *Journal of Broadcasting and Electronic Media, 34*, 37–53.

Potter, W. J. (1986). Perceived reality and the cultivation hypothesis. *Journal of Broadcasting and Electronic Media, 30*, 159–174.

Potter, W. J. (1988). Perceived reality in television effects research. *Journal of Broadcasting and Electronic Media, 32*, 23–41.

Rubin, A. M. (1977). Television usage, attitudes and viewing behaviors of children and adolescents. *Journal of Broadcasting, 21*, 355–369.

Rubin, A. M. (1979). Television use by children and adolescents. *Human Communication Research, 5*, 109–120.

Rubin, A. M. (1981b). A multivariate analysis of "60 Minutes" viewing motivations. *Journalism Quarterly, 58*, 529–534.

Rubin, A. M. (1983). Television uses and gratifications: The interactions of viewing patterns and motivations. *Journal of Broadcasting, 27*, 37–51.

Rubin, A. M., and Perse, E. M. (1987). Audience activity and soap opera involvement: A uses and effects investigation. *Human Communication Research, 14*, 246–268.

Rubin, A. M., Perse, E. M., and Powell, R. A. (1985). Loneliness, parasocial interaction, and local television news viewing. *Human Communication Research, 12*, 155–180.

Perceived Realism Scale*

Instructions: Here are some statements people may make about television. For each statement please circle the number that best expresses your own feelings. If you *strongly agree* with the statement, circle a 5. If you *agree*, circle a 4. If you *agree some and disagree some*, circle a 3. If you *disagree*, circle a 2. If you *strongly disagree*, circle a 1.

1. Television presents things as they really are in life.
2. If I see something on TV, I can't be sure it really is that way.
3. Television lets me really see how other people live.
4. TV does not show life as it really is.
5. Television lets me see what happens in other places as if I were really there.

Note. Items 2 and 4 are reverse-coded for data analysis.

Personal Involvement Inventory

Involvement is a significant construct in mass communication and advertising research. It is expected to mediate attitudes and behavioral responses to messages, issues, and objects. Involvement signifies arousal, interest, and motivation (Munson & McQuarrie, 1987). It is typically treated as a mediating variable in assessing whether a message such as an advertisement is relevant to the consumer. In advertising research, personal relevance suggests the felt importance of the advertisement, product, or purchasing decision. Personal elements such as needs and relevance, stimulus elements such as product alternatives and communication sources, and situational elements such as use and occasion are antecedents of involvement (Zaichkowsky, 1986).

The Personal Involvement Inventory (PII) is a unidimensional construct of an object's perceived relevance based on personal needs and interests. To develop the PII, Zaichkowsky (1985) first generated a list of 168 bipolar word pairs and had three expert judges rate whether the word pairs represent involvement across advertisements, products, and purchase decisions. She then deleted unrepresentative word pairs and had five new judges rate the representativeness of the remaining 43 word pairs. This content validity procedure resulted in 23 word pairs that achieved 80% agreement. Deeming 23 too few a number for data collection, Zaichkowsky added 7 additional items.

Zaichkowsky (1985) administered these 30 items for two product classes (watches and athletic shoes) to 152 undergraduate students to assess internal consistency and stability; 26 items had item-total correlations of .50 or better and a Cronbach alpha of .95. She deleted six adjective pairs with low item-total correlations. A factor analysis largely supported a single-factor solution for the 24 items in each product class. Test–retest reliability for these 24 items with 55 psychology students and 26 MBA students resulted in a final 20-item scale with test–retest correlations of at least .88 and Cronbach alphas of at least .95 for four tested products. Zaichkowsky argued that the 20 items provide a good sampling of items to represent in-

Profile by Alan M. Rubin.

volvement and are superior to a smaller number of items due to the applicability to different product categories.

The PII is a 20-item, 7-point, summated semantic differential scale, with possible scores ranging from 20 to 140. The measure takes about 2 minutes to complete for each object being judged.

RELIABILITY

The PII has proven consistent and unidimensional. Mobley, Bearden, and Teel (1988) reported Cronbach alphas of .96 and .97 for two classes of products (shirts and tennis shoes). Celuch and Evans (1989) noted Cronbach alphas of .93 and .96 for high- and low-involvement products. Ram and Jung (1989) reported a .92 alpha for five product categories.

Munson and McQuarrie (1987) sought to produce a shortened version of the PII that a more general, noncollege population could understand. They discarded 4 of the 20 PII adjective pairs to form a Modified Personal Involvement Inventory (MPII): superfluous–vital, mundane–fascinating, significant–insignificant, and fundamental–trivial. Using several products as stimuli, they tested 80 undergraduate and 50 graduate business students. They noted a .95 Cronbach alpha for the MPII but weaker MPII test–retest correlations averaging .69 across a 1-week period than Zaichkowsky (1985) observed for the PII. Munson and McQuarrie reported one major factor, attitudinal involvement, and one minor factor, arousal involvement, for the 16-item MPII.

VALIDITY

Besides the initial content validity assessment, Zaichkowsky (1985) did three other validity checks. First, to support content validity, she had two expert judges sort open-ended responses from 45 MBA students into low-, medium-, and high-involvement categories for three types of products. She noted significant chi-square relationships when she compared these responses to respondents' answers to the 20-item PII, also collapsed into low, medium, and high categories. Second, Zaichkowsky reported criterion-related validity via a repeated-measures ANOVA by comparing 68 undergraduate students' PII scores for 21 products classified as being high or low in involvement in earlier studies. Third, she supported the PII's construct validity by assessing 57 staff members' responses to five statements representing theoretical propositions about involvement (e.g., "I would be interested in reading information about how the product is made") with their PII scores for three kinds of products (instant coffee, laundry detergent, and color TV).

She found that the PII tapped the involvement construct concerning search-ing for product information, evaluating competing brands, perceiving dif-ferences among brands, and having a brand preference.

Celuch and Evans (1989) considered the PII and the Consumer Involve-ment Profile (CIP) (Laurent & Kapferer, 1985), which is a multidimensional measure of involvement. Celuch and Evans supported convergent validity between the PII and CIP, especially for low-involvement products. They observed discriminant validity of both measures in terms of innovativeness and information-processing confidence, especially for high-involvement products, but not in one's attitude toward the object or toward the act of buying. Goldsmith and Emmert (1991) used a multitrait–multimethod matrix analysis to support the convergent, discriminant, and criterion-related validity of the PII, the CIP, and the Involvement Scale (Mittal, 1989).

Ram and Jung (1989) found that involvement, as measured by the PII, related positively to the frequency of using five products (e.g., videocassette recorders and personal computers). Ratchford (1987) observed a .76 corre-lation between that study's measure of involvement and the PII. To sup-port convergent validity of the MPII, Munson and McQuarrie (1987) re-ported that the salience of the summed involvement scores reflected the high- and low-involvement nature of 12 products ranging from automobiles to canned corn. To support predictive validity, they found that scores on the 16-item MPII significantly predicted three consequences of involvement: information search and choice, brand comprehension, and brand differen-tiation.

COMMENTS

There has been ample discussion about the conceptual meaning of involve-ment and whether involvement is a unidimensional or multidimensional construct. McQuarrie and Munson (1987) criticized the PII for "the absence of a multi-dimensional approach and the danger of attitude contamination" (p. 37). Laurent and Kapferer (1985) proposed the CIP as a multidimen-sional measure of involvement (i.e., interest, pleasure, self-image, risk im-portance, and probability of mispurchase). Ratchford (1987), though, con-tended that only interest and risk importance actually measure involvement, and that the CIP's other three dimensions are antecedents to involvement. According to Mittal (1989), the common feature of all definitions of in-volvement is an "activated motivational state," that is, a motivational state that is activated by a stimulus or goal object such as a task or a decision. Mittal suggested that six of the PII items measure involvement: relevant, important, of concern, matters, means a lot, and significant. The other items assess attitudes or involvement antecedents.

LOCATION

Zaichkowsky, J. L. (1985). Measuring the involvement construct. *Journal of Consumer Research, 12,* 341–352.

REFERENCES

Celuch, K., & Evans, R. (1989). An analysis of the convergent and discriminant validity of the Personal Involvement Inventory and the Consumer Involvement Profile. *Psychological Reports, 65,* 1291–1297.

Goldsmith, R. E., & Emmert, J. (1991). Measuring product category involvement: A multitrait–multimethod study. *Journal of Business Research, 23,* 363–371.

Laurent, G., & Kapferer, J. (1985). Measuring consumer involvement profiles. *Journal of Marketing Research, 22,* 41–53.

McQuarrie, E. F., & Munson, J. M. (1987). The Zaichkowsky Personal Involvement Inventory: Modification and extension. *Advances in Consumer Research, 14,* 36–40.

Mittal, B. (1989). A theoretical analysis of two recent measures of involvement. *Advances in Consumer Research, 16,* 697–702.

Mobley, M. F., Bearden, W. O., & Teel, J. E. (1988). An investigation of individual responses to tensile price claims. *Journal of Consumer Research, 15,* 273–279.

Munson, J. M., & McQuarrie, E. F. (1987). The factorial and predictive validities of a revised measure of Zaichkowsky's Personal Involvement Inventory. *Educational and Psychological Measurement, 47,* 773–782.

Ram, S., & Jung, H. (1989). The link between involvement, use innovativeness and product usage. *Advances in Consumer Research, 16,* 160–166.

Ratchford, B. T. (1987). New insights about the FCB grid. *Journal of Advertising Research, 27*(4), 24–38.

Zaichkowsky, J. L. (1986). Conceptualizing involvement. *Journal of Advertising, 15*(2), 4–14, 34.

Personal Involvement Inventory*

Instructions: The purpose of this study is to measure people's involvement with (various products they regularly purchase or have purchased in the past). We need you to judge various [products] against a series of descriptive scales according to how *you* perceive the product. Here is how you are to use these scales:

---

*Copyright 1985 by the University of Chicago Press. Reprinted by permission.

If you feel that the [product] that appears at the top of the page is *very closely related* to one end of the scale, you should place your check mark as follows:

Unimportant : _X_ :___:___:___:___:___:___: Important

or

Unimportant :___:___:___:___:___:___: _X_ : Important

If you feel that the [product] is "Quite closely related" to one or the other end of the scale (but not extremely), place your checkmark as follows:

Unimportant :___: _X_ :___:___:___:___:___: Important

or

Unimportant :___:___:___:___:___: _X_ :___: Important

If you feel that the [product] seems "only slightly related" (but not really neutral) to one end of the scale, place your checkmark as follows:

Unimportant :___:___: _X_ :___:___:___:___: Important

or

Unimportant :___:___:___:___: _X_ :___:___: Important

Important:

1. Be sure that you check every scale for every [product]; do not omit any.
2. Never put more than one check mark on a single scale.

Make each item a separate and independent judgment. Work at fairly high speed through this questionnaire. Do not worry or puzzle over individual items. It is your first impressions, the immediate feelings about the items, that we want. On the other hand, please do not be careless, because we want your true impressions.

Any questions?

[Insert name of object to be judged.]

Important :___:___:___:___:___:___:___: Unimportant*

Of no concern :___:___:___:___:___:___:___: Of concern to me

Irrelevant :___:___:___:___:___:___:___: Relevant

Means a lot to me :___:___:___:___:___:___:___: Means nothing to me*

Useless :___:___:___:___:___:___:___: Useful

Valuable :___:___:___:___:___:___:___: Worthless*

Trivial :___:___:___:___:___:___:___: Fundamental

Beneficial :___:___:___:___:___:___:___: Not beneficial*

Matters to me :___:___:___:___:___:___:___: Doesn't matter*

Uninterested :___:___:___:___:___:___:___: Interested

Significant :___:___:___:___:___:___:___: Insignificant*

Vital :___:___:___:___:___:___:___: Superfluous*

Boring :___:___:___:___:___:___:___: Interesting

Unexciting :___:___:___:___:___:___:___: Exciting
Appealing :___:___:___:___:___:___:___: Unappealing*
Mundane :___:___:___:___:___:___:___: Fascinating
Essential :___:___:___:___:___:___:___: Nonessential*
Undesirable :___:___:___:___:___:___:___: Desirable
Wanted :___:___:___:___:___:___:___: Unwanted*
Not needed :___:___:___:___:___:___:___: Needed

Note. Items on the left are scored (1) for *low involvement* and on the right (7) for *high involvement*. An asterisk indicates that the item is reverse-scored.

Personal Report of Communication Apprehension

Probably no other construct in our discipline has commanded more attention of researchers and teachers alike than communication apprehension (CA). The construct first appeared in our literature in 1970 in an article published by McCroskey. In an attempt to understand why individuals apparently had trouble talking to others, McCroskey examined persons' trait or dispositional anxieties about communicating. Conceptualized originally and in more recent writings as the level of fear or anxiety associated with either real or anticipated communication encounters, CA refers to *oral* communication encounters only. In recent years, the construct has been expanded to include not only *trait*, but more *state*-like orientations as well; that is, persons may be apprehensive across all or most communication situations (trait) or their anxieties may be associated with particular contexts (generalized-context CA), individuals (person–group CA), or even more state-like, particular persons at a given point in time (situational CA).

The most popular and most valid measure of trait-like CA is McCroskey's (1982) Personal Report of Communication Apprehension (PRCA-24). This 24-item, Likert-type instrument assesses individuals' communication apprehension across four contexts: public, small group, meeting, and dyadic or interpersonal encounters. Each context is represented by six items. Even though the measure is generally scored by summing participants' responses across all 24 items, four generalized-context scores can also be obtained. In this way, respondents or researchers can examine the relative degree of apprehension between and among common communication situations as well. Factor analysis consistently reveals the measure to be construed as either a unidimensional measure of trait CA and/or four individual factors of generalized-context CA. Thus, the measure may be scored separately for each context or an overall CA score may be computed. The instrument is self-report; it requires approximately 15 minutes to complete.

Profile by Michael J. Beatty.

RELIABILITY

The PRCA-24 is internally consistent. Alpha reliability estimates for all 24 items ranges from .93 to .95 (McCroskey, Beatty, Kearney, & Plax, 1985). Reliability estimates for the individual composites are only slightly lower (McCroskey & Beatty, 1984). The 24-B measure also demonstrated considerable stability across time; test–retest reliability coefficients greater than .80 have been reported (Rubin, Graham, & Mignerey, 1990).

VALIDITY

Published studies support the construct and criterion-related validity of the PRCA-24. McCroskey and Beatty (1984) found that all four context-based scores predicted self-reported state anxiety experienced in a related context (e.g., public speaking). This finding has been replicated for the public speaking component of the PRCA-24 (Beatty, 1987, 1988; Beatty, Balfantz, & Kuwabara, 1989; Beatty & Friedland, 1990). Moreover, public-speaking context scores have been shown to predict avoidance and withdrawal behavior (Beatty, 1987) and speech duration (Beatty, Forst, & Stewart, 1986). Also, PRCA-24 total scores correlate negatively (−.70) with assertiveness (McCroskey et al., 1985). Booth-Butterfield (1988) found that high CA students who anticipated interaction reported greater anxiety and lower recall of lecture material than did those not anticipating social interaction. Research also indicates that PRCA-24 scores reflect expected changes due to therapy (e.g., Ayres & Hopf, 1990).

COMMENTS

A number of instruments have been developed that purportedly measure individuals' trait-like communication apprehension, including earlier versions of the PRCA-24. Most of those instruments are merely parallel forms of this one. While some measures may tap different contexts or target different persons or groups, the PRCA-24 continues to be the instrument of choice. With its repeatedly high reliability estimates and its well-documented validity, the PRCA-24 is highly recommended as a means of assessing persons' trait or generalized-context CA.

LOCATION

McCroskey, J. C. (1982). *An introduction to rhetorical communication* (4th ed.). Englewood Cliffs, NJ: Prentice Hall.

McCroskey, J. C., Beatty, M. J., Kearney, P., & Plax, T. G. (1985). The content validity of the PRCA-24 as a measure of communication apprehension across communication contexts. *Communication Quarterly, 33,* 165–173.

Richmond, V. P., & McCroskey, J. C. (1985). *Communication apprehension, avoidance, and effectiveness.* Scottsdale, AZ: Gorsuch Scarisbrick.

REFERENCES

Ayres, J., & Hopf, T. S. (1990). The long-term effect of visualization in the classroom: A brief research report. *Communication Education, 39,* 75–78.

Beatty, M. J. (1987). Communication apprehension as a determinate of avoidance, withdrawal and performance anxiety. *Communication Quarterly, 35,* 202–217.

Beatty, M. J. (1988). Situational and predispositional correlates of public speaking anxiety. *Communication Education, 37,* 28–39.

Beatty, M. J., Balfantz, G. L., & Kuwabara, A. Y. (1989). Trait-like qualities of selected variables assumed to be transient causes of performance state anxiety. *Communication Education, 38,* 277–289.

Beatty, M. J., Forst, E. C., & Stewart, R. A. (1986). Communication apprehension and motivation as predictors of public speaking duration. *Communication Education, 35,* 143–146.

Beatty, M. J., & Friedland, M. H. (1990). Public speaking state anxiety as a function of selected situational and predispositional variables. *Communication Education, 39,* 142–147.

Booth-Butterfield, S. (1988). Inhibition and student recall of instructional messages. *Communication Education, 37,* 312–324.

McCroskey, J. C. (1970). Measures of communication-bound anxiety. *Speech Monographs, 37,* 269–277.

McCroskey, J. C., & Beatty, M. J. (1984). Communication apprehension and accumulated communication state anxiety experiences: A research note. *Communication Monographs, 51,* 79–84.

Rubin, R. B., Graham, E. E., & Mignerey, J. T. (1990). A longitudinal study of college students' communication competence. *Communication Education, 39,* 1–14.

Personal Report of Communication Apprehension (PRCA-24)*

Instructions: This instrument is composed of 24 statements concerning your feelings about communication with other people. Please indicate in the space provided the degree to which each statement applies to you by marking whether you (1) strongly agree, (2) agree, (3) are undecided, (4) disagree, or

---

(5) strongly disagree with each statement. There are no right or wrong answers. Many of the statements are similar to other statements. Do not be concerned about this. Work quickly, just record your first impression.

[Editors' note: Respondents write the number corresponding to their response in blanks provided beside each item.]

1. I dislike participating in group discussions.
2. Generally, I am comfortable while participating in a group discussion.
3. I am tense and nervous while participating in group discussions.
4. I like to get involved in group discussions.
5. Engaging in a group discussion with new people makes me tense and nervous.
6. I am calm and relaxed while participating in group discussions.
7. Generally, I am nervous when I have to participate in a meeting.
8. Usually I am calm and relaxed while participating in meetings.
9. I am very calm and relaxed when I am called upon to express an opinion at a meeting.
10. I am afraid to express myself at meetings.
11. Communicating at meetings usually makes me uncomfortable.
12. I am very relaxed when answering questions at a meeting.
13. While participating in a conversation with a new acquaintance, I feel very nervous.
14. I have no fear of speaking up in conversations.
15. Ordinarily I am very tense and nervous in conversations.
16. Ordinarily I am very calm and relaxed in conversations.
17. While conversing with a new acquaintance, I feel very relaxed.
18. I'm afraid to speak up in conversations.
19. I have no fear of giving a speech.
20. Certain parts of my body feel very tense and rigid while giving a speech.
21. I feel relaxed while giving a speech.
22. My thoughts become confused and jumbled when I am giving a speech.
23. I face the prospect of giving a speech with confidence.
24. While giving a speech I get so nervous, I forget facts I really know.

Scoring:
Group = 18 − (1) + (2) − (3) + (4) − (5) + (6)
Meeting = 18 − (7) + (8) + (9) − (10) − (11) + (12)
Dyadic = 18 − (13) + (14) − (15) + (16) + (17) − (18)
Public = 18 + (19) − (20) + (21) − (22) + (23) − (24)
Overall CA = Group + Meeting + Dyadic + Public

Note. Items should be mixed to avoid response set error variance.

Political Media Gratifications Scale

Blumler and McQuail (1969) conducted an extensive investigation into the role of TV in the 1964 British general election. They sought to apply the uses and gratifications (U&G) perspective to political broadcasts. U&G is audience centered and holds that how people use media influences the gratifications they receive from exposure. Blumler and McQuail were interested in uncovering the reasons people watched or avoided political broadcasts.

After extensive interviews, Blumler and McQuail (1969) developed an instrument that included 11 different reasons for watching and 9 for avoiding political broadcasts. Respondents reported to interviewers which statements corresponded to their own reasons. The gratifications sought (GS) from political broadcasting clustered into three dimensions: Political Reasons (i.e., reinforcement and vote guidance); Surveillance (e.g., keeping up with the issues); and Excitement (e.g., seeing which party will win). Blumler and McQuail defined motivation to view as the ratio of the number of reasons for watching to the number of reasons for avoiding political broadcasts.

McLeod and Becker (1974) adapted the British statements to the U.S. political arena. They reduced the number of GS statements to eight and the number of avoidances statements to seven. McLeod and Becker asked respondents to report on a 3-point scale whether a statement applied to them *a lot*, *a little*, or *not at all*. Their analysis identified five gratification factors (Surveillance, Vote Guidance, Anticipated Communication, Excitement, and Reinforcement) and three TV avoidances (Partisanship, Relaxation, and Alienation).

McLeod and Becker's (1974) U.S. adaptation of the Political Media Gratifications Scale (PMGS) has been used in various political and news contexts for several research purposes: (a) to validate gratifications measures, (b) to test the distinction between gratifications sought and obtained, and (c) to test a transactional model (incorporating media exposure and GS) of political effects.

The U.S. adaptation by McLeod and Becker (1974) of Blumler and McQuail's (1969) items is presented here. The PMGS takes less than 5 min-

Profile by Elizabeth M. Perse.

utes to complete. The statements were adapted for use in such contexts as public affairs and political news (Becker, 1979), attending political rallies (Sanders & Kaid, 1981), specific political campaigns (e.g., Garramone, 1984; McLeod, Bybee, & Durall, 1982), and newspaper reading (Becker, 1979). Respondents use the 3-point response options to indicate how much each statement applies to them personally. The statements were also modified to measure gratifications obtained, using 3-point response options (*helpful*, *somewhat helpful*, and *not at all helpful*) (McLeod et al., 1982).

RELIABILITY

After principal-components analysis with varimax rotation of the seven gratifications sought from public affairs and political broadcasts, McLeod and McDonald (1985) reported a Cronbach alpha of .69 for both the three-item Surveillance and the four-item Communication Utility factors. Few other studies report the internal consistency of the dimensions of GS and avoidances. Most studies use the items as individual indicators or use factor scores in analyses.

McLeod and Becker (1981) reported that there is evidence for test–retest stability. Even though the referents differed (i.e., the first concerned news about current event and politics; the second concerned presidential campaigns) there was an average item cross-time correlation of .30 over a 12-month period. This was stronger than the average interitem correlation at a single time. McDonald and Glynn (1984) used Lisrel to test the 12-month stability of Surveillance and Communication Utility dimensions. They found a stability estimate (correcting for attenuation due to unreliability) of .68 for Surveillance and .44 for Communication Utility.

VALIDITY

The GS dimensions have been shown to have content validity. Becker (1979) reported results of a study that supported the completeness of McLeod and Becker's (1974) list. Adults were asked open-ended questions with probes designed to uncover as many reasons as possible for media exposure about local elections and politics. Although some gratifications were more salient to respondents, they included all items in the scale. Becker, though, noted that the avoidance dimensions were incomplete; people also avoided political news because of perceived bias in the reports.

There is also evidence of discriminant validity. McLeod et al. (1982) reacted to the criticisms that U&G research confounds differences between what people seek and what they receive from media exposure. They used

separate measures of gratifications sought and obtained (using similar statements but different response options). Principal-components analyses with
varimax rotation suggested that the two constructs had somewhat different
factor structures, partially supporting their conceptual distinction.

Studies of political effects provided evidence of construct validity.
Blumler and McQuail (1969), for example, observed that strong party sup-
porters were more likely to report watching political broadcasts for reinforcement reasons and less likely to watch for vote guidance. McDonald and
Glynn's (1984) analysis of panel data also supported the construct validity
of Surveillance and Communication Utility dimensions. They found support for the hypothesis that viewers who find cognitive utility would be more
likely to develop social utility for political information. Over time, Surveillance predicted Communication Utility, whereas Communication Utility
did not predict Surveillance.

McLeod and Becker (1974) set out to validate their gratification measures by testing whether the inclusion of gratifications added significantly
to the explained variance of different political effects. They used a strict test,
adding the gratifications and avoidances measures after the exposure measures. The gratifications and avoidances contributed significantly to most
early campaign effects, including probability of voting, campaign activity,
and convention and political advertising viewing. The measures only partially predicted such late campaign effects as political discussion, election-
night media use, and voting-intention change. McLeod and Becker suggested
that other variables might have a stronger influence closer to the election.

COMMENTS

The PMGS has been widely used in political communication contexts with
several adult samples. Its value has been in descriptions of the audience and
theoretical development of models for explaining the connections between
gratifications sought and obtained and media exposure (McLeod et al., 1982;
McLeod & McDonald, 1985). It is the only widely used GS measure that
includes reasons for avoiding media content. The Blumler and McQuail
(1969) scale was also adapted by Palmgreen, Wenner, and Rayburn (1980)
in developing the expectancy-value approach to U&G.

LOCATION

Blumler, J. G., & McQuail, D. (1969). *Television in politics: Its uses and influence.*
       Chicago: University of Chicago Press.
McLeod, J. M., & Becker, L. B. (1974). Testing the validity of gratification mea-

sures through political effects analysis. In J. G. Blumler & E. Katz (Eds.), *The uses of mass communications: Current perspectives on gratifications research* (pp. 137–164). Beverly Hills, CA: Sage.

REFERENCES

Becker, L. B. (1979). Measurement of gratifications. *Communication Research, 6,* 54-73.

Garramone, G. M. (1984). Motivational models: Replication across media for political campaign content. *Journalism Quarterly, 61,* 537–541, 691.

McDonald, D. G., & Glynn, C. J. (1984). The stability of media gratifications. *Journalism Quarterly, 61,* 542–549, 741.

McLeod, J. M., & Becker, L. B. (1981). The uses and gratifications approach. In D. D. Nimmo & K. R. Sanders (Eds.), *Handbook of political communication* (pp. 67–99). Beverly Hills, CA: Sage.

McLeod, J. M., Bybee, C. R., & Durall, J. A. (1982). Evaluating media performance by gratifications sought and received. *Journalism Quarterly, 59,* 3–12, 59.

McLeod, J. M., & McDonald, D. G. (1985). Beyond simple exposure: Media orientations and their impact on political processes. *Communication Research, 12,* 3–34.

Palmgreen, P., Wenner, L. A., & Rayburn, J. D., II. (1980). Relations between gratifications sought and obtained: A study of television news. *Communication Research, 7,* 161–192.

Sanders, K. R., & Kaid, L. L. (1981). Political rallies: Their uses and effects. *Central States Speech Journal, 32,* 1–11.

Political Media Gratifications Scale*: Television Gratifications

Instructions: Here is a list of statements that different people have made when asked why they watch television shows that feature political candidates. For each statement on the list, please tell me whether it applies to you *a lot, a little,* or *not at all.*

1. To judge what political leaders are like.
2. To see what a candidate would do if elected.
3. To keep up with the main issues of the day.
4. To help make up my mind how to vote in an election.
5. To use as ammunition in arguments with others.
6. To judge who is likely to win an election.
7. To enjoy the excitement of an election race.
8. To remind me of my candidate's strong points.

---

*Copyright 1974 by the University of Chicago Press. Reprinted by permission.

Television Avoidances

Instructions: Here is a list of statements that different people have given for avoiding television shows that feature political candidates. For each statement on the list, please tell whether it applies to you *a lot, a little,* or *not at all.*

1. Because I am not much interested in politics.
2. Because my mind is already made up.
3. Because I prefer to relax when watching television.
4. Because you can't always trust what politicians tell you on television.
5. Because some candidates talk down to the audience.
6. Because some candidates talk over one's head.
7. Because they hardly ever have anything to say.

Quality Marriage Index

Norton (1983) conceptualized marital quality as an individual's evaluation of the "goodness of the relationship gestalt" (p. 143). Norton used three important criteria in developing the Quality Marriage Index (QMI); he hoped to improve on earlier measures of marital satisfaction (such as Spanier's [1976] Dyadic Adjustment Scale). First, he argued that self-reported global evaluative judgments be used to assess relationships. Global items are semantically similar to one another and yet independent of other covariates such as communication, conflict, and affection. If global measures are employed, he argued, the researcher is free to explore variables related to marital quality without fear that the construct of interest is embedded in the dependent variable. Second, because global assessments of marital satisfaction tend to yield positively skewed data, Norton (1983) suggested that scores be standardized before they are added (for specific instructions, see p. 149). Third, Norton suggested that the measure of marriage quality be limited to just a few items, to remain parsimonious.

The QMI was developed as a result of work on another scale, the Partner Communication Scale (PCS) (Montgomery & Norton, 1980). The PCS was mailed to 507 couples across four states and consisted of 261 items; only 20 items were analyzed for the QMI. The focus of this scale is communication in a quality marriage. Montgomery and Norton employed four criteria to extract the most cohesive set of evaluative variables: (a) the item must be both descriptive and evaluative of the whole relationship, (b) the item must display face validity, (c) the intercorrelations among these items must be extremely high, and (d) the item must have a high primary factor loading. The resulting index was a six-item, self-report, global measure of marital quality that takes less than 1 minute to complete. People evaluate their marital quality by responding to five items using Likert scales that range from *very strong disagreement* (1) to *very strong agreement* (7) and one item that asks respondents to assess the degree of happiness in their marriage on a scale that ranges from *very unhappy* (1) to *perfectly happy* (10). Although the index was designed to be used for assessing marital quality, researchers have employed the measure successfully in nonmarital relationships as well (Baxter & Bullis, 1986).

Profile by Elizabeth E. Graham.

RELIABILITY

Norton did not provide any reliability information for the QMI. However, Baxter (1990), interested in how people manage contradictions in relationships, reported a Cronbach alpha of .95. Baxter and Bullis (1986) and Van-Lear (1991) also reported high Cronbach alphas (.88 and .93, respectively), even though they modified the index for use in romantic nonmarital relationships. Finally, Perse, Pavitt, and Burggraf (1990) reported a Cronbach alpha of .96. The index appears internally consistent.

VALIDITY

Covariates that are independent of marital quality were used to investigate the construct validity of the index (Norton, 1983). For example, as similarity of attitudes increases, so does perceived marital quality. Norton also reported that those with low QMI scores have talked about ending their relationship.

Other researchers also investigated the validity of the QMI. For example, evidence of concurrent validity was found via significant correlations between the QMI and the Kansas Marital Satisfaction Scale (Schumm et al., 1986). Baxter and Bullis (1986) reported a positive correlation between relationship commitment and satisfaction, providing evidence of criterion-related validity. Schumm et al. (1986) also attempted to establish the discriminant validity of the QMI, although the high correlations between satisfaction with taxes and the QMI suggests that future research needs to investigate discriminant validity further.

COMMENTS

The QMI is a global evaluative assessment of marital happiness and therefore avoids many of the problems associated with traditional measures of marital quality. Although the QMI has not been used extensively, it appears to be a valid and reliable means of assessing marital satisfaction.

LOCATION

Norton, R. (1983). Measuring marital quality: A critical look at the dependent variable. *Journal of Marriage and the Family, 45,* 141–151.

REFERENCES

Baxter, L. A. (1990). Dialectical contradictions in relationship development. *Journal of Social and Personal Relationships, 7*, 69–88.

Baxter, L. A., & Bullis, C. (1986). Turning points in developing romantic relationships. *Human Communication Research, 12*, 469–493.

Montgomery, B., & Norton, R. W. (1980, November). *Grounding for a research program investigating marital communication.* Paper presented at the annual meeting of the Speech Communication Association, New York.

Perse, E. M., Pavitt, C., & Burggraf, C. (1990). Implicit theories of marriage and evaluations of marriage on television. *Human Communication Research, 16*, 387–408.

Schumm, W. R., Paff-Bergen, L. A., Hatch, R. C., Obiorah, F. C., Copeland, J. M., Meens, L. D., & Bugaighis, M. A. (1986). Concurrent and discriminant validity of the Kansas Marital Satisfaction Scale. *Journal of Marriage and the Family, 48*, 381–387.

Spanier, G. B. (1976). Measuring dyadic adjustment: New scales for assessing the quality of marriage and similar dyads. *Journal of Marriage and the Family, 38*, 15–28.

VanLear, C. A. (1991). Testing a cyclical model of communicative openness in relationship development: Two longitudinal studies. *Communication Monographs, 58*, 337–361.

Quality Marriage Index*

Instructions: For Items 1 through 5, use the following scale:

Very strong disagreement = 1
Moderate disagreement = 2
Slight disagreement = 3
Neutral = 4
Slight agreement = 5
Moderate agreement = 6
Very strong agreement = 7

For Item 6, indicate how happy you are by using the following scale:

Very unhappy   1   2   3   4   5   6   7   8   9   10   Perfectly happy

1. We have a good marriage.
2. My relationship with my partner is very stable.
3. Our marriage is strong.
4. My relationship with my partner makes me happy.
5. I really feel like part of a team with my partner.
6. The degree of happiness, everything considered, in your marriage.

Receiver Apprehension Test

We know that people, as sources of communication, are often inhibited in their ability to express themselves frequently or competently to others. A primary reason for that inhibition is communication apprehension. Similarly, we know that people as receivers in communication exchanges often fail to process or decode information adequately. Wheeless (1975) identified receiver apprehension as one potential cause of the inability to listen or decode communication as accurately and efficiently as one might desire. According to Wheeless, receiver apprehension is a learned, trait-like disposition of anxiety or fear about listening. Specifically, receiver apprehension refers to "the fear of misinterpreting, inadequately processing, and/or not being able to adjust psychologically to messages sent by others" (p. 263).

To assess individuals' levels of receiver apprehension, Wheeless (1975) developed a 20-item, Likert-type instrument with response options ranging from *strongly agree* (5) to *strongly disagree* (1). Items on this instrument are designed to measure how persons generally respond while functioning in their role as "receiver." People are asked to self-report how they generally feel when receiving messages from (or listening to) others. Research reveals the RAT to be a unidimensional measure, with all items having their primary loadings on the first unrotated factor (Wheeless, 1975). Consequently, after recoding positively worded items, responses are summed across all 20 items to reveal a total RAT score. The instrument takes only about 10 minutes to complete.

RELIABILITY

The RAT appears to be internally consistent. Wheeless (1975) reported a split-half reliability of .91. Beatty, Behnke, and Henderson (1980) reported an alpha reliability coefficient of .81 for the RAT. Other studies report reliabilities in the upper .80 to lower .90 range.

Profile by Michael J. Beatty.

VALIDITY

The results of numerous studies support the construct validity of the RAT. Beatty et al. (1980) found that RAT scores significantly predicted listeners' self-reported state anxiety associated with two separate difficult listening tasks. Beatty (1981) found a moderate and negative relationship between RAT scores and assimilation scores, which assess the amount of information assimilation across a wide range of topics. Roberts (1984) reported a significant correlation between RAT scores and physiological arousal (tympanic temperature) during a listening task. Beatty (1985) found that RAT scores functioned in a manner consistent with assimilation theory. Specifically, RAT scores were basically stable, but they were increased by the anticipation of a difficult listening task.

Beatty et al. (1980) reported evidence regarding concurrent validity. They found a positive and moderate correlation between RAT scores and trait anxiety scores (administered with instructions to respond in terms of how subjects generally feel while listening to difficult or provocative material).

COMMENTS

In the early development of the RAT, Wheeless (1975) factored individuals' responses to both the receiver-oriented RAT and source-oriented Personal Report of Communication Apprehension items. Reasoning that persons might be apprehensive as sources, but not as receivers (and vice versa), Wheeless found responses factored separately, with all items loading on their respective factors. In short, people responded to the two scales quite differently. With that same sample of 324 college students, Wheeless also found that persons "experienced significantly lower apprehension as receivers than as sources" (p. 267). According to Wheeless, "this result is not surprising. We would probably expect persons to be much less apprehensive generally about receiving information than about functioning as a communication source" (p. 267). Even so, approximately 10% of the respondents scored over one standard deviation above the mean and, thus, could be classified as highly apprehensive about receiving or decoding information.

LOCATION

Wheeless, L. R. (1975). An investigation of receiver apprehension and social context dimensions of communication apprehension. *Speech Teacher, 24,* 261–268.

REFERENCES

Beatty, M. J. (1981). Receiver apprehension as a function of cognitive backlog. *Western Journal of Speech Communication, 45*, 277–281.

Beatty, M. J. (1985). Effects of anticipating listening (state) anxiety on the stability of receiver apprehension scores. *Central States Speech Journal, 36*, 72–76.

Beatty, M. J., Behnke, R. R., & Henderson, L. S. (1980). An empirical validation of the Receiver Apprehension Test as a measure of trait listening anxiety. *Western Journal of Speech Communication, 44*, 132–136.

Roberts, C. V. (1984). A physiological validation of the Receiver Apprehension Test. *Communication Research Reports, 1*, 126–129.

Receiver Apprehension Test*

Instructions: The following statements apply to how various people feel about receiving communication. Indicate if these statements apply to how you feel by noting whether you (5) *strongly agree*, (4) *agree*, (3) *are undecided*, (2) *disagree*, or (1) *strongly disagree*.

1. I feel comfortable when listening to others on the phone.
2. It is often difficult for me to concentrate on what others are saying.
3. When listening to members of the opposite sex I find it easy to concentrate on what is being said.
4. I have no fear of being a listener as a member of an audience.
5. I feel relaxed when listening to new ideas.
6. I would rather not have to listen to other people at all.
7. I am generally overexcited and rattled when others are speaking to me.
8. I often feel uncomfortable when listening to others.
9. My thoughts become confused and jumbled when reading important information.
10. I often have difficulty concentrating on what others are saying.
11. Receiving new information makes me feel restless.
12. Watching television makes me nervous.
13. When on a date I find myself tense and self-conscious when listening to my date.
14. I enjoy being a good listener.
15. I generally find it easy to concentrate on what is being said.
16. I seek out the opportunity to listen to new ideas.

---

17. I have difficulty concentrating on instructions others give me.
18. It is hard to listen or concentrate on what other people are saying unless I know them well.
19. I feel tense when listening as a member of a social gathering.
20. Television programs that attempt to change my mind about something make me nervous.

Note. Scores for Items 1, 3, 4, 5, 14, 15, and 16 are reverse-coded before all items are summed.

Relational
Communication Scale

Burgoon and Hale (1984) conceptualized relational communication as the verbal and nonverbal themes present in people's communication that define an interpersonal relationship. Based on a thorough analysis and synthesis of the literature, 12 relational communication dimensions were derived: Dominance–Submission, Intimacy, Affection–Hostility, Intensity of Involvement, Inclusion–Exclusion, Trust, Depth–Superficiality, Emotional Arousal, Composure, Similarity, Formality, and Task–Social Orientation.

To develop the Relational Communication Scale (RCS), Burgoon and Hale (1987) first canvassed related measures and constructed 32 items that reflected the relational topoi. Next, Burgoon and Hale generated a few possible factor solutions for the 12 dimensions of relational communication; they ranged from a 4-factor orthogonal (20-item) solution accounting for 51% of the variance to a 10-factor oblique (60-item) solution accounting for 57% of the variance. They recommended using an 8-factor solution, and, depending on one's measurement objectives, the 4-factor orthogonal solution might be preferable.

The eight factors (and a sample item for each) are: Immediacy/Affection ("Person A was highly involved in the conversation"), Similarity/Depth ("A didn't care what B thinks"), Receptivity/Trust ("A wanted B to trust him/her"), Composure ("A was calm and poised with B"), Formality ("A made the interaction very formal"), Dominance ("A was dominating the conversation"), Equality ("A didn't treat B as an equal"), and Task Orientation ("A wanted to stick to the main purpose of the interaction"). This solution best captured "the relational meanings that are imbedded in all communication interchanges" (Burgoon & Hale, 1987, p. 40).

Although primarily designed as a self-report measure, the RCS may also be used as an other-report (e.g., Burgoon, Olney, & Coker, 1987) and observer-report measure (Burgoon & Newton, 1991). The original scale contained 64 Likert items that range from *strongly disagree* (1) to *strongly agree* (5). Generally this scale has been used in dyadic relationships; however, the RCS is versatile and can be adapted for use in interpersonal, family, health

Profile by Elizabeth E. Graham.

care, and mass communication settings. It takes respondents about 10 minutes to complete.

RELIABILITY

Employing different versions of the RCS, Burgoon and Hale (1987) reported coefficient alphas for the eight dimensions that range from .42 to .88. Other researchers, using different versions of the scale, reported similar results (Buller, LePoire, Aune, & Eloy, 1992; Kelley & Burgoon, 1991).

VALIDITY

Burgoon and Hale (1987) reported several validity studies for the different RCS versions. For example, in a series of criterion-related validity studies, they asked respondents to discuss a social or moral problem with a friend and a stranger. In each pair, one respondent secretly served as a confederate. In a third of the conditions, the confederate increased nonverbal immediacy, in another third, the confederate reduced nonverbal immediacy, and the remaining third was instructed to act as naturally as possible. Respondents completed the 32-item instrument (as well as the Personal Report of Communication Apprehension and the Unwillingness-to-Communicate Scale) as it pertained to the recently completed interaction.

The results indicated that the RCS is capable of discriminating: "(1) immediate from nonimmediate behaviors, (2) high from low gaze levels, (3) pleasant from hostile voices, (4) high from low reward communicators, (5) male from female communicators, (6) dimensions of credibility, and (7) dimensions of personality" (Burgoon & Hale, 1987, p. 40). Burgoon and associates have elaborated on many of these findings in subsequent research (e.g., Buller & Aune, 1988; Buller & Burgoon, 1986; Burgoon, Coker, & Coker, 1986; Burgoon & Hale, 1988; Burgoon, Olney, & Coker, 1987; Burgoon, Newton, Walther, & Baesler, 1989; Burgoon, Pfau, Birk, & Manusov, 1987; Burgoon, Walther, & Baesler, 1992).

The RCS has utility beyond dyadic contexts. For example, Burgoon, Pfau, Parrott, et al. (1987), interested in the communication between physicians and patients, reported that increases in receptivity, immediacy, composure, similarity, formality, and less dominance by the physician were responsible for greater patient satisfaction. In an attempt to interface personal and mediated communication, Pfau (1990) concluded that "relational messages account for more influence than content messages in both television and interpersonal communication, whereas content messages are responsible for more influence than relational messages in print, radio, and public address" (p. 204). Furthermore, Walther and Burgoon (1992) reported that computer-mediated groups mirror face-to-face groups in that both experience an increase in relational communication over time. These studies contributed to the construct validity of the RCS.

COMMENTS

The RCS appears to be a valid measure as evidenced by the vast amount of validity research conducted. Although some of the dimensions initially had more variable or lower reliabilities, they improved in later investigations. Future research should investigate the test–retest reliability of the RCS.

LOCATION

Burgoon, J. K., & Hale, J. L. (1987). Validation and measurement of the fundamental themes of relational communication. *Communication Monographs, 54,* 19–41.

REFERENCES

Buller, D. B, & Aune, R. K. (1988). The effects of vocalics and nonverbal sensitivity on compliance: A speech accommodation theory explanation. *Human Communication Research, 14,* 301–332.

Buller, D. B, & Burgoon, J. K. (1986). The effects of vocalics and nonverbal sensitivity on compliance: A replication and extension. *Human Communication Research, 13,* 126–144.

Buller, D. B., LePoire, B. A., Aune, R. K., & Eloy, S. V. (1992). Social perceptions as mediators of the effect of speech rate similarity on compliance. *Human Communication Research, 19,* 286–311.

Burgoon, J. K., & Coker, D. A., & Coker, R. A. (1986). Communicative effects of gaze behavior: A test of two contrasting explanations. *Human Communication Research, 12,* 495–524.

Burgoon, J. K., & Hale, J. L. (1984). The fundamental topoi of relational communication. *Communication Monographs, 51,* 193–214.

Burgoon, J. K., & Hale, J. L. (1988). Nonverbal expectancy violations: Model elaboration and application to immediacy behaviors. *Communication Monographs, 55,* 58–79.

Burgoon, J. K., & Newton, D. A. (1991). Applying a social meaning model to relational message interpretations of conversational involvement: Comparing observer and participant perspectives. *Southern Communication Journal, 56,* 96–113.

Burgoon, J. K., Newton, D. A., Walther, J. B., & Baesler, E. J. (1989). Nonverbal expectancy violations and conversational involvement. *Journal of Nonverbal Behavior, 13,* 97–119.

Burgoon, J. K., Olney, C. A., & Coker, R. A. (1987). The effects of communicator characteristics on patterns of reciprocity and compensation. *Journal of Nonverbal Behavior, 11,* 146–165.

Burgoon, J. K., Pfau, M., Birk, T., & Manusov, V. (1987). Nonverbal communication performance and perceptions associated with reticence: Replications and classroom implications. *Communication Education, 36,* 119–130.

Burgoon, J. K., Pfau, M., Parrott, R., Birk, T., Coker, R., & Burgoon, M. (1987). Relational communication, satisfaction, compliance-gaining strategies, and compliance in communication between physicians and patients. *Communication Monographs, 54,* 307–324.

Burgoon, J. K., Walther, J. B., & Baesler, E. J. (1992). Interpretations, evaluations, and consequences of interpersonal touch. *Human Communication Research, 19,* 237–263.

Kelley, D. L., & Burgoon, J. K. (1991). Understanding marital satisfaction and couple type as functions of relational expectations. *Human Communication Research, 18,* 40–69.

Pfau, M. (1990). A channel approach to television influence. *Journal of Broadcasting and Electronic Media, 34,* 195–214.

Walther, J. B., & Burgoon, J. K. (1992). Relational communication in computer-mediated interaction. *Human Communication Research, 19,* 50–88.

Relational Communication Scale*

Instructions: Below is a series of statements about the conversation you just completed with your partner. For each one, please circle a number from 1 to 7, depending on the degree to which you agree or disagree with the statement. A 7 means you *strongly agree*, a 6 means you *agree*, a 5 means you *agree somewhat*, a 4 means you are *neutral or unsure*, a 3 means you *disagree somewhat*, a 2 means you *disagree*, and a 1 means you *strongly disagree*. You may circle 1, 2, 3, 4, 5, 6, or 7. Please complete all items.

Strongly disagree	Disagree	Disagree somewhat	Neutral or unsure	Agree somewhat	Agree	Strongly agree
1	2	3	4	5	6	7

[Editors' note: The items listed below represent the eight dimensions recommended by the scale authors; they advocate choosing at least four items per dimension (when possible) from the following pool of items to reflect the dimensions one desires to measure and the length of measure desired.]

Immediacy/Affection (Intimacy I)

1. He/she was intensely involved in our conversation.
2. He/she did not want a deeper relationship between us.
3. He/she was not attracted to me.
4. He/she found the conversation stimulating.
5. He/she communicated coldness rather than warmth.
6. He/she created a sense of distance between us.
7. He/she acted bored by our conversation.
8. He/she was interested in talking to me.
9. He/she showed enthusiasm while talking to me.

Similarity/Depth (Intimacy II)

10. He/she made me feel he/she was similar to me.
11. He/she tried to move the conversation to a deeper level.
12. He/she acted like we were good friends.
13. He/she seemed to desire further communication with me.
14. He/she seemed to care if I liked him/her.

Receptivity/Trust (Intimacy III)

15. He/she was sincere.
16. He/she was interested in talking with me.
17. He/she wanted me to trust him/her.
18. He/she was willing to listen to me.
19. He/she was open to my ideas.
20. He/she was honest in communicating with me.

Composure

21. He/she felt very tense talking to me.
22. He/she was calm and poised with me.
23. He/she felt very relaxed talking with me.
24. He/she seemed nervous in my presence.
25. He/she was comfortable interacting with me.

Formality

26. He/she made the interaction very formal.
27. He/she wanted the discussion to be casual.
28. He/she wanted the discussion to be informal.

Dominance

29. He/she attempted to persuade me.
30. He/she didn't attempt to influence me.
31. He/she tried to control the interaction.
32. He/she tried to gain my approval.
33. He/she didn't try to win my favor.
34. He/she had the upper hand in the conversation.

Equality

35. He/she considered us equals.
36. He/she did not treat me as an equal.
37. He/she wanted to cooperate with me.

Task Orientation

38. He/she wanted to stick to the main purpose of the interaction.
39. He/she was more interested in social conversation than the task at hand.
40. He/she was very work-oriented.
41. He/she was more interested in working on the task at hand than having social conversation.

Note. Items should be arranged randomly before administration.

Items 2, 3, 5, 6, 7, 21, 24, 27, 28, 30, 33, 36, and 39 should be reverse-coded prior to scoring.

Relational
Dimensions Instrument

Fitzpatrick (1976, 1977) developed the Relational Dimensions Instrument (RDI) in an effort to organize marital interaction research and to create a typology of relationships. She argued that Kantor and Lehr's (1975) Access and Target dimensions are central to definitions of relational life and she used these dimensions as a framework for this measure. Access dimensions refer to space, time, and energy and describe how couples organize their surroundings and personal space. Target dimensions refer to affect, power, and meaning. Fitzpatrick and Best (1979) concluded that "given the pervasiveness of these factors, it seems reasonable to assume that relational partners make decisions about how to organize their energy, space, and time to achieve affect, power and meaning in their lives" (p. 169).

To develop the RDI, Fitzpatrick (1976, 1977) first drew 200 access–target and autonomy–interdependence items from the work of Kantor and Lehr (1975). After they assessed for redundancy, 184 items remained (approximately 25 items for each of the eight dimensions: Energy, Space, Time, Affect, Power, Meaning, Autonomy, and Interdependence). Questionnaires containing the 184 items were administered to over 900 married subjects.

Factor analysis revealed a 64-item, eight-factor instrument (Fitzpatrick, 1976, 1977). First, Sharing consisted of all of Kantor and Lehr's (1975) six dimensions. It suggests an openness, caring, and concern between partners and is represented by items such as "Sex is very important in our relationship." Second, Ideology of Traditionalism reflects many of Kantor and Lehr's meaning items and suggests a strong commitment to traditional values, customs, and rules; an example item is: "Our wedding ceremony was (will be) very important to us." Third, Ideology of Uncertainty and Change also reflects many of Kantor and Lehr's meaning items yet encompasses an openness to uncertainty and change; spontaneity, novelty, and humor define this factor; a sample item is: "There seem to be many minor crises in our lives." Fourth, Assertiveness taps the power dimension of a relationship; an example item is: "We cook and eat our meals separately, even when we are both at home." Fifth, Temporal Regularity reflects an adherence to time and sched-

Profile by Elizabeth E. Graham.

314

ules; it is represented by items such as "In our house, we keep a fairly regular daily time schedule." Sixth, Conflict Avoidance suggests the sharing of only positive feelings; an example item is: "It is better to hide one's true feelings in order to avoid hurting your spouse/mate." Seventh, Undifferentiated Space refers to sharing of personal property as well as space and is represented by items such as "I open my spouse's personal mail without asking permission." Eighth, Autonomy concerns individual space and time apart; a sample item is: "We can go for long periods of time without spending much time together as a couple." Individuals are categorized according to their self-reported responses to three dimensional measures: ideology (traditionalism, uncertainty), interdependence (sharing, autonomy, undifferentiated space, and temporal regularity), and communication (assertiveness and conflict avoidance).

In addition to item and factor analyses, Fitzpatrick (1976, 1977) conducted a linear typal analysis with 68 couples to isolate relational types. "Independents" thrive on uncertainty, autonomy, and change and are opposed to traditional values. Independents do not avoid conflict, typically engage in a moderate amount of sharing, put up few psychological or physical boundaries, and report being less socially constrained. "Separates" report being socially constrained and separate from their partner yet not independent or autonomous. In addition, separates report engaging in very little sharing or conflict. "Traditionals" engage in a high degree of sharing and are most comfortable with temporal regularity. They also espouse traditional values and attitudes including limited autonomy and, generally, do not avoid conflict.

The next step in the development of the RDI involved comparing individuals' relational definitions with those of their partners (Fitzpatrick, 1976, 1977). Spouses were classified as separates, traditionals, or independents and then husband–wife responses were compared and couples classified as either pure (those in which both partners agree that their relationship is best defined as traditional, independent, or separate) or mixed (couples that do not share the same relational definition). Through repeated research (Fitzpatrick, 1976, 1977; Fitzpatrick & Best, 1979), only four of the possible couple types emerged with any regularity: traditional, independent, separate, and traditional–separate. Sixty percent of the sample couples were categorized as one of the four types (Fitzpatrick, 1988). Respondents complete the RDI about their relationship dyad. The RDI uses Likert and frequency scales and requires about 25 minutes for completion.

RELIABILITY

Fitzpatrick (1976, 1977) reported an overall Cronbach alpha of .71 for the RDI. However, two of the RDI's eight subscales (Conflict Avoidance and

Undifferentiated Space) had especially low reliabilities. To remedy this, Fitzpatrick and Indvik (1982) added 13 items from the original pool of items; the resulting alphas for the 77-item instrument were sharing, .88; ideology of traditionalism, .80; temporal regularity, .82; assertiveness, .65; autonomy, .46; ideology of uncertainty and change, .60; undifferentiated space, .52; and conflict avoidance, .60. Other researchers reported similar results (Kelley & Burgoon, 1991).

VALIDITY

Various studies found evidence of construct validity of the RDI. For example, Fitzpatrick (1976, 1977), interested in expressive and instrumental communication of couples, found that traditionals are more frank in their communication with one another and also communicate vulnerability more frequently than do either independents or separates. Their analysis also revealed that independents were "less socially restrained in their communication than either *traditionals* or *separates*" (Fitzpatrick, 1977, p. 273). Fitzpatrick and Indvik (1982) provided evidence of construct validity by regenerating the typology in reference to the instrumental and expressive domains of relationships. This was accomplished by administering measures of sex-role orientation to a sample of 224 married couples drawn from a large metropolitan area. Not surprisingly, traditional and separate couples, as well as separate–traditionals, were oriented toward conventional male and female role behavior. Traditional couples were very normative in that the husband engaged in instrumental communication and the wife engaged in expressive communication, yet in separate relationships, both partners were instrumental and neither was expressive. Interestingly, the most expressive communication was used by the traditional wife of a separate husband. Independent couples reported the use of both instrumental and expressive forms of communication. However, as the wife exhibited more instrumental behavior, the husband did not necessarily engage in more expressive communication. Despite the fact that traditional couples adhere to sex-role orientations and behaviors, Burggraf and Sillars (1987) found no evidence to suggest that there are any sex differences within couple types.

   Fitzpatrick and Best (1979) and Guerrero and Eloy (1992) provided evidence of criterion validity. Their research indicated that dyadic adjustment (Spanier, 1976), cohesiveness, consensus, affectual expression, and satisfaction between relational partners could discriminate between couple types. For example, traditional couples reported more satisfaction, consensus, and cohesion than did any other couple type. However, VanLear and Zietlow (1990) analyzed three approaches to marital satisfaction and found that traditionals and independents were most satisfied and separates were least satisfied. Fitzpatrick and Best (1979) also found that the RDI can discriminate between those in agreement on couple type and those in disagreement over couple type: A couple that shares a relational definition was more cohesive and experienced more agreement on many relational issues than was a couple that did not share the same relational definition.

Marital types have been associated with a wide variety of perceptual communication variables, thus adding substantially to the criterion and construct validity of the RDI. Sillars, Pike, Jones, and Redmon (1983), for example, compared the three pure couple types with conflict behavior and found that the major discriminating factor between the couple types was avoidance of communication. Williamson and Fitzpatrick (1985) reported that couple types, as defined by the RDI, employ different control strategies, and Witteman and Fitzpatrick (1986) indicated that marital types utilize different patterns of compliance-gaining strategies. Finally, Sillars and associates (Sillars, Burggraf, Yost, & Zietlow, 1992; Sillars, Weisberg, Burggraf, & Wilson, 1987) investigated themes across marital types. As expected, traditional couples emphasized communal themes, independents espoused a balance between individual and communal themes, and separates relied on individual themes. Finally, Segrin and Fitzpatrick (1992) reported an association between couple type, depression, and verbal aggression. They concluded that separates suffer from the most depression and exhibit the most verbal aggression and traditionals report the least depression and verbal aggression. As Fitzpatrick (1987) noted, "the range and diversity of the interaction differences among these couple types indicates that the typology is not artifactual" (p. 137).

COMMENTS

Although the RDI was designed to study married couples, Fitzpatrick (1984) proposed that it has measurement utility in premarital romantic relationships as well. Similarly, the RDI was established for use in personal relationships; however, two studies employed the RDI to assess perceptions of married couples on TV (Fallis, Fitzpatrick, & Friestad, 1985; Perse, Pavitt, & Burggraf, 1990). The RDI has also been modified by employing only two of the original eight factors. The two subscales, Sharing and Traditionalism, are capable of defining relational types because they are so large and inclusive of the other six dimensions (Sillars et al., 1983).

Baxter (1988) summarized many of the strengths and weaknesses of the RDI. She applauded the vast amount of validity information amassed on behalf of the RDI yet was less enthused about the reliability of the RDI. Four subscales—Autonomy, Undifferentiated Space, Ideology of Uncertainty and Change, and Conflict Avoidance—have relatively low reliabilities.

Baxter also calls for more test–retest reliability information. She also noted that the majority of the research is based on pure couple types, yet a full 40% of the sampled couples are categorized as mixed types. Thus, she argued, it is difficult to draw any definitive conclusion concerning the mixed couple types. Yet, Baxter (1988) noted "the RDI appears to be tapping some unique features of the marital relationship which other measures used with adult marital relationships do not gauge" (p. 202).

LOCATION

Fitzpatrick, M. A. (1976). A typological examination of communication in enduring relationships (Doctoral dissertation, Temple University, 1976). *Dissertation Abstracts International*, *38*, 414.

Fitzpatrick, M. A. (1988). *Between husbands and wives*. Beverly Hills, CA: Sage.

Fitzpatrick, M. A., & Indvik, J. (1982). The instrumental and expressive domains of marital communication. *Human Communication Research*, *8*, 195–213.

REFERENCES

Baxter, L. A. (1988). Dyadic personal relationships: Measurement options. In C. H. Tardy (Ed.), *A handbook for the study of human communication: Methods and instruments for observing, measuring, and assessing communication processes* (pp. 193–228). Norwood, NJ: Ablex.

Burggraf, C. S., & Sillars, A. L. (1987). A critical examination of sex differences in marital communication. *Communication Monographs*, *54*, 276–294.

Fallis, S. F., Fitzpatrick, M. A., & Friestad, M. S. (1985). Spouses' discussion of television portrayals of close relationships. *Communication Research*, *12*, 59–81.

Fitzpatrick, M. A. (1977). A typological approach to communication in relationships. *Communication Yearbook*, *1*, 263–275.

Fitzpatrick, M. A. (1984). A typological approach to marital interaction: Recent theory and research. *Advances in Experimental Social Psychology*, *18*, 1–47.

Fitzpatrick, M. A. (1987). Marriage and verbal intimacy. In V. J. Derlega & J. H. Berg (Eds.), *Self-disclosure: Theory, research, and therapy* (pp. 131–154). New York: Plenum Press.

Fitzpatrick, M. A., & Best, P. (1979). Dyadic adjustment in relational types: Consensus, cohesion, affectual expression, and satisfaction in enduring relationships. *Communication Monographs*, *46*, 167–178.

Guerrero, L., & Eloy, S. (1992). Relational satisfaction and jealousy across marital types. *Communication Reports*, *4*, 23–31.

Kantor, D., & Lehr, W. (1975). *Inside the family*. New York: Harper & Row.

Kelley, D. L., & Burgoon, J. K. (1991). Understanding marital satisfaction and couple type as functions of relational expectations. *Human Communication Research*, *18*, 40–69.

Perse, E. M., Pavitt, C., & Burggraf, C. S. (1990). Implicit theories of marriage and evaluations of marriage on television. *Human Communication Research, 16,* 387–408.

Segrin, C., & Fitzpatrick, M. A. (1992). Depression and verbal aggressiveness in different marital types. *Communication Studies, 43,* 79–91.

Sillars, A. L., Burggraf, C. S., Yost, S., & Zietlow, P. H. (1992). Conversational themes and marital relationship definitions: Quantitative and qualitative investigations. *Human Communication Research, 19,* 124–154.

Sillars, A. L., Pike, G. R., Jones, T. S., & Redmon, K. (1983). Communication and conflict in marriage. *Communication Yearbook, 7,* 414–429.

Sillars, A. L., Weisberg, J., Burggraf, C. S., & Wilson, E. A. (1987). Content themes in marital communication. *Human Communication Research, 13,* 495–528.

Spanier, G. B. (1976). Measuring dyadic adjustment: New scales for assessing the quality of marriage and similar dyads. *Journal of Marriage and the Family, 38,* 15–28.

VanLear, C. A. Jr., & Zietlow, P. H. (1990). Toward a contingency approach to marital interaction: An empirical investigation of three approaches. *Communication Monographs, 57,* 202–218.

Williamson, R. N., & Fitzpatrick, M. A. (1985). Two approaches to marital interaction: Relational control patterns in marital types. *Communication Monographs, 52,* 236–252.

Witteman, H., & Fitzpatrick, M. A. (1986). Compliance-gaining in marital interaction: Power bases, processes, and outcome. *Communication Monographs, 53,* 130–143.

Relational Dimensions Instrument*

This questionnaire is concerned with how husbands and wives communicate with one another and how they organize their family life. The answers will provide information about couples in ongoing relationships and will have direct practical application in counseling and marital enrichment programs. Your responses will be used for the purposes of research only. All responses will be kept confidential and anonymous, so please do not sign your name.

Instructions: Although the questionnaire is rather lengthy, much of it requires only short answers and can be completed rather quickly. There are no right or wrong answers to these questions, so try to answer them as honestly as possible. Give each question a moment's thought and then answer it. Please answer the questions without help from your partner. Your partner should not see your answers nor try to help you with them. Please feel free to add comments if none of the responses describe how you feel or fit your situation. Thank you for participating in this project.

On the following pages, you will find a number of statements. Each statement is followed by a scale. This scale requires you to make a judgment of how frequently a particular activity or behavior occurs *or* how frequently a given statement can be considered true for you or your relationship. Please *circle* the number that best shows how you feel about the statement.

Always	Usually	Often	Occasionally	Often not	Usually not	Never
1	2	3	4	5	6	7

[Editors' note: The numbers 1 to 7 appear after each statement.]

1. We eat our meals (i.e., the ones at home) at the same time every day.
2. I open my spouse's/mate's personal mail without asking permission.
3. My spouse/mate tells me (i.e., tries to influence) what magazines or books to read and/or what television shows to watch.
4. I have my own private workspace (study, workshop, utility room, etc.).
5. My spouse/mate reassures and comforts me when I am feeling low.
6. If I can avoid arguing about some problems, they will disappear.
7. In our house, we keep a fairly regular daily time schedule.
8. My mate complains if I open his/her personal mail without permission.
9. I tell (i.e., try to influence) my spouse/mate which magazines or books to read and/or what television shows to watch.
10. My spouse has his/her own private workspace (workshop, utility room, study, and so on).
11. We tell each other how much we love or care about each other.
12. Our time schedule varies quite a bit from day to day.
13. It bothers me if a guest goes into our refrigerator or fixes himself/herself some coffee in our home.
14. My spouse/mate *forces* me to do things that I do not want to do.

Instructions: The next set of questions is followed by scales which ask for a judgment of how strongly you agree or disagree with particular statements concerning a variety of issues. Please *circle* the number that best shows how you feel about the statement.

Strongly agree	Agree	Moderately agree	Undecided	Moderately disagree	Disagree	Strongly disagree
1	2	3	4	5	6	7

[Editors' note: The numbers 1 to 7 appear after each statement.]

15. It is important for a couple (or a family) to attend church (synagogue) and, when possible, to attend together.
16. Life is filled with so many contradictions that I am not certain how to interpret what it all means.

17. It is better to hide one's true feelings in order to avoid hurting your spouse/mate.
18. I think it is important for one to have some private space which is all his/her own and separate from one's mate.
19. Our society, as we see it, needs to regain faith in the law and in our institutions.
20. Relationships should not interfere with each person's pursuit to discover his/her own potential.
21. I think that we joke around and have more fun than most couples.
22. Partners should be frank and spontaneous in conversations with one another even if it leads to disagreements.
23. A woman should take her husband's last name when she marries.
24. In marriage/close relationships, there should be no constraints or restrictions on individual freedom.

Note. The items presented here are the three top-loading (including negative loadings) items reported in Fitzpatrick and Indvik (1982). For the entire measure and instructions on how to calculate marital types, see Fitzpatrick (1988).

Sharing: 5, 11, 21; Autonomy: 4, 10, 18; Traditionalism: 15, 19, 23; Uncertainty: 16, 20, 24; Conflict Avoidance: 6, 17, 22; Space: 2, 8, 13; Temporal Regularity: 1, 7, 12; Assertiveness: 3, 9, 14.

Scoring Instructions: Reverse-coding for all items and again reverse-coding for Items 8, 12, 13, 15, and 22.

Revised Self-Disclosure Scale

Wheeless and Grotz (1976) developed a topic-free multidimensional measure of self-disclosure, the Revised Self-Disclosure Scale (RSDS), to improve on earlier measures of self-disclosure (e.g., Self-Disclosure Inventory [Jourard & Lasakow, 1958]). They conceptualized self-disclosure as "any message about the self that a person communicates to another" (Wheeless & Grotz, 1976, p. 338), either self-disclosure to a particular individual (RSDS) (Wheeless & Grotz, 1976) or a general predisposition to disclose to other people (Wheeless, 1976). The authors conceived of self-disclosure as comprising eight dimensions: Frequency, Duration, Honesty, Accuracy, Intimacy, Disclosive Intent, Positive or Negative Information, and Disclosure Relevance to Other Topics.

The RSDS was developed in a series of studies (Wheeless & Grotz, 1976, 1977; Wheeless, 1976, 1978). First, 32 items were written to reflect the eight components of self-disclosure. Next, a diverse sample of subjects completed the RSDS about one of 20 disclosure targets (e.g., mother, spouse, and doctor). The orthogonal rotation accounted for 60% of the variance and revealed a 15-item, five-factor solution: Intent to Disclose, Amount of Disclosure, Positive–Negative Nature of Self-Disclosure, Honesty/Accuracy of Disclosure, and Depth Control of Disclosure. Oblique rotation produced a 17-item, six-factor solution that also accounted for 60% of the variance. The sixth factor was disregarded because of low reliability (.25). Wheeless and Grotz (1976) concluded that because both rotations yielded similar factor structures, the results could be interpreted as supporting the existence of at least five independent dimensions of self-disclosure.

To improve the reliability of the subscales, Wheeless (1976) added eight items to each of the five dimensions of self-disclosure. The results of a principal-components factor analysis utilizing orthogonal rotation revealed a 31-item, five-factor solution; the factors were identical to those derived earlier. Respondents require about 5 minutes to self-report how they communicate with a specific target person by responding to 31 items using Likert scales that range from 7 (*strongly agree*) to 1 (*strongly disagree*). The same dimensions and items may be used to measure general disclosiveness; here, respondents are requested to complete the instrument to reflect how they communicate with other people in general (Wheeless, 1978).

Profile by Elizabeth E. Graham.

RELIABILITY

Wheeless (1978) reported the following reliabilities for the RSDS dimensions: intent, .85; amount, .88; positiveness/negativeness, .91; depth, .84; and honesty, .87. Various researchers have employed the RSDS and have reported coefficient alphas ranging from .81 to .91 (Stacks & Stone, 1984; Wheeless, Nesser, & McCroskey, 1986). The reliabilities for the General Disclosiveness Scale (GSD) ranged from .65 to .90 (Wheeless, 1978).

VALIDITY

Many of the hypothesized dimensions of self-disclosure were also found empirically, thus providing some evidence of content validity (Wheeless & Grotz, 1976). Several studies assessed the construct validity of the RSDS. For example, Wheeless (1976) reported that perceptions of solidarity were accompanied by higher levels of self-disclosure. Furthermore, self-disclosure and trustworthiness were related (Wheeless, 1978; Wheeless & Grotz, 1977) and served as predictors of interpersonal solidarity (Wheeless, 1978).

Several studies concluded that the more apprehensive students are, the less likely they are to engage in self-disclosure (Stacks & Stone, 1984; Wheeless et al., 1986). In addition, Hurt and Gonzalez (1988) reported that hearing students were not likely to disclose to hearing-impaired students and hearing-impaired students were not likely to disclose to hearing students.

Gudykunst and associates (Gudykunst, Forgas, Franklyn-Stokes, Schmidt, & Moylan, 1992; Gudykunst & Hammer, 1988; Gudykunst, Nishida, & Chua, 1986; Gudykunst, Nishida, & Schmidt, 1989) investigated the role of uncertainty reduction in interethnic and intercultural relationships. Although they used only the depth dimension of the RSDS in their analysis, their results indicated that there are differences in self-disclosure for high- and low-intimacy dyads as well as for people of different races and cultures. These results provide further evidence of the construct validity of the self-disclosure measure. In addition to the numerous studies that provided construct validity of the RSDS, two studies (Wheeless et al., 1986; Wheeless, 1978) confirmed the factor structure of the RSDS, providing further evidence of the construct validity of this measure.

COMMENTS

The RSDS appears to be both reliable and valid. The versatility of the RSDS is probably its biggest strength. Wheeless (1978) created a measure of general disclosiveness (GSD) as well as self-disclosure with a specific person (RSDS). Both measures were developed in a systematic fashion with careful attention paid to the network of concepts that may be theoretically related to self-disclosure. As Tardy (1988) suggested, future research should establish the convergent validity of the RSDS.

LOCATION

Wheeless, L. R. (1978). A follow-up study of the relationships among trust, disclosure, and interpersonal solidarity. *Human Communication Research, 4,* 143–157.

REFERENCES

Gudykunst, W. B., Forgas, J. P., Franklyn-Stokes, A., Schmidt, K. L., & Moylan, S. (1992). The influence of social identity and intimacy of relationship on interethnic communication: An extension of findings from the United States to Australia and England. *Communication Reports, 5,* 90–98.

Gudykunst, W. B., & Hammer, M. R. (1988). The influence of social identity and intimacy of interethnic relationships on uncertainty reduction processes. *Human Communication Research, 14,* 569–601.

Gudykunst, W. B., Nishida, T., & Chua, E. (1986). Uncertainty reduction in Japanese-North American dyads. *Communication Research Reports, 3,* 39–46.

Gudykunst, W. B., Nishida, T., & Schmidt, K. L. (1989). The influence of cultural, relational, and personality factors on uncertainty reduction processes. *Western Journal of Speech Communication, 53,* 13–29.

Hurt, H. T., & Gonzalez, T. (1988). Communication apprehension and distorted self-disclosure: The hidden disabilities of hearing-impaired students. *Communication Education, 37,* 106–117.

Jourard, S. M., & Lasakow, P. (1958). Some factors in self-disclosure. *Journal of Abnormal and Social Psychology, 56,* 91–98.

Stacks, D. W., & Stone, J. D. (1984). An examination of the effect of basic speech courses, self-concept, and self-disclosure on communication apprehension. *Communication Education, 33,* 317–331.

Tardy, C. H. (1988). Self-disclosure: Objectives and methods of measurement. In C. H. Tardy (Ed.), *A handbook for the study of human communication: Methods and instruments for observing, measuring, and assessing communication processes* (pp. 323–346). Norwood, NJ: Ablex.

Wheeless, L. R. (1976). Self-disclosure and interpersonal solidarity: Measurement, validation, and relationships. *Human Communication Research, 3,* 47–61.

Wheeless, L. R., & Grotz, J. (1976). Conceptualization and measurement of reported self-disclosure. *Human Communication Research, 2,* 338–346.

Wheeless, L. R., & Grotz, J. (1977). The measurement of trust and its relationship to self-disclosure. *Human Communication Research, 3,* 250–257.

Wheeless, L. R., Nesser, K., & McCroskey, J. C. (1986). The relationships of self-disclosure and disclosiveness to high and low communication apprehension. *Communication Research Reports*, *3*, 129–134.

Revised Self-Disclosure Scale*

Instructions: Please mark the following statements to reflect how *you* communicate *with [specific target person]*. Indicate the degree to which the following statements reflect how you communicate with this person by marking whether you (7) *strongly agree*, (6) *agree*; (5) *moderately agree*, (4) *are undecided*, (3) *moderately disagree*, (2) *disagree*, or (1) *strongly disagree*. Record the number of your response in the space provided. Work quickly and just record your first impressions.

Intended Disclosure
1. When I wish, my self-disclosures are always accurate reflections of who I really am.
2. When I express my personal feelings, I am always aware of what I am doing and saying.
3. When I reveal my feelings about myself, I consciously intend to do so.
4. When I am self-disclosing, I am consciously aware of what I am revealing.

Amount
5. I do not often talk about myself.
6. My statements of my feelings are usually brief.
7. I usually talk about myself for fairly long periods at a time.
8. My conversation lasts the least time when I am discussing myself.
9. I often talk about myself.
10. I often discuss my feelings about myself.
11. Only infrequently do I express my personal beliefs and opinions.

Positive–Negative
12. I usually disclose positive things about myself.
13. On the whole, my disclosures about myself are more negative than positive.
14. I normally reveal "bad" feelings I have about myself.
15. I normally "express" my good feelings about myself.
16. I often reveal more undesirable things about myself than desirable things.

---

17. I usually disclose negative things about myself.
18. On the whole, my disclosures about myself are more positive than negative.

Control of Depth
19. I intimately disclose who I really am, openly and fully in my conversation.
20. Once I get started, my self-disclosures last a long time.
21. I often disclose intimate, personal things about myself without hesitation.
22. I feel that I sometimes do *not* control my self-disclosure of personal or intimate things I tell about myself.
23. Once I get started, I intimately and fully reveal myself in my self-disclosures.

Honesty–Accuracy
24. I cannot reveal myself when I want to because I do not know myself thoroughly enough.
25. I am often not confident that my expressions of my own feelings, emotions, and experiences are true reflections of myself.
26. I always feel completely sincere when I reveal my own feelings and experiences.
27. My self-disclosures are completely accurate reflections of who I really am.
28. I am not always honest in my self-disclosures.
29. My statements about my feelings, emotions, and experiences are always accurate self-perceptions.
30. I am always honest in my self-disclosures.
31. I do not always feel completely sincere when I reveal my own feelings, emotions, behaviors or experiences.

Note. Items 5, 6, 8, 11, 13, 14, 16, 17, 24, 25, 28, and 31 must be reverse-coded before computing mean scores. Items should be randomly arranged and subscale labels removed before administration.

For the General Disclosiveness Scale, all content is the same, but the instructions read "Please mark the following statements to reflect how *you* communicate *with other people in general*," rather than "how *you* communicate *with* [*specific target person*]."

Source Credibility Scale—Berlo

Source credibility (SC) refers to the believability of sources of information. Berlo, Lemert, and Mertz (1970) sought to extend the work of Hovland, Janis, and Kelley (1953) in this area. Hovland and his colleagues suggested two dimensions of credibility: Perceived Expertness and Perceived Trustworthiness. Berlo et al. sought to provide empirical evidence to establish the criteria "used by receivers to evaluate information sources" (p. 564).

From interviews and literature reviews Berlo et al. (1970) first generated 128 pairs of bipolar adjectives "to describe highly acceptable or unacceptable sources" (p. 566). Due to computer limitations, they had six faculty members judge the scales for redundancy and reduced the pool to 83 items. They selected interpersonal sources (i.e., three well-known acquaintances whose opinions they respected, did not respect, and neither respected nor lacked respect for), public sources without context (e.g., the American Broadcasting Company), public sources with relevant context (e.g., Churchill on foreign policy), and public sources with irrelevant context (e.g., Khrushchev on art).

They conducted two factor-analytic studies. First, they had college students rate 18 sources on each of the 83 bipolar-adjective scales. "Scales were reversed randomly, and pages were ordered randomly within sets" (Berlo et al., 1970, p. 566). Responses from the college-student sample produced four SC factors: Safety, Qualification, Dynamism, and Sociability. They questioned the value of the last factor.

Second, they administered 35 scales to randomly selected Lansing, Michigan, adult residents with a minimum of sixth-grade education. During in-home interviews, respondents were asked to rate 12 sources on each of the 35 bipolar-adjective scales. Responses produced three SC factors explaining 60% of the variance: Safety (e.g., kind–cruel and friendly–unfriendly); Qualification (e.g., trained–untrained and experienced–inexperienced); and Dynamism (e.g., aggressive–meek and bold–timid).

Many authors have used or cited Berlo et al.'s (1970) multidimensional measure. It has served as the basis for constructing or modifying other SC measures, and for relating SC to other variables, including profane language (Bostrom, Basehart, & Rossiter, 1973), subordinate satisfaction (Falcione,

Profile by Alan M. Rubin.

327

1973), eye contact (Beebe, 1974), communicator responsibility (Kaplan & Sharp, 1974), selection of reporters' statements (Counts, 1975), listener personality (Rosenfeld & Plax, 1975), behavior in work units (O'Reilly & Roberts, 1976), argumentativeness (Infante, 1981), camera shot and witness presentational style (Kaminski & Miller, 1984), and leadership (Posner & Kouzes, 1988).

The Source Credibility Scale (SCS) uses a series of bipolar adjectives that are usually randomly ordered when presented to respondents. Berlo et al. (1970) suggested that researchers use a 15-item version that best represents the three dimensions of source credibility. The scale takes about 5 minutes to complete. As noted above, items from the SCS have often been combined with other measures, such as McCroskey's (1966) credibility measure, in forming revised credibility measures.

RELIABILITY

Berlo et al. (1970) did not address reliability, and some researchers have mixed information about the reliability of this measure. Infante, Parker, Clarke, Wilson, and Nathu (1983) reported Cronbach alphas of .67, .73, and .82 for three-item Expertise, Trustworthiness, and Dynamism indices. Infante (1981) earlier reported alpha coefficients of .87 and .92 for three-item Expertise (i.e., qualification) and five-item Dynamism factors. After factor analyzing the 15 Safety, Qualification, and Dynamism SC items, Kaminski and Miller (1984) reported alpha coefficients of .72, .72, and .85 for the respective dimensions. Posner and Kouzes (1988) adapted the SC items to 5-point Likert-type scales, yielding a .90 coefficient alpha for their credibility index.

Typically, though, researchers such as Falcione (1974) either failed to report reliability or combined the Berlo et al. (1970) measures with those of other researchers. Smith (1977), for example, used nine of the Berlo et al. items in her credibility instrument for which she reported a .90 Cronbach alpha.

VALIDITY

Berlo et al. (1970) also did not directly address validity but did discuss the three dimensions in light of Hovland et al.'s (1953) two credibility dimensions. The initial assessment of the item pool by faculty members provided face or content validity. With a few exceptions, there has been little extended discussion about construct validity but claims that the items have face validity.

Infante et al. (1983) pointed out that a major criticism of the SC semantic differential scales is that the factor structure is unstable. Their factor analysis of the nine items produced only Trustworthiness and Dynamism dimensions, which calls into question the SC Scale's construct validity. They also explored a unidimensional measure by summing all nine subscales, which produced a .83 coefficient alpha. Infante et al. used only nine SCS items in this analysis and it was not clear if all items came from Berlo et al. (1970).

Carbone (1975) supported concurrent validity by observing .85 and .53 correlations between Berlo et al. (1970) and McCroskey's (1966) Expertness and Trustworthiness measures. Infante (1980) supported criterion-related validity of the SC measures, finding significant canonical relationships between Trustworthiness, Expertise, and Dynamism (using three items each from the Berlo et al. scales) and responses to the source such as favorableness, global attitude, and intent to listen.

COMMENTS

Some have questioned the stability and generalizability of Berlo et al.'s (1970) dimensions. Applbaum and Anatol (1972), for example, used the 15 most representative items from Berlo et al. (1970) along with items from McCroskey (1966) and others, and noted that the factor structure of SC varies across situations. Cronkhite and Liska (1976) critiqued factor-analytic approaches to studying credibility and questioned the interpretation and generalizability of Berlo et al.'s (1970) measures. Tuppen (1974) suggested that two of the Berlo et al. items (i.e., logical–illogical and believable–unbelievable) cross-loaded on Safety and Qualification dimensions, and that two additional clusters involving respect, trust, and scholarship should have been interpreted.

LOCATION

Berlo, D. K., Lemert, J. B., & Mertz, R. J. (1970). Dimensions for evaluating the acceptability of message sources. *Public Opinion Quarterly*, *33*, 563–576.

REFERENCES

Applbaum, R. F., & Anatol, K. W. E. (1972). The factor structure of source credibility as a function of the speaking situation. *Speech Monographs*, *39*, 216–222.
Beebe, S. A. (1974). Eye contact: A nonverbal determinant of speaker credibility. *Speech Teacher*, *23*, 21–25.

Bostrom, R. N., Basehart, J. R., & Rossiter, C. M., Jr. (1973). The effects of three types of profane language in persuasive messages. *Journal of Communication*, *23*, 461–475.

Carbone, T. (1975). Stylistic variables as related to source credibility: A content analysis approach. *Speech Monographs*, *42*, 99–106.

Counts, T. M., Jr. (1975). The influence of message and source on selection of statements by reporters. *Journalism Quarterly*, *52*, 443–449.

Cronkhite, G., & Liska, J. (1976). A critique of factor analytic approaches to the study of credibility. *Communication Monographs*, *43*, 91–107.

Falcione, R. L. (1973). The relationship of supervisor credibility to subordinate satisfaction. *Personnel Journal*, *52*, 800–803.

Falcione, R. L. (1974). The factor structure of source credibility scales for immediate superiors in the organizational context. *Central States Speech Journal*, *25*, 63–66.

Hovland, C. I., Janis, I. L., & Kelley, H. H. (1953). *Communication and persuasion.* New Haven, CT: Yale University Press.

Infante, D. A. (1980). The construct validity of semantic differential scales for the measurement of source credibility. *Communication Quarterly*, *28*(2), 19–26.

Infante, D. A. (1981). Trait argumentativeness as a predictor of communicative behavior in situations requiring argument. *Central States Speech Journal*, *32*, 265–272.

Infante, D. A., Parker, K. R., Clarke, C. H., Wilson, L., & Nathu, I. A. (1983). A comparison of factor and functional approaches to source credibility. *Communication Quarterly*, *31*, 43–48.

Kaminski, E. P., & Miller, G. R. (1984). How jurors respond to videotaped witnesses. *Journal of Communication*, *34*(1), 88–102.

Kaplan, S. J., & Sharp, H. W., Jr. (1974). The effect of responsibility attributions on message source evaluation. *Speech Monographs*, *41*, 364–370.

McCroskey, J. C. (1966). Scales for the measurement of ethos. *Speech Monographs*, *33*, 65–72.

O'Reilly, C. A., & Roberts, K. H. (1976). Relationships among components of credibility and communication behaviors in work units. *Journal of Applied Psychology*, *61*, 99–102.

Posner, B. Z., & Kouzes, J. M. (1988). Relating leadership and credibility. *Psychological Reports*, *63*, 527–530.

Rosenfeld, L. B., & Plax, T. G. (1975). The relationship of listener personality to perceptions of three dimensions of credibility. *Central States Speech Journal*, *26*, 274–278.

Smith, M. J. (1977). The effects of threats to attitudinal freedom as a function of message quality and initial receiver attitude. *Communication Monographs*, *44*, 196–206.

Tuppen, C. J. S. (1974). Dimensions of communicator credibility: An oblique solution. *Speech Monographs*, *41*, 253–260.

Source Credibility Scale—Berlo*

[Editors' note: No specific instructions were provided by Berlo et al. (1970), but respondents were asked to evaluate specific sources—such as "a person you know well whose opinion you respect highly," "Adlai Stevenson on the United Nations," or "Mickey Mantle on organized crime"—on each of the following scales.]

<u>Safety factor</u>

Kind	: ___:___:___:___:___:___:___ : Cruel
Safe	: ___:___:___:___:___:___:___ : Dangerous
Friendly	: ___:___:___:___:___:___:___ : Unfriendly
Just	: ___:___:___:___:___:___:___ : Unjust
Honest	: ___:___:___:___:___:___:___ : Dishonest

<u>Qualification factor</u>

Trained	: ___:___:___:___:___:___:___ : Untrained
Experienced	: ___:___:___:___:___:___:___ : Inexperienced
Qualified	: ___:___:___:___:___:___:___ : Unqualified
Skilled	: ___:___:___:___:___:___:___ : Unskilled
Informed	: ___:___:___:___:___:___:___ : Uninformed

<u>Dynamism factor</u>

Aggressive	: ___:___:___:___:___:___:___ : Meek
Emphatic	: ___:___:___:___:___:___:___ : Hesitant
Bold	: ___:___:___:___:___:___:___ : Timid
Active	: ___:___:___:___:___:___:___ : Passive
Energetic	: ___:___:___:___:___:___:___ : Tired

Note. Scales are randomly reversed and arranged when presented to respondents.

Source Credibility
Scale—McCroskey

Source credibility—ethos, prestige, or image—was originally conceived as a unidimensional attitude a receiver has about a source, but this changed in the mid-1960s when two lines of research began promoting it as a multidimensional attitude. Berlo, Lemert, and Mertz (1970) identified Safety, Qualification, and Dynamism dimensions of credibility for media sources; this work was informed by Hovland, Janis, and Kelley's persuasion research and by Osgood, Suci, and Tannenbaum's semantic differential methodology. McCroskey's (1966) research focused on credibility of people—speakers, peers, teachers, and so forth. These two lines of research guided communication research from the 1970s onward and McCroskey's work is discussed here.

McCroskey (1966) drew on both social psychology and rhetoric to create a 5-point Likert-type scale for two source credibility dimensions: Authoritativeness (22 items) and Character (20 items). He conducted seven studies to develop and test this credibility instrument, and in so doing, he also created two six-item 7-point semantic differential scales, each requiring less than 2 minutes to complete. Almost all of the research that uses McCroskey's scales uses the semantic differential format.

McCroskey, Jenson, and Valencia (1973; see also McCroskey, Hamilton, & Weiner, 1974) revised and extended the 7-point semantic differential instrument and found five dimensions (containing three bipolar constructs each) of source credibility for peers and spouses: Sociability, Character, Competence, Composure, and Extroversion. This scale takes respondents less than 3 minutes to complete. Versions of this scale also were created to assess credibility of teachers (McCroskey, Holdridge, & Toomb, 1974; see also Burgoon, Pfau, Birk, & Manusov, 1987; Rubin & Feezel, 1986) and mass media news sources (McCroskey & Jenson, 1975).

McCroskey's (1966) original scales have been used to confirm that high- and low-credibility speakers are actually perceived in this way (Carbone, 1975; Mehrley & McCroskey, 1970) and to assess credibility of trial witnesses (Kaminski & Miller, 1984; Pryor & Buchanan, 1984) and immedi-

Profile by Rebecca M. Rubin.

ate superiors in organizations (Falcione, 1974). They have also been used to assess the impact on credibility of (a) message sidededness and evidence (McCroskey, Young, & Scott, 1972), (b) rate of speech and gender (Wheeless, 1971), (c) discrepancy between one's own and another's stand on an issue (Mortensen & Sereno, 1970), (d) nonverbal cues (Arnold, 1973), (e) richness of fantasy and refutation skills (Infante, 1975), (f) one's own counterarguing ability (Brandt, 1979), (g) agreeing with the message (Infante, 1972), (h) social status and dialect (Bochner & Bochner, 1973), and (i) effect of humor and interesting speeches (Gruner, 1970). The newer 15-item scale has been used to examine the effect of attire (Bassett, 1979), reticence (Burgoon & Koper, 1984), relational communication (Pfau & Kang, 1991), and vocal hostility (Buller & Aune, 1988; Buller & Burgoon, 1986) on credibility.

RELIABILITY

McCroskey (1966) reported (a) split-half reliabilities for the Likert-type scales ranging from .94 to .98 for Authoritativeness and from .93 to .98 for Character and (b) Hoyt internal consistency reliabilities ranging from .94 to .98 for Authoritativeness and .93 to .97 for Character. The six-item semantic differential scales had alphas of .93 (Authoritativeness) and .92 (Character). Brandt (1979) reported an alpha of .95 for the Authoritativeness scale. Kaminski and Miller (1984) factor-analyzed the Likert-type scales, which reduced the Authoritativeness scale to 7 items (.85 alpha) and the Character scale to 10 (.90 alpha).

McCroskey et al. (1973) reported internal consistency ratings for the 15-item semantic differential of .39 for Extroversion, .64 for Character, .80 for Composure, .84 for Competence, and .86 for Sociability. Reliabilities for later versions ranged from (a) .79 to .96 (McCroskey, Hamilton, & Weiner, 1974), (b) .83 to .93 (Bassett, 1979), (c) .68 to .90 (Andersen & Withrow, 1981), (d) .74 to .89 (Buller & Burgoon, 1986), and (e) .71 to .88 (Burgoon & Koper, 1984). This version now appears to have a sufficient level of internal consistency.

VALIDITY

Little validity evidence for the Likert-type instrument exists. One study tested the construct validity of the Authoritativeness and Character scales and of the Berlo et al. (1970) scale; Carbone (1975) found that high- and low-credibility sources differed significantly on the two McCroskey dimensions and on the three Berlo et al. dimensions. McCroskey (1966) found that the Authoritativeness dimension was indeed related (.92 correlation) to psychological authoritativeness.

Most researchers have used the semantic differential version of Mc-Croskey's (1966) credibility scales, either alone or with other scales; in general, the evidence suggests that semantic differential scales have face and criterion-related validity. Speakers are perceived as more credible when they (a) use a normal speech rate and are male (Wheeless, 1971), (b) are higher in richness of fantasy and more effective in refutation (Infante, 1975), (c) use humor and interesting information in the speech (Gruner, 1970), (d) are of higher social status (dialect and syntax) (Bochner & Bochner, 1973), (e) have lower anxiety levels during testimony (Pryor & Buchanan, 1984), (f) use evidence in messages (McCroskey et al., 1972), and (g) use of powerful language by witnesses (Johnson & Vinson, 1990). Listeners who disagreed with the desirability of consequences of a speaker's position (Infante, 1972) or with the speaker's stand on the issue (Mortensen & Sereno, 1970) viewed the speaker as lower in credibility; those who could not effectively counterargue viewed the speaker as higher in credibility (Brandt, 1979).

Those who have used the 15-item semantic differential scale have found that (a) interaction behavior is a predictor of all five dimensions of credibility (McCroskey, Hamilton, & Wiener, 1974), (b) high-status clothing produced higher ratings on competence (Bassett, 1979), and (c) nonverbal expressiveness is related positively to Sociability and Character and negatively to Composure and Competence (Andersen & Withrow, 1981).

The 15-item semantic differential has not always factored into five dimensions, which calls into question the scale's construct validity. Sociability and Character sometimes loaded on the same dimension in the factor analysis (Buller & Aune, 1988; Buller & Burgoon, 1986; McCroskey & Jenson, 1975), and sometimes the context makes a difference (Applbaum & Anatol, 1972).

Applbaum and Anatol (1973) tested the stability of the scales by combining the six-item semantic differentials with two other sets of semantic differentials (containing at least two other dimensions). McCroskey's two factors did not emerge from this study, probably because the items interacted with the additional items. Their data on test–retest indicated that all the semantic differential scales were relatively stable over a 1-week period. However, Infante (1980) found that Expertise (Authoritativeness) and Trustworthiness (Character) were indeed two main dimensions of source credibility. Dynamism also emerged as a dimension, but as McCroskey and Young (1981) indicated, Dynamism is a different type of dimension (perhaps a potency measure instead of an evaluation one).

COMMENTS

All in all, McCroskey's scales have been used in numerous studies over the years. The 1966 article has been cited over 100 times in the literature, and many of these citations are to research studies that have used all or part of the scales. The semantic differential format seems to have emerged as the predominant method of scaling.

Although many researchers have, over the years, used one or the other scale, often they combine the semantic differential scales into a large battery of semantic differential scales (sometimes with those published by others) and then factor-analyze the scales to see what dimensions of source credibility emerge, just as Tucker (1971) recommended. This procedure has generated controversy about the most appropriate technique: factor analysis of semantic differential scales (Infante, 1980), use of existing Likert-type scales (McCroskey & Young, 1981), use of a functional approach to scale construction (Cronkhite & Liska, 1976), or use of a constructivistic approach to credibility (Delia, 1976).

When McCroskey et al. (1973) recommended using a standard set of scales to measure credibility in future research involving people, Cronkhite and Liska (1976) argued that the scales could not be used in this way because semantic differential scales, especially those that people generate for themselves, are used to identify meaning and only factor analysis of the scales permits meaning to emerge. Infante, Parker, Clarke, Wilson, and Nathu (1983) found that the functional and factor approaches explained about the same amount of variance in other indicators of credibility.

Today, questions still remain about the credibility scale's content validity: Are all dimensions of credibility represented in the scale? In light of recent research on communication competence, it is possible that some overlap exists between the two constructs.

LOCATION

McCroskey, J. C. (1966). Scales for the measurement of ethos. *Speech Monographs*, *33*, 65–72.

McCroskey, J. C., Hamilton, P. R., & Weiner, A. M. (1974). The effect of interaction behavior on source credibility, homophily, and interpersonal attraction. *Human Communication Research*, *1*, 42–52.

McCroskey, J. C., Jenson, T., & Valencia, C. (1973, April). *Measurement of the credibility of peers and spouses*. Paper presented at the meeting of the International Communication Association, Montreal.

REFERENCES

Andersen, J. F., & Withrow, J. G. (1981). The impact of lecturer nonverbal expressiveness on improving mediated instruction. *Communication Education, 30*, 342–353.

Arnold, W. E. (1973). The effect of nonverbal cues on source credibility. *Central States Speech Journal, 24*, 227–230.

Applbaum, R., & Anatol, K. W. E. (1972). The factor structure of source credibility as a function of the speaking situation. *Speech Monographs, 39*, 216–222.

Applbaum, R. L., & Anatol, K. W. E. (1973). Dimensions of source credibility: A test for reproducibility. *Speech Monographs, 40*, 231–237.

Bassett, R. E. (1979). Effects of source attire on judgments of credibility. *Central States Speech Journal, 30*, 282–285.

Berlo, D. K., Lemert, J. B., & Mertz, R. J. (1970). Dimensions for evaluating the acceptability of message sources. *Public Opinion Quarterly, 33*, 563–576.

Bochner, B., & Bochner, A. (1973). The effects of social status and social dialect on listener responses. *Central States Speech Journal, 24*, 75–82.

Brandt, D. (1979). Listener propensity to counterargue, distraction, and resistance to persuasion. *Central States Speech Journal, 30*, 321–331.

Buller, D. B., & Aune, R. K. (1988). The effects of vocalics and nonverbal sensitivity on compliance: A speech accommodation theory explanation. *Human Communication Research, 14*, 301–332.

Buller, D. B., & Burgoon, J. K. (1986). The effects of vocalics and nonverbal sensitivity on compliance: A replication and extension. *Human Communication Research, 13*, 126–144.

Burgoon, J. K., & Koper, R. J. (1984). Nonverbal and relational communication associated with reticence. *Human Communication Research, 10*, 601–626.

Burgoon, J. K., Pfau, M., Birk, T., & Manusov, V. (1987). Nonverbal communication performance and perceptions associated with reticence: Replications and classroom implications. *Communication Education, 36*, 119–130.

Carbone, T. (1975). Stylistic variables as related to source credibility: A content analysis approach. *Speech Monographs, 42*, 99–106.

Cronkhite, G., & Liska, J. (1976). A critique of factor analytic approaches to the study of credibility. *Communication Monographs, 43*, 91–107.

Delia, J. G. (1976). A constructivist analysis of the concept of credibility. *Quarterly Journal of Speech, 62*, 361–375.

Falcione, R. L. (1974). The factor structure of source credibility scales for immediate superiors in the organizational context. *Central States Speech Journal, 25*, 63–66.

Gruner, C. (1970). The effects of humor in dull and interesting informative speeches. *Central States Speech Journal, 21*, 160–166.

Infante, D. (1972). The function of perceptions of consequences in attitude formation and communicator image formation. *Central States Speech Journal, 23*, 174–180.

Infante, D. (1975). Richness of fantasy and beliefs about attempts to refute a proposal as determinants of attitude. *Speech Monographs, 42*, 75–79.

Infante, D. A. (1980). The construct validity of semantic differential scales for the measurement of source credibility. *Communication Quarterly*, *28*, 19–26.

Infante, D. A., Parker, K. R., Clarke, C. H., Wilson, L., & Nathu, I. A. (1983). A comparison of factor and functional approaches to source credibility. *Communication Quarterly*, *31*, 43–48.

Johnson, C., & Vinson, L. (1990). Placement and frequency of powerless talk and impression formation. *Communication Quarterly*, *38*, 325–333.

Kaminski, E. P., & Miller, G. R. (1984). How jurors respond to videotaped witnesses. *Journal of Communication*, *34*(1), 88–102.

McCroskey, J. C., Holdridge, W., & Toomb, J. K. (1974). An instrument for measuring the source credibility of basic speech communication instructors. *Speech Teacher*, *23*, 26–33.

McCroskey, J. C., & Jenson, T. A. (1975). Image of mass media news sources. *Journal of Broadcasting*, *19*, 169–180.

McCroskey, J. C., & Young, T. J. (1981). Ethos and credibility: The construct and its measurement after three decades. *Central States Speech Journal*, *32*, 24–34.

McCroskey, J., Young, T., & Scott, M. (1972). The effects of message sidedness and evidence on inoculation against counterpersuasion in small group communication. *Speech Monographs*, *39*, 205–212.

Mehrley, R., & McCroskey, J. (1970). Opinionated statements and attitude intensity as predictors of attitude change and source credibility. *Speech Monographs*, *37*, 47–52.

Mortensen, C., & Sereno, K. (1970). The influence of ego-involvement and discrepancy on perceptions of communication. *Speech Monographs*, *37*, 127–134.

Pfau, M., & Kang, J. G. (1991). The impact of relational messages on candidate influence in televised political debates. *Communication Studies*, *42*, 114–128.

Pryor, B., & Buchanan, R. W. (1984). The effects of a defendant's demeanor on juror perceptions of credibility and guilt. *Journal of Communication*, *34*(3), 92–99.

Rubin, R. B., & Feezel, J. D. (1986). Elements of teacher communication competence. *Communication Education*, *35*, 254–268.

Tucker, R. K. (1971). On the McCroskey scales for the measurement of *ethos*. *Central States Speech Journal*, *22*, 127–129.

Wheeless, L. (1971). Some effects of time-compressed speech on persuasion. *Journal of Broadcasting*, *15*, 415–420.

Source Credibility Scale—McCroskey:
12-Item Semantic Differential*

Instructions: On the scales below, please indicate your feelings about_____
_____. Circle the number between the adjectives which best represents
your feelings about _____. Numbers "1" and "7" indicate a very
strong feeling. Numbers "2" and "6" indicate a strong feeling. Numbers
"3" and "5" indicate a fairly weak feeling. Number "4" indicates you are
undecided or do not understand the adjectives themselves. Please work
quickly. There are no right or wrong answers.

<u>Authoritativeness</u>

Reliable	1	2	3	4	5	6	7	Unreliable*
Uninformed	1	2	3	4	5	6	7	Informed
Unqualified	1	2	3	4	5	6	7	Qualified
Intelligent	1	2	3	4	5	6	7	Unintelligent*
Valuable	1	2	3	4	5	6	7	Worthless*
Inexpert	1	2	3	4	5	6	7	Expert

<u>Character</u>

Honest	1	2	3	4	5	6	7	Dishonest*
Unfriendly	1	2	3	4	5	6	7	Friendly
Pleasant	1	2	3	4	5	6	7	Unpleasant*
Selfish	1	2	3	4	5	6	7	Unselfish
Awful	1	2	3	4	5	6	7	Nice
Virtuous	1	2	3	4	5	6	7	Sinful*

Note. Items are presented here grouped by dimension. Users should randomly order
the bipolar adjectives to avoid response set error variance. Reverse scoring should
be performed for items with asterisks.

15-Item Semantic Differential**

Instructions: On the scales below, please indicate your feelings about _____
_____. Circle the number between the adjectives which best represents
your feelings about _____. Numbers "1" and "7" indicate a very
strong feeling. Numbers "2" and "6" indicate a strong feeling. Numbers
"3" and "5" indicate a fairly weak feeling. Number "4" indicates you are

undecided or do not understand the adjectives themselves. Please work quickly. There are no right or wrong answers.

Sociability

Good-natured	1	2	3	4	5	6	7	Irritable*
Cheerful	1	2	3	4	5	6	7	Gloomy*
Unfriendly	1	2	3	4	5	6	7	Friendly

Extroversion

Timid	1	2	3	4	5	6	7	Bold
Verbal	1	2	3	4	5	6	7	Quiet*
Talkative	1	2	3	4	5	6	7	Silent*

Competence

Expert	1	2	3	4	5	6	7	Inexpert*
Unintelligent	1	2	3	4	5	6	7	Intelligent
Intellectual	1	2	3	4	5	6	7	Narrow*

Composure

Poised	1	2	3	4	5	6	7	Nervous*
Tense	1	2	3	4	5	6	7	Relaxed
Calm	1	2	3	4	5	6	7	Anxious*

Character

Dishonest	1	2	3	4	5	6	7	Honest
Unsympathetic	1	2	3	4	5	6	7	Sympathetic
Good	1	2	3	4	5	6	7	Bad*

Note. Items are presented here grouped by dimension. Users should randomly order the bipolar adjectives to avoid response set error variance. Reverse scoring should be performed for items with asterisks.

Speakers' Perceptions of Situational Causes of Anxiety

Even though we know that communication apprehension (CA) is often regarded as a trait-like, predispositional anxiety or fear toward communicating with others, more recent research examines the influence of situational causes of that anxiety or fear. Specifically, Buss (1980) proposed that seven situational factors could give rise to CA during public speaking performances: novelty, formality, subordinate status, conspicuousness, unfamiliarity, dissimilarity, and degree of attention. Drawing on the writing apprehension literature, McCroskey (1984) later identified an eighth cause as well: degree of evaluation. Taken together or individually, these eight situational factors could trigger high, albeit temporary, apprehension during public speaking, regardless of prior trait CA levels.

To assess the validity of that claim, Beatty (1988) developed a measure that assesses the original seven situational factors identified by Buss (1980). (Beatty argued that the eighth factor, evaluation, was more accurately interpreted to be an individual difference variable, rather than a situational factor; thus, evaluation was omitted from his measure). Beatty designed the measure so that speakers themselves assess the psychological impact of each situational factor. Only speakers involved in those situations, he reasoned, can assess accurately whether any given situation is novel or routine, familiar or unfamiliar, etc.

The resulting measure, the Speakers' Perceptions of Situational Causes of Anxiety (SPSCA) scale, is a 14-item, Likert-type instrument. Two items measure each of the seven original situational causes. The instrument is administered immediately after a public speaking performance. It requires approximately 10 minutes to complete.

RELIABILITY

Alpha reliability coefficients for each situational cause range from .60 to .72 (Beatty, 1988; Beatty, Balfantz, & Kuwabara, 1989; Beatty & Friedland, 1990).

Profile by Michael J. Beatty.

VALIDITY

Studies provide some evidence for the construct validity of the instrument. For example, Beatty (1988) found that subjects delivering a speech from the front of the classroom reported significantly higher scores on the Formality dimension than did those giving a report from their desk to an audience seated in a circular arrangement. Subjects speaking without the benefit of a lectern reported significantly more *conspicuousness* than did those speaking from behind a lectern. In two separate studies, Beatty found that Novelty scores decreased with speaking experience (Beatty, 1988; Beatty et al., 1989). He also found Subordinate Status scores consistently correlated with self-reported public speaking anxiety and context-based (Public Speaking) CA.

COMMENTS

In the published literature, each of the seven situational dimensions has been scored separately to preserve the conceptual framework appearing in the situationalists' literature. Because the measure was initially designed for immediate administration, often in conjunction with other postperformance measures, the number of items was necessarily restricted. As a consequence of these two parameters, the reliabilities are somewhat lower than many self-report measures. However, the correlation matrices reported in Beatty (1988) and Beatty et al. (1989) indicated correlations among many of the situational dimensions. Therefore, unless theoretical adherence to the situational parameters is desired, factor analysis (or some other data reduction technique) is likely to produce a more parsimonious set of constructs (consisting of two items; thus, higher reliability) and is, therefore, recommended.

LOCATION

Beatty, M. J. (1988). Situational and predispositional correlates of public speaking anxiety. *Communication Education, 37*, 28–39.

REFERENCES

Beatty, M. J., Balfantz, G. L., & Kuwabara, A. Y. (1989). Trait-like qualities of selected variables assumed to be transient causes of performance state anxiety. *Communication Education, 38*, 277–289.
Beatty, M. J., & Friedland, M. H. (1990). Public speaking state anxiety as a func-

tion of selected situational and predispositional variables. *Communication Education, 39,* 142–147.

Buss, A. H. (1980). *Self-consciousness and social anxiety.* San Francisco: W. H. Freeman.
McCroskey, J. C. (1984). The communication apprehension perspective. In J. A. Daly & J. C. McCroskey (Eds.), *Avoiding communication: Shyness, reticence, and communication apprehension* (pp. 13–38). Beverly Hills, CA: Sage.

Speakers' Perceptions of Situational Causes of Anxiety*

Instructions: Please respond to the following items in terms of how you felt during your presentation. Circle one of the letters for each question: SA = *strongly agree,* A = *agree,* N = *undecided or neutral,* D = *disagree,* and SD = *strongly disagree.*

[Editors' note: Respondents use the above scale for each of the following items.]

1. Making a presentation like this one was a new experience for me [Novelty].
2. I would describe the situation as formal [Formality].
3. The other students in class seemed to be better at this type of presentation than I am [Subordinate Status].
4. I felt that I was the center of attention during my talk [Conspicuousness].
5. I am not familiar with many of the students in class [Unfamiliarity].
6. The students in class seem very different from me [Dissimilarity].
7. The students were paying close attention during my talk [Degree of attention from others].
8. This experience was different from previous experiences as a communicator [Novelty].
9. The expectations for my behavior and performance were rigid and inflexible [Formality].
10. The other students seem to know more about my topic than I do [Subordinate Status].
11. I felt conspicuous during my presentation [Conspicuousness].
12. Most of the students in class are strangers [Unfamiliarity].
13. I seem to have little in common with the students in this class [Dissimilarity].
14. I felt that the students were watching and listening during my talk [Degree of attention from others].

Note. Bracketed information on the seven situational causes does not appear on scale when administered.

Student Motivation Scale

The first situational (state) motivation scale to be used in the communication literature was devised by Beatty and Payne (1985). They defined state motivation as a temporary condition in which individuals direct high levels of concentration and attention toward the competent completion of a task. More directly interested in instructional communication, Christophel (1990) differentiated students' trait from state motivation in the classroom. Whereas trait motivation can be defined as a relatively enduring predisposition toward school or learning, state motivation refers to students' attitudes toward a particular class or subject. Correspondingly, Richmond (1990) attempted to differentiate students' compliant behavior from motivated behavior by reasoning that the former relied on the preferences of another person (e.g., the teacher), while the latter was a manifestation of the student's own desires or needs. "Key here," claimed Richmond, "is the probability that motivated behavior will occur regardless of the presence of others, whereas the compliant behavior will only occur in the presence (physical and/or psychological) of the compliance-seeking person" (p. 1983).

The original version of the Student Motivation Scale (SMS) was a simple single-item semantic differential scale (Beatty, Behnke, & Froelich, 1980) and was later expanded to include three or four bipolar adjectives (Beatty, Forst, & Stewart, 1986; Beatty & Payne, 1985). Later, a fifth pair was added (Richmond, 1990). The literature measuring motivational states in students now includes as many as 12 sets of bipolar, semantic differential items (Christophel, 1990). In the most recent 12-item version, students are asked to complete the SMS twice (Christophel, 1990): First, to assess students' trait motivation toward school, students are asked to indicate how they "*feel in general* about taking classes at the University" (p. 327). Second, to measure students' state motivation toward a specific class, students are asked to indicate how they "*feel about this specific class*" (p. 327). This most recent 12-item instrument takes 5–10 minutes to complete.

Profile by Michael J. Beatty.

RELIABILITY

Available research indicates that the various combinations of items used to measure motivation demonstrate acceptable to excellent reliability. Beatty and Payne (1985) reported alpha coefficients of .93 and .96 for two administrations of their 4-item version. Beatty et al. (1986) obtained an alpha coefficient of .79 for a 3-item instrument. Richmond (1990) reported alpha co-efficient of .94 for a 5-item scale. Christophel (1990) observed reliability coefficients ranging from .95 to .96 for a 12-item measure.

VALIDITY

Considerable evidence for the construct validity of these scales has been published. Beatty et al. (1980) found that subjects promised extra credit proportional to their comprehension of audiotaped material reported significantly higher scores on a "motivated–unmotivated" bipolar-adjective scale than did subjects who were not offered the incentive. Furthermore, scores on the motivation scale correlated with state anxiety scores ($r = .66$) and with scores on a single item referring to the importance of the bonus points ($r = .52$). Beatty and Payne (1985) reported that (a) extra credit incentives produced higher scores on the four-item measure than did a nonincentive condition when students were engaged in a writing task, and (b) scores on the motivation measure were positively and significantly related to the length of written responses. Beatty et al. (1986) found that motivation scores interacted with communication apprehension in the prediction of the duration of student speeches; the simple correlation between motivation and speech duration was .54. Other studies indicated that variations of the motivation instrument are associated with teachers' use of power strategies, teacher immediacy, and various dimensions of student learning (cognitive, affective, learning loss, etc.) (Christophel, 1990; Richmond, 1990).

COMMENTS

Like most paper-and-pencil tests of psychological constructs, reliability estimates are often a function of the number of items employed in the scale; the more the items, the greater the reliability. The SMS is no exception. Christophel's (1990) 12-item SMS resulted in higher reliability estimates than did prior versions which contained only 3, 4, or 5 items. Consequently, researchers might be better off using the longer version.

Moreover, using the SMS to measure either trait and/or state student motivations toward learning in general or toward a class in particular may be an important consideration in future research. Like other trait and state measures, we might expect the trait version to contribute to some instructional outcomes, while the state version may predict others. To convert the SMS to a trait (or state) motivation scale, only the directions for completing the instrument need to be changed with the trait version referencing school or learning more generally, and the state version referencing a specific class or subject matter.

LOCATION

Christophel, D. M. (1990). The relationships among teacher immediacy behaviors, student motivation, and learning. *Communication Education, 39*, 323–340.
Richmond, V. P. (1990). Communication in the classroom: Power and motivation. *Communication Education, 39*, 181–195.

REFERENCES

Beatty, M. J., Behnke, R. R., & Froelich, D. L. (1980). Effects of achievement incentive and presentation rate on listening comprehension. *Quarterly Journal of Speech, 66*, 193–200.
Beatty, M. J., Forst, E. C., & Stewart, R. A. (1986). Communication apprehension and motivation as predictors of public speaking duration. *Communication Education, 35*, 143–146.
Beatty, M. J. & Payne, S. K. (1985). Is construct differentiation loquacity?: A motivational perspective. *Human Communication Research, 11*, 605–612.

Student Motivation Scale*

[Editors' note: The following set of scales has been used in various combinations to measure student motivation.]

Instructions: Please circle the number toward either word which best represents your feelings about _____.

1.	Motivated	1	2	3	4	5	6	7	Unmotivated
2.	Interested	1	2	3	4	5	6	7	Uninterested
3.	Involved	1	2	3	4	5	6	7	Uninvolved
4.	Not stimulated	1	2	3	4	5	6	7	Stimulated
5.	Don't want to study	1	2	3	4	5	6	7	Want to study

6.	Inspired	1	2	3	4	5	6	7	Uninspired
7.	Unchallenged	1	2	3	4	5	6	7	Challenged
8.	Uninvigorated	1	2	3	4	5	6	7	Invigorated
9.	Unenthused	1	2	3	4	5	6	7	Enthused
10.	Excited	1	2	3	4	5	6	7	Not excited
11.	Aroused	1	2	3	4	5	6	7	Not aroused
12.	Not fascinated	1	2	3	4	5	6	7	Fascinated
13.	Dreading it	1	2	3	4	5	6	7	Looking forward to it
14.	Important	1	2	3	4	5	6	7	Unimportant
15.	Useful	1	2	3	4	5	6	7	Useless
16.	Helpful	1	2	3	4	5	6	7	Harmful

Note. Items 1, 14, 15, and 16 were used by Beatty and Payne (1985); Items 1, 2, and 3 were used by Beatty, Forst, and Stewart (1986); Items 1, 2, 3, 10 (Excited–Bored), and 13 were used by Richmond (1990); Items 1–12 were used by Christophel (1990); and Items 1 and 14 were used by Beatty, Behnke, and Froelich (1980).

Items 1, 2, 3, 6, 10, 11, 14, 15, and 16 are reverse-coded before summing.

Student Resistance Strategies

Discovering that students' likelihood of compliance with or resistance to teachers' persuasive messages was a function of teacher's immediacy (Kearney, Plax, Smith, & Sorensen, 1988), Burroughs, Kearney, and Plax (1989) developed an instrument to assess the variety of strategies that college students might use in their resistance attempts. Conceptually, the typology of resistance techniques refers to those strategies or resources available to students in their attempts to reciprocally influence teachers.

Similar to the typology of Behavior Alteration Techniques developed by Kearney, Plax, Richmond, and McCroskey (1985), the Student Resistance Strategies (SRS) comprise an inductively derived typology specific to college student use in the instructional environment. Each of the 19 strategies is operationalized with multiple, rather than single, representative messages derived from students. Factor analysis reveals that the strategies can be reduced to two interpretable dimensions: teacher owned and student owned (Kearney, Plax, & Burroughs, 1991). Teacher-owned strategies target the teacher as the source of the problem. In other words, students employ messages that blame the teacher for their own resistance. Conversely, student-owned strategies suggest that students themselves, not the teacher, actually *own* the reasons for their resistance.

The five strategies indicative of teacher ownership include Teacher Advice, Teacher Blame, Appeal to Powerful Others, Modeling Teacher Behavior, and Modeling Teacher Affect. Five strategies comprising student ownership include Deception, Ignoring the Teacher, Priorities, Hostile Defensive, and Student Rebuttal. Because this is still a relatively new instrument, future research should incorporate all 19 techniques and subsequently factor-analyze participants' responses in an effort to confirm the stability of the two-factor, 10-item solution.

When assessing students' resistance in the classroom, students are asked to indicate how likely they would be to use each of the resistance categories in their efforts to resist teacher demands or requests. Response options range from *extremely likely* (7) to *extremely unlikely* (1). Resistance strategy category labels are omitted from the questionnaire; only messages representing each category are supplied. The scale takes about 15 minutes to complete.

Profile by Patricia Kearney.

RELIABILITY

Alpha reliability estimates for each dimension of the resistance categories are high. Across four separate stimulus conditions, reliability estimates ranged from .88 to .93 for teacher-owned, and from .86 to .91 for student-owned strategies (Kearney et al., 1991).

VALIDITY

Two studies provide indicators of the SRS typology's content validity. First, rather than relying solely on researcher-generated categories, Burroughs et al. (1989) had 574 college students inductively derive resistance messages that they would (or did) use to avoid complying with a teacher's request/demand. Almost 3,000 individual messages were constructed and subsequently coded into the 19 resistance categories. Second, Kearney et al. (1991) validated the existence of all 19 strategies by asking students to indicate their likelihood of employing each category type in their resistance attempts with selected teachers. Resulting frequencies, means, and standard deviations indicated that all 19 categories would be used, with some strategies more likely to be used than others. This was true for both student constructed responses (free recall) and student selections from the category list.

As for construct validity, college students reported that they would be significantly more likely to use teacher-owned strategies to resist nonimmediate (distant, aloof) than immediate (warm, close) teachers. Conversely, students reported greater likelihood of using student-owned strategies with immediate than with nonimmediate teachers. Follow-up qualitative data analysis revealed that students' strategy preferences were based primarily on attributions they made about their teachers. With immediate teachers, the attributions were overwhelmingly positive and students "owned" the problem and selected parallel strategies. With nonimmediate teachers, however, the attributions were negative; thus, students blamed the teacher and selected teacher-owned resistance techniques.

COMMENTS

These resistance categories may or may not be representative of those strategies secondary and/or elementary students might use in their resistance attempts. To determine if the teacher-owned and student-owned factors are generalizable across grade levels, alternative resistance messages should be written to reflect more accurately those messages a 5th- or an 11th-grade student might use.

Conceivably, some students may never resist their teacher's demands or they may never select a given resistance technique. Unfortunately, the current response options, from *extremely unlikely* to *extremely likely*, do not reflect that option. Future research might consider an alternative response range (e.g., 0 = *never* to 4 = *always*).

LOCATION

Burroughs, N. F., Kearney, P., & Plax, T. G. (1989). Compliance–resistance in the college classroom. *Communication Education, 38*, 214–229.
Kearney, P., Plax, T. G., & Burroughs, N. F. (1991). An attributional analysis of college students' resistance decisions. *Communication Education, 40*, 325–342.

REFERENCES

Kearney, P., Plax, T. G., Richmond, V. P., & McCroskey, J. C. (1985). Power in the classroom: III. Teacher communication techniques and messages. *Communication Education, 34*, 19–28.
Kearney, P., Plax, T. G., Smith, V. R., & Sorensen, G. (1988). Effects of teacher immediacy and strategy type on college student resistance to on-task demands. *Communication Education, 37*, 54–67.

Student Resistance Strategies*

Instructions: Below you will find a series of statements or behaviors that a student might say or do to avoid going along with a teacher's request or demand. Please read all of the statements that are grouped together in each category and then indicate how likely you would be to use statements of that type in an effort to resist a demand your teacher has just made of you.

Even though you might not use these exact statements to avoid going along with your teacher's demand, keep in mind that these statements are merely examples of a particular type of resistance strategy you might use. Do the same for the rest of the remaining categories of statements. Use a 1–7 scale, with 7 = *extremely likely* and 1 = *extremely unlikely*. Respond quickly!

[Editors' note: Respondents use the 7-point scale to indicate likelihood of using each strategy.]

---

1. I would offer the teacher advice by saying something like the following: "Prepare yourself better so you give better lectures." "Be more expressive; everything will work out to your advantage." "You should relate more with students before trying to give any advice." "If you open up, we'll tend to be more willing to do what you want." [Teacher Advice]

2. I would resist by claiming that "the teacher is boring." "The teacher makes me feel uneasy." "It is boring; I don't get anything out of it." "You don't seem prepared yourself." "If you weren't so boring, I would do what you want." [Teacher Blame]

3. I would simply drop the class. I won't participate as much. I won't go to class. I'll sit in the back of the room. [Avoidance]

4. I'll do only enough work to get by. Although I would comply with the teacher's demands, I would do so unwillingly. I'll come more prepared, but not be interested at all. Grudgingly, I'll come prepared. [Reluctant Compliance]

5. I won't come prepared at all. I'll leave my book at home. I'll continue to come unprepared to get on the teacher's nerves. I'll keep coming to class, but I won't be prepared. [Active Resistance]

6. I'll act like I'm prepared for class even though I may not be. I may be prepared, but play dumb for spite. I might tell the teacher I would make an effort, but wouldn't. I'll make up some lies about why I'm not performing well in this class. [Deception]

7. I'll go to the teacher's office and try to talk to him/her. After class I would explain my behavior. I would talk to the teacher and explain how I feel and how others perceive him/her in class. [Direct Communication]

8. I'll disrupt the class by leaving to get needed materials. I would be noisy in class. I'll ask questions in a monotone voice without interest. I'll be a wise-guy in class. [Disruption]

9. I would offer some type of excuse like: "I don't feel well." "I don't understand the topic." "I can remember things without writing stuff down." "I forgot." "My car broke down." "The class is so easy I don't need to stay caught up." [Excuses]

10. I would simply ignore the teacher's request, but come to class anyway. I probably wouldn't say anything; just do what I was doing before. I would simply let the teacher's request go in one ear and out the other. [Ignoring the Teacher]

11. I would tell the teacher I had other priorities, like: "I have other homework so I can't prepare well for this one." "I have kids and they take up my time." "I'm too busy." "This class is not as important as my others." "I only took this class for general education requirements." [Priorities]

12. I would challenge the teacher's authority by asserting: "Do others in class have to do this?" "No one else is doing it, so why should I?" "Do you really take this class seriously?" "If it's such a good idea, why don't you do it?" [Challenge the Teacher's Basis of Power]

13. I would rally up student support. For instance, I would talk to others in class to see if they feel the same. I would tell my classmates not to go to class. I might get others to go along with me in not doing what the teacher wants. [Rally Student Support]

14. I would talk to someone in higher authority. For instance, I might complain to the department Chair that this instructor is incompetent and can't motivate the class. I would make a complaint to the Dean about the teacher's practices. I would talk to my advisor. I would threaten to go to the Dean. [Appeal to Powerful Others]

15. I would indicate to the teacher that I would participate more if he/she were more enthusiastic about what he/she is doing. Or, I might say, "You aren't enjoying it, so how can I?" "If you're not going to make the effort to teach well, I won't make an effort to listen." "You don't do it, so why should I?" [Modeling Teacher Behavior]

16. I would tell the teacher that if he/she doesn't care about us students, why should I care about what he/she wants? Or, I would say, "You don't seem to care about this class, why should I?" "You have no concern for this class yourself." [Modeling Teacher Affect]

17. I'd take a more active stance and tell the teacher that "I'm old enough to know how I can do in this class." "Right or wrong, that's the way I am." "I'm surprised you even noticed I'm in your class." "Lead your own life." "My behavior is my business." [Hostile Defensive]

18. I would argue that "I know what works for me; I don't need your advice." "I don't need this grade anyway." "I'm doing just fine without changing my behavior." "We'll see when the test comes up." [Student Rebuttal]

19. I'll get even by expressing my dissatisfaction with the teacher/course on evaluations at the end of the term. I won't recommend this teacher/class to others. I'll write a letter to put in the teacher's personnel file. I'll steal or hide the teacher's lecture notes/test. [Revenge]

Note. Generally, a very specific demand is inserted into the instructions. The student is asked to imagine him/herself in a hypothetical situation with a teacher who asks him/her to "come to class more prepared from now on." Testing the relationship between teacher immediacy and resistance, that same research described the hypothetical teacher as being either high or low in generalized (and specific) immediacy and employing either prosocial or antisocial behavior alteration techniques (Burroughs, Kearney, & Plax, 1989; Kearney, Plax, & Burroughs, 1991).

Category labels in brackets should be omitted from the actual questionnaire during administration.

Teacher Credibility

Teacher credibility refers to students' attitudes toward or evaluation of their teachers. Even though rhetorical scholars and communication researchers may disagree over the particular dimensions that comprise the credibility construct, all agree that credibility is multidimensional. After several years of intensive study of the construct and its associative operationalizations, McCroskey and his colleagues concluded that five basic dimensions represent credibility (Competence, Character, Composure, Sociability, and Extroversion) and those dimensions might change across sources and types of subjects. What soon followed was the development and testing of a separate teacher credibility scale (McCroskey, Holdridge, & Toomb, 1974).

Subsequent to that research, however, McCroskey and Young (1981) questioned the validity of those conclusions. They argued instead that the credibility construct had been distorted conceptually and theoretically to include dimensions that assessed person perception rather than evaluation. In an effort to achieve conceptual and operational isomorphism, then, McCroskey and Young (1981) returned to some of their earlier work, which established credibility as two-dimensional: Competence (or Authoritativeness) and Character. Moreover, they maintained that both dimensions remain fairly stable across public figures, teachers, and other sources. Consequently, they argued that a separate teacher credibility scale was no longer desirable or particularly useful.

Two types of scales can be used to measure the Competence and Character dimensions of credibility. The first is a Likert-type scale with 22 items written for the Competence factor and 20 items for Character (McCroskey, 1966). Wording of the scales must be modified to target the specific source of "teacher." The second, more concise measure, is a 12-item semantic differential scale (see McCroskey, 1966, for one version and McCroskey & Young, 1981, for a slightly different version). The correlation between the Likert and semantic differential Competence scales was .85 and between the two Character scales, .82 (McCroskey, 1966). Only the more recent semantic differential scale is offered below (McCroskey & Young, 1981).

When assessing teacher credibility, students are asked to evaluate their instructor in terms of the specific bipolar adjectives listed on a 7-point scale.

Profile by Patricia Kearney.

Responses are subsequently recoded so that higher scores reflect perceptions of higher teacher credibility. The scale takes less than 5 minutes to complete.

RELIABILITY

Reliability estimates of this specific 12-item semantic differential scale as well as other versions using the same and additional adjective pairs, are always high. Reported estimates range from .84 to .93 for the Competence dimension and .86 to .93 for Character (Beatty & Behnke, 1980; Beatty & Zahn, 1990; McCroskey, 1966; McCroskey & Young, 1981; Powers, Nitcavic, & Koerner, 1990).

VALIDITY

A large body of research supports the validity of the credibility scale. The most definitive work on the scale's content validity is McCroskey and Young (1981), which addresses the isomorphism between operational and historical, conceptual definitions of the construct. In explanation, while a number of other scales attempt to measure credibility, McCroskey and Young maintained that those assessments attempt to measure characteristics and perceptions well beyond the original definition of ethos or credibility.

Evidence of concurrent validity is reported in McCroskey's (1966) initial publication of both the Likert and semantic differential credibility measures, with obtained correlations between the two measures above .80. Factor structures across items generated to measure credibility typically result in at least the two dimensions of competence and character. This finding is generally consistent even though the labels for factors may differ (Beatty & Zahn, 1990; Beatty & Behnke, 1980; McCroskey & Young, 1981; Powers et al., 1990).

The Competence and Character subscales of teacher credibility have been shown to predict differentially to other criterion variables, including positive teacher vocalics and constructive teacher comments (Beatty & Behnke, 1980), student ratings of the course and teacher (Beatty & Zahn, 1990), desire to take additional courses from the same instructor (McCroskey, Holdridge, & Toomb, 1974), and overall teacher evaluations (Scott & Nussbaum, 1981).

LOCATION

McCroskey, J. C., & Young, T. J. (1981). Ethos and credibility: The construct and its measurement after decades. *Central States Speech Journal, 32*, 24–34.

REFERENCES

Beatty, M. J., & Behnke, R. R. (1980). Teacher credibility as a function of verbal content and paralinguistic cues. *Communication Quarterly, 28,* 55–59.

Beatty, M. J., & Zahn, C. J. (1990). Are student ratings of communication instructors due to "easy" grading practices? An analysis of teacher credibility and student-reported performance levels. *Communication Education, 39,* 275–282.

McCroskey, J. C. (1966). Special reports: Scales for the measurement of ethos. *Speech Monographs, 33,* 65–72.

McCroskey, J. C., Holdridge, W., & Toomb, J. K. (1974). An instrument for measuring the source credibility of basic speech communication instructors. *Speech Teacher, 33,* 26–33.

Powers, W. G., Nitcavic, R., & Koerner, D. (1990). Teacher characteristics: A college level perspective. *Communication Education, 39,* 227–233.

Scott, M. D., & Nussbaum, J. F. (1981). Student perceptions of instructor communication behaviors and their relationship to student evaluation. *Communication Education, 30,* 44–53.

Teacher Credibility*

Instructions: The following are a series of attitude scales. You are asked to evaluate your instructor in terms of the adjectives on each side. For example, if you think your instructor is very tall you might mark the following scale as below:

Tall __X__ ___ ___ ___ ___ ___ ___ Short

Of course, if you consider your instructor to be shorter, you would mark your "X" nearer the "short" adjective. The middle space on each scale should be considered "neutral." Mark this space if you feel neither adjective on the scale applies to your instructor or if you feel both apply equally.

My instructor in this course is:

Intelligent ___ ___ ___ ___ ___ ___ ___	Unintelligent
Untrained ___ ___ ___ ___ ___ ___ ___	Trained
Expert ___ ___ ___ ___ ___ ___ ___	Inexpert
Uninformed ___ ___ ___ ___ ___ ___ ___	Informed
Competent ___ ___ ___ ___ ___ ___ ___	Incompetent
Stupid ___ ___ ___ ___ ___ ___ ___	Bright
Sinful ___ ___ ___ ___ ___ ___ ___	Virtuous
Dishonest ___ ___ ___ ___ ___ ___ ___	Honest

Unselfish   ___   ___   ___   ___   ___   ___   ___   Selfish

Sympathetic   ___   ___   ___   ___   ___   ___   ___   Unsympathetic

High character   ___   ___   ___   ___   ___   ___   ___   Low character

Untrustworthy   ___   ___   ___   ___   ___   ___   ___   Trustworthy

Note. Some of the more current research assessing teacher characteristics has students reference "the instructor you have in the class that meets just before (or after) this one" in an effort to increase the sample size and diversity of teachers targeted.

The first six adjective pairs measure teacher competence; the second set of six assesses teacher character. Items should be recoded so that higher scores indicate higher overall credibility.

Teacher Satisfaction Scale

The construct, teacher satisfaction, is closely aligned with job satisfaction more generally. Plax, Kearney, and Downs (1986) were interested specifically in teachers' attitudes or affect toward their primary job responsibility, teaching. Whereas more generalized measures of job satisfaction assessed workers' attitudes toward pay, coworkers, working conditions, and other important factors, Plax et al. reasoned that teachers' job satisfaction is reflected primarily in their classroom experiences with students. Consequently, the Teacher Satisfaction Scale (SAT) was developed to assess teachers' attitudes about (a) teaching in global terms and (b) their own students.

The SAT is composed of six items, three measuring teachers' satisfaction toward the teaching profession and three measuring their satisfaction with the students they teach. Response options range from *never* (1) to *always* (5) or *very dissatisfying* (1) to *very satisfying* (5). Based on elementary, secondary, and college teachers' responses, factor analyses revealed that the SAT could be treated as either a single, unidimensional measure of teachers' overall satisfaction or two related assessments of satisfaction toward (a) teaching and (b) students.

RELIABILITY

The SAT appears to be internally consistent. In two separate studies reported by Plax et al. (1986), alpha reliability estimates were .88 and .85 for the teaching factor and .85 and .86 for the student factor. When the instrument was considered unidimensional, overall reliability estimates were .76 and .91.

VALIDITY

There is some evidence of construct validity for the SAT. Plax et al. (1986) found significant relationships between the satisfaction dimensions and teachers' use of behavior alteration techniques. In general, they found that

Profile by Michael J. Beatty.

356

"teachers may be more or less satisfied as a function of their abilities to effectively manage students" (p. 385). This finding was replicated across elementary, secondary, and college teacher samples.

COMMENTS

The SAT improves on prior job satisfaction instruments by assessing teachers' satisfaction toward their primary job responsibilities, teaching and dealing with students. Even so, Plax et al. (1986) recommend that the scale be expanded to include other potentially relevant job factors. Specifically, the authors suggested that teachers themselves be asked to derive inductively those issues that influence their level of satisfaction toward their chosen profession. A number of other, relevant in-class factors may emerge, including class size, instructional resources, and students' individual differences.

LOCATION

Plax, T. G., Kearney, P., & Downs, T. M. (1986). Communicating control in the classroom and satisfaction with teaching and students. *Communication Education*, *35*, 379–388.

Teacher Satisfaction Scale*

1. Have you ever considered quitting teaching?

   Never   Seldom   Sometimes   Usually   Always

2. Everything considered, how satisfying has teaching been for you?

   Very satisfying   Satisfying   Somewhat satisfying, somewhat dissatisfying   Dissatisfying   Very Dissatisfying

3. If you had your life to live over, do you think you would go into teaching as a profession?

   Definitely   Probably   Possibly   Probably not   Definitely not

4. Are you generally comfortable with the cooperation exhibited by your students in your classes?

   Never   Seldom   Sometimes   Usually   Always

---

*Copyright 1986 by the Speech Communication Association. Reprinted by permission.

5. In general, how satisfied are you with the motivation of the students you teach?

| Very satisfied | Satisfied | Somewhat satisfied, somewhat dissatisfied | Dissatisfied | Very dissatisfied |

6. How satisfied are you with the general level of students' abilities in your classes?

| Very satisfied | Satisfied | Somewhat satisfied, somewhat dissatisfied | Dissatisfied | Very dissatisfied |

Note. Items 1–3 are satisfaction with teaching and Items 4–6 are satisfaction toward students.

Teacher
Self-Disclosure Instrument

Teacher self-disclosure "refers to teacher statements in the classroom about self that may or may not be related to subject content, but reveal information about the teacher that students are unlikely to learn from other sources" (Sorensen, 1989, p. 260). Prior research on teacher self-disclosure examined more gestalt impressions of the teacher's disclosure. Specifically, Downs, Javidi, and Nussbaum (1988) revealed "topics" or categories of teacher disclosure; others investigated perceptions of another's disclosure based on honesty, valence, amount and depth, and intent (Wheeless, Young, & Nesser, 1978).

In an extension of that research, Sorensen (1989) devised a low-inference Teacher Self-Disclosure Instrument (TSDI) that identifies specific disclosures associated with either "good" or "poor" teachers. The TDSI comprises 150 different teacher statements; however, a shorter 32-item version is reported here. (The original instrument isolated disclosure statements indicative of good and poor teachers, as well as two additional categories of neutral and mixed.) Students reported that the first 16 items reflected good teachers, whereas the second 16 items were associated with poor teachers. Employing a simulated experimental design, good teachers were differentiated from poor teachers based on students' perceptions of teacher solidarity, immediacy, and students' affect.

An examination of the resulting disclosure profiles revealed that students attributed to good teachers more positively worded disclosures and sentiments that showed a concern for students and others. Students thought that poor teachers, on the other hand, would be more likely to use statements that showed a lack of tolerance for others, employ more source-oriented statements (particularly about their own achievements), and reveal a pessimistic or negative outlook on life (Sorensen, 1989).

The 32-item version of the TSDI takes about 5 minutes to complete. Students use a 4-point scale, ranging from *very likely* (4) to *very unlikely* (1), to indicate how likely it is that their instructors would make the 32 statements.

Profile by Patricia Kearney.

RELIABILITY

No reliability coefficients are reported. The disclosure statements were not originally intended as a scaled instrument. Instead, items or statements reflecting either good or poor teachers were discriminated on the basis of a series of student's t-tests.

VALIDITY

In terms of the construct validity of the TSDI, Sorensen (1989) found that simulated good and poor teacher profiles were perceived differently on measures of students' generalized perceptions of the level of intent, honesty, amount, and valence (positive–negative) of that self-disclosure. In particular, good and poor teacher profiles accounted for 21% of the variance on the Positiveness–Negativeness dimension of self-disclosure. Students perceived the teacher in the good-teacher disclosure profile as using significantly more positive disclosures than the simulated poor teacher.

COMMENTS

Because this instrument is new to our discipline, we recommend that future researchers factor-analyze responses to the 32-item scale to substantiate further the good–poor teacher underlying dimensions. Moreover, reliabilities for each of those resulting dimensions should be computed.

The TSDI offers instructional communication researchers and teachers a low-inference alternative to other, high-inference self-disclosure scales currently available. In terms of teacher training, prospective teachers might be asked to indicate how likely they would be to use statements of each type in their classroom instruction followed by a discussion on students' perceptions of each type. Researchers might also consider investigating the appropriateness of each disclosure type for the multicultural/multiethnic classroom.

LOCATION

Sorensen, G. (1989). The relationship among teachers' self-disclosive statements, students' perceptions, and affective learning. *Communication Education*, *38*, 259–276.

REFERENCES

Downs, V. C., Javidi, M., & Nussbaum, J. F. (1988). An analysis of teachers' verbal communication within the college classroom: Use of humor, self-disclosure, and narratives. *Communication Education, 37,* 127–141.

Wheeless, L. R., Young, M. K., & Nesser, I. K. (1978, April). *Observational measurement of the perceived self-disclosure of another person.* Paper presented at the annual meeting of the Eastern Communication Association, Boston.

Teacher Self-Disclosure Instrument*

Instructions. Below is a sample of statements made by college instructors in a typical college classroom with somewhere between 25 and 40 students. Rate each of these statements according to how likely you think *your instructor* is to make that statement or a similar statement of that type. Rate each statement using the following scale: (4) *very likely,* (3) *somewhat likely,* (2) *somewhat unlikely,* or (1) *very unlikely.*

[Editors' note: Respondents use the above scale to respond to the following items.]

1. I care about my students.
2. I'll go out of my way to avoid hurting someone.
3. Men should be able to cry as an emotional release.
4. I love my family more than anyone in the world.
5. There's nothing better than a good book to raise my spirit.
6. I am truly in love with my spouse.
7. I paint for relaxation.
8. I've tried to teach my children that race, religion or social class shouldn't affect their relations with people.
9. I'm a giving person.
10. One of my favorite authors is Mark Twain.
11. I enjoy playing with my children.
12. Tennis is my favorite game.
13. I believe in the human rights movement.
14. You can be great, no matter what you do.
15. If you cheat, you are cheating yourself.
16. I'd love to spend a year or two traveling around the country, meeting people.

---

17. I enjoy going out and getting drunk.
18. Most people who get married don't stay married.
19. I can't stand a child who whines.
20. Children deserve to be spanked whenever they do something wrong.
21. I just cut my hair and I hate it.
22. I don't like men with long hair.
23. I voted for Nixon and I'd do it again.
24. Baseball is too slow a game to be our national pastime.
25. I've never really had a vacation.
26. I have a violent temper.
27. I find it difficult to respond rationally when I'm criticized.
28. I suspect people's motives when they compliment me.
29. There are times when I feel I've wasted my life.
30. When someone criticizes an idea I have or something I do, I can't help taking it personally.
31. People who go to church generally don't practice religious principles in their own lives.
32. Poor people get too much welfare.

Note. The original disclosure instrument asked students to rate how likely a "good" (or "poor") teacher is to make each statement. Alternatively, students could assess "the teacher they have in the course immediately preceding (or following) this class" in order to elicit a greater diversity and number of targeted teachers.

Positive statements are 1–16 and negative statements are 17–32. To avoid response bias, items should be randomly arranged for the actual test administration.

Team-Review Questionnaire

Team building is the most popular and widely used intervention for organizational development. A review of the literature, however, reveals that there are no consistent definitions of what an effective team is or what the processes of building teams are. Liebowitz and De Meuse (1982) described team building as "a long term, data based intervention in which intact work groups experientially learn . . . to increase their skills for effective teamwork. It is a direct attempt to assist the group in becoming more adept at identifying, diagnosing, and solving its own problems, usually with the aid of a behavioral science consultant" (p. 2).

There are a number of instruments designed to analyze the status of team interaction, but most of these have been developed by consultants and are not available without cost (e.g., Team Excellence Questionnaire [Larson & LaFasto, 1989] and Team Interaction Profile [Wilson Learning, 1985]). Francis and Young (1979), on the other hand, encouraged innovation with their Team-Review Questionnaire (TRQ) and suggested researchers "freely copy these sheets, but for internal and non-profit use only" (p. 39).

The TRQ is composed of 108 statements, measuring the following 12 team characteristics.

1. *Effective Leadership*. The team manager is committed and able to develop a team approach, and management in the team is seen as a shared function.
2. *Suitable Membership*. Members are capable of contributing a "mix" of skills that provides for an appropriate balance.
3. *Team Commitment*. Members feel individual commitment to the aims of the team and are willing to devote personal energy to building the team and supporting other team members.
4. *Team Climate*. People feel relaxed, able to be direct and open, and prepared to take risks.
5. *Team Achievement*. Objectives are clear and felt to be worthwhile, targets for performance are felt to be stretching but achievable, energy is devoted to the achievement of results, and team performance is reviewed frequently.

Profile by Cal W. Downs, with assistance from John Gribas.

6. *Corporate Role*. The team has contributed to corporate planning and has an important role in the overall organization.
7. *Work Methods*. The team has developed lively, systematic, and effective ways to solve problems together.
8. *Team Organization*. Roles and communication patterns are clear and administrative procedures support a team approach.
9. *Critiquing*. Errors and weaknesses are examined without personal attack to enable the group to learn from experience.
10. *Individual Development*. Member development is sought and the team can cope with strong individual contributions.
11. *Creative Capacity*. New ideas are created through member interaction, innovative risk taking is rewarded, and the team will support new ideas from individual members or from outside.
12. *Intergroup Relations*. There is regular contact and review of collective priorities with other teams; individuals are encouraged to work with members of other teams.

Each of the 12 factors has nine items, and because the instrument is specifically designed to pinpoint weaknesses, all items are worded negatively to suggest a problem. In the original version, respondents simply reported whether they believed the statement was generally "true" or generally "false" in describing their teams. The number of true items for each factor was then tabulated across respondents and the 12 factors rank-ordered in terms of probable problems. Gribas (1990) substituted a 7-point Likert scale, arguing that this permitted more sophisticated analyses.

RELIABILITY

Francis and Young (1979) have not promoted the TRQ as an experimental tool, and they offer no statistical analysis of its reliability. Gribas (1990), however, calculated internal reliability scores in his study of participants in community theaters. Because they did not seem to fit his sample, he omitted the Corporate Role and Intergroup Relations dimensions from his study. Cronbach alphas for the other 10 factors ranged from .86 to .92, which indicate a high degree of reliability and also offer justification for dealing with the factors as distinct and cohesive units. Gribas also correlated each item on a factor with the overall factor score. Only four had correlation coefficients lower than .50. While these results give some insights into the instrument, more work is needed to verify its reliability.

VALIDITY

No statistical data are available to support the construct validity of this instrument, yet there is some evidence of face validity. Downs (1989), for example, has used this instrument with managers from a number of organizations, and their evaluations of it have generally been positive. The managers felt that it covers the most important areas of effective teams.

The TRQ factors are also similar to those found in other instruments. For example, Larson and LaFasto (1989) identified the following eight factors: Clear Elevating Goal, Results-Driven Structure, Competent Team Members, Unified Commitment, Collaborative Climate, Standards of Excellence, and External Support and Recognition. Abelson and Woodman (1983) identified seven factors: Duplication of Effort, Ambiguous Responsibility, Lack of Trust, Need for More Commitment, Role Ambiguity, Poor Management of Resources, and Unclear Goals. Therefore, the factors measured by the TRQ are ones that are commonly found in the team-building literature.

COMMENTS

The TRQ is based not on systematic research but on extensive work in organizations. Although Francis and Young (1979) indicated, "our suggestions are in line with current behavioral science research" (p. 2), they have not built a research-based rationale for their instrument. Their primary purpose is "to help a work team address its strengths and weaknesses" (p. 39).

The lack of research about the TRQ, of course, makes building a case for it difficult. Furthermore, the TRQ has some problems as well as some strengths. First, its length enables it to cover a great many aspects of organizational life, but it also makes it more unwieldy than other shorter instruments. Factor analysis would enable one not only to determine the adequacy of the 12-factor structure but also to shorten the total instrument. Of course, securing enough responses to factor-analyze 108 items would require some rather large teams. Second, the fact that the items are worded negatively is objectionable to some people because it stresses problems. Third, the true–false response format probably needs altering in the Gribas fashion if important analytical work is to be done. A format allowing for indication of degree of problem would offer better descriptions of team status and certainly would allow for more advanced statistical analysis of the responses. Fourth, the instrument has a bias in favor of participative leadership as being the most effective leadership type. Gribas and Downs (1991), however, noted that "effective" leadership as measured by the TRQ had a negative correlation to member satisfaction among actors and directors. In other words, they perceived tight direction as more effective. While this bias is not a weakness of the instrument necessarily, researchers need to look at its orientation in terms of specific organization types and relevant contingencies.

Despite the lack of prior analysis, this instrument was included in this volume because it also has some strong points. It is an excellent tool to use in assessing the status of teams as a means of organizational development. Downs has used it successfully with engineering organizations, and Simons (1982) used it in a pre- and posttest format to measure the success of team building in the staffs of residence halls. And when something has such practical applications, it ought to offer advantages for research as well. It is also thorough in its coverage of the organization, even though not all the factors might be applicable to every organization as Gribas (1990) demonstrated. Furthermore, there is a specificity about the items that has strong appeal. Although some instruments deal in rather high levels of abstraction, the TRQ items are rather specific. Finally, the scoring can be done quickly.

LOCATION

Francis, D., & Young, D. (1979). *Improving work groups: A practical manual for team building*. La Jolla, CA: University Associates.

REFERENCES

Abelson, M. A., & Woodman, R. W. (1983). Review of research on team effectiveness: Implications for teams in schools. *School Psychology Review, 12,* 125–136.

Downs, C. W. (1989, November). *Teamwork: A review*. Paper presented at the meeting of the Speech Communication Association, San Francisco.

Gribas, J. (1990). *Characteristics of temporary teams: Perceptions among community theatre casts and directors*. Unpublished master's thesis, University of Kansas, Lawrence.

Gribas, J., & Downs, C. W. (1991, May). *Characteristics of temporary teams*. Paper presented at the meeting of the International Communication Association, Chicago.

Larson, C. E., & LaFasto, F. M. J. (1989). *Teamwork: What must go right/what can go wrong*. Newbury Park, CA: Sage.

Liebowitz, S. J., & De Meuse, K. P. (1982). The application of team building. *Human Relations, 35,* 1–18.

Simons, K. (1982). *The effects of team building on University of Kansas residence hall staffs*. Unpublished master's thesis, University of Kansas, Lawrence.

Wilson Learning. (1985). *Team Interaction Profile*. Eden Prairie, MN: Author.

*   *   *

Permission to reprint the Team-Review Questionnaire was denied by the copyright holders.

Television Affinity Scale

TV affinity is an attitude toward the medium that reflects the importance people assign to TV or specific programs. Greenberg (1974) first reported using a three-item Likert scale to measure the intensity of one's attachment to TV. Rubin (1977, 1979) used that measure, and later increased it to five items (Rubin, 1981a). Adaptations of the Television Affinity Scale (TAS) have been used to measure affinity with soap operas (Perse, 1986; Rubin & Perse, 1987), TV news and information programs (Rubin, 1981b; Rubin, Perse, & Powell, 1985), religious programs (Abelman, 1987, 1988), and talk radio (Armstrong & Rubin, 1989).

Affinity measures have been used often in uses and gratifications studies in which affinity is not usually the primary focus of the research. Affinity is usually used to mediate or moderate the relationships between other TV viewing variables such as motives and exposure. Only a few studies have treated affinity as a criterion variable (Austin & Myers, 1984; Rubin, 1983).

In early studies, affinity was correlated with viewing motives to explore the meaning of reasons for using TV (e.g., Greenberg, 1974; Rubin, 1979; Rubin & Rubin, 1982b). Other research considered how affinity related to ritualistic and instrumental media orientations (Rubin, 1983) and to watching various TV programs such as *60 Minutes* (Rubin, 1981b) and the *700 Club* (Abelman, 1988). In recent research, affinity has been a predictor variable for viewing outcomes such as parasocial interaction (Rubin et al., 1985), soap opera cultivation (Perse, 1986), and soap opera involvement (Rubin & Perse, 1987).

Most studies using adaptations of the scale report the items they used. The TAS used by Rubin and Rubin (1982a) is given below. Earlier studies (e.g., Rubin, 1979, 1981a) used a negatively worded Item 2, "If the television wasn't working, I would not miss it," but the double negative made it confusing. Respondents mark their agreement with the statements using 5-point Likert scales, from *strongly disagree* (1) to *strongly agree* (5). Averaged scores are usually used in analyses. The scale takes about 1 minute to complete. The items are often mingled with other attitudinal statements.

Profile by Elizabeth M. Perse.

368 MEASURE PROFILES

RELIABILITY

Although Greenberg (1974) did not report the reliability of the original three-item scale, four- and five-item versions are internally consistent. Cronbach alphas for the four-item version range from .75 to .83; alphas for the five-item version range from .79 to .93. Four-item versions usually exclude the negatively worded item to increase reliability. The scale has been used reliably with different samples: children (Rubin, 1979), traditional and nontraditional college students (Austin & Myers, 1984; Conway & Rubin, 1991; Perse, 1986; Rubin & Perse, 1987; Rubin et al., 1985), adults (Abelman, 1988; Conway & Rubin, 1991; Rubin, 1981a, 1983), and elders (Rubin & Rubin, 1982a, 1982b). Although affinity is conceptualized as an attitude toward TV, studies have not assessed the scale's test–retest stability.

VALIDITY

Establishing validity for the TAS has not been a primary research focus. Although there is no discussion of scale development in the literature, the scale items appear to have face validity. That is, the items seem to be assessing a sense of TV importance and attachment to the medium. Researchers have found that the more motivated people are to watch TV, the more important they believe TV to be (Greenberg, 1974; Rubin, 1979, 1981a; Rubin & Rubin, 1982b).

Because affinity measures how important people believe TV or its content is, analyses do provide support for construct validity. Several authors point out that TV should be more important to respondents who have fewer opportunities for mass or interpersonal communication. For example, using contextual age measures, Rubin and Rubin (1982a) observed that affinity was negatively related to self-reliance in an elder sample. Talk-radio affinity also related to perceptions of being less mobile, more frequent talk-radio telephoning behavior, avoiding interpersonal interaction, and receiving fewer rewards from communicating with others (Armstrong & Rubin, 1989). And, Austin and Myers (1984) observed that deaf respondents report greater affinity for TV than do hearing viewers. They explained that TV's importance might reflect its role as a social surrogate for the deaf.

Later studies that tested multivariate relationships among variables suggest the scale's criterion-related validity. Affinity is a predictor of parasocial interaction, or feelings of interaction with TV personalities (Rubin & Perse, 1987; Rubin et al., 1985). Soap opera affinity also predicted planning to watch a favorite soap opera, engaging in fewer distracting activities when watching, and thinking about and talking about the program after watching (Rubin & Perse, 1987).

COMMENTS

Although there is evidence for the scale's reliability and validity, affinity scores are usually low. On 5-point scales, averaged affinity scores have ranged from 1.45 to 3.38. Most scores are in the 2.00–3.00 range suggesting that most respondents do not see TV or specific programs as extremely important in their lives.

Research using the TAS has been restricted to uses and gratifications research. Because few studies have focused on affinity as an outcome variable (cf. Rubin, 1983), little is known about various influences on attachment to different media. Because of its positive relationship to exposure and initial results that support links to viewing outcomes, affinity might have utility for media effects studies.

LOCATION

Rubin, A. M. (1981a). An examination of television viewing motivations. *Communication Research, 8*, 141–165.

Rubin, A. M., & Rubin, R. B. (1982a). Contextual age and television use. *Human Communication Research, 8*, 228–244.

REFERENCES

Abelman, R. (1987). Religious television uses and gratifications. *Journal of Broadcasting and Electronic Media, 31*, 293–307.

Abelman, R. (1988). Motivations for viewing "The 700 Club." *Journalism Quarterly, 65*, 112–118, 164.

Armstrong, C. B., & Rubin, A. M. (1989). Talk radio as interpersonal communication. *Journal of Communication, 39*(2), 84–94.

Austin, B. A., & Myers, J. W. (1984). Hearing-impaired viewers of prime-time television. *Journal of Communication, 34*(4), 60–71.

Conway, J. C., & Rubin, A. M. (1991). Psychological predictors of television viewing motivation. *Communication Research, 18*, 443–463.

Greenberg, B. S. (1974). Gratifications of television viewing and their correlates for British children. In J. G. Blumler & E. Katz (Eds.), *The uses of mass communications: Current perspectives on gratifications research* (pp. 71–92). Beverly Hills, CA: Sage.

Perse, E. M. (1986). Soap opera viewing patterns of college students and cultivation. *Journal of Broadcasting and Electronic Media, 30*, 175–193.

Rubin, A. M. (1977). Television usage, attitudes and viewing behaviors of children and adolescents. *Journal of Broadcasting, 21*, 355–369.

Rubin, A. M. (1979). Television use by children and adolescents. *Human Communication Research, 5*, 109–120.

Rubin, A. M. (1981b). A multivariate analysis of "60 Minutes" viewing motivations. *Journalism Quarterly, 58*, 529–534.

Rubin, A. M. (1983). Television uses and gratifications: The interactions of viewing patterns and motivations. *Journal of Broadcasting, 27*, 37–51.

Rubin, A. M., & Perse, E. M. (1987). Audience activity and soap opera involvement: A uses and effects investigation. *Human Communication Research, 14*, 246–268.

Rubin, A. M., Perse, E. M., & Powell, R. A. (1985). Loneliness, parasocial interaction, and local television news viewing. *Human Communication Research, 12*, 155–180.

Rubin, A. M., & Rubin, R. B. (1982b). Older persons' TV viewing patterns and motivations. *Communication Research, 9*, 287–313.

Television Affinity Scale*

Instructions: Here are some statements people may make about themselves (or about television). For each statement please circle the number that best expresses your own feelings. If you *strongly agree* with the statement, circle a 5. If you *agree*, circle a 4. If you *agree some and disagree some*, circle a 3. If you *disagree*, circle a 2. If you *strongly disagree*, circle a 1.

1. Watching television is one of the more important things I do each day.
2. If the television set wasn't working, I would really miss it.
3. Watching television is very important in my life.
4. I could easily do without television for several days.
5. I would feel lost without television to watch.

Note. Item 4 is reverse-coded for data analysis.

Television Viewing
Motives Scale

Uses and gratifications (U&G) is an audience-centered mass communication perspective. It assumes people actively seek media to satisfy communication needs, and research examines the reasons people use media (Katz, Blumler, & Gurevitch, 1974). Early U&G studies focused on media motives and their links to behaviors, attitudes, and demographics.

Greenberg (1974) developed his Viewing Motivation Scale to assess why children use TV. To create the scale, Greenberg asked British 9-, 12-, and 15-year-olds to write essays about why they like to watch TV. Content analysis of the 180 essays yielded eight clusters of reasons: to pass time, to forget, to learn about things, to learn about myself, for arousal, for relaxation, for companionship, and as a habit. Greenberg created 31 statements reflecting the eight sets of reasons and administered the scale to a large sample of British children and adolescents. Factor analysis identified eight factors accounting for 56% of the variance: Six of the dimensions drawn from the essays were replicated; the two Learning dimensions merged into one factor; and the Pass Time dimension split between two factors.

Rubin (1977, 1979) adapted Greenberg's scale for use with U.S. children and adolescents. Based on a pretest with children, Rubin shortened the scale to 24 statements to reduce respondent fatigue. He chose the three items with the highest factor loadings in each of Greenberg's eight dimensions. Rubin found that the two learning dimensions and the two habit and pass-time dimensions merged in two of the six factors.

Greenberg's scale and Rubin's adaptation are the most widely used measures of viewing motivation. The scales have been adapted to several contexts, such as TV use by college students (Bantz, 1982; Finn & Gorr, 1988), adults (Rubin, 1981a, 1983, 1984), and elders (Ostman & Jeffers, 1983; Rubin & Rubin, 1982); watching TV news and information (Rubin, 1981b; Rubin & Perse, 1987b), public TV (Palmgreen & Rayburn, 1979), music TV (Sun & Lull, 1986), soap operas (Rubin & Perse, 1987a), and religious TV (Abelman, 1987); and listening to talk radio (Armstrong & Rubin, 1989).

Profile by Elizabeth M. Perse.

The 27-item Television Viewing Motives Scale (TVMS) used by Rubin (1983) is profiled here. This scale is adapted from Greenberg (1974) and Rubin (1979, 1981a). It takes about 5 minutes to complete, but twice as long for children. Respondents are asked to specify how much each of the statements is like their own reasons for watching TV: *exactly* (5), *a lot* (4), *somewhat* (3), *not much* (2), or *not at all* (1). Items are randomly or alternately presented based on motive dimension. Others have used different response categories (see Babrow, 1988, p. 478, for a summary). Rubin (1981a) also included a specific-content dimension.

Scale items are treated as indicators of underlying motive dimensions (Babrow, 1988). Items are usually subjected to data reduction methods, such as factor or cluster analysis, to uncover the latent motive structure. Motive clusters or factors are then used in subsequent analyses to describe media use and to test hypotheses about media behaviors and outcomes.

RELIABILITY

Motive dimensions have been reliable. Greenberg (1974) reported interitem correlations for his eight factors ranging from .29 (Pass Time) to .44 (Arousal). Rubin (1977) reported somewhat higher interitem correlations for his six factors, ranging from .40 (Pass Time/Habit) to .50 (Companionship). Greenberg (1974) and Rubin (1979) also showed stability of motives across age groups of children and adolescents.

Cronbach alphas also support the reliability of motive dimensions. Finn and Gorr (1988) reported alphas ranging from .68 (Escape) to .87 (Entertainment). Rubin (1979) reported reliabilities ranging from .62 (Relaxation) to .81 (Learning), and Conway and Rubin (1991) reported alphas ranging from .69 (Relaxation) to .82 (Pass Time). Rubin and Perse's (1987a) soap opera motive factors' reliability ranged from .71 (Social Utility) to .87 (Entertainment). Finn (1992) reported alphas of .87 and .86 for Combined Mood Management (i.e., relaxation, arousal, entertainment, and information) and Social Compensation (i.e., companionship, habit, pass time, and escape) dimensions of TV viewing motivation based on Rubin's (1981a, 1983) scales.

VALIDITY

Greenberg's (1974) method of creating viewing-motive statements supports its content validity. Rubin (1981a) took additional steps to ensure content validity of the scale with a U.S. sample. He recruited 270 persons, ranging from children to the elderly, to provide open-ended statements of why they watch TV. He used those responses to clarify categories of motives and to revise the scale. He also supported construct validity of the scale by finding a .93 Kendall's Coefficient of Concordance comparing rankings of open-ended viewing-motivation responses to responses to the 30 Likert motive items for his sample of 626 persons.

The results of other studies point out that the scale may not be a complete inventory of motives for specific programs or other genres or media. Babrow (1987) and Sun and Lull (1986), for example, found that freely elicited reasons for watching soap operas and MTV, respectively, yielded additional dimensions unique to the genres, as did Furno-Lamude and Anderson (1992) for rerun TV programs.

Several studies provide concurrent and criterion-related validity for motive dimensions. Greenberg (1974) noted that different viewing motives relate predictably to other variables. He found that (a) believing TV content was realistic predicted watching TV to learn, (b) spending less time with homework and more total TV watching explained habit motives, and (c) watching more TV, science fiction, and action-adventure programs and an expressed willingness to commit violence predicted arousal motives. Similarly, Rubin (1983) found that all viewing motives but escape predicted TV exposure and attachment. That is, the more motivated people are to watch TV, the more they watch and the more important they think TV is.

Rubin and Perse (1987b) found validity for news-viewing motives via links to news-viewing activity. Pass-time motives related to engaging in more distractions when watching the news; more salient information motives and less salient entertainment motives related to more cognitive involvement with news stories. Rubin and Perse (1987a) also found that voyeuristic soap opera viewing motives, which focus on the attraction and appeal of the characters, were linked with parasocial interaction with a soap opera character. Watching soap operas for social utility reasons was associated with greater postviewing discussion.

Finn and Gorr (1988) provided some evidence of construct validity for Rubin's (1983) scale. They predicted that TV viewing motives would arise, in part, from needs related to inadequacies in the social environment. Supporting their hypothesis, they found social compensation motives such as companionship and escape were linked to greater loneliness, shyness, and reduced social support.

COMMENTS

Several have offered suggestions for using media-motive scales. First, there are conceptual assumptions and corresponding methodological implications in measuring motives (Babrow, 1988). Second, there is a conceptual difference between factors that account for the most variance and factors that are most salient to respondents (Sun & Lull, 1986). Third, media motives may reflect both more goal-directed instrumental and less purposive ritualized media orientations (Rubin, 1984), as well as proactive (Mood Management) and passive (Social Compensation) dimensions (Finn, 1992). Fourth, statement order may introduce response bias (Finn & Gorr, 1988). Fifth, different statistical packages and procedures can yield different factor analysis results (Dobos & Dimmick, 1988).

LOCATION

Greenberg, B. S. (1974). Gratifications of television viewing and their correlates for British children. In J. G. Blumler & E. Katz (Eds.), *The uses of mass communications: Current perspectives on gratifications research* (pp. 71–92). Beverly Hills, CA: Sage.

Rubin, A. M. (1981a). An examination of television viewing motivations. *Communication Research, 8,* 141–165.

Rubin, A. M. (1983). Television uses and gratifications: The interactions of viewing patterns and motivations. *Journal of Broadcasting, 27,* 37–51.

REFERENCES

Abelman, R. (1987). Religious television uses and gratification. *Journal of Broadcasting and Electronic Media, 31,* 293–307.

Armstrong, C. B., & Rubin, A. M. (1989). Talk radio as interpersonal communication. *Journal of Communication, 39*(2), 84–94.

Babrow, A. S. (1987). Student motives for watching soap operas. *Journal of Broadcasting and Electronic Media, 31,* 309–321.

Babrow, A. S. (1988). Theory and method in research on audience motives. *Journal of Broadcasting and Electronic Media, 32,* 471–487.

Bantz, C. R. (1982). Exploring uses and gratifications: A comparison of reported uses of television and reported uses of favorite program type. *Communication Research, 9,* 352–379.

Conway, J. C., & Rubin, A. M. (1991). Psychological predictors of television viewing motivation. *Communication Research, 18,* 443–464.

Dobos, J., & Dimmick, J. (1988). Factor analysis and gratification constructs. *Journal of Broadcasting and Electronic Media, 32,* 335–350.

Finn, S. (1992). Television addiction? An evaluation of four competing media-use models. *Journalism Quarterly, 69,* 422–435.

Finn, S., & Gorr, M. B. (1988). Social isolation and social support as correlates of television viewing motivations. *Communication Research, 15,* 135–158.

Furno-Lamude, D., & Anderson, J. (1992). The uses and gratifications of rerun viewing. *Journalism Quarterly, 69,* 362–372.

Katz, E., Blumler, J. G., & Gurevitch, M. (1974). Utilization of mass communication by the individual. In J. G. Blumler & E. Katz (Eds.), *The uses of mass communications: Current perspectives on gratifications research* (pp. 19–32). Beverly Hills, CA: Sage.

Ostman, R. E., & Jeffers, D. W. (1983). Life stage and motives for television use. *International Journal of Aging and Human Development, 17*, 315–322.

Palmgreen, P., & Rayburn, J. D., II. (1979). Uses and gratifications and exposure to public television: A discrepancy approach. *Communication Research, 6*, 155–179.

Rubin, A. M. (1977). Television usage, attitudes and viewing behaviors of children and adolescents. *Journal of Broadcasting, 21*, 355–369.

Rubin, A. M. (1979). Television use by children and adolescents. *Human Communication Research, 5*, 109–120.

Rubin, A. M. (1981b). A multivariate analysis of "60 Minutes" viewing motivations. *Journalism Quarterly, 58*, 529–534.

Rubin, A. M. (1984). Ritualized and instrumental television viewing. *Journal of Communication, 34*(3), 67–77.

Rubin, A. M., & Perse, E. M. (1987a). Audience activity and soap opera involvement: A uses and effects investigation. *Human Communication Research, 14*, 246–268.

Rubin, A. M., & Perse, E. M. (1987b). Audience activity and television news gratifications. *Communication Research, 14*, 58–84.

Rubin, A. M., & Rubin, R. B. (1982). Older persons' TV viewing patterns and motivations. *Communication Research, 9*, 287–313.

Sun, S-W., & Lull, J. (1986). The adolescent audience for music videos and why they watch. *Journal of Communication, 36*(1), 115–125.

Television Viewing Motives Scale*

Instructions: Here are some reasons that people have given for why they watch television. Please circle the number to indicate whether each reason is *exactly* (5), *a lot* (4), *somewhat* (3), *not much* (2), or *not at all* (1) like your own reason for watching television.

[Editors' note: Response options are presented for each item as shown for Item 1.]

I watch television . . .

<u>Relaxation</u>
1. Because it relaxes me.   5   4   3   2   1
2. Because it allows me to unwind.
3. Because it's a pleasant rest.

Companionship
1. So I won't have to be alone.
2. When there's no one else to talk to or be with.
3. Because it makes me feel less lonely.

Habit
1. Just because it's there.
2. Because I just like to watch.
3. Because it's a habit, just something I do.

Pass Time
1. When I have nothing better to do.
2. Because it passes the time away, particularly when I'm bored.
3. Because it gives me something to do to occupy my time.

Entertainment
1. Because it entertains me.
2. Because it's enjoyable.
3. Because it amuses me.

Social Interaction
1. Because it's something to do when friends come over.
2. So I can talk with other people about what's on.
3. So I can be with other members of the family or friends who are watching.

Information
1. Because it helps me learn things about myself and others.
2. So I can learn how to do things which I haven't done before.
3. So I could learn about what could happen to me.

Arousal
1. Because it's thrilling.
2. Because it's exciting.
3. Because it peps me up.

Escape
1. So I can forget about school, work, or other things.
2. So I can get away from the rest of the family or others.
3. So I can get away from what I'm doing.

Note. Category labels should be removed and items arranged randomly.

Three-Dimensional Communication Load Scale

"Some research indicates that the majority of corporate managers, especially those at the operating level, regard 'information overload' as an academic, rather than a real issue" (Chung & Goldhaber, 1991, p. 3). Intuitively, however, it makes sense that the sheer amount of information to be processed can be overwhelming to managers and that the amount is actually increasing as new technologies generate information easily and allow it to be shared quickly. Therefore, communication load in organizations is a topic often discussed among organizational writers, but difficulties in measuring it have inhibited scholars from conducting much research on the topic. Consequently, the scale by Chung and Goldhaber offers help not only in measuring communication load but also in refining the concept.

Chung and Goldhaber (1991) based their concept of communication load on the works of Galbraith (1977) and Weick (1979). Galbraith viewed organizations as information-processing systems and called attention to the need to match an organization's capabilities for processing information with the actual load encountered. When the two are not equal, either overload or underload results. Weick's emphasis, on the other hand, was on the process of organizing, and he viewed organizations as activities rather than structures or entities. By means of act–response–adjustment communication, "organizational members reduce the equivocality in data input and, thus, transform equivocal raw data into information" (Chung & Goldhaber, 1991, p. 4). This theory leads to the designation of one function of communication being to reduce equivocality and increase certainty.

Often load is described merely in terms of quantity. However, Chung and Goldhaber concluded that communication load has three dimensions:

> Communication load is a measure of the extent to which, in a given period of time, an organization's members perceive more *quantity*, *complexity*, and/or *equivocality* in the information than an individual desires, needs, or can handle in the process of communication . . . if an organization member perceives A degrees of quantity, B degrees of complexity, and C degrees of equivocality in the information for communication, and desires, needs, or can handle A'

Profile by Cal W. Downs, with assistance from Jensen Chung.

377

degrees of quantity, B' degrees of complexity and C' degrees of equivocality, then the measure of this individual's communication load, X is $X = f(A-A', B-B', C-C')$. (Chung & Goldhaber, 1991, p. 8, italics added)

Quantity is defined in terms of the perceived amount of messages received and sent within a certain period. A sample question is: How often do you receive more information than you can process? Other studies have actually tried to count symbols and messages, but definitions of information make this difficult. Complexity is also based on perception. It is defined as the perceived amount of decisions to be made about those messages sent or received in the same period of time, and this concept may be typified by the question "How often do you receive information that requires you to make too many decisions?" Equivocality is operationalized as the "perceived amount of discussions or explanations related to information received or sent in a given period of time" (Chung & Goldhaber, 1991, p. 10). A representative question is: "Sometimes, you may receive information that needs too many explanations in order for it to be useful to you. How often does this occur?"

The scale has only 10 questions, which are answered on a 6-point scale ranging from *very often* (6) to *never* (0). Linked with each question is a follow-up question: "Do you feel that this is a situation that needs to be improved?" These questions use the same response format. The scale requires only about 5 minutes for completion.

RELIABILITY

This instrument is quite new and, therefore, does not have a history of use by other researchers. However, Chung and Goldhaber (1991) reported results of a study in which the instrument was given to 467 managers in 12 organizations (6 from Taiwan and 6 from the United States). Types of organizations included colleges, hospitals, newspapers, chemical companies, grocery companies, banks, and power companies. Cronbach alphas ranged from .88 to .92.

VALIDITY

In their studies of the 12 organizations, Chung and Goldhaber (1991) found that overload was a problem for managers in the organizations, but contrary to their hypothesis, there were no statistical differences across levels of management in terms of the quantity dimension of communication load. However, they found that middle managers experience greater complexity and equivocality than do first-level and top managers. When the Taiwanese and U.S. managers were contrasted, an interesting difference surfaced. In terms of load in general, U.S. middle managers felt the greatest communication load, whereas the Taiwanese first-level managers felt the greatest burden of communication load.

Construct validity was confirmed through exploratory factor analysis using an oblique rotation, using the Harris–Kaiser method with power set at .50. A four-factor solution accounted for 92% of the variance and confirmed the three dimensions. Quantity accounted for 56% of the variance, Complexity accounted for 17%, and Equivocality accounted for 11%. Interfactor correlations revealed that Complexity and Equivocality correlated at .20, thus indicating that they are related, but still distinct.

COMMENTS

The instrument is obviously short and easy to use. Respondents can answer it in under 5 minutes. Furthermore, the wording is easy to follow and should be understandable for people at any level of an organization. The data are self-report, perceptual data, and some people may find this objectionable. However, perceptions may be what is needed to be measured in terms of load because the very term "communication load" carries with it a connotation of feelings and of subjective judgment ("There are times I feel overloaded and times I don't").

The concept of communication load is one that needed refining, and this instrument helps to do that. Chung and Goldhaber are quite analytical about the tributaries of theories and research that led them to their conclusions. And their preliminary analyses supported their definitions of the construct.

Two of the contributions made so far have been not only to examine how different levels of management differ in terms of load, but also to contrast managers in different countries. Their immediate analysis of these differences revolved around the different emphasis on socioemotional communication and task communication. Therefore, this concept may be valuable in understanding differences across cultures.

As Chung and Goldhaber (1991) suggested, continued work needs to be done to differentiate between information load and communication load: "For example, managers with heavier communication loads may not need more information. Installation of an information system for some individuals or certain managerial levels may turn out to be a waste of resources" (p. 24). Therefore, there are very practical implications that can be associated with the measurement of communication load.

LOCATION

Chung, C. J., & Goldhaber, G. (1991, May). *Measuring communication load: A three-dimensional instrument*. Paper presented at the meeting of the International Communication Association, Chicago.

REFERENCES

Galbraith, J. R. (1977). *Organization design*. Reading, MA: Addison-Wesley.
Weick, K. E. (1979). *The social psychology of organizing* (2nd ed.). Reading, MA: Addison-Wesley.

Three-Dimensional Communication Load Scale*

Instructions
   1. On these scales under each question, a "6" indicates *very often* or *very much so*, the lower numbers (5, 4, . . . 1) indicate a lesser amount, and "0" indicates *never* or *not at all*.
   2. Please complete all the questions by *circling* the number that best represents your opinion.
   3. Do *not* write your name on the questionnaire.
   4. In the following questions, the word "information" refers to messages in your communication through face-to-face conversation, meetings, telephone, memos, letters, or other channels. It includes reports, answers, requests, commands, and other directives.

[Editors' note: The following scales are used with each set of questions:

6	5	4	3	2	1	0		6	5	4	3	2	1	0
Very often						Never		Very much so						Not at all]

In a typical workweek, approximately:

   1. How often do you feel you generally have too many phone calls, meetings, memos, letters, face-to-face conversations, etc. in this organization?
      Do you feel this is a situation (having too many phone calls, meetings, memos, etc.) that needs to be improved?
   2. How often do you receive more information than you *need* in order to do your job effectively?

Do you feel this is a situation (receiving more information than you need) that needs to be improved?

3. How often do you receive more information than you *can* process?

   Do you feel this is a situation that needs to be improved?

4. How often do you receive information that requires you to make too many decisions?

   Do you feel this is a situation that needs to be improved?

5. Sometimes, you may receive information that needs too many explanations in order for it to be useful to you. How often does this occur?

   Do you feel this is a situation that needs to be improved?

6. How often does your communicating with others involve making too many decisions?

   Do you feel this is a situation that needs to be improved?

7. Sometimes, the information you need to explain to others is ambiguous or confusing in nature. How often is the information you explain ambiguous?

   Do you feel this is a situation that needs to be improved?

8. Sometimes, you may have more discussions than you *wish to* about the confusing or ambiguous information. How often does this occur?

   Do you feel this is a situation that needs to be improved?

9. How often do you feel you have to *send* more information than you *wish to*?

   Do you feel this is a situation that needs to be improved?

Note. Items 1, 3, and 9 are quantity items; Items 4, 6, and 7 are complexity items; and Items 2, 5, and 8 are equivocality items.

Unwillingness-to-Communicate Scale

Burgoon (1976) created a scale to measure unwillingness-to-communicate, a predisposition or "chronic tendency to avoid and/or devalue oral communication" (p. 60). Refinement of early versions of the scale resulted in a 26-item instrument that contained two main dimensions: Approach–Avoidance (.80 alpha) and Reward (.68 alpha).

Approach–Avoidance (AA) is "the degree to which individuals feel anxiety and fears about interpersonal encounters and are inclined to actively participate in them or not" and Reward (R) reflects "the degree to which people perceive that friends and family don't seek them out for conversation and opinions, and that interactions with others are manipulative and untruthful" (Burgoon & Hale, 1983b, p. 240).

The Unwillingness-to-Communicate Scale (UCS) today consists of 20 items, 10 for each dimension. Respondents indicate amount of agreement with each statement using 7-point Likert-type scales. Approach–Avoidance (likelihood of participating in communication) and Reward (finding communication rewarding) dimensions are created. It takes respondents less than 5 minutes to complete the measure.

RELIABILITY

This instrument appears to have sufficient reliability. Split-half reliabilities are good: For the 26-item UCS, split-half reliability was .88 (Burgoon & Burgoon, 1974), and for the 20-item UCS, it was .86 for UCS-AA and .82 for UCS-R (Burgoon, 1977). Coefficient alphas are also very good. Alphas for the UCS-AA dimension have ranged from .85 (Buller & Burgoon, 1986) to .98 (Burgoon & Hale, 1983a). Coefficient alphas for the UCS-R dimension have ranged from .70 (Buller & Burgoon, 1986) to .95 (Burgoon, Pfau, Birk, & Manusov, 1987).

Profile by Rebecca B. Rubin.

VALIDITY

There is sufficient criterion-related validity data on this measure. The UCS-AA dimension significantly predicts a group member's total participation, information giving, information seeking, and satisfaction with the decision (as indicated by the group), while UCS-R predicts individual members' satisfaction with the decision (Burgoon, 1977). The UCS also accounted for more variance in small group communication behavior than did anomia or communication apprehension (Burgoon & Burgoon, 1974). The UCS-AA also significantly predicted reduced language intensity (Burgoon & Hale, 1983a). And there is a significant difference between talk-radio callers and noncallers on the UCS-R dimension; callers found communication less rewarding and avoided personal communication when possible (Armstrong & Rubin, 1989).

Others provided evidence for concurrent validity. Daly (1978) found the UCS-AA dimension positively correlated with social anxiety, avoidance, tension, communication apprehension, social sensitivity, verbal reticence, social avoidance and distress, exhibitionism, and sociability. Bostrom and Waldhart (1988) found significant correlations between UCS-AA and self-esteem, recreational communication (negative) and rhetorical sensitivity (negative); UCS-R was positively related to communication apprehension and negatively related to amount of recreational communication. Burgoon and Hale (1983b) found UCS related to communication apprehension, nonverbal expressiveness, and ease, enjoyment, and reward in writing. Also, Kelly (1982) reported that the UCS-R was correlated at low levels with communication apprehension, reticence, and shyness, while the UCS-AA was highly correlated with these constructs. An earlier version of the UCS correlated with communication apprehension, anomia, and alienation (Burgoon, 1976; Burgoon & Burgoon, 1974). Infante and Rancer (1982) found that UCS correlated negatively with the tendency to approach arguments and positively with the tendency to avoid arguments.

During her search for differences between high and low reticents on nonverbal behavior, Burgoon has provided evidence of construct validity. Burgoon and Koper (1984) found that the highly reticent were perceived by strangers as more anxious, tense, depressed and unanimated, detached, apathetic, and less task attractive; nonaffiliated nonverbal behaviors were also examined in conditions of moderate and high stress and the highly reticent used increased body tension, self-touching, and protective behaviors. Burgoon et al. (1987) later found that reticents who avoid communication had lower scores on gestures, vocal animation, relaxation, and long face/head adaptors; they were also viewed as lower on the composure and extraversion components of credibility. Those reticents who saw communication as less rewarding were less flexible nonverbally and their messages were rated lower in intimacy/similarity.

Another construct validity study examined the stability of the dimensions. Samter and Burleson (1984) used principal-components factor analysis with varimax rotation and found two factors that were similar to Burgoon's. Nine items loaded on the UCS-AA dimension (alpha of .85) and seven on the UCS-R dimension (alpha of .55). UCS-AA was significantly correlated with (a) number of units of comforting behavior (negatively), (b) frequency of communication (negatively), (c) number of topic-relevant units (negatively), and (d) proportion of acknowledgement (positive). UCS-R was negatively related to proportion of acknowledgements and positively related to number of topic-relevant units. A second study again found the two factors; 10 items loaded on UCS-AA (.88 alpha) and 8 loaded on UCS-R (.80 alpha) (Burleson & Samter, 1985). UCS was unrelated to construct differentiation and emotional empathy, but UCS-R was related negatively to construct abstractness. In a later work, Samter (1992) found only seven items loaded on the Approach–Avoidance dimension and six on the Reward dimension.

COMMENTS

The scale appears to be very reliable and valid. It has good face validity and the evidence for construct, criterion, and concurrent validity is mounting. The UCS has been used in interpersonal, instructional, and mass communication research. The construct appears to tap more than communication apprehension; future research should examine more carefully the reward dimension of the UCS and how it is related to other similar constructs such as inclusion, opinion leadership, and trust. Also, future research should provide test–retest reliability information.

LOCATION

Burgoon, J. K. (1976). The Unwillingness-to-Communicate Scale: Development and validation. *Communication Monographs, 43*, 60–69.

REFERENCES

Armstrong, C. B., & Rubin, A. M. (1989). Talk radio as interpersonal communication. *Journal of Communication, 39*(2), 84–94.

Bostrom, R. N., & Waldhart, E. S. (1988). Memory models and the measurement of listening. *Communication Education, 37*, 1–13.

Buller, D. B., & Burgoon, J. K. (1986). The effects of vocalics and nonverbal sensitivity on compliance: A replication and extension. *Human Communication Research, 13,* 126–144.

Burgoon, J. K. (1977). Unwillingness to communicate as a predictor of small group discussion behaviors and evaluations. *Central States Speech Journal, 28,* 122–133.

Burgoon, J. K., & Burgoon, M. (1974). Unwillingness-to-communicate, anomia-alienation, and communication apprehension as predictors of small group communication. *Journal of Psychology, 88,* 31–38.

Burgoon, J. K., & Hale, J. L. (1983a). Dimensions of communication reticence and their impact on verbal encoding. *Communication Quarterly, 31,* 302–312.

Burgoon, J. K., & Hale, J. L. (1983b). A research note on the dimensions of communication reticence. *Communication Quarterly, 31,* 238–248.

Burgoon, J. K., & Koper, R. J. (1984). Nonverbal and relational communication associated with reticence. *Human Communication Research, 10,* 601–626.

Burgoon, J. K., Pfau, M., Birk, T., & Manusov, V. (1987). Nonverbal communication performance and perceptions associated with reticence: Replications and classroom implications. *Communication Education, 36,* 119–130.

Burleson, B. R., & Samter, W. (1985). Individual differences in the perception of comforting messages: An exploratory investigation. *Central States Speech Journal, 36,* 39–50.

Daly, J. A. (1978). The assessment of social-communicative anxiety via self-reports: A comparison of measures. *Communication Monographs, 45,* 204–218.

Infante, D. A., & Rancer, A. S. (1982). A conceptualization and measure of argumentativeness. *Journal of Personality Assessment, 46,* 72–80.

Kelly, L. (1982). A rose by any other name is still a rose: A comparative analysis of reticence, communication apprehension, unwillingness to communicate, and shyness. *Human Communication Research, 8,* 99–113.

Samter, W. (1992). Communicative characteristics of the lonely person's friendship circle. *Communication Research, 19,* 212–239.

Samter, W., & Burleson, B. R. (1984). Cognitive and motivational influences on spontaneous comforting behavior. *Human Communication Research, 11,* 231–260.

Unwillingness-to-Communicate Scale*

Instructions: Below are a series of statements about communication. There are no right or wrong answers. Indicate the degree to which each statement applies to you by circling a number from 1 to 7. A 1 means you *strongly disagree,* a 2 means you *disagree,* a 3 means you *disagree somewhat,* a 4 means you are *neutral* or *unsure,* a 5 means you *agree somewhat,* a 6 means you *agree,* and a 7 means you *strongly agree.*

Strongly   Strongly
disagree   agree

    1   2   3   4   5   6   7

[Editors' note: Respondents use the above scale to respond to the following items.]

1. I am afraid to speak up in conversations.
2. I talk less because I'm shy.
3. I like to get involved in group discussions.
4. I talk a lot because I am not shy.
5. My friends and family don't listen to my ideas and suggestions.
6. I think my friends are truthful with me.
7. I don't ask for advice from family or friends when I have to make decisions.
8. I believe my friends and family understand my feelings.
9. I have no fears about expressing myself in a group.
10. My family doesn't enjoy discussing my interests and activities with me.
11. I avoid group discussions.
12. My friends seek my opinions and advice.
13. I am afraid to express myself in a group.
14. During a conversation, I prefer to talk rather than listen.
15. Other people are friendly only because they want something out of me.
16. I find it easy to make conversation with strangers.
17. My friends and family listen to my ideas and suggestions.
18. Talking to other people is just a waste of time.
19. I feel nervous when I have to speak to others.
20. I don't think my friends are honest in their communication with me.

Note. Approach–Avoidance items are: 1, 2, 3, 4, 9, 11, 13, 14, 16, and 19; Reward items are: 5, 6, 7, 8, 10, 12, 15, 17, 18, and 20.
   Items 1, 2, 5, 7, 10, 11, 13, 15, 18, 19, and 20 should be reverse-scored.

Verbal Aggressiveness Scale

Verbal aggressiveness (VA) is "a personality trait that predisposes persons to attack the self-concepts of other people instead of, or in addition to, their positions on topics of communication" (Infante & Wigley, 1986, p. 61). Teasing, ridicule, profanity, character attacks, and insults are forms of verbally aggressive messages that often lead to relational outcomes such as anger, embarrassment, and hurt feelings. Infante and Wigley (1986) created the Verbal Aggressiveness Scale (VAS) to measure this trait and to test a model of skill deficiency that suggests that physical aggression results when people lack the verbal skills necessary to argue constructively.

Over 200 students completed the first version (30 items) of the VAS (Infante & Wigley, 1986). Factor and item analysis resulted in a one-dimensional, 20-item scale, with 10 items positively worded and 10 negatively worded. Later, 427 students completed the scale to develop norms; the mean was 49.10, the median was 48.82, and the standard deviation was 9.79. The coefficient alpha in both samples was .81. Factor analysis revealed the positively and negatively worded dimensions.

The VAS contains 20 items and takes about 10 minutes to self-administer. Responses range from *almost never true* (1) to *almost always true* (5). Scores are summed after reversing coding of positive items; high scores reflect high levels of VA.

RELIABILITY

Coefficient alpha levels of the 20-item VAS have been consistently high. Infante and Wigley (1986) reported alphas of .81. Rancer, Kosberg, and Silvestri (1992) reported an alpha of .85. And Rancer, Baukus, and Amato (1986) reported a .72 coefficient alpha.

Adaptations of the scale are also internally consistent. Boster and Levine (1988) reported a .79 alpha after deleting four items as a result of confirmatory factor analysis. Bayer and Cegala (1992), after rewording several items, found an alpha level of .81. Ten-item versions tapped (a) one's VA when talking with

Profile by Rebecca B. Rubin.

one's spouse (alpha = .79) and a report of one's spouse's VA level (alpha = .89) (Infante, Chandler, & Rudd, 1989) and (b) a superior's or subordinate's VA (alphas ranged from .90 to .92) (Infante & Gorden, 1989, 1991). A 5-item VA scale was less internally consistent (alpha = .68) (Infante & Gorden, 1987).

The construct appears stable over time. Test–retest reliability (4 weeks) was .82 and the session means did not differ significantly (Infante & Wigley, 1986).

VALIDITY

In the original study, Infante and Wigley (1986) examined the concurrent validity of the VAS; they found it to be related to Assault and Verbal Hostility measures. VA was inversely related to cognitive complexity and social desirability. Consistent with the conceptualization, VA has been found to be unrelated to argumentativeness (Infante & Wigley, 1986; Rancer et al., 1992). Later research shows VA negatively correlated with self-esteem (Rancer et al., 1992). Men seem to have higher VA levels than do women (Harmon, Klopf, & Ishii, 1990; Infante & Wigley, 1986).

One line of research examined VA in relation to message strategies. Boster and Levine (1988) looked at VA as a predictor of compliance-gaining messages and found situationally bound effects. Lim (1990) adapted the VAS for an other-report format and found verbal aggression was used with partners who use unfriendly resistance to persuasion strategies. When resistance to persuasion was strong, VA increased sharply over time, but when resistance was weak, the VA was more gradual but started at a higher level. Infante (1989) created argumentative and verbally aggressive strategies and asked people how they would respond to others who used them. People, and especially women, preferred the argumentative to the verbally aggressive strategies. Later research revealed that verbally aggressive people used more teasing, competence attacks, swearing, and nonverbal emblems (Infante, Riddle, Horvath, & Tumlin, 1992).

Another line of research investigated the link to physical abuse predicted in the original model of verbal aggression. First, Infante et al. (1989) found VA higher in violent marriages. In these marriages, wives reported their own argumentativeness to be low and their spouses' VA levels to be high. Rancer et al. (1986) examined the construct validity of the VAS and failed to find predicted differences in marital satisfaction between couples with similar and dissimilar verbal aggression styles. Infante, Sabourin, Rudd, and Shannon (1990) adapted the VAS for wives' recall of VA messages by abusive husbands; verbally aggressive messages were much more frequent in disagreements ending in violence. Payne and Sabourin (1990) found that (a) VA was inversely related to a husband's satisfaction with the marriage and (b) a wife's perception of her husband's VA was inversely related to her own marital satisfaction. And Segrin and Fitzpatrick (1992) discovered that a wife's VA is related to her husband's depression, but a husband's VA is unrelated to his wife's depression.

Perceptions of others' VA levels figured prominently in two additional lines of research. Downs, Kaid, and Ragan (1990) reworded 16 of the VAS items to reflect a conversation between Dan Rather and George Bush; as predicted, the researchers found an inverse relationship between VA and communicator image, with VA accounting for over 20% of the variance and argumentativeness accounting for over 27% of the variance. "Verbal aggression had a significant negative effect on Bush's image but a positive effect for Rather" (Downs et al., 1990, p. 107). Bush's perceived VA was higher than Rather's, who had a higher image overall.

Finally, Infante and Gorden have been interested in perceptions of coworker VA. They found that subordinates' perceptions of their supervisor's VA were negatively related and argumentativeness positively related to satisfaction with superior, respect of employee rights, and perceptions that the supervisor is effective in upward communication (Infante & Gorden, 1985). High VA was also related inversely to friendly, attentive, impression leaving, and relaxed communicator styles and to communicator image (Infante & Gorden, 1987). Infante and Gorden (1991) later examined the verbal aggression and argumentativeness of organizational superiors. The VAS was used along with friendly, attentive, and relaxed style components to create affirming and nonaffirming style profiles. The nonaffirming style resulted in lower organizational commitment, satisfaction with superior, and satisfaction with work. "Subordinates were more dissatisfied with their superiors when the subordinates believed they were victims of their supervisors' verbally abusive behavior" (p. 300). Superiors were more satisfied with subordinates low in VA, high in argumentativeness, and high in communicator style (Infante & Gorden, 1989).

COMMENTS

This measure has spawned a large number of research studies since its conception in 1986. The measure appears reliable and valid. Future research might examine the content and predictive validity of the measure.

LOCATION

Infante, D. A., & Wigley, C. J., III. (1986). Verbal aggressiveness: An interpersonal model and measure. *Communication Monographs, 53,* 61–69.

REFERENCES

Bayer, C. L., & Cegala, D. J. (1992). Trait verbal aggressiveness and argumentativeness: Relations with parenting style. *Western Journal of Communication, 56,* 301–310.

Boster, F. J., & Levine, T. (1988). Individual differences and compliance gaining message selection: The effects of verbal aggressiveness, argumentativeness, dogmatism, and negativism. *Communication Research Reports, 2,* 114–119.

Downs, V. C., Kaid, L. L., & Ragan, S. (1990). The impact of argumentativeness and verbal aggression on communicator image: The exchange between George Bush and Dan Rather. *Western Journal of Speech Communication, 54,* 99–112.

Harmon, C. M., Klopf, D. W., & Ishii, S. (1990). Verbal aggression among Japanese and American students. *Perceptual and Motor Skills, 70,* 1130.

Infante, D. A. (1989). Response to high argumentatives: Message and sex differences. *Southern Communication Journal, 54,* 159–170.

Infante, D. A., Chandler, T. A., & Rudd, J. E. (1989). Test of an argumentative skill deficiency model of interspousal violence. *Communication Monographs, 56,* 163–177.

Infante, D. A., & Gorden, W. I. (1985). Superiors' argumentativeness and verbal aggressiveness as predictors of subordinates' satisfaction. *Human Communication Research, 12,* 117–125.

Infante, D. A., & Gorden, W. I. (1987). Superior and subordinate communication profiles: Implications for independent-mindedness and upward effectiveness. *Central States Speech Journal, 38,* 73–80.

Infante, D. A., & Gorden, W. I. (1989). Argumentativeness and affirming communicator style as predictors of satisfaction/dissatisfaction with subordinates. *Communication Quarterly, 37,* 81–90.

Infante, D. A., & Gorden, W. I. (1991). How employees see the boss: Test of an argumentative and affirming model of supervisors' communicative behavior. *Western Journal of Speech Communication, 55,* 294–304.

Infante, D. A., Riddle, B. L., Horvath, C. L., & Tumlin, S. A. (1992). Verbal aggressiveness: Messages and reasons. *Communication Quarterly, 40,* 116–126.

Infante, D. A., Sabourin, T. C., Rudd, J. E., & Shannon, E. A. (1990). Verbal aggression in violent and nonviolent marital disputes. *Communication Quarterly, 38,* 361–371.

Lim, T-S. (1990). The influences of receivers' resistance on persuaders' verbal aggressiveness. *Communication Quarterly, 38,* 170–188.

Payne, M. J., & Sabourin, T. C. (1990). Argumentative skill deficiency and its relationship to quality of marriage. *Communication Research Reports, 7,* 121–124.

Rancer, A. S., Baukus, R. A., & Amato, P. P. (1986). Argumentativeness, verbal aggressiveness and marital satisfaction. *Communication Research Reports, 3,* 28–32.

Rancer, A. S., Kosberg, R. L., & Silvestri, V. N. (1992). The relationship between self-esteem and aggressive communication predispositions. *Communication Research Reports, 9,* 23–32.

Segrin, C., & Fitzpatrick, M. A. (1992). Depression and verbal aggressiveness in different marital types. *Communication Studies, 43,* 79–91.

Verbal Aggressiveness Scale*

Instructions: This survey is concerned with how we try to get people to comply with our wishes. Indicate how often each statement is true for you personally when you try to influence other persons. Use the following scale:

1 = Almost never true
2 = Rarely true
3 = Occasionally true
4 = Often true
5 = Almost always true

1. I am extremely careful to avoid attacking individuals' intelligence when I attack their ideas.
2. When individuals are very stubborn, I use insults to soften the stubbornness.
3. I try very hard to avoid having other people feel bad about themselves when I try to influence them.
4. When people refuse to do a task I know is important, without good reason, I tell them they are unreasonable.
5. When others do things I regard as stupid, I try to be extremely gentle with them.
6. If individuals I am trying to influence really deserve it, I attack their character.
7. When people behave in ways that are in very poor taste, I insult them in order to shock them into proper behavior.
8. I try to make people feel good about themselves even when their ideas are stupid.
9. When people simply will not budge on a matter of importance I lose my temper and say rather strong things to them.
10. When people criticize my shortcomings, I take it in good humor and do not try to get back at them.
11. When individuals insult me, I get a lot of pleasure out of really telling them off.
12. When I dislike individuals greatly, I try not to show it in what I say or how I say it.
13. I like poking fun at people who do things which are very stupid in order to stimulate their intelligence.
14. When I attack persons' ideas, I try not to damage their self-concepts.
15. When I try to influence people, I make a great effort not to offend them.
16. When people do things which are mean or cruel, I attack their character in order to help correct their behavior.
17. I refuse to participate in arguments when they involve personal attacks.

---

*Copyright 1986 by the Speech Communication Association. Reprinted by permission.

18. When nothing seems to work in trying to influence others, I yell and scream in order to get some movement from them.
19. When I am not able to refute others' positions, I try to make them feel defensive in order to weaken their positions.
20. When an argument shifts to personal attacks, I try very hard to change the subject.

Note. Sum the scores on the 20 items after reversing the scoring for Items 1, 3, 5, 8, 10, 12, 14, 15, 17, and 20.

Verbal Immediacy Behaviors

Perceptions of immediacy, or physical and psychological closeness, are affected not only by a person's nonverbal behaviors but also by an individual's verbal behaviors. Mehrabian (1967, 1981) characterized verbal immediacy along stylistic or linguistic dimensions, including the extent to which a person uses present (as opposed to past) verb tense, inclusive references (we vs. I), probability (will vs. may), ownership or responsibility (I think she's nice vs. most people think she's nice), and so on. As a content-analytic approach, this procedure assesses the attitudes of the speaker and the degree of like or dislike the speaker associates with another.

Consistent with that conceptualization, Gorham (1988) asked students to list specific behaviors that characterized "the best teachers they had had throughout all their years of school" (p. 43). These behaviors were then categorized into a list of 21 different teacher behaviors. Of these, 19 were verbal behaviors exclusively; a 20th was added to contrast the linguistic variable of inclusivity (I and my vs. we and our). The resulting 20 verbal behaviors were then given to a second sample of students to assess the frequency with which their teacher used each behavior. Factor analysis revealed that all items had their highest loading on the first unrotated factor. Item-total correlations indicated that all items correlated above .45 except for three, which correlated below .25. Thus, these three were subsequently dropped from the Verbal Immediacy Behaviors (VIB) instrument (Gorham, 1988; Gorham & Zakahi, 1990).

Assessments of verbal immediacy typically include students' perceptions of their teacher's verbal behaviors or teachers' self-reports of their own behaviors. Response options range from *never engage in that behavior* (0) to *very often* (4). The 17-item Likert-type scale takes about 5 minutes to complete.

RELIABILITY

The 17-item measure of verbal immediacy has demonstrated consistently high reliability. Alpha and split-half reliabilities for students' assessments

Profile by Patricia Kearney.

range from .83 to .94, and was reported at .89 for teachers' self-reports (Christophel, 1990; Gorham, 1988; Gorham & Zakahi, 1990; Powell & Harville, 1990).

VALIDITY

In terms of the instrument's content validity, Gorham's (1988) data revealed that all 17 verbal immediacy items loaded on the same single factor as did the 14 nonverbal behaviors previously identified as immediacy behaviors (Richmond, Gorham, & McCroskey, 1987). To date, no research has examined the relationship between the VIB instrument and either the Generalized Immediacy Scale or the Behavioral Indicants of Immediacy Scale previously generated by Andersen (1979). Nevertheless, the VIB instrument improves upon other gestalt assessments of immediacy by its ability to isolate and identify particular verbal behaviors. On the other hand, this measure does not rely on linguistic components that may prove too difficult for observers to monitor.

Verbal immediacy behaviors have been found to correlate positively and significantly with affective learning (and behavioral commitment) and cognitive learning but negatively with learning loss (Gorham, 1988; Gorham & Zakahi, 1990). These findings hold true for students in the multicultural classroom as well; however, the magnitude of this association varies by ethnic group (Sanders & Wiseman, 1990). Both student reports of their teachers' verbal immediacy and teachers' self-reports were also substantially and positively related. Finally, verbal immediacy was correlated with students' motivation or interest in taking the class (Christophel, 1990) and perceptions of teacher clarity (Powell & Harville, 1990).

COMMENTS

Research on immediacy in the classroom should rely on assessments of both verbal and nonverbal immediacy. Whether the more gestalt instrument of Generalized Immediacy (Andersen, 1979) or the low-inference assessments of verbal (Gorham, 1988) and nonverbal (Richmond, Gorham, & McCroskey, 1986) behaviors are used depends primarily on the researcher's need to identify more general or specific properties of the construct.

LOCATION

Gorham, J. (1988). The relationship between verbal teacher immediacy behaviors and student learning. *Communication Education*, 37, 40–53.

REFERENCES

Andersen, J. F. (1979). Teacher immediacy as a predictor of teaching effectiveness. *Communication Yearbook, 3*, 543–559.

Christophel, D. (1990). The relationships among teacher immediacy behaviors, student motivation, and learning. *Communication Education, 39*, 323–340.

Gorham, J., & Zakahi, W. R. (1990). A comparison of teacher and student perceptions of immediacy and learning: Monitoring process and product. *Communication Education, 39*, 354–368.

Mehrabian, A. (1967). Attitudes inferred from non-immediacy of verbal communications. *Journal of Verbal Learning and Verbal Behavior, 6*, 294–295.

Mehrabian, A. (1981). *Silent messages: Implicit communication of emotions and attitudes* (2nd ed.). Belmont, CA: Wadsworth.

Powell, R. G., & Harville, B. (1990). The effects of teacher immediacy and clarity on instructional outcomes: An intercultural assessment. *Communication Education, 39*, 369–379.

Richmond, V. P., Gorham, J. S., & McCroskey, J. C. (1987). The relationship between selected immediacy behaviors and cognitive learning. *Communication Yearbook, 10*, 574–590.

Sanders, J. A., & Wiseman, R. L. (1990). The effects of verbal and nonverbal teacher immediacy on perceived cognitive, affective, and behavioral learning in the multicultural classroom. *Communication Education, 39*, 341–353.

Verbal Immediacy Behaviors*

Instructions: Below are a series of descriptions of things some teachers have been observed saying in some classes. Please respond to each of the statements in terms of the way you perceive your teacher communicating towards you or others in your class. For each item, indicate how often your teacher responds this way when teaching. Use the scale: 0 = *never*; 1 = *rarely*; 2 = *occasionally*; 3 = *often*; and 4 = *very often*.

1. Uses personal examples or talks about experiences she/he has had outside of class.
2. Asks questions or encourages students to talk.
3. Gets into discussions based on something a student brings up even when this doesn't seem to be part of his/her lecture plan.
4. Uses humor in class.
5. Addresses students by name.
6. Addresses me by name.
7. Gets into conversations with individual students before or after class.

---

8. Has initiated conversations with me before, after or outside of class.
9. Refers to class as "our" class or what "we" are doing.
10. Provides feedback on my individual work through comments on papers, oral discussions, etc.
11. Calls on students to answer questions even if they have not indicated that they want to talk.
12. Asks how students feel about an assignment, due date or discussion topic.
13. Invites students to telephone or meet with him/her outside of class if they have questions or want to discuss something.
14. Asks questions that solicit viewpoints or opinions.
15. Praises students' work, actions or comments.
16. Will have discussions about things unrelated to class with individual students or with the class as a whole.
17. Is addressed by his/her first name by the students.

Note. Item 11 is *non*immediate. Coding should be reversed before summing.

Index

Note. *Measures that are profiled in this volume (in Part II) are indicated by capital letters.*

397